LEGISLATION AND STATUTORY INTERPRETATION

by

William N. Eskridge, Jr.
John A. Garver Professor of Jurisprudence,
Yale Law School

Philip P. Frickey
Irving Younger Professor of Law,
University of Minnesota Law School

Elizabeth Garrett
Professor of Law and Deputy Dean for Academic Affairs,
University of Chicago Law School

NEW YORK, NEW YORK
FOUNDATION PRESS

2000

Cover design: Keith Stout, New York, New York

Cover Photograph: President Lyndon Johnson signing the Civil Rights Act of 1964. Courtesy of the Lyndon Baines Johnson Library, University of Texas.

To my brother Henry, sister Betsy, and cousins Nicki, Tom, Allen, Truman, Martha, Sally, Anne, Heather, and Holly

W.N.E., Jr.

To Alex and Beth, my youthful enthusiasts for process and interpretation

P.P.F.

To my parents, to Laura, and especially to Sarah

E.G.

Preface

This book seeks to provide a comprehensive overview of the legislative process and statutory interpretation. We have attempted to integrate our analysis not only with our own casebook on these subjects,[1] but with all the other major casebooks as well, and thus this book should be useful to any law student taking a course in this area. Attorneys should find much of interest in our treatment of statutory creation and interpretation as well.

Professors Eskridge and Frickey thank the deans of their respective schools, Anthony Kronman and E. Thomas Sullivan, for summer research grants supporting this project. The James H. Douglas, Jr. Fund for the Study of Law and Government at the University of Chicago Law School provided support to Professor Garrett for her work on this book. George Mader and Alina McLauchlan contributed outstanding research assistance. Our special thanks goes to Adrian Vermeule, who read most of the manuscript and gave us excellent comments and suggestions.

William N. Eskridge, Jr.
New Haven, Connecticut

Philip P. Frickey
Minneapolis, Minnesota

Elizabeth Garrett
Chicago, Illinois

November 1999

---

[1] Eskridge & Frickey, *Cases and Materials on Legislation: Statutes and the Creation of Public Policy* (West Pub. Co., 2d ed. 1995), with a 1998 supplement written with Professor Garrett. The three of us are now at work on a third edition.

A Note on Citation Practice

Following Chapter 1, references to the major casebooks on legislative process and statutory interpretation are provided in abbreviated form, as follows:

"Eskridge & Frickey": William Eskridge, Jr. & Philip Frickey, *Cases and Materials on Legislation: Statutes and the Creation of Public Policy* (2d ed. 1995)

"Eskridge, Frickey & Garrett Supp.": 1998 supplement to the Eskridge & Frickey book, co-authored by Elizabeth Garrett

"Hetzel, Libonati & Williams": Otto Hetzel, Michael Libonati & Robert Williams, *Legislative Law and Process: Cases and Materials* (2d ed. 1993)

"Issacharoff, Karlan & Pildes": Samuel Issacharoff, Pamela Karlan & Richard Pildes, *The Law of Democracy: Legal Structures of the Political Process* (1998)

"Lowenstein": Daniel Hays Lowenstein, *Election Law: Cases and Materials* (1995)

"Mikva & Lane": Abner Mikva & Eric Lane, *Legislative Process* (1995)

"Popkin": William Popkin, *Materials on Legislation: Political Language and the Political Process* (2d ed. 1997)

Table of Contents

Table of Cases

TABLE OF CASES

TABLE OF CASES

An Introduction to Legislation

Less than two decades ago, Robert Weisberg accurately observed that "[t]he general contemporary American view of statutory interpretation is that there is not a great deal to say about the subject. As a result, nothing else as important in the law receives so little attention."[1] The experiences of two of us as law students in the mid-1970s confirm this observation. We studied no integrated approach to legislative processes and their products. At best, students of that era might have gleaned something generally useful from discussions of interpretation in areas governed by statutes, such as tax or labor law. To the extent that law professors troubled themselves with whether their students picked up statutory skills, the hope was that the exposure to different, essentially random pieces of the interpretation puzzle would eventually reveal the big picture. Unfortunately, as Judge Posner, writing contemporaneously with Professor Weisberg, pointed out, teachers of specific statutory courses could barely find the time to cover the substantive material of the subject. Furthermore, they lacked casebooks or other teaching materials that provided systematic access to the larger issues of statutory interpretation and the legislative process.[2]

In the past dozen or so years, a flood of scholarly and pedagogical materials on the legislative process and its products has inundated the law schools.[3] This explosion in materials on legislation resulted from

---

[1]Robert Weisberg, *The Calabresian Judicial Artist: Statutes and the New Legal Process*, 35 Stan. L. Rev. 213, 213 (1983) (footnote omitted).

[2]See Richard Posner, *Statutory Interpretation — in the Classroom and in the Courtroom*, 50 U. Chi. L. Rev. 800, 802 (1983).

[3]For example, three new casebooks on legislation were published during this period. See William Eskridge, Jr. & Philip Frickey, *Cases and Materials on Legislation: Statutes and the Creation of Public Policy* (2d ed. 1995; 1st ed. 1988); Abner Mikva & Eric Lane, *Legislative Process* (1995); William Popkin, *Materials on Legislation: Political Language and the Political Process* (2d ed. 1997; 1st ed. 1993). In addition, one casebook that appeared in 1980 entered its second edition. See Otto Hetzel, Michael Libonati & Robert Williams, *Legislative Law and Process: Cases and Materials* (2d ed. 1993). Two new casebooks on representative structures and processes also appeared. See Samuel Issacharoff,

a variety of factors, including closer attention to empirical and normative theories of the legislative process, a consideration of statutory interpretation as worthy of both high scholarly theory and practical, professionally oriented pedagogy, and a dramatic series of debates among Supreme Court Justices about the judiciary's institutional role in construing legislative products.[4] In addition, important questions relevant to the legislative process have caught the attention of scholars, judges, and the media. Courts have recently decided cases concerning term limits for state and federal lawmakers, the constitutionality of aspects of the federal budget process, methods of apportionment, and the role of political parties in campaign finance arrangements.

From the perspective of the law student, we believe that the most important development is that academic law is catching up with legal practice. Statutory interpretation is what most lawyers do for a good deal of their time. Today, the boundaries of most legal inquiry are structured by statutes and administrative regulations, not the common law.[5]

For many law students, however, this realization can be frightening. Leaving the comfortable methods of the common law — burned into every American law student's brain by the standard first-year law school curriculum — and turning to the legislative process and the interpretation of statutes can be a daunting and frustrating task. The common law is created by judges on a case-by-case, contextually

---

Pamela Karlan & Richard Pildes, *The Law of Democracy: Legal Structures of the Political Process* (1998); Daniel Hays Lowenstein, *Election Law: Cases and Materials* (1995). Legislation topics have been the subject of countless commentaries as well.

[4]See Philip Frickey, *Legislative Processes and Products*, 46 J. Legal Educ. 469 (1996); Philip Frickey, *From the Big Sleep to the Big Heat: The Revival of Theory in Statutory Interpretation*, 77 Minn. L. Rev. 241 (1992); William Eskridge, Jr. & Philip Frickey, *Legislation Scholarship and Pedagogy in the Post-Legal Process Era*, 48 U. Pitt. L. Rev. 691 (1987).

[5]See Guido Calabresi, *A Common Law for the Age of Statutes* 1 (1982), labeling this effect the "statutorification" of American law. See also Antonin Scalia, *A Matter of Interpretation: Federal Courts and the Law* 13 (1997), proclaiming that "[w]e live in an age of legislation, and most new law is statutory law."

sensitive basis, usually within the framework of argument constructed by adversary counsel representing individuals with concrete stakes in the outcome. This source of law resides in appellate opinions written in discursive form. What is authoritative about it is the holding (as opposed to dicta) of the opinion within that context.

Contrast law by statute. It resides in canonical, not discursive form.[6] These often-terse legal commands come not from judges, but from democratically elected legislators. The process of statutory creation is not a highly proceduralized adversary system of argument by lawyers culminating in a discursive opinion seemingly rooted in logic or adherence to precedent. Rather, the legislative process is an often-chaotic process of lobbying by interest groups and of assessments by legislators of the public interest and of their own, sometimes less public-regarding needs (such as reelection). In short, the common law and statutes may appear to be quite different creatures created by quite different institutions for quite different reasons. Moreover, students accustomed to the relatively orderly and deliberative process of judicial decisionmaking may find it tempting to dismiss the legislative process as merely the operation of politics conducted in an environment virtually bereft of principled behavior. How can a process so chaotic and unpredictable, affected by competing pressures and a multitude of organized groups, be susceptible to rigorous academic analysis? Perhaps more important for the law student, how can the academic study of legislation contribute to the process of training lawyers?

---

[6]To take a simple example, contrast a statute outlawing employment discrimination on account of race ("it shall be an unlawful employment practice for any employer to alter the employment relationship with any employee in any way on account of race") with a common law opinion either (1) implying a covenant of good faith in the employment contract under which the employer impliedly promised not to disadvantage employees on account of race or (2) creating a new tort, "intentional employment discrimination." Imagine that you are the law clerk required to write such an opinion. Consider the research and considerations that you will face. Compare your imaginary opinion with the statutory language quoted above. Now, suppose that you are an assistant to a state legislator in a state that does not have an employment discrimination statute and that you have been asked to draft one. Consider the research and considerations that you will face. Compare your statutory language to the imaginary judicial opinion you created earlier.

Of course, even if common law methodology cannot be directly transposed to statutory questions, statutory interpretation need not be viewed as some foreign and complex intellectual endeavor. A common rhetorical claim is that courts should simply discover the law; for statutes, that instruction might rather simply translate into judges' adhering to what the statutory text seems to say. This limited judicial role might seem especially appropriate for statutory interpretation, for the judge is finding meaning in the law created by a co-equal and democratically elected branch. Therefore, structural constitutional considerations might require the judge to avoid techniques that allow judicial prejudices to slip into the analysis. Similarly, Jeremy Waldron argues that strict attention to statutory text may be required by the nature of a legislature, "a large gathering of disparate individuals who purport to act collectively in the name of the whole community but who can never be sure exactly what it is that they have settled on, as a collective body, except by reference to a given form of words in front of them."[7]

Of course, if interpretation were that simple, there would be little reason for this book — or, for that matter, for people to hire attorneys to analyze and advocate different sides of statutory problems. Let us consider some of the competing factors in what might at first glance look like a simple statutory case.[8]

Suppose that the California traffic code provides as follows:

> The driver of a vehicle intending to turn to the left or to complete a U-turn at an intersection shall yield the right-of-way to all vehicles approaching from the opposite direction which are close enough to constitute a hazard at any time during the turning movement.

A driver is stopped in the left-turn lane at a red light. Just as the light turns green, the driver quickly turns left in front of the opposing

---

[7]Jeremy Waldron, *The Dignity of Legislation*, 54 Md. L. Rev. 633, 654 (1995). In another writing, Waldron argues that legislators work in the "circumstances of politics," which require that the words enacted by lawmakers, despite the difficulties of collective action, be accorded special authority. See Jeremy Waldron, *Legislation, Authority, and Voting*, 84 Geo. L.J. 2185 (1996).

[8]See *People v. Marsh*, 8 Cal. App. 4th Supp. 1, 11 Cal. Rptr. 2d 768 (1992).

traffic before the other drivers can move. Has the driver violated the law?

Before considering the statute in question, imagine that this were a question of common law. It would be simple, would it not? The driver did not act as a reasonable person in the circumstances and should be subject to damages if her actions harmed anyone. If the jurisdiction still permitted courts to create common law crimes, perhaps this behavior should amount to a crime as well.

But, alas, it is not that simple in California today. We must figure out what the statute means, not what reasonable care in the absence of a statutory mandate might be. Read the statutory text carefully. Can you make a solid textual argument, based on the plain meaning of the words, that the driver did not violate the statute? Yes. The statute speaks of yielding to "approaching vehicles." The vehicles pointing in the opposite direction had not yet begun to move and therefore should not be considered to be "approaching."

This is, arguably, the simplest answer to the problem. It might seem to have the virtue of limiting judicial discretion and honoring the words chosen by the democratically elected legislature. But is this the right answer? To what extent might the judge consider the dysfunctionality of this conclusion, which encourages reckless driving? Or, because the statute is the legislature's baby and not the court's, are all questions of functionality and policy surrounding a statute to be decided by the legislature? In that case, perhaps the only legitimate solution to a drafting problem is to hope for a legislative amendment in the future. Should the court be more willing to depart from the literal text if the judge is convinced that the legislative oversight is a result of a scrivener's drafting error? In other words, to what extent should a judge conceptualize her role to be that of *the faithful agent of statutory text*?[9]

Might the judge justify an interpretation that departs from the ordinary and literal meaning of the text by asking what the legislature "intended" its words to mean in these circumstances? It is difficult to draft clear commands, in part because drafters lack the omni-

---

[9]For a more elaborate examination of interpretive theories rooted in textual meaning, see Chapter 6, Part II.

science to foresee all circumstances that might arise. We also might feel that it is more respectful for the agent (the judge) to adhere to what the principal (the legislature) probably would have wanted, rather than to a wooden and literal interpretation of words that turn out to be poorly chosen in a given context. Indeed, we might think that "interpretation" is best understood not as literal application of dictionary definitions, but instead as attempting to unlock the message the speaker intended to send. Thus, perhaps statutory text cannot be interpreted properly without this inquiry.

Yet the notion of "legislative intent" is inherently problematic. How can a large group of people have any specific, actual intent about the meaning of words used in a statute? A majority vote might only have been possible because the members of the enacting coalition understood its vague or ambiguous language in very different ways or because they had different expectations regarding the ways courts would fill statutory gaps. Even if the notion of a monolithic legislative intent is viable, how do we use that concept in the context of problems that were not foreseen at the time of enactment? The best that we might be able to do is imaginatively reconstruct what the legislature would have intended had it foreseen our precise problem, but such a judicial inquiry is obviously fraught with opportunities for disguised judicial discretion and potential abuse.

Furthermore, even if unified legislative intent might be a useful legal fiction, evidentiary problems abound. May judges examine the legislative history of a statute (e.g., floor debates of legislators, reports of legislative committees, records of amendments to the proposal that were rejected) as an aid to discerning legislative intent, or are such sources likely to be at best unhelpful and at worst misleading? Do judges have the expertise to make sense of the legislative documents? Like most modern lawyers, they are relatively unaware of the intricacies of the legislative process and thus perhaps not likely to determine accurately which legislative signals are credible sources of intent and which are strategically placed by those who did not have the votes to enact their proposals.[10] In short, to

---

[10]For an example, see the discussion of the *Montana Wilderness Association v. United States Forest Service* case in Chapter 3, Part IA.

what extent should the judge conceptualize her role to be that of *the faithful agent of the enacting legislature*, and what are the limitations of that approach?[11]

An expanded inquiry would transcend statutory textual meaning and legislative intent to address more directly concerns of practicality and functionality. At common law, at least in theory, judges attempt to find the "best" answers they can consistent with precedent and policy. Should statutory interpretation be so very different? In our California traffic example, it is evident that it makes sense to criminalize the act of turning left by "jumping the light." That may accord more closely with the larger legislative purpose behind the enactment. Lawmakers might well have wanted to eliminate the mischief caused by reckless driving generally, not just in the circumstances literally described in the statute. Is there any strong reason to let poor drafting and inattentive lawmakers stand in the way of the most sensible legal regime? Of course, a judge who wishes to impose the functional outcome can hide behind reconstructed legislative intent ("had the legislators thought of this problem, they would want it resolved this way"). Similarly, the judge can apply presumptions about the nature of statutes — statutes, like all other forms of law, are instruments for achieving public purposes — and about legislators — legislators are reasonable people pursuing reasonable purposes reasonably — to justify the best interpretation. Again, however, because the judge is actually deciding what is reasonable and functional rather than deferring to another authority, these approaches may seem disingenuous and obscure the source of the legal requirement. In short, to what extent may the judge be *the faithful agent of a well-functioning regulatory regime*, in this context, a functional traffic code?[12]

Finally, to what extent may the judge consider broader issues of law? Statutes are, after all, law, and they must fit within the broader legal framework. There are many policy-based canons of interpretation that attempt to bring broader legal process values into the

---

[11]For a more elaborate consideration of interpretive theories based on legislative intent, see Chapter 6, Part I.

[12]For more discussion of interpretive theories rooted in such considerations, see Chapter 6, Part III.

interpretive framework.[13] One that might apply here is the rule of lenity, a canon that instructs judges to read ambiguities in criminal statutes in favor of the defendant. Potential justifications for this canon include the notions that people deserve fair notice of what constitutes a crime (which also justifies the constitutional requirement that criminal statutes must avoid vagueness) and that prosecutorial discretion should be limited (which derives from the constitutional notion of due process of law). Should the judge apply the rule of lenity and let this defendant off the hook? Or was defendant's conduct so obviously wrongful that she cannot claim lack of fair notice or unfair prosecutorial conduct? In short, to what extent may the judge consider *broader legal process issues*, including constitutional values, in interpreting a statute?[14]

All of this analysis complicates a decision relating to a simple traffic incident, and most of it would be legally irrelevant if American courts had definitively chosen one of these methods to the exclusion of others. If that were true, the law student could happily become an expert in that particular method and relegate all the rest to those of us who ruminate academically. Alas, that is not the case. What Henry Hart and Albert Sacks wrote a generation ago remains true:

> Do not expect anybody's theory of statutory interpretation, whether it is your own or somebody else's, to be an accurate statement of what courts actually do with statutes. The hard truth of the matter is that American courts have no intelligible, generally accepted, and consistently applied theory of statutory interpretation.
>
> When an effort is made to formulate a sound and workable theory, therefore, the most that can be hoped for is that it will have some foundation in experience and in the best practice of the wisest judges, and that it will be well calculated to serve the ultimate purposes of law.[15]

---

[13]See Chapter 9 for a discussion of such substantive canons.

[14]For greater consideration of such issues, see Chapter 6, Parts IC & IIIA; Chapter 9.

[15]Henry Hart, Jr. & Albert Sacks, *The Legal Process: Basic Problems in the Making and Application of Law* 1169 (William Eskridge, Jr. & Philip Frickey publication editors, 1994) (from the 1958 "tentative edition").

Although this state of affairs may be troublesome to the law student, note well that it is a boon to the practitioner. If there is no simple, universally accepted approach to interpreting statutes, and if (as we have already glimpsed) the interpretive models competing for judicial acceptance are rooted in conflicting assumptions, there is ample room for the skill and imagination of the able practitioner. Advocating a particular side in a close statutory case is an art, not a science. What that calls for is neither mechanical analysis nor the scientific method, but instead a learned rhetorical form of argumentation and reasoning.

Moreover, because no single method controls, attorneys are encouraged to craft their arguments as cumulative rhetoric, taking the most convincing pieces of whatever approaches best fit their side of the case. This cumulative argumentation has many advantages. The attorney covers all the bases, thereby incidentally including whatever approach the particular judge might favor as well as rebutting counter-arguments based on different approaches. Indeed, our experience is consistent with the views of Hart and Sacks: most judges are not single-minded theoreticians in statutory interpretation, but instead undertake a cumulative inquiry examining all possibilities. For these judges, the cumulative inquiry is simply a pragmatic way of identifying and weighing the values at stake in any given statutory case.[16]

The cumulative method also helps narrow the range of conflict in a case. A pragmatic approach to interpretation moves the dispute away from abstract arguments — e.g., the importance of preserving the integrity of the statutory text versus the importance of identifying and adhering to what legislators probably would have wanted the court to do — to much more specific ones that arise in the facts of the case. Perhaps even judges who disagree about the appropriate strategies of statutory interpretation can nevertheless agree about the

---

[16]See William Eskridge, Jr. & Philip Frickey, *Statutory Interpretation as Practical Reasoning*, 42 Stan. L. Rev. 321 (1990) (discussing the pragmatic approach taken by many members of the judiciary in interpreting statutes); Nicholas Zeppos, *The Use of Authority in Statutory Interpretation: An Empirical Analysis*, 70 Tex. L. Rev. 1073 (1992) (providing evidence that judges undertake this approach). See Chapter 6, Part IIIB for a diagram representing our pragmatic methodology.

right outcome; often counsel will not be particularly concerned about the court's reasoning, or whether all members agree about how they reach a particular conclusion, as long as her client wins the case.

Consider an illustration. To return to our seemingly simple California traffic code issue, let us examine how an attorney representing the defendant will urge the court to acquit her client. The obvious starting argument will be based on statutory text. The statute consists of words chosen by the legislature to bind the citizenry, the attorney will argue, and the surest source of meaning for the statute is what the ordinary reader of the English language would make of those words. The legislature chose the word "approaching," and that word simply cannot describe vehicles at rest.

If this attorney does her research, she will happily discover that many years ago a California appellate court had a similar question before it and answered it consistently with her current argument. In 1956, the relevant traffic code provision required the driver intending to turn left to "yield the right of way to any vehicle approaching from the opposite direction which is within the intersection or so close thereto as to constitute an immediate hazard." In *People v. Bull*,[17] the court stated (arguably in dicta) that this old provision did not cover someone who jumped the light to turn left:

> * * * There was, of course, no car other than the defendant's within the intersection and none that might be said to be approaching, as the defendant made his left turn. This is so, because all others, involved, were stationary and so not approaching. It would be a contradiction in terms to say that a *standing* car was *approaching*. But the word is used in the statute, and may not be discarded.

The obvious response by the prosecutor will be that such a literal, acontextual, and wooden interpretation of the word "approaching" defeats the evident will of the legislature. The attorneys could — and, we think, should — present arguments about the more abstract issues involved in the choice among textual integrity, legislative intent, and statutory functionality. But, if the defense attorney does even further research, she will find support for a more specific and

---

[17]144 Cal. App. 2d Supp. 860, 862, 301 P.2d 311, 312 (1956).

contextual response, which requires a somewhat elaborate explanation.

Based on solid research, the defense counsel has an excellent argument that the legislature has actually anticipated our situation and intends that the driver be free from criminality. In response to the *Bull* decision, the legislature amended the traffic code provision to require left-turning drivers to yield to any vehicle "which has approached or is approaching." A year later, the appellate court understood this amendment to overturn the outcome in *Bull*: "[T]he necessity of yielding the right of way is no longer limited to vehicles in motion, but applies as well to those not in motion, if they have arrived so close to the intersection as to constitute a hazard to the driver as he makes his left turn."[18] Then in 1988 the legislature again amended the provision, deleting the phrase "which has approached."

What could this most recent amendment mean, defense counsel will argue, other than that the legislature intended to return the law of California to *Bull*? She will argue, more than a little slyly, that the prosecutor surely does not wish to suggest that the legislature enacted a law for no reason at all! And, she will continue, it is reasonable for the court to presume that the legislature is familiar with the state of the case law interpreting a statute when it amends the statute. Indeed, California case law had already recognized the strength of such reasoning. Like other American courts, California appellate opinions state that "reenactment of a statute implies approval of prior judicial interpretations of the words and phrases used in the statute," and that "when legislation has been judicially construed and a subsequent statute on the same or an analogous subject is framed in the identical language, it will ordinarily be presumed that the Legislature intended that the language as used in the later enactment would be given a like interpretation."[19]

The prosecutor can still respond that the defense attorney's conclusion is ridiculous and an extraordinarily dysfunctional approach to managing a traffic code. But note that the defense counsel seems to have a "double gotcha" here: both the plain

---

[18]*People v. Miller*, 161 Cal. App. 2d Supp. 842, 844, 327 P.2d 236, 238 (1958).

[19]*People v. Marsh*, 8 Cal. App. 4th Supp. 1, 4, 11 Cal. Rptr. 2d 768, 770 (1992).

meaning of the statute and the apparent intent of the legislature support her argument. How can judicial impressions of functionality trump both the text of the law and the imputed intent of the law-creator (the legislature)? Defense counsel's cumulative argument (statutory text plus legislative intent, in part ascertained through the use of canons of construction) is much more powerful than either component of the argument standing alone.[20]

If the law is nonsensical, defense counsel might continue, it is up to the legislature to fix the problem. This normative point about the way law arguably should work could be reinforced by an empirical observation: surely the prosecutors of California — a small group of like-minded and highly motivated professionals — would be easy to organize for legislative action.[21] Indeed, the response to the interpretation in *Bull* provides a pertinent example of legislative attention to these matters, proving the ability of lawmakers to correct any drafting errors in the statute.

Defense counsel's arguments are excellent. Indeed, in *People v. Marsh*,[22] on which our example is based, the court of appeals acknowledged that the argument "that the Legislature, having deleted any reference to stationary vehicles, must have intended to restore the rule of *Bull*" was "neatly crafted and assiduously researched." Unfortunately for the defendant, however, the court concluded that the arguments were "ultimately unavailing." The court wrote:

> Simply stating the proposition in plain language seems to refute it. No one can seriously argue allocation of right-of-way should be reduced to a contest of reaction times. Putting people into 4,000-pound, combustion-powered, gasoline-laden machines; stressing them out in a daily commute; and then telling them right-of-way is simply a matter of whether they are quick enough to "get

---

[20]To borrow (and take slightly out of context) a phrase of Judge Posner's, this cumulative-although-theoretically-impure argument prefers the "sturdy mongrel" to the "sickly pedigreed purebred." See Richard Posner, *What Has Pragmatism To Offer Law?*, 63 S. Cal. L. Rev. 1653, 1664 (1990).

[21]See Chapter 3, Part IIB; see also William Eskridge, *Jr., Overriding Supreme Court Statutory Interpretation Decisions*, 101 Yale L.J. 331, 335-37 (1991) (finding that statutory overrides of Supreme Court opinions are more likely under similar circumstances).

[22]8 Cal. App. 4th Supp. 1, 4, 11 Cal. Rptr. 2d 768, 770 (1992).

off the line" before the other drivers seems like such a patently bad idea that it would be insulting to ascribe it to the Legislature. And we will not. * * *

In fact, there simply was no "rule of *Bull*." Appellate department decisions are not binding authority, especially with regard to dicta therein, so there was never a rule capable of "restoration" by the subsequent legislative amendment.

More importantly, the "rules" appellant cites were, after all, self-constructed by the courts to guide them in determining the intent of the Legislature. The ultimate task before us is not to grade appellant's argument or harmonize legislation and prior appellate interpretation, but to discern the Legislature's intent. [Citing a precedent.]

Penal Code section 4 provides, "The rule of the common law, that penal statutes ought to be strictly construed, has no application to this code. All its provisions are to be construed according to the fair import of their terms, with a view to effect its objects and to promote justice." This rule applies with equal force to penal provisions of other codes such as the Vehicle Code. [Citing precedents.]

Approaching this statute "with a view to effect its objects," we are absolutely convinced that the legislative intent was to interpret "approaching" as a reference to direction rather than motion. We hold that a fair interpretation of the words "approaching from the opposite direction" includes all vehicles coming from that direction whether or not their progress has been momentarily interrupted by traffic control devices.

It may be that the Legislature could more clearly have expressed itself with a word like "opposing" or "facing"; but nothing in the law requires such clarity, and one need only spend a few minutes with a thesaurus to realize this is an awkward concept to phrase. The wording they came up with is plenty clear enough for most people, and we are satisfied the driving public correctly understands the section. As long as common usage recognizes "traffic that has stopped" (an oxymoron) and "traffic that is moving" (a redundancy), we see no reason why the Legislature cannot employ such usage in referring to stationary "approaching" cars.

To hold otherwise would encourage semantic precision, and words like "diametrical," at the expense of the understanding of most motorists. It would also encourage traffic patterns unimaginably masochistic. If that was the Legislature's intent, it will have to speak more clearly; otherwise, the law is clear enough.

In short, the court opted for functionality and its common-sense view of the "best" answer. Although we generally agree with this approach, the student must recognize that the contrary — much more formal and legalistic — approach once obtained judicial support in California (in the *Bull* case) and would likely be adopted by many judges on today's federal and state courts. Indeed, as we later examine at length, the "new textualism," which views statutory words, as supplemented by the canons of interpretation, as essentially the only sources of statutory meaning, has been on the ascendancy in the United States Supreme Court for a decade.[23] It is worth noting, however, that even the *Marsh* court, which was comfortable with a dynamic approach to interpretation, felt somewhat constrained by the words of the statute. The judge interpreted "approaching" as a reference to a direction; he did not ignore the language of the statute entirely. Rather, he adopted a relatively strained, and certainly not obvious, meaning on the basis of his common-sense understandings and his view of the overall purpose of the traffic law.

Our simple point is that the court in *Marsh* had a choice: it could have taken the *Bull* approach or a more functional approach. To say that the court had a choice, however, is not to suggest that it was playing a game with no rules. Under our legal traditions, the court was compelled to issue an opinion addressing the formal argument about the meaning of "approaching" and either accepting it or rejecting it in favor of its functional counterpart. Moreover, the judge's consideration of this question was shaped by the presentations of the attorneys representing the two sides. Had defense counsel not made such a good argument — in effect, revealed to the judge the existence of a line of reasoning that resonated powerfully with our accepted traditions of statutory interpretation — the judge could have disposed of the case more quickly, perhaps in an unpublished opinion. In a nutshell, this case reveals what the attorney's task in statutory

---

[23]See Chapter 6, Part IIB.

interpretation in adversary situations is all about: constructing a persuasive argument that convinces the decisionmaker that the interpretive question meshes with our interpretive traditions in such a way that it should be answered favorably for the attorney's client.

It should be obvious that these arguments are heavily shaped by institutional considerations and informed by an understanding of the details of the legislative process. For example, in *Marsh*, is it realistic to think that the California legislature intended anything about the question at issue there? Is it accurate to assume in all cases that legislators are reasonable people pursuing reasonable purposes reasonably? Even if that is sometimes a stretch of faith, would our law nonetheless work better if we make the assumption anyway? Is it fair to presume that legislators know the details of judicial opinions interpreting statutes they are amending, or that they are familiar with laws that use similar language? Is it enough for the members of the committee considering the bill to be aware of such precedents? Is it sufficient that only certain legislative staff members have the requisite knowledge? How much textual clarity should we expect from legislative drafters? Will the interpretive methods used by judges create incentives for legislators to write laws more clearly? How much discretion can we afford to give judicial interpreters, who might use their discretion to displace the judgments of the democratically elected legislature?

* * *

One payoff to the study of legislation is the development of expertise in constructing statutory arguments. This book is designed in part to introduce you to the American interpretive traditions and how they might be sculpted by advocates.[24] The book also introduces

---

[24] Judge Posner's comments about the goals of legal education make this point nicely:

> The most important thing that law school imparts to its students is a feel for the outer bounds of permissible legal argumentation at the time when the education is being imparted. (Later those bounds will change, of course.) What "thinking like a lawyer" means is not the use of special analytic powers but an awareness of approximately how plastic law is at the frontiers — neither infinitely plastic * * * nor rigid and predetermined, as many laypersons think — and of the permissible "moves" in

the other core subject matter covered in law school legislation courses, such as legislative structure and processes. As you can already see from *Marsh* and our traffic provision, the reality of the legislative process is intimately related to the interpretive payoff we hope to provide to you.

For instance, much of the rhetoric, and even some of the reality, of judicial interpretation of statutes is couched in terms of assumptions or beliefs about legislative capacities and processes. Recall, for example, the "rule" that defense counsel in *Marsh* suggested: the court should assume that the California legislature, when it most recently amended the statute in question, not only was aware of the old *Bull* case, but that it also intended to revive that approach to the statute. (To that contention, the court in question responded, in effect, "bull.") The relevance of the legislative process is not limited to the role it plays in the selection of interpretive methods. In most cases, losing parties can turn to the legislature to change the statute. Understanding the role of interest groups in the legislature suggests that such a result is unlikely here.[25] People who will be prosecuted under the statute in the future cannot easily form organized groups to try to influence lawmakers with convincing arguments and campaign contributions. Nor are lawmakers apt to be sympathetic to entreaties to change laws in ways that appear to undermine traffic safety; support for such proposals can be portrayed in the next election as symbolic of a legislator's poor judgment or inattention to automobile safety. In contrast, California prosecutors are a relatively small and easily organized group with substantial credibility in the legislative process. Should the court in *Marsh* have ruled for the defendant, thereby encouraging the prosecutors to persuade the legislature to clean up the problem if a strict construction of the statute really diverged from lawmakers' wishes?

---

arguing for, or against, a change in the law. It is neither method nor doctrine, but a repertoire of acceptable arguments and a feel for the degree and character of doctrinal stability, or, more generally, for the contours of a professional culture — a professional culture lovable to some, hateful to others.

Richard Posner, *The Problems of Jurisprudence* 100 (1990).

[25]See Chapter 3, Part II.

In the end, much of our jurisprudential disagreement about how to interpret statutes represents a tension between our common law tradition and our democratic tradition. Law students, in particular, tend to think of law as being made incrementally by judges, fine-tuned on a case-by-case basis in light of judicial precedent, the customs of our people, and functional considerations. In this sense, although *Marsh* is not technically a common law opinion because it interprets a statute rather than the common law, the methodological approach of the court in *Marsh* has a strong common law flavor to it. Yet we live in a democracy, where today most of our law is made not by judges in common law cases but by popularly elected legislators adopting statutes and by administrative agencies promulgating rules and regulations. Although it is beyond the scope of this book to study the administrative process, which is guided by statutory directives and influenced by legislative oversight, we hope to introduce the reader to the structure and processes by which statutes are created. These subjects are worthy of study in their own right — they raise a variety of interesting and practical legal questions, as well as provide an important piece necessary for solving the broader statutory interpretation puzzle.

2

Theories of Representation

Federal and state governments in our country are *representative democracies*: citizens vote for representatives, who debate about and enact legislation. Representatives are accountable to citizens because they must frequently run for reelection. This political arrangement reflects a constitutional choice that laws will rarely be adopted or ratified by direct popular vote. Is this a wise choice? If so, is there still an appropriate role for popular initiatives and referenda? Who should be eligible to serve in the legislature, and how should representatives be chosen? What is their proper role in the legislature? Underlying one's analysis of all the questions is one's theory of representation. Such a theory must be more than descriptive, for the legitimacy of law depends in part on the extent of popular trust or, conversely, on the degree of the electorate's alienation, engendered by the relationship between the citizenry and their representatives. Consider three kinds of theories about representation.

Liberal theories[1] view citizens as rational actors who need government to achieve cooperative goals and to resolve differences among themselves. Every citizen is an autonomous person with a great degree of freedom to pursue her own goals, subject to limits set by law. The legitimacy of law rests, at least in part, on its procedural pedigree: it is adopted by representatives elected by the citizenry, each of whom has the same right to vote and to organize into interest groups pressing their views and proposals in the legislature. Correla-

---

[1]Liberal theories draw from the ideas generated by Hobbes, Locke, Bentham, Madison, and Mill. Classic accounts by American authors include Arthur Bentley, *The Process of Government* (1908); Robert Dahl, *A Preface to Democratic Theory* (1956) (essentially an exegesis of Madison); David Truman, *The Governmental Process* (1953). See also Henry Hart, Jr. & Albert Sacks, *The Legal Process: Basic Problems in the Making and Application of Law* 1169 (William Eskridge, Jr. & Philip Frickey publication editors, 1994) (from the 1958 "tentative edition"). Public choice theory is a reductionist form of liberalism. See James Buchanan & Gordon Tullock, *The Calculus of Consent* (1962); Anthony Downs, *An Economic Theory of Democracy* (1957). More recent accounts of liberal theory reveal its potential for nuance and suppleness. See, e.g., Robert Dahl, *Dilemmas of Pluralist Democracy* (1982); Amy Gutmann, *Liberal Equality* (1980); John Rawls, *Political Liberalism* (1996); John Rawls, *A Theory of Justice* (1971).

tively, citizens have an obligation to obey the law and to seek any changes in it through the duly established procedures. Under the simplest liberal theory, the representative pursues the interests of her constituents as their collective agent. Legislating is a process whereby representative-agents reflecting different interests bargain and logroll[2] until most of the relevant interests are satisfied. Once a sufficient coalition has been assembled through a series of trades and negotiation, legislation will be adopted. Lawmaking then is merely the result of aggregating the preferences of a majority of representatives, who mirror the preferences of a majority of their constituents.

Republican theories[3] tend to view citizens as less autonomous and more profoundly affected by the community around them. In contrast to simpler versions of liberalism, republicanism supposes that people are constituted by government and law as well as vice versa. Individuals' preferences are not fixed; rather, they are endogenous, that is, shaped in part by the deliberative process of enacting legislation, as well as by other interactions and experiences. At its best, law not only protects citizens against violence from others, but it also creates opportunities for positive human flourishing. That flourishing, in turn, encourages citizens to participate actively in the law-creating process. Citizens have an obligation to obey the law because they have been able to enjoy the benefits of the community. Legitimate mandates are adopted by representatives after a deliberative process that is public regarding, but the legitimacy of law rests upon its substantive guarantees as well as procedural justice. A lawmaker's constituency is the public good, and her role is to deliberate as a trustee for the people.

The foregoing account paints liberal and republican theories in starkly, and excessively, dichotomous terms. Liberals can and do posit theories of representation that allow a role for evolving

---

[2]Logrolling is vote-trading: A will trade her support for a dam that B wants, in return for B's willingness to support A's tobacco subsidy. The vote trade may occur even if neither A nor B thinks the other project worthwhile.

[3]See Arthur Maass, *Congress and the Common Good* (1980); Philip Pettit, *Republicanism: A Theory of Freedom and Government* (1997); Gordon Wood, *The Creation of the American Republic, 1776-1787* (1969); *Symposium on Republicanism*, 97 Yale L.J. 1493 (1988). For a skeptical account, see Daniel Rodgers, *Republicanism: The Career of a Concept*, 79 J. Am. Hist. 11 (1992).

preferences and that rely on deliberation to sort out public-regarding solutions from self-interested ones. Republicans can and do posit theories of representation that recognize and valorize citizen autonomy and that treat some preferences as exogenous in the short term. The most eminent theorist of representation, Hanna Pitkin, offered a basis for synthesizing liberal and republican theories when she insisted that "representing . . . means acting in the interest of the represented, in a manner responsive to them."[4] One can imagine other syntheses of these two philosophical traditions, perhaps influenced in part by our third group of theories.

Critical theories[5] are skeptical that "representation" amounts to anything more than a social construct. The interests emphasized by liberals are a product of the political process, as are the public interest and deliberation stressed by republicans. Not only are citizens nonautonomous, contrary to liberalism, but their political participation and deliberation are infected by structures and discourses of subordination, undermining the republican project. The social construct of representation is both contingent (it depends on citizens' belief in it) and historically situated (the belief is grounded in possibly illegitimate practices of subordination). Critical theorists focus more on the representation of groups than of individuals (liberalism) or the common weal (republicanism). In their view, a good system of representation must include a politics of presence: members of historically subordinated groups (classically, blacks and women, perhaps also gays and poor people) must be in the legislature in sufficient numbers to influence outcomes.[6] According to critical theory, legislator heterogeneity, along lines of race and sex at least, is needed for legitimate representation. The inability of a legislature of white men to understand minority perspectives undermines legislators' ability to represent the interests of minority constituencies

---

[4]Hanna Pitkin, *The Concept of Representation* 209 (1967).

[5]See Lani Guinier, *The Tyranny of the Majority: Fundamental Fairness and Representative Democracy* (1994); Melissa Williams, *Voice, Trust, and Memory: Marginalized Groups and the Failings of Liberal Representation* (1998); Iris Young, *Justice and the Politics of Difference* (1990).

[6]Compare the differently motivated idea of the "mirror of representation" among the constitutional Framers. See Jack Rakove, *Original Meanings: Politics and Ideas in the Making of the Constitution* 203-43 (1996).

(liberalism) or to take account of them in the process of deliberation (republicanism).

Rather than endorsing any one theory, our goal is to help the reader see what different questions each theory raises about a few of the legal and constitutional issues implicated in a representative democracy and how the different theories point to distinct and sometimes competing resolutions of those issues. The application of the different theories may also illuminate the values underlying them and the problems associated with them. In this chapter we will discuss the theories of representation through three concrete applications, and throughout the rest of the book we will continue to relate this theoretical framework to issues of the legislative process and statutory interpretation.

I. Direct versus Representative Democracy[7]

Do representatives provide better governance than direct enactment of laws by popular vote? The Framers of the Constitution thought so for both liberal and republican reasons, and critical theory advances additional reasons for representative rather than direct democracy. The Framers, however, did not address the issue currently important: In a system of representative democracy, can popular plebiscites serve useful purposes in monitoring or prodding elected representatives? In other words, is some form of hybrid system best of all? A final question is of particular importance to lawyers: How should the judiciary approach the products of direct democracy in jurisdictions that have a hybrid system of government? The judicial stance toward direct legislation should be informed by the theoretical considerations. For example, a republican might be concerned that the absence of extensive public deliberation on most ballot questions, as well as the inability to reach compromises and amend such proposals, will lead to laws that do not serve the public interest. The courts could provide an additional filter for the products of direct democracy if they applied more aggressive review and perhaps even opened up litigation challenging ballot questions

---

[7]Issues of direct democracy are treated in Eskridge & Frickey 325-82; Issacharoff, Karlan & Pildes 665-712; Hetzel, Libonati & Williams 927-48; Lowenstein 259-95, 545-80; Mikva & Lane 729-54; Popkin 853-76.

beyond the adversaries in a particular case to encourage the participation of a wide range of interests.[8] In addition, republicans are likely to favor reforms of direct democracy that require public hearings throughout the state before a vote, some sort of legislative involvement before the election, or two votes of the citizens in order to pass any proposition. How do such requirements affect the outcome of direct democracy? How appropriate is aggressive judicial review of statutes adopted not by the representatives of voters but by citizen-legislators themselves?

A. *Should We Have a Representative Democracy?*

What could be more legitimate than laws adopted by a popular vote? From a liberal point of view, this is the most direct way for individuals to express their preferences, and a majority-wins rule is an appealing way to aggregate political preferences. From a republican point of view, popular initiatives promise to engage the citizenry in lawmaking and stimulate public deliberation over important issues of the day. These opportunities for the exercise of civic virtue are seen as most likely to occur in the context of a small homogeneous republic like ancient Athens or modern Switzerland. The Framers and most subsequent political thinkers have maintained that direct democracy cannot work in a large populous republic like the United States or even in most of its states. Deliberation and aggregation of preferences for such large numbers of people would be difficult for complex issues and well-nigh impossible to accomplish for every important matter of policy. Note, however, that this kind of pragmatic argument may be less persuasive in an age of instant and low-cost communication. An "internet democracy" could inform people of political choices, assemble their feedback, formulate proposals, and subject them to instantaneous votes without undue fuss. There must be deeper objections to direct democracy in this era of facile communication.

---

[8]Compare Jane Schacter, *The Pursuit of "Popular Intent": Interpretive Dilemmas in Direct Democracy*, 105 Yale L.J. 107, 155-56 (1995) (making such a proposal) with Philip Frickey, *Interpretation on the Borderline: Constitution, Canons, Direct Democracy*, 1996 Ann. Surv. Am. L. 477, 493 (arguing that Schacter's proposal would not have much impact on public law).

Typically, James Madison said it best. In *Federalist* No. 10, he painted a fearful picture of the citizenry as naturally selfish and easily prone to emotional judgments. Freedoms assured by democracy can be the polity's undoing, or, as Madison put it, "[l]iberty is to faction what air is to fire,"[9] for the sustaining force of the polity simultaneously produces other forces that could destroy it. Selfishness and passion stimulate us to take advantage of our liberty and to form factions, which seek to enlist the state's power in private projects. To the extent that the state becomes the instrument for factional politics, it will lose its legitimacy. Madison recognized that the majority-wins precept would control factions in those cases where most people rejected their proposals, but he claimed that squalid majorities could form, perhaps only temporarily, to oppress the vulnerable and obnoxious among us.

Direct democracy provides no check on the people's tendency toward a short-sighted politics of passion, punishment, and partiality. A representative democracy, on the other hand, could weed out the proposals most responsive to "temporary or partial considerations" because elected lawmakers would deliberate and choose sounder proposals.[10] "Under such a regulation, it may well happen that the public voice pronounced by the representatives of the people, will be more consonant to the public good, than if pronounced by the people themselves convened for that purpose."[11] Madison's essay is a brilliant defense of representative government, in part because it can appeal to an audience holding different theories of representation. Liberals find inspiration in his emphasis on the dangers that temporary majorities pose to individual rights and interests. Critical thinkers join liberals in fearing the tendency of popular majorities to penalize despised minorities. Republicans are attracted to Madison's reliance on reasoned deliberation as the best way to avoid unwise laws.

Madison himself recognized an immediate objection to his defense of representative over direct democracy: "Men of factious tempers, of local prejudices, or of sinister designs, may, by intrigue,

---

[9]*The Federalist* No. 10, at 78 (J. Madison) (Clinton Rossiter ed., 1961).

[10]*Id.* at 82.

[11]*Id.*

by corruption, or by other means, first obtain the suffrages, and then betray the interests of the people."[12] Today this is called an *agency problem*: agents of the people may betray their principals' interests or the public's interest by self-dealing, by favoring an undeserving faction (or, in modern terminology, facilitating rent-seeking[13]), or even by making lazy, uninformed political choices. Madison's response to the agency problem was to argue that it is less urgent in a large republic than in a small one. Larger republics have a greater pool of possible representatives so that better people will be elected. Furthermore, the substantial numbers of contending interests will better monitor policymakers and detect any shirking or bad behavior. This assertion strikes many as speculative, unfalsifiable, and unpersuasive. The beady-eyed Madison who authored the critically incisive first part of *Federalist* No. 10 became a utopian Pollyanna at the end.[14]

The question might be posed comparatively: Do the costs and risks of direct democracy exceed those of representative democracy? (The question whether one is presumptively more legitimate than the other is also worth considering, but it may be impossible to answer with confidence or consensus.) From a liberal point of view, would direct democracy be more likely than representative democracy to invade individual rights and to over-regulate? From a republican point of view, does the legislature's ability to deliberate about issues over long periods of time, to assemble facts and expert guidance, and

---

[12]*Id.*

[13]"Rent-seeking refers to the attempt to obtain economic rents (i.e., payments for the use of an economic asset in excess of the market price) through government intervention in the market." Jonathan Macey, *Promoting Public-Regarding Legislation Through Statutory Interpretation: An Interest Group Model*, 86 Colum. L. Rev. 223, 224 n.6 (1986).

[14]There is a tendency by critics of direct democracy also to take a cynical view of the popular voting process and a romantic view of the legislative process. See Lynn Baker, *Direct Democracy and Discrimination: A Public Choice Perspective*, 67 Chi.-Kent L. Rev. 707, 751 (1991); Richard Briffault, *Distrust of Democracy*, 63 Tex. L. Rev. 1347 (1985) (book review); Clayton Gillette, *Is Direct Democracy Anti-Democratic?*, 34 Willamette L. Rev. 609 (1998), all making this point in excellent analyses of the critics of direct democracy. We add that the opposite is typically true for staunch defenders of direct democracy. See, e.g., Richard Parker, *"Here, the People Rule": A Constitutional Populist Manifesto* (1994).

to amend proposals to reflect new information contribute more reliably to the common good than direct democracy's ability to reflect the will of the people and to elicit greater citizen involvement? From a critical point of view, does direct democracy imperil historically disadvantaged minorities more than representative democracy does — or does it offer politically active minorities the opportunity to obtain affirmative state protection to remedy their disadvantages? Consider these inquiries not just as a theoretical debate over what should or might be the best system of democratic government, but also in light of the mixed system already in place in most state and local governments. This hybrid system is our political reality; no theoretical arguments about representation are likely to lead to its repeal.

B. *Representative plus Direct Democracy*

Most states — but not the federal government — enjoy a mixed system, in which most laws are enacted by a legislature, but which allows the possibility of popular initiation if the legislature does not act (the *initiative*) or popular override of laws that the legislature does enact (the *referendum*).[15] A mixed system might be preferable to either direct or representative democracy standing alone — or it might be worse than either. Direct democracy might stimulate dawdling representatives to deal with matters of pressing popular interest in order to stave off a more extreme ballot question. The ability of the citizenry to legislate might circumvent entrenched interests opposed to reform and monitor self-dealing and rent-seeking in the legislature. For example, few are surprised that term limits proposals have been enacted largely through initiatives or that most significant state campaign finance reform packages are proposed as direct legislation. As the ballot pamphlet in the 1911 California vote

---

[15]According to *The Book of the States, 1998-99*, at 210 (1998), almost half the states have initiatives and virtually all have referenda:

	Changes to statutes	Changes to constitutions	Totals
Initiatives	22	18	24
Referenda	25	49	49

to adopt the initiative explained: "It is not intended and will not be a substitute for legislation, but will constitute that safeguard which the people should retain for themselves to supplement the work of the legislature by initiating those measures which the legislature either viciously or negligently refuses to enact; and to hold the legislature in check."[16] On the other hand, direct democracy might merely increase the influence of special interests that can exert influence over popular lawmaking by virtue of superior wealth and organization. Or representatives might refuse to compromise in the traditional legislative arena if they know they can submit their more extreme proposals to a popular vote. They might expect to win the vote, or they might hope that the presence of the question on the ballot will manipulate voter turnout in a way that increases their chances for reelection.

Although direct democracy has coexisted with representative democracy in some states for most of the century, scholars are only beginning to study its systematic effects. The interest of legal academics and political scientists may have been sparked in part by the resurgence of direct democracy as a vital form of policymaking.[17] Although new work is shedding light on the issues surrounding direct democracy, the studies often reach inconsistent or uncertain conclusions on key issues.[18] Furthermore, evaluations of the data are significantly influenced by one's normative values. For example, a finding that direct democracy results in outcomes closer to the

---

[16]Constitutional Amendment 22, California Ballot Pamphlet, Special Election (Oct. 11, 1911).

[17]For example, in California, "[s]ince November 1978, forty initiatives have been approved by the voters, an average of four in each two-year election cycle, and nearly as many as in all the years before 1978. . . . Since the 1960s, when nine initiatives qualified for the ballot, the total has doubled in every decade . . . . " Peter Schrag, *Paradise Lost: California's Experience, America's Future* 194 (1998). See also David Magleby, *Direct Legislation: Voting on Ballot Propositions in the United States* 70, 205-06 (1984) (documenting the increasing use of direct democracy).

[18]See, e.g., Thomas Cronin, *Direct Democracy: The Politics of Initiative, Referendum, and Recall* 207-22 (1989) (mixed perspective on direct democracy); Magleby, *supra* note 17 (skeptical of direct democracy); *Referendums: A Comparative Study of Practice and Theory* 224 (David Butler & Austin Ranney eds. 1978) (more positive perspective on direct democracy).

preferences of the median voter[19] may be disturbing to one who worries that the median voter may be insufficiently attentive to minority interests. Even at this early stage of scholarly work, however, we can begin to draw some conclusions about the role of direct democracy in a hybrid system of governance.

An important charge leveled at ballot initiatives concerns whether the laws accurately reflect popular preferences or whether they are predominantly a tool of well-funded interests and individuals. Qualifying a question for the ballot and mounting a campaign to pass it are both very costly activities. Before a question can appear on the ballot, supporters must collect thousands of signatures within a limited period of time. For example, in California 430,000 signatures were needed to qualify a statutory question for the 1996 ballot; a constitutional change required approximately 250,000 more signatures.[20] To ensure that their proposals survive this hurdle, groups are increasingly turning to paid petition circulators, paying up to $1.50 per name in California. The total amount of money required for paid circulators is substantial. Analysts estimate that the circulation drive alone — before any expenses are incurred in the campaign to pass the question — costs between $1,000,000 and $2,000,000 in California.[21] Ordinary people cannot hope to compete in such a costly process; indeed, the groups that can participate successfully will be disproportionately those that can raise large sums of money. Thus, the agenda of direct democracy will not necessarily reflect the concerns of the average voter; it will be shaped to a large extent by well-funded and passionate interest groups.[22]

---

[19]See Elisabeth Gerber, *Legislative Response to the Threat of Popular Initiatives*, 40 Am. J. Pol. Sci. 99 (1996) (legislators in states that allow initiatives pass parental consent laws that more closely resemble median voters' preferences than legislators in states without initiatives).

[20]See Elaine Korry & Bob Edwards, *Ballot Initiatives Submitted by Internet*, (NPR's Morning Edition, Nov. 7, 1996). See also Magleby, *supra* note 17, at 61.

[21]See David Broder, *Taking the Initiative on Petitions: Signatures for a Price*, Wash. Post Nat'l Wkly. Ed., April 20, 1998, at A28 ($2,000,000 estimate); Charlene Wear Simmons, *California's Statewide Initiative Process* 9 (1997) ($1,000,000 estimate).

[22]See Elizabeth Garrett, *Money, Agenda Setting, and Direct Democracy*, 77 Tex. L. Rev. 1845 (1999).

Even if the issues that appear on the ballot do not necessarily track the interests of ordinary people, perhaps the outcome of the election reflects their preferences. Again, however, we have reason to be skeptical. First, the binary format of direct legislation prevents voters from expressing views on a range of policy proposals and, to some extent, from expressing the intensity of their preferences. Citizens must vote "yes" or "no" on proposals that are often complicated, multifaceted, and nuanced. Ballot proposals are drafted by the groups that circulate the petitions to qualify them for the ballot; there is no opportunity during the campaign to amend the proposals. In contrast, opinion polls, letter-writing campaigns, media coverage, and lobbying enable legislators to get some idea of voters' complex preferences. Legislators can refine proposals in light of the intensity of preferences of their constituents or colleagues.

Second, most who cast their vote on a ballot question do so on the basis of very little information. Ballot measures are often too lengthy and complex for the average voter to digest. In the 1988 and 1990 elections in California, for example, voters considered thirteen initiatives that each exceeded 5,000 words, including one proposal of 15,633 words, or approximately 62 double-spaced, typed pages.[23] Voters receive most of their information about an initiative through political advertising and news stories, so how the media characterize a ballot measure plays a pivotal role in how voters perceive it. This low-information environment makes republicans uneasy about the initiative process. How legitimate, they might ask, is law that results from the votes of uninformed and perhaps confused citizen-legislators?[24] Even if elected representatives also sometimes vote on the basis of inadequate information, they participate in a forum conducive to deliberation and they can rely on congressional staff to make considered recommendations. Furthermore, some people react to the complexity of the initiative proposals and the absence of reliable information by abstaining from the process entirely. Thus, while

---

[23]See Schacter, *supra* note 8, at 136.

[24]For an unusual republican-sounding decision invalidating a term limits initiative on the ground that the voter-legislators did not know what they were deciding, see *Jones v. Bates*, 127 F.3d 839 (9th Cir.), *rev'd en banc*, *Bates v. Jones*, 131 F.3d 843 (9th Cir. 1997), *cert. denied*, 118 S.Ct. 1302 (1998). See also Eskridge, Frickey & Garrett Supp. 141-152.

those concerned with the measure will vote, the average voter, and particularly the less sophisticated voter, is likely to forego voting. Such a skew in citizen participation calls into question claims that direct democracy reflects the will of the majority.

Notwithstanding all these difficulties undermining direct democracy's ability to reflect citizen preferences accurately, it might not be an entirely inadequate method to discern popular views on important issues. First, it is a more targeted way than the legislative process for the public to affect governance. Most voters have little idea how their legislators vote on particular issues, and most legislator influence occurs behind the scenes. A vote on an initiative proposal allows citizens to become lawmakers and directly affect the outcome on a particular issue; thus, it is a more transparent outlet for citizen involvement. In addition, a voter may not need full information about a ballot question to vote in a way consistent with her preferences. People have limited time and attention for politics and often decide how to vote on the basis of informational shortcuts, like party affiliation in candidate elections.[25] If the information they obtain through ads and news stories is sufficient for them to make choices that serve their interests, a liberal might argue that they are voting rationally and acceptably. The republican might still prefer a more substantial and sophisticated deliberative process than that afforded by the environment of direct democracy.

A final criticism leveled at the ability of direct democracy to mirror stable majority preferences may be a product of the absence of structured deliberation. Madison argued that representatives are less responsive to petty and passing popular fancies than is the public because representatives' reflective decisionmaking mediates temporary and intolerant public sentiment. Of course, that assertion may not be empirically true; as legislators rely more on opinion polls, focus groups, electronic communication and the like, they may also react to the immediate demands of their constituents without

---

[25]See Arthur Lupia, *Shortcuts Versus Encyclopedias: Information and Voting Behavior in California Insurance Reform Elections*, 88 Am. Pol. Sci. Rev. 63 (1994) (describing inevitability of informational shortcuts and identifying ones in direct democracy that allow voters to vote consistently with their interests).

sufficient analysis of the long-term implications of proposals.[26] Certainly, however, there are dramatic examples of initiatives that have deeply resonated with the citizenry during the campaign and that have had long-range consequences that may have been unintended. Perhaps the most famous is California's Proposition 13, which greatly reduced property taxes and stimulated an era of direct democracy in California. As a result of this and subsequent tax-cutting and tax-freezing initiatives, state and local governments have been disabled from responding to new problems or even maintaining previous levels of educational and other services.[27] Arguably, here the availability of direct democracy encouraged short-sighted lawmaking: taxes were cut without regard to the effect on the mix of public services, and programs were then been adopted without sufficient means to pay for them. Changing laws adopted by popular vote once their long-term effects become apparent is difficult; in many cases, constitutional provisions and even statutes that are the product of direct democracy can be changed only by a second popular vote. Madison's nightmare may be playing out at the state level, and in a way that entrenches many unfortunate decisions for a very long time.

The foregoing provides reasons to view cautiously the argument that direct democracy produces policies more in accord with the preferences of the average voter. Indeed, political scientists who have tested for such an effect have only sometimes found a statistically significant one.[28] But even if direct democracy succeeds on this dimension, it is not clearly desirable. As Madison realized, majorities may oppress minorities, and not just the rich and propertied (the objects of Madison's solicitude), but especially racial, ethnic, and sexual orientation minorities. Critical scholars argue that ballot questions hurt people of color, as white majorities have repeatedly been willing to withdraw civil rights protections through passage of

---

[26]See Lawrence Grossman, *The Electronic Republic: Reshaping Democracy in the Information Age* (1995); Alan Rosenthal, *The Decline of Representative Democracy: Process, Participation, and Power in State Legislatures* (1998).

[27]See Schrag, *supra* note 17, at 154-56.

[28]Compare, e.g., Gerber, *supra* note 19 (finding some effect) with Edward Lascher et al., *Gun Behind the Door? Ballot Initiatives, State Policies, and Public Opinion*, 58 J. Pol. 760 (1996) (no significant effect).

popular initiatives and referenda.[29] Recent initiatives have targeted immigrants and gay people for special disabilities. Between 1959 and 1993, there were 38 ballot measures seeking to withdraw legislated civil rights for gay people. Thirty of those measures were adopted by the voters — a 79% success rate that has not been replicated for any other subject matter (direct democracy's overall success rate is about one-third). Moreover, this record contrasts with the relatively pro-gay record of legislatures during this period.[30]

Students of direct democracy are divided over whether the process is progressive or conservative in nature, or exhibits no systematic tendencies.[31] On social issues, the direct democracy agenda has tended to be politically conservative in recent years, as illustrated by the ballot questions on sexual orientation, immigration, and affirmative action. Even when such questions are rejected by the people, the intolerant rhetoric of the campaigns can cause lasting harm to the interests of minority groups. But with respect to environmental concerns, animal rights, and economic issues, direct democracy has often supported politically liberal causes.[32] In addition, many state reforms of campaign finance laws, lobbying regulations, and ethics rules have been propelled by direct democracy, particularly when the governance proposals conflict with the self-interest of legislators.

---

[29]See, e.g., Derrick Bell, Jr., *The Referendum: Democracy's Barrier to Racial Equality*, 54 Wash. L. Rev. 1, 18-21 (1978); Lawrence Sager, *Insular Majorities Unabated:* Warth v. Seldin *and* City of Eastlake v. Forest City Enterprises, Inc., 91 Harv. L. Rev. 1373, 1411-12, 1414-16, 1418-23 (1978).

[30]See Barbara Gamble, *Putting Civil Rights to a Popular Vote*, 41 Am. J. Pol. Sci. 245, 254 (1997).

[31]Compare Cronin, *supra* note 18, at 98, and Magleby, *supra* note 17, at 190-91 (concluding that direct democracy has mixed record on these scores), with Gamble, *supra* note 30 (direct democracy exacerbates society's tendency to discriminate against minorities).

[32]See Benjamin Barber, *Strong Democracy: Participatory Politics for a New Age* 284 (1984) (direct democracy broke legislative logjams to ban disposable soft-drink containers in several states, to open up some states to legalized gambling, and to defeat right-to-work proposals). The national initiative proposal of the 1970's was supported by such liberals as Senator James Abourezk (D-S.D.) and Ralph Nader.

To the extent that the initiative and referendum result in the enactment of legislation oppressing or singling out minorities, courts could play a role in invalidating or limiting those laws. In fact, half of all initiatives passed by voters have been challenged in court, and, in more than half of those cases, courts struck down part or all of the initiatives.[33] The appropriate role of the judiciary in direct democracy is thus a vital question and one that implicates the theories of representation.

C. *The Role of the Courts in Policing Direct Democracy*

Article IV, Section 4 of the Constitution requires Congress to "guarantee to every State [a] Republican Form of Government." This clause might be read to assure that the states follow a reasonable variation of the republican government defended in *Federalist* No. 10 and therefore to invalidate direct democracy provisions in state constitutions. The Supreme Court and state courts have traditionally held the obligations of the Guarantee Clause to be nonjusticiable,[34] but Guarantee Clause concerns might suggest that the judiciary should scrutinize the fruits of direct democracy more vigorously than the products of representative democracy.[35] On the other hand, special judicial rules for assessing initiatives and referenda might be inappropriate given the perceived legitimacy of such measures. The countermajoritarian difficulty with judicial review applies most vividly here.

---

[33]See Kenneth Miller, *The Role of Courts in the Initiative Process: A Search for Standards*, paper presented at the 1999 Annual Meeting of the American Political Science Association.

[34]See *Pacific States Tel. & Tel. Co. v. Oregon*, 223 U.S. 118 (1912). Strongly contra is Hans Linde, *When Initiative Lawmaking Is Not "Republican Government": The Campaign Against Homosexuality*, 72 Or. L. Rev. 19 (1993). See generally Arthur Bonfield, *The Guarantee Clause of Article IV, Section 4: A Study in Constitutional Desuetude*, 46 Minn. L. Rev. 513 (1962).

[35]See Justice Hans Linde's opinion in *Oregon Education Ass'n v. Phillips*, 727 P.2d 602 (Or. 1986); Bell, *supra* note 29; Julian Eule, *Judicial Review of Direct Democracy*, 99 Yale L.J. 1503 (1990). But see Robin Charlow, *Judicial Review, Equal Protection and the Problem with Plebiscites*, 79 Cornell L. Rev. 527, 607-09 (1994); Mark Tushnet, *Fear of Voting: Differential Standards of Judicial Review of Direct Legislation*, 1996 Ann. Surv. Am. L. 373.

Perhaps a middle ground is possible. Concerns with direct democracy are sharpest when its measures appear to undermine individual civil rights, so courts could adopt more activist strategies in protecting such rights. Political scientist David Magleby, a critic of direct democracy, opines that its baleful consequences have been mitigated because courts "have been active in protecting individual rights, minimizing the harmful effects of short-term majorities on minority and individual rights."[36] Sometimes a higher level of judicial activism is explicitly contemplated by the state constitutional law creating initiatives and referenda. The Massachusetts Constitution, for example, provides that initiatives cannot touch upon enumerated matters such as religious freedoms nor invade specified individual rights.[37] Typically, however, judicial activism is fueled by skepticism about the process of direct democracy itself, both its lack of filters to calm the momentary passions of the people and its susceptibility to use by majorities to harm disfavored groups. Consider the following Supreme Court decisions in light of the theories of representation described earlier.

The earliest cases along these lines were brought by racial minorities. In *Hunter v. Erickson*,[38] the Supreme Court evaluated an initiative that amended the Akron, Ohio city charter to suspend the operation of an existing city ordinance assuring "equal opportunity to all persons to live in decent housing facilities regardless of race, color, religion, ancestry or national origin" and to require that the city's electorate approve future racial, religious, or ancestral housing discrimination ordinances before they could take effect. The Supreme Court invalidated the amendment on equal protection grounds, as an explicit racial classification treating racial housing matters differently from other housing matters. Although a liberal theory might defer to the popular will, the racial classification clearly implicated republican and critical concerns. It also raised liberal

---

[36]Magleby, *supra* note 17. See also Magleby, *Let the Voters Decide? An Assessment of the Initiative and Referendum Process*, 66 U. Colo. L. Rev. 13, 40-42 (1995).

[37]See Mass. Const. amend. Art. XLVIII Pt. 2, § 2.

[38]393 U.S. 385 (1969). See also *Reitman v. Mulkey*, 387 U.S. 369 (1967), which invalidated a California referendum overriding a civil rights statute.

concerns that the anti-apartheid goals of the Fourteenth Amendment were being undermined.

Consistent with its equal protection jurisprudence requiring a showing of discriminatory intent in order to trigger strict scrutiny of policies with no racial classifications but with race-based effects, the Court applied *Hunter* cautiously in subsequent cases. In *James v. Valtierra*,[39] the Supreme Court upheld an amendment to the California Constitution bringing all public housing decisions under California's referendum provisions. The Court rejected the invitation to extend *Hunter* to laws that do not expressly utilize race-based classifications. In *Washington v. Seattle School District No. 1*,[40] the Court held that a state initiative designed to terminate the use of mandatory busing for purposes of racial integration in the public schools violated the Equal Protection Clause. It reached this decision consistently with *Valtierra* because it decided that the initiative used the racial nature of an issue to define the governmental decision-making structure, thereby imposing substantial and unique burdens on racial minorities.

As race-inspired initiatives briefly waned somewhat after this period of judicial hostility to them,[41] sexuality-based ones have waxed — and have presented courts the question of how expansively to read *Hunter*. In 1992, Colorado voters adopted a state constitutional amendment prohibiting any law or policy "whereby homosexual, lesbian or bisexual orientation, conduct, practices or relationships shall constitute or otherwise be the basis of or entitle any person or class of persons to have or claim any minority status, quota prefer-

---

[39]402 U.S. 137 (1971).

[40]458 U.S. 457 (1982). Contrast *Crawford v. Board of Educ.*, 458 U.S. 527 (1982), which upheld a facially neutral initiative against equal protection challenge.

[41]Such initiatives are experiencing a resurgence, however, as voters consider proposals prohibiting race-based affirmative action programs. See, e.g., California's Prop. 209, Nov. 5, 1996 (enacted as Cal. Const. Art. I, § 31). Moreover, anti-immigrant initiatives and proposals hostile to bilingual education may be prompted in part by racial bias. See, e.g., California's Prop. 187, Nov. 8, 1994 (enacted as Cal. Penal Code, § 113) (making illegal aliens ineligible for public social services, such as health care and education); California's Prop. 227, June 2, 1998 (prohibiting bilingual education), enjoined from implementation by *Valeria G. v. Wilson*, 12 F. Supp. 2d 1007 (N.D. Cal. 1998)

ences, protected status or claim of discrimination." The main purpose of the initiative was to preempt local ordinances protecting against sexual orientation discrimination, similar to *Hunter* but without implicating the core purpose of the Reconstruction Amendments. Invoking *Hunter* nonetheless, the Colorado Supreme Court in *Evans v. Romer*[42] invalidated the initiative because it denied gay people access to the normal political process (majority vote in city councils and county commissions) for effectuating their rights, thereby denying gays a fundamental right of political participation. The court's approach reflected both republican and critical concerns that popular majorities were trying to drive gay people back into their accustomed political closets. A dissenting opinion pressed the liberal objection that, in cases unrelated to the core (race-based) concerns of the Fourteenth Amendment, the democratic process allows majorities at the state or national level to abrogate rules developed at the local level. The dissent also pressed a republican objection that the people speaking collectively ought to have discretion to express disapproval of "lifestyles" they find less desirable.[43] The state supreme court majority did not persuasively refute these objections, but, using the analogy of the Fourteenth Amendment's anti-racism goal, it might have developed a theory specifying which traditionally or currently disempowered groups deserve judicial protection.[44]

On appeal in *Romer v. Evans*,[45] the U.S. Supreme Court ignored the state court's theory but nonetheless affirmed, reading the *Hunter* line of cases to monitor prejudice-based motives as well as racially based classifications in direct democracy. The initiative violated the

---

[42]882 P.2d 1335 (Colo. 1994), *aff'd*, 517 U.S. 620 (1996).

[43]See *id.* at 1362-64 (Erickson, J., dissenting).

[44]See Caren Dubnoff, Romer v. Evans: *A Legal and Political Analysis*, 15 L. & Ineq. J. 275 (1997); Pamela Karlan, *Just Politics? Five Not So Easy Pieces of the 1995 Term*, 34 Hous. L. Rev. 289, 296 (1997); Nicholas Zeppos, *The Dynamics of Democracy: Travel, Premature Predation, and the Components of Political Identity*, 50 Vand. L. Rev. 445 (1997).

[45]517 U.S. 620 (1996). The reach of *Romer* is unclear, in part because the Supreme Court later denied review of a decision upholding a similarly worded city charter amendment adopted by popular referendum. See *Equality Foundation of Greater Cincinnati v. City of Cincinnati*, 128 F.3d 289 (6th Cir. 1997), *cert. denied*, 119 S.Ct. 365 (1998).

Equal Protection Clause, the Court ruled, because "its sheer breadth is so discontinuous with the reasons offered for it that the amendment seems inexplicable by anything but animus toward the class that it affects." The Court characterized the initiative as a "status-based" law aimed at a class of citizens; such laws violate the core equal protection command that " 'a bare . . . desire to harm a politically unpopular group cannot constitute a *legitimate* government interest.' "[46]

The state had defended the law as a way of concentrating scarce enforcement resources on race and sex discrimination, protecting the privacy rights of landlords and parents who did not want gay people in their houses and schools, and sending a public message that homosexuality is not an approved "lifestyle." Do these arguments sound like animus? Some liberals would have a hard time reaching that conclusion, for the initiative left gay people free to overturn its results using the state or national political process.[47] Commentators have found republican and critical possibilities in *Romer*. As a consequence of legal persecution and witch-hunting, gay people have traditionally been closeted, which has impaired their ability to organize as a political group with power to influence the legislative process.[48] Republican and critical theories of representation are skeptical of measures that turn back efforts to undo the psychic and political damage of previous state discrimination.

Furthermore, these theorists' emphasis on the quality and content of deliberation might make them particularly uncomfortable with a law adopted on the basis of the popular arguments deployed during the initiative campaign. Gay people were characterized as AIDS-diseased because of their "voracious," "high-risk," and promiscuous sexual lives. In other material, they were described as a wealthy group seeking "special rights" so they could be free to "attack" the

---

[46]517 U.S. at 632 (first quotation), 634-35 (second), quoting *Department of Agriculture v. Moreno*, 413 U.S. 528, 534 (1973).

[47]See *Romer*, 517 U.S. at 636 (Scalia, J., dissenting); Robert Bork, *Slouching Towards Gomorrah* 112-14 (1996).

[48]See William Eskridge, Jr., *Gaylaw: Challenging the Apartheid of the Closet* ch. 6 (1999); Bruce Ackerman, *Beyond* Carolene Products, 98 Harv. L. Rev. 713 (1985).

family and the church and to "indoctrinate" and recruit the state's young people.[49] These kinds of arguments were not only counterfactual (for example, lesbians suffer fewer diseases than other groups, including heterosexuals), but they also reinforced social perceptions of gay people as a "pariah group." Defenders of *Romer* invoke a republican and critical principle against state actions that tend to create or reinforce prejudice against pariah groups.[50]

Concerns related to the status of the targeted group can justify aggressive judicial review in ways that may resonate with some liberals. John Hart Ely argues that the most defensible approach for judicial review in a democratic society is a *representation-reinforcing role*. This approach to judicial review is "an 'antitrust' as opposed to a regulatory orientation. [R]ather than dictate substantive results it intervenes only when the 'market,' in our case the political market, is systematically malfunctioning. (A referee analogy is also not far off: the referee is to intervene only when one team is gaining unfair advantage, not because the 'wrong' team has scored.)" According to Ely, the political market is failing, and therefore "undeserving of trust, when (1) the ins are choking off the channels of political change to ensure that they will stay in and the outs will stay out, or (2) though no one is actually denied a voice or a vote, representatives beholden to an effective majority are systematically disadvantaging some minority out of simple hostility or a prejudiced refusal to recognize commonalities of interest, and thereby denying that minority the protection afforded other groups by a representative system."[51]

The Court in *Romer* could have identified both kinds of anticompetitive behavior on the part of powerful political interests. First, strongly entrenched "ins" sought to disrupt the process by which gay people were becoming politically mobilized. Recent

---

[49]See Robert Nagel, *Playing Defense*, 6 Wm. & Mary Bill of Rts. J. 167, 191-99 (1997) (appendix reproducing key voter information pamphlet).

[50]See Daniel Farber & Suzanna Sherry, *The Pariah Principle*, 13 Const. Comm. 257 (1996). See also Akhil Amar, *Attainder and Amendment 2:* Romer's *Rightness*, 95 Mich. L. Rev. 203 (1996); Michael Seidman, Romer's *Radicalism: The Unexpected Revival of Warren Court Activism*, 1996 Sup. Ct. Rev. 67.

[51]John Hart Ely, *Democracy and Distrust: A Theory of Judicial Review* 102-03 (1980); see *United States v. Carolene Prods. Co.*, 304 U.S. 144, 153 n.4 (1938), which inspired Ely's theory.

efforts by groups supporting gay rights have led to the enactment of local laws protecting out-of-the-closet folks from job and other discriminations. Second, the initiative stripped gay people of the antidiscrimination rules enjoyed by everyone else in Colorado — including straight people who, after the initiative, became the only beneficiaries of the local antidiscrimination laws gay people had lobbied for. Under all the theories of representation we have discussed, initiatives with these effects on the autonomy of citizens, particularly historically disempowered ones, should trigger special scrutiny by reviewing courts.[52]

II. Qualification and Election of Representatives[53]

The process for choosing representatives in our country looks liberal: almost any adult citizen can vote and run for public office, and each vote is weighted the same. The apparent triumph of liberalism reflects more than a century's worth of constitutional amendment and judicial decisionmaking, but the process is not quite as unencumbered as it appears. It is regulated in significant respects: laws deny ballot access to new political parties, to some independent candidates, and (for many state offices) to incumbents who have served a specified maximum term; laws refuse to extend the voting franchise to noncitizens and criminals; and laws gerrymander (i.e., manipulate) electoral districts to achieve partisan or racial goals. Although courts have invalidated some of these regulations, most have survived judicial scrutiny.

A restriction on or manipulation of electoral qualifications and voting rules is the paradigm case for activist representation-reinforcing judicial review as explained by Ely or applied by the various courts in *Romer*. The major theories of representation would pose objections to most attempts to impose qualifications on the right to

---

[52]And one study concludes that courts are more aggressive in reviewing initiatives that target minorities or restrict political speech than in reviewing ballot questions on other subjects. See Miller, *supra* note 33.

[53]Issues of electoral and office qualifications are analyzed in Eskridge & Frickey 124-206 (plus Eskridge, Frickey & Garrett Supp. 5-23); Hetzel, Libonati & Williams 297-323, 377-86; Issacharoff, Karlan & Pildes 17-115, 122-177, 367-423, 441-615, 695-712; Lowenstein 21-257, 297-424, 687-716; Mikva & Lane 308-437.

vote. Liberal theory, which has largely driven the evolution of public law in this area, would support extensive deregulation, especially as to suffrage. The liberal position on qualifications for candidates, particularly those adopted by popular vote of the citizens, is more complicated, as we will discuss. Republicans worry that most restrictions on voting and service (except those imposing term limits on office holders) have been adopted by legislators and political parties. These entrenched political interests have incentives to structure politics so that they can remain in power, perhaps at the expense of the voters and the public interest. Some voting exclusions and gerrymanders are intended to perpetuate the under-representation of traditionally excluded minorities, a particular concern for critical theorists.

Given these concerns and the close relationship between such restrictions and issues of representation, judicial review policing the rules for choosing representatives is more defensible, and less susceptible to charges of countermajoritarianism, than aggressive review of direct democracy. Yet judicial review has been disappoint-ing — both too timid to correct agency problems and other dys-functions impairing representation, and too rigid to provide real solutions even when judges seize the moment and question laws that appear to disadvantage new participants in the process. We will next apply the theories of representation to some of these questions and then continue our analysis in Chapter 4 with a more detailed discus-sion of ballot access regulations.

A. *Who Is Eligible to Serve as a Representative?*

The Philadelphia Convention hotly debated the Committee of Detail's proposal that the "Legislature of the United States shall have authority to establish such uniform qualifications of the members of each House, with regard to property, as to the said Legislature shall seem expedient." Madison urged its rejection, stating that the proposal would vest "an improper & dangerous power in the Legisla-ture," which could "subvert" the Constitution "by limiting the number capable of being elected" so as to keep outsiders out of the legislature.[54] The Convention accepted Madison's arguments and amended the Committee's draft to remove any mention of congressional power to set additional qualifications. The final version of the Qualifications Clauses of the Constitution set few limits on who can be a congressional representative.[55] Article I, Section 2 requires only that a member of the U.S. House of Representatives be at least 25 years of age, a U.S. citizen for seven years or more, and an "Inhabitant" of the state from which elected. Article I, Section 3 requires only that a member of the U.S. Senate be at least 30 years of age, a U.S. citizen for nine years or more, and an "Inhabitant" of the state from which elected. During the ratification debates, Alexander Hamilton argued that "the true principle of a republic is, that the people should choose whom they please to govern them. Representation is imperfect in proportion as the current of popular favor is checked. The great source of free government, popular election, should be perfectly pure, and the most unbounded liberty allowed."[56]

Several important Supreme Court cases have applied the Framers' liberal reading of the Qualifications Clauses to invalidate federal and state regulations. *Powell v. McCormack*[57] decided whether Congress could refuse to seat a representative who met the constitutional qualifications. A House special committee found that Representative Adam Clayton Powell of New York met the formal requirements for membership in the House of Representatives but urged his censure because of various frauds on the public. By a vote of 248 to 176, the full House amended the special committee's resolution to require Powell's exclusion from the House and then adopted the amended resolution by a vote of 307 to 116.

A virtually unanimous Supreme Court ruled first that the case did not present the Court with a nonjusticiable political question because the Constitution provided sufficiently clear legal standards to resolve

---

[54]2 *Records of the Federal Convention of 1787*, at 249-50 (Max Farrand rev. ed. 1966).

[55]For state constitutional provisions to similar effect, see Mikva & Lane 400.

[56]2 *Debates on the Federal Constitution* 257 (J. Elliott ed. 1876).

[57]395 U.S. 486 (1969), excerpted and discussed in Eskridge & Frickey 187-99; Hetzel, Libonati & Williams 303-16; Issacharoff, Karlan & Pildes 707-08; Mikva & Lane 400-07.

the controversy. Second, it held that the House Qualifications Clause, which reflected a complete list of criteria for inclusion in the national legislature, could not be changed or supplemented by Congress. As the Court demonstrated, its holding was consistent with the liberal precepts announced by Madison and Hamilton at the Philadelphia Convention and ratification debates, respectively. The Court finally concluded that the House was not empowered to exclude Powell from his seat even if (as the Court assumed, arguendo) the House had the authority under Article I, Section 5, to expel Powell by a two-thirds vote.

Powell is a remarkable decision in several ways. The Supreme Court has sometimes refused to interfere with the operation of the legislative process, but *Powell* and the reapportionment cases (discussed below) ushered in a period when the Supreme Court has routinely enforced constitutional precepts of representation to overturn congressional decisions.[58] Equally important, *Powell* stands as a strong statement of a liberal baseline for national representation: the minimal criteria of the Qualifications Clauses cannot be augmented by Congress.[59] The most dramatic test of that baseline occurred because of the recent term limits movement.

After the 1994 election cycle, 22 states had adopted amendments to their constitutions limiting the number of terms that could be served by their representatives in Congress. Supporters of term limits argue that members tend to become "lifers" in the legislature, impelling them toward timidity in pressing bold policy innovations that might be controversial. Long-time incumbents also become part of cozy ossified triangles, in which legislators, executive branch bureaucrats, and interest groups create self-interested policy that undermines the public interest. Although voters claim to resent the lifetime legislator phenomenon, they continue to return their own incumbent to office, lest they find themselves ineffectively repre-

---

[58]See, e.g., *United States v. Munoz-Flores*, 495 U.S. 385 (1990) (revenue bills must originate in the House); *INS v. Chadha*, 462 U.S. 919, 941 (1983) (bicameralism and presentment required for all legislative acts).

[59]*Powell* also has a critical edge, explicitly noted in Justice Douglas's concurring opinion: because Powell was an African-American representative with substantial seniority and was chair of the education committee, his exclusion had "racist overtones." *Powell*, 395 U.S. at 553 (Douglas, J., concurring).

sented by an inexperienced junior member in an institution governed by powerful norms of seniority.[60] Mandatory term limits are an effort to "throw [all] the rascals out" and replace them with citizen-representatives who, like the legendary Cincinnatus, will leave their plows and work for the public good for a short while. As these arguments suggest, liberals as well as republicans have supported term limits — the former to improve legislator responsiveness to the electorate and the latter to improve deliberation, civic virtue, and popular participation.[61] Critical scholars might support term limits because challengers of diverse backgrounds could more easily win in races for open seats than in races against powerful and wealthy incumbents.

Many political science scholars remain skeptical of term limits, for liberal as well as republican reasons.[62] At the state level, it is not clear that term limits are needed, as half of the legislators in lower state chambers and a third in upper chambers leave after six years in

---

[60]Such voters are in a prisoners' dilemma. If they all vote out their respective incumbents, they are potentially better off. But if one group of voters defects and reelects its incumbent representative, while other voters remain faithful to the term limit idea, then the first group wins a big prize (a representative with seniority and savvy) and the other groups get the sucker's payoff (a rookie representative with less power who is easily rolled by the savvy one). Knowing this, voters will, against their better judgment, tend to return seniority-laden incumbents even when challengers would promote policies closer to the voters' preferences. See Einer Elhauge, *Are Term Limits Undemocratic?*, 64 U. Chi. L. Rev. 83, 85-86 (1997). To avoid this, the term limits movement adopted a national strategy, winning 13 state adoptions in 1992; some of the amendments delayed their effective dates so that term limits would not be imposed until a significant number of other states also adopted such limits. See John Carey, *Term Limits and Legislative Representation* 12 (1996).

[61]See Robert Kurfirst, *Term-Limit Logic: Paradigms and Paradoxes*, 29 Polity 119 (1996) (different theories of representation have generated arguments for term limits); George Will, *Restoration: Congress, Term Limits, and the Recovery of Deliberative Democracy* (1992).

[62]See Linda Cohen & Mathew Spitzer, *Term Limits*, 80 Geo. L.J. 477 (1992); Nelson Polsby, *Restoration Comedy*, 102 Yale L.J. 1515 (1993) (scathing review of Will, *Restoration*); Alan Rosenthal, *The Effect of Term Limits on Legislatures: A Comment*, in *Limiting Legislative Terms* 205-08 (Michael Malbin & Gerald Benjamin eds. 1992), excerpted in Mikva & Lane 427-30; *Legislative Term Limits: Public Choice Perspectives* (Bernard Grofman ed. 1996).

office.[63] Careers are lengthier in Congress, although the Congresses elected in 1992 and 1994 contained many new faces.[64] Others object that term limits will deprive legislatures of their most experienced members (it takes a few terms just to learn the ropes), without producing corresponding advantages in the quality of deliberation or in the content of legislation. Furthermore, even with term limits, the citizen-legislator may remain a mythical creature as term-limited politicians adopt strategies of moving from office to office to maintain long-term political careers.[65] Term limits on state offices have not eliminated the career politicians; the experience in California, where people like Willie Brown move from the legislature to other positions in city or state government, demonstrates the ability of ambitious politicians to alter their behavior to comport with new rules. Nor do term limits ameliorate the threat of interest group influence. Term-limited representatives may not be as interested in campaign contributions from interest groups, but there is probably little real difference in the appetite for campaign money of current long-time incumbents and politicians who move from office to office when term limits force a change. Moreover, term limits might provide interest groups a different influential tool: the offer of post-service jobs for the term-limited representative.

Whatever their political utility, term limits have been challenged as violating both state and federal constitutional requirements. Term limits on state legislators have generally been upheld against constitutional attack. The leading case is *Legislature of the State of California v. Eu,*[66] which balanced the interests of incumbents to stay in office and of voters to have the choice of reelecting them against

---

[63]See Gary Montcrief et al., *For Whom the Bell Tolls: Term Limits and State Legislatures*, 17 Legis. Studs. Q. 37, 39-42 (1992).

[64]Even with this significant turnover in recent Congresses, institutionalized term limits would result in greater and more systematic turnover. See W. Robert Reed & D. Eric Schansberg, *The House Under Term Limits: What Would It Look Like?,* 76 Soc. Sci. Q. 699 (1995) (estimating turnover under six-year limits and twelve-year limits).

[65]See Elizabeth Garrett, *Term Limitations and the Myth of the Citizen-Legislator*, 81 Cornell L. Rev. 623, 656-658 (1996).

[66]816 P.2d 1309 (Cal. 1991), *cert. denied*, 503 U.S. 919 (1992). Accord, *Bates v. Jones*, 131 F.3d 843 (9th Cir. 1997) (en banc).

the state's interest in ending the "incumbent's advantage" in elections. The court found that no fundamental rights had been critically burdened (voters have no "right" to vote for a particular candidate) and that the state's interest was considerable.

Term limits on federal lawmakers have not fared as well in the courts. In *U.S. Term Limits, Inc. v. Thornton*,[67] the U.S. Supreme Court held that state-imposed term limits on federal representatives violate the Qualifications Clauses as they are properly understood in light of *Powell v. McCormack*. Although some argued that *Powell* made *Thornton* an easy case, the Court divided 5-4, with a spirited dissenting opinion that distinguished between additional qualifications imposed by Congress and those imposed by the states themselves. While current members of Congress might have self-serving reasons for adopting particular qualifications, voters, either acting directly or through state legislators, have no such conflict of interest that might cast into doubt the motives behind the additional requirements for congressional service. Thus, *Powell*'s holding did not necessarily dictate the outcome of *Thornton*.

Much of the debate between the majority and the dissent related to the original understanding of the Qualifications Clauses and early state practice under them. More interestingly for our purposes, the dissent essentially charged the majority with betraying liberal premises of representation and undermining the possibility of republican governance. The first charge was inspired by the fact that the Arkansas term limits provision at issue, like virtually all others adopted in 1992 and 1994, was the result of a popular initiative. How could the Court invalidate term limits by invoking the principle of free voter choice, when the voters had unequivocally chosen to adopt term limits? As Justice Thomas wrote in dissent: "[T]he authority to narrow the field of candidates . . . may be part and parcel of the right to elect Members of Congress. That is, the right to choose may include the right to winnow."[68] The dissent's second, more republican-sounding charge was inspired by the ways in which congressional incumbents have insulated themselves from serious challenge. Among other things, they have voted themselves franking

---

[67]514 U.S. 779 (1995).

[68]*Id.* at 881 (Thomas, J., dissenting).

and staff privileges to ingratiate themselves with the voters, and they have adopted campaign finance rules making it hard for potential challengers to raise the great sums of money needed to buy the name recognition available to incumbents at taxpayers' expense. From the perspective of preventing the "ins" from entrenching themselves, term limits can be justified as a way to level the playing field so that challengers have a realistic chance to serve in Congress.

B. *The Right to Political Participation: Voting and Choice*

It is ironic that a nation committed to freedom and democracy disallowed most people from voting for representatives at the time of its founding and for several generations thereafter. Women, slaves and their descendants, and people who did not own property were disenfranchised for much of the nation's history, either by direct prohibitions or by indirect measures such as literacy tests and poll taxes. Most of the bars to voting have been repealed — by constitutional amendment,[69] federal voting rights laws,[70] and Supreme Court decisions. The Court in *Harper v. Virginia State Board of Elections*[71] anticipated the Twenty-Fourth Amendment in striking down poll taxes. The Court ruled that " 'the political franchise of voting' " is a " 'fundamental political right, because preservative of all rights.' "[72] The Court extended *Harper* to strike down most laws requiring property ownership in limited purpose elections[73] and most durational residence requirements.[74]

---

[69]See U.S. Const., amend. XV (no discrimination on account of race in access to the franchise), amend. XIX (no discrimination on account of sex), amend. XXIV (poll taxes abolished), amend. XXVI (18 year-olds may vote).

[70]See Voting Rights Act of 1965, Pub. L. No. 89-110, 79 Stat. 437.

[71]383 U.S. 663 (1966)

[72]*Id.* at 667, quoting *Yick Wo v. Hopkins*, 118 U.S. 356, 370 (1886).

[73]See *Kramer v. Union Free Sch. Dist. No. 15*, 395 U.S. 621 (1969), followed in *Cipriano v. Houma*, 395 U.S. 701 (1969); *Phoenix v. Kolodziejski*, 399 U.S. 204 (1970); *Quinn v. Millsap*, 491 U.S. 95 (1989), but distinguished in *Salyer Land Co. v. Tulare Lake Basin Water Storage Dist.*, 410 U.S. 719 (1973); *Ball v. James*, 451 U.S. 355 (1981).

[74]See *Dunn v. Blumstein*, 405 U.S. 330 (1972), distinguished in *Rosario v. Rockefeller*, 410 U.S. 752 (1973).

All these cases reflect the liberal principle that "[a]ny unjustified discrimination in determining who may participate in political affairs or in the selection of public officials undermines the legitimacy of representative government."[75] Notwithstanding such rhetoric, the right to vote remains regulated, both directly and indirectly, mostly for republican reasons: to exclude voters who are not part of the political community and to avoid voter confusion. Although liberal and critical theorists strongly object to many of these regulations, the Supreme Court has shown only sporadic inclination to disturb them. We will discuss here the first set of regulations, affecting who can vote, and return to ballot access laws, which are ostensibly designed to combat voter confusion, in Chapter 4.

Admittedly, there are few direct and general exclusions from the right to vote in our polity. The main ones are for people under the age of eighteen; noncitizens; and people convicted of serious crimes. One may argue about the age at which citizens should be entitled to vote, but the principle underlying this exclusion is robust: people under a certain age are not mature enough to form reasoned political preferences (liberalism), and they may not have enough of a stake in society to sustain serious deliberative duties (republicanism). The second exclusion is based upon a republican principle: only serious stakeholders should exercise the right to choose representatives. The Supreme Court has ruled that states cannot discriminate generally against hiring noncitizens for the civil service but can do so for offices that are at "the heart of representative government."[76] This logic augurs against a successful constitutional claim by noncitizens seeking the right to vote. But excluding noncitizens from voting can be questioned on liberal, republican, and critical grounds. If a noncitizen has paid taxes, sent her children to school, and participated in the civic and economic life of the community for a significant period of time, why should she not be able to vote, at least in school board and other local elections? Also, the exclusion of noncitizens

---

[75]*Kramer*, 395 U.S. at 626.

[76]*Bernal v. Fainter*, 467 U.S. 216, 216 (1984). Compare *Sugarman v. Dougall*, 413 U.S. 634 (1973) (states cannot generally discriminate), with *Ambach v. Norwick*, 441 U.S. 68 (1979) (state can discriminate against noncitizens in public school teacher hiring).

falls primarily on marginalized groups, such as Latinos and poor people.

Nearly four-fifths of the states have laws excluding citizens convicted of serious crimes from voting or holding elective office.[77] These laws would appear questionable under liberal premises: once the felon has paid his debt to society, he should be free to rejoin the polity. They are defended by the republican argument that felons have forfeited the full rights of citizenship by their criminal acts. The Supreme Court upheld California's exclusionary law in *Richardson v. Ramirez*.[78] The Court distinguished *Harper* and its progeny on the ground that Section 2 of the Fourteenth Amendment explicitly contemplated that the states can deny "the right to vote" by reason of "participation in rebellion [i.e., the Civil War], or other crime." Therefore, the Framers of Section 1 of the Amendment (where the Equal Protection Clause resides) could not have intended for the right to vote to be absolute. As a construction of the U.S. Constitution, *Ramirez* does not bar states from construing their own constitutions to invalidate laws disenfranchising felons, but many such laws are embedded in their states' constitutions. We are aware of no successful challenge brought on state or federal right-to-vote grounds.[79]

There does remain a doctrinal, and critically inspired, basis for challenging such laws, insofar as they disproportionately affect African-American men. In some jurisdictions, the bar disables 10-20% of black men from voting or holding office.[80] The Supreme Court struck down such a law in *Hunter v. Underwood*.[81] The Alabama Constitution of 1901 disenfranchised all persons convicted

---

[77]See Steven Snyder, *Let My People Run: The Rights of Voters and Candidates Under State Laws Barring Felons from Holding Elective Office*, 4 J.L. & Pol. 543 (1988) (app. A). Currently, 39 states do not allow certain felons, most notably those with vote-fraud convictions, to appear on the ballot.

[78]418 U.S. 24 (1974).

[79]Interestingly, the reasoning of *U.S. Term Limits v. Thornton* suggests that states cannot disqualify felons from running for federal office. See *U.S. Term Limits v. Thornton*, 514 U.S. at 917.

[80]See Michael Fletcher, *Voting Rights for Felons Win Support: 13% of Black Men Ineligible with Ban*, Wash. Post, Feb. 22, 1999, at A1.

[81]471 U.S. 222 (1985).

of crimes involving "moral turpitude," including rape, murder, sodomy, adultery, vagrancy, and wife beating. The law not only had a disproportionate effect on blacks (ten times as many blacks as whites were disenfranchised), but it was also motivated by racial animus, as it was adopted as part of the state's post-Reconstruction campaign to minimize black political power. *Hunter v. Underwood* was an easy case because of the strong evidence of racist motives. Critical theories of representation would maintain that the Court should extend that decision's result to cases where there is a significant racially disproportionate impact and evidence that the rule has been retained due to an invidious desire to marginalize racial minorities' voting power. Although the Court has been generally unwilling to invalidate facially neutral laws having substantial and disproportionate racial impact without solid evidence that the law was adopted or maintained for discriminatory reasons, it has ratified a lower court judgment to that effect in at least one constitutional voting case, where a fundamental right as well as arguable race discrimination were involved.[82]

C. *Fair Aggregation of Votes and Gerrymandering*

The right to vote involves not only the formal right to cast a vote, but also a right to a fair aggregation of votes. For example, if Joan is one of 100,000 voters choosing a representative for Congress, her vote is worth less, or "diluted," if Sarah is one of only 10,000 voters choosing a member of Congress in the neighboring district. The Supreme Court in *Wesberry v. Sanders*[83] held that this arrangement violates Article I, Section 2 of the Constitution, which requires that the members of the House of Representatives be "apportioned among the several States according to their respective Numbers." In an opinion inspired more by theories of representation than by legal criteria, the Court ruled that Section 2 requires that "as nearly as is practicable one [person's] vote in a congressional election is to be

---

[82]See *Rogers v. Lodge*, 458 U.S. 613 (1982), where the majority affirmed a holding that an at-large electoral system with strong racially disproportionate impact had been maintained for racially discriminatory reasons. The outcome was hotly challenged by dissenting Justices Stevens, Powell, and Rehnquist.

[83]376 U.S. 1 (1964).

worth as much as another's."[84] This famous "one person, one vote" standard not only promotes the liberal goal of assuring formal equality in the aggregation of votes, it serves republican and critical values of overturning districting schemes that blatantly over-represented rural interests and under-represented urban and suburban ones.[85]

Wesberry has been a much heralded opinion for these reasons, as well as for its virtue of being easy to administer.[86] Before *Wesberry*, the Court had ruled in *Baker v. Carr*[87] that state reapportionment issues are justiciable. After *Wesberry,* the Court in *Reynolds v. Sims*[88] held that apportionment in state legislatures must conform to the "one person, one vote" rule pursuant to the Equal Protection Clause.[89] Chief Justice Warren's opinion for the Court is the leading statement of a liberal philosophy of representation. It held that voting is a fundamental constitutional right triggering strict equal protection scrutiny and that such a right is abridged by malapportionment. In rejecting the state's argument that its districts were justified by history and geographical compactness, Warren memorably said: "Legislators represent people, not trees or acres," and the people thus

---

[84]*Id.* at 8.

[85]See Robert Dixon, Jr., *Democratic Representation: Reapportionment in Law and Politics* (1968).

[86]See *Kirkpatrick v. Preisler*, 394 U.S. 526, 530-31 (1969) (striking down redistricting plan leaving deviation of 5.97% between most and least populous congressional districts); *White v. Weiser*, 412 U.S. 783 (1973) (striking down plan leaving deviation of 4.13%); *Karcher v. Daggett*, 462 U.S. 725 (1983) (striking down plan with deviation of 0.6984% and rejecting a de minimis exception to the one person, one vote rule).

[87]369 U.S. 186 (1962). *Baker* remains the leading case articulating criteria for the Court's application of the political question doctrine and inaugurated a period of great judicial activism as to issues of representation, as this chapter demonstrates.

[88]377 U.S. 533 (1964).

[89]In *Avery v. Midland County*, 390 U.S. 474 (1968), the Court held that the one person, one vote rule applies to local governments. See also *Hadley v. Junior College Dist.*, 397 U.S. 50 (1970).

represented cannot be subject to denial of the franchise or "dilution" of it.[90]

The equal representation assured in state legislatures is both broader and narrower than that assured in the federal legislature. It is broader because the precept applies to both houses of bicameral state legislatures, not just the lower house. *Reynolds* noted that the U.S. Senate flouts the one person, one vote principle and is saved only by its being embedded in the Constitution.[91] The logic of one person, one vote would be undermined, the Court held, if one chamber were exempt from it, for the "unrepresentative" chamber could then obstruct laws pressed by the "representative" one. This is a notably strong endorsement of a liberal theory of representation, at the expense of the republican argument that an "unrepresentative" upper chamber is useful to slow down hasty but popular proposals. Warren might also have been influenced by the critical insight that chambers constituted without following one person, one vote tended to be biased against civil rights interests. The equal representation guarantee for state legislatures is also narrower than that for the national legislature. Unlike apportionment of congressional districts under Article I, Section 2, demonstrable population deviation among districts has been upheld in the context of state legislatures.[92]

One of most significant effects of the one person, one vote revolution has been to make *partisan gerrymandering* easier and more pervasive. Gerrymandering is easier because *Reynolds* de-emphasized historical and geographic concerns relative to the over-riding concern of numerical equality. To meet the exacting numerical standards, states often had to depart from territorial boundaries. Furthermore, opportunities for gerrymandering are more frequent because one person, one vote requires states to redraw their federal

---

[90]*Reynolds*, 377 U.S. at 562.

[91]See U.S. Const. Art. V (structure of Senate cannot be amended out of the Constitution).

[92]For example, deviations under 10% have been routinely upheld. See *Connor v. Finch*, 431 U.S. 407 (1977); *White v. Regester*, 412 U.S. 755 (1973). Even an apportionment plan that contains a higher deviation may be upheld if it is deemed necessary to achieving legitimate state interests. See, e.g., *Brown v. Thomson*, 462 U.S. 835 (1983).

and state district lines after every census in order to achieve the numerical precision demanded by the Court. Not surprisingly, given the overwhelming incentives for politicians to take advantage of such opportunities, partisan gerrymandering has been vigorously pursued in the last generation. Although the Supreme Court in *Davis v. Bandemer*[93] followed *Baker* to hold partisan gerrymanders reviewable, the Court's standard was vague. It held that "unconstitutional discrimination occurs only when the electoral system is arranged in a manner that will consistently degrade a voter's or a group of voters' influence on the political process as a whole."[94] Under that standard, no partisan gerrymander has been invalidated by a federal appellate court under the Equal Protection Clause.

The one person, one vote rule also would have made *racial gerrymandering* easier and more pervasive for the same reasons, but that process was disrupted and eventually rechanneled by the adoption of the Voting Rights Act in 1965.[95] To begin with, the Voting Rights Act and its early jurisprudence reflect critical as well as liberal theories of representation.[96] As amended in 1982, § 2 of the statute bars electoral schemes that "result[] in a denial or abridgment of the right . . . to vote on account of race or color."[97] This "discrimi-

---

[93]478 U.S. 109 (1986).

[94]*Id.* at 110. Justice White delivered the judgment of the Court and wrote a plurality opinion for four Justices. He first ruled that political gerrymander challenges are justiciable under *Baker*, a conclusion joined by two dissenting Justices. He next articulated a vague standard for reviewing such gerrymanders (quoted in text) and upheld the gerrymander under that standard; three Justices concurred in dismissing the constitutional challenge, but not in the plurality's reasoning, because they considered the controversy nonjusticiable. For critique of the plurality, see Samuel Issacharoff, *Judging Politics: The Elusive Quest for Judicial Review of Political Fairness*, 71 Tex. L. Rev. 1643 (1993).

[95]Pub. L. No. 89-110, 79 Stat. 437, codified as 42 U.S.C. § 1973 *et seq.*

[96]See generally Kathryn Abrams, *Relationships of Representation in Voting Rights Act Jurisprudence*, 71 Tex. L. Rev. 1409 (1993); Chandler Davidson, *The Voting Rights Act: A Brief History*, in *Controversies in Minority Voting: The Voting Rights Act in Perspective* 7 (Bernard Grofman & Chandler Davidson eds. 1992); Samuel Issacharoff, *Polarized Voting and the Political Process: The Transformation of Voting Rights Jurisprudence*, 90 Mich. L. Rev. 1833 (1992).

[97]42 U.S.C. § 1973(a), construed in *Thornburgh v. Gingles*, 478 U.S. 30 (1986).

natory result" provision authorizes a more aggressive judicial review of voting schemes than the "discriminatory intent" review the Supreme Court normally follows in race cases such as *James v. Valtierra* and *Hunter v. Underwood*. A liberal justification for more aggressive review is the documented history of subterfuges used to deny or dilute the right to vote for people of color. Given such history, an inquiry that allows more judicial intrusion into the political process is appropriate. Indeed, § 5 of the Voting Rights Act is particularly far-reaching, requiring official "preclearance" of electoral changes by jurisdictions (mainly in the South) found to have systematically excluded blacks.[98]

Critical theory offers a more controversial justification for aggressive judicial and executive branch review in cases of possible racial vote dilution.[99] Because white people are in the majority most of the time and tend not to vote for nonwhite candidates, minorities tend to be under-represented in legislatures, especially when elections are at-large rather than by smaller, more homogeneous districts.[100] For critical theory, it is important for racial minorities to serve in the legislature, because their voices and the intensity of their concerns cannot be fully internalized by even the most sympathetic white representative. Women and gay people have some of the same concerns, and critical theorists point to their under-representation as partial causes for the undistinguished legislative performances in hearings concerning Anita Hill's sexual harassment charges against Clarence Thomas and in the debates about excluding gay people from the armed services. Also, it is symbolically important that the legislature reflect the diversity of the country. Consistent with these theories, racial bloc voting and the absence of people of color in the legislature are two indications that can support a finding of a violation of § 2 of the Voting Rights Act.[101] Furthermore, since the 1980s, the

---

[98]See 42 U.S.C. § 1973c.

[99]See Keith Bybee, *Mistaken Identity: The Supreme Court and the Politics of Minority Representation* (1998); Guinier, *supra* note 5; Williams, *supra* note 5.

[100]Where voting is racially polarized, a racial minority will find it easier to win in a subdistrict where her race is a majority and impossible to win in the at-large district. Congress abolished at-large House districts which existed in several states in Pub. L. No. 90-196, 81 Stat. 581 (1967).

[101]See *Gingles*, 478 U.S. at 48-51.

Justice Department has exercised its § 5 preclearance authority to press for more "majority-minority" districts in the South. These efforts yielded an unprecedented number of racial minorities in the House of Representatives in the 1990s.

The movement toward *proportional representation* of racial minorities and perhaps women has stimulated liberal and republican responses. Some critics argue that the current response of packing racial minorities into homogeneous districts ghettoizes those minorities and marginalizes their representatives in the legislature.[102] Would minorities be better off with more representatives who had to pay attention to their interests because they are a powerful and organized constituency, rather than with a few representatives of minority districts who specialize in protecting only their interests? The answer to this question is not clear.

Much clearer has been the liberal response: by deploying race-based classifications or acting with racially motivated intent, creators of majority-minority districts make distinctions between white and black voters based solely on their race. Such discrimination is constitutionally questionable for the same reason as race-based affirmative action, argue the critics.[103] The Supreme Court in *Shaw v. Reno*[104] opened race-based districting to moderately aggressive judicial review. Since *Shaw*, the Court has struck down several majority-minority districts and disapproved the Department of Justice's construction of § 5.[105] These cases reflect the Court's strong turn away from critical implications of the Voting Rights Act and its interpretation in the Burger and Warren Courts and toward the same kind of liberal understanding of representation found in *Wesberry* and *Reynolds*.

---

[102]See Carol Swain, *Black Faces, Black Interests: The Representation of African Americans in Congress* (1993).

[103]See Abigail Thernstrom, *Whose Votes Count? Affirmative Action and Minority Voting Rights* (1987); Stephan Thernstrom & Abigail Thernstrom, *America in Black and White: One Nation, Indivisible* (1997).

[104]509 U.S. 630 (1993).

[105]See *Bush v. Vera*, 517 U.S. 952 (1996); *Shaw v. Hunt*, 517 U.S. 899 (1996); *Miller v. Johnson*, 515 U.S. 900 (1995); *United States v. Hays*, 515 U.S. 737 (1995).

III. "Corruption" in Representatives' Deliberations[106]

All theories of representation are concerned with corruption of the deliberative process, but different theories emphasize different conceptions of corruption. For example, all theories would criticize *self-dealing*, the representative's putting her own goals ahead of those of others, but they would have different visions of what constitutes self-dealing. Liberals might criticize a representative for putting her own financial or perhaps even ideological interests ahead of those of her constituents; republicans might also consider all special-interest deals corrupt, even when desired by voters in the legislator's district; and critical theorists would consider it self-dealing for a representative to be insensitive to the perspectives of minorities. The discussion of bribery and conflicts of interest in this Part will explore these differences. We will return to these themes when we discuss in more detail campaign finance reform laws (Chapter 4) and when we study various rules of the legislative process designed to militate against special-interest legislation (Chapter 5).

The theories are in particular conflict with respect to the role of money in politics. Some liberals are untroubled, and even enthusiastic, about the role of money; most of them are at least skeptical that it can be effectively regulated. Republican and critical theorists are very concerned about money, especially corporate money, because it can reinforce existing patterns of dominance and subordination that politics, optimistically, might hope to displace. Supporters of regulation, however, must face the dilemma that the incumbent representatives who have the responsibility for passing laws that regulate money in politics are the very people who benefit from its ubiquity the most. Even the sunniest republican doubts that the majority of pigs at the trough will agree to a diet plan that benefits the public good.

---

[106]Issues of legislative corruption are examined in Eskridge & Frickey 276-92; Issacharoff, Karlan & Pildes 632-47, 649-55; Lowenstein 425-75; Mikva & Lane 507-19; Popkin 745-50. The role of money in politics is examined in Eskridge & Frickey 206-38; Isaacharoff, Karlan & Pildes 616-64; Lowenstein 477-797; Mikva & Lane 448-79; Popkin 750-81.

A. *Corruption the Old-Fashioned Way: Bribery*

Senator Sludgepump receives $100,000 in return for her agreement to introduce private bills in Congress to suspend the deportation of a specified noncitizen. The senator and the donor have committed serious offenses. It is a crime for someone to give and for a legislator to receive a *bribe* or an *unlawful gratuity*.[107] The federal statute and most state laws consider it a bribe when (1) a public official obtains anything of value (2) in return for an official act, and (3) the public official and/or private person acted with "corrupt intent." The last element is the primary distinction between bribery and unlawful gratuity offenses. Payments to a public official for acts that would have occurred in any event are probably unlawful gratuities and not bribes.[108] Sludgepump at the very least has taken an unlawful gratuity, and, if corrupt intent can be shown, she has taken a bribe.

What exactly is wrong with taking a bribe? Important to the moral opprobrium of bribery is that the representative's judgment is being influenced by a factor extraneous to the representative function, whether that function be as agent of her constituency, trustee for the public interest, or voice for women and other groups that have been marginalized in the political process.[109] Would it matter to the analysis if Sludgepump could show that her constituents favored the action she took, that it was in the public interest, or that it was taken for the benefit of excluded voices? Such evidence could support a mens rea argument (Sludgepump is only guilty of taking an unlawful gratuity), but we are doubtful that argument would be successful.

---

[107]The federal bribery statute, 18 U.S.C. § 201(b)-(c), makes both bribery and unlawful gratuities illegal for covered federal officials. Most states have separate statutes regulating the two activities. See Eskridge & Frickey 277-78; Lowenstein 425-76; Popkin 743-44.

[108]See *United States v. Campbell*, 684 F.2d 141 (D.C. Cir. 1982). It is now established that the payment must relate to some identifiable official act, not merely to the fact that the recipient occupies an important office, to be considered an unlawful gratuity. See *United States v. Sun-Diamond Growers*, 119 S.Ct. 1402 (1999).

[109]See Daniel Lowenstein, *Political Bribery and the Intermediate Theory of Politics*, 32 UCLA L. Rev. 784 (1985); Beth Nolan, *Public Interest, Private Income: Conflicts and Control Limits on the Outside Income of Government Officials*, 87 Nw. U.L. Rev. 57, 71-80 (1992); John Noonan, Jr., *Bribes* 704 (1984).

Just as important as the nature of the action is the secrecy of the bribe, the personal benefit to Sludgepump, and the effect of the appearance of agency or trusteeship failure on the voters' trust in institutions of governance.[110]

B. *Other Regulation of Corrupt Conflicts of Interest*

Bribery and unlawful gratuity statutes are merely the tip of the regulatory iceberg in the area of corrupt representation. Sludge-pump's agreement might also be prosecuted under federal statutes making it a serious crime to engage in extortion, which the Supreme Court has defined to include demanding a bribe for an official act.[111] Indeed, the fact that interest groups tend to give money to politicians of different ideologies, both political parties, and sometimes competitors for the same office may suggest that they feel threatened by lawmakers whose actions can hurt them as well as benefit them. An environment where private parties seem willing to buy protection from any likely officeholder makes claims of extortion believable. Sludgepump might also be susceptible to a prosecution for mail or wire fraud, a charge which applies to fraudulent schemes designed to deprive the citizenry of the intangible right to honest representation.[112] Unlike federal bribery and unlawful gratuity statutes, which affect only federal public officials, federal statutes criminalizing extortion, mail fraud, and wire fraud are used regularly by federal prosecutors to indict local and state officials who have not been charged under state anti-corruption statutes. This practice raises federalism concerns, but it might be justified on representation-reinforcing grounds. Federal prosecutors may be the only effective monitors of local corruption if local district attorneys are themselves corrupt, cowed, or underfunded.

---

[110]The "corrupt" senator might have a procedural defense based on the Speech or Debate Clause in the Constitution, which is discussed in Chapter 5, Part I.

[111]See 18 U.S.C. § 1951, applied to bribe-taking by public officials where there was a quid pro quo in *Evans v. United States*, 504 U.S. 255 (1992); and *McCormick v. United States*, 500 U.S. 257 (1991). See James Lindgren, *The Elusive Distinction Between Bribery and Extortion: From the Common Law to the Hobbs Act*, 35 UCLA L. Rev. 815 (1988).

[112]See 18 U.S.C. §§ 1341, 1343; see also *id.* § 1346, overriding *McNally v. United States*, 483 U.S. 350 (1987).

Many of the criminal prohibitions discussed above require a *quid pro quo*, namely, Sludgepump's agreement to introduce legislation in return for the $100,000. Even without a proven *quid pro quo*, such a lavish gift has the appearance of great impropriety and raises strong inferences of corruption. For this reason, Congress and most state legislatures are adopting prophylactic rules flatly prohibiting gifts to legislators or their staffs in excess of specified modest values.[113] The appearance of impropriety associated with lavish gifts to representatives is part of the general public's discomfort with the close relationship between lobbyists and elected officials. In addition to prohibiting the amount of in-kind benefits like presents, travel, golf, and fancy meals that lobbyists can shower on representatives, laws and congressional rules also require disclosure of the contacts between them.[114] We will discuss the regulation of lobbying in more depth in Chapter 5, where we will consider, in light of the theories of representation, the justifications for lobbying disclosure laws and other more burdensome regulations on such political speech and activity.

Another set of anti-corruption laws prohibits gifts disguised as acceptable payments to representatives. Of course, the largest set of such payments take the form of campaign contributions, the subject of the final section of this chapter and extended discussion in Chapter 4. But campaign contributions are not the only such presumptively acceptable payment to representatives; consider, for example, honoraria for speeches and appearances. In 1995, the Supreme Court considered the constitutionality of a law barring federal employees from accepting any compensation for making speeches or writing articles.[115] The concern prompting the law was a finding that "because their salaries are so inadequate, many members of Congress are supplementing their official compensation by accepting substantial amounts of 'honoraria' for meeting with interest groups which

---

[113]See, e.g., Senate Rule XXXV and House Rule XXVI, cl. 5(a), as amended and strengthened in the 106th Congress.

[114]See Lobbying Disclosure Act of 1995, Pub. L. No. 104-65, 109 Stat. 691, codified at 2 U.S.C. §§ 1601-1607.

[115]See *United States v. National Treasury Employees Union*, 513 U.S. 454 (1995).

desire to influence their votes."[116]   Although the Court struck down the law as it applied to lower-level executive branch employees, such as a mail handler who had given lectures on the Quaker religion, it left untouched the honoraria ban with respect to members of Congress. The record of abuse of honoraria by representatives who would speak for a few minutes at a breakfast of Armani-clad tax lobbyists only hours before voting on an omnibus tax relief bill was sufficiently strong to justify the prophylactic measure's burden on speech.

So far, we have focused on Senator Sludgepump's receiving money in return for her work on the private bill. Bribery and related laws might be interpreted to reach beyond the secret selling of one's legislative influence for money or any valuable but tangible thing. Would it be a crime for Senator Sludgepump to agree to support a bill exempting labor unions from certain tax liabilities, in return for a promise by unions to contribute $100,000 to her reelection campaign? Or, has she committed a crime if she agrees to support the labor union bill in return for another senator's support for a bill benefitting her constituents? In language that sounds politically naive today, a New York state judge in 1903 opined that "[t]he interests of public service require that public officers shall act honestly and fairly upon propositions laid before them for consideration, and shall [not] enter into bargains with their fellow legislators or officers or with others for the giving or withholding of their votes, conditioned upon their receiving any valuable favor, political or otherwise, for themselves or for others."[117]   Such an interpretation that criminalizes routine behavior in the legislative process seems absurd. However, the plain language of the bribery acts would seem to reach vote trading — a vote is something of value to a public official — particularly if one understands corruption to include voting for a proposal not because that representative supports it on the merits but for instrumental or strategic reasons.

In short, if you view the legislative representative as a trustee for the public good, you might be inclined to label logrolling as bribery,

---

[116]*Id.* at 457-58 (citing the Report of the 1989 Quadrennial Commission on Executive, Legislative and Judicial Salaries).

[117]*People ex rel. Dickinson v. Van de Carr*, 87 App. Div. 386, 84 N.Y.S. 461 (N.Y. App. 1903), excerpted and discussed in Eskridge & Frickey 279-82.

as well as campaign contributions that carry a commitment by the legislator to vote in specified ways on future issues. If you view the legislator as simply an agent of popular desires, you might want to limit bribery prosecutions to those cases where the representative benefits personally and not to prosecute in those cases where the representative is merely making political tradeoffs that serve the interests of her constituents. In thinking about this issue, consider also the political speech and association values implicated in a group's making campaign contributions to a candidate who will assure it that she supports its agenda.

C. *Money in Politics — Does It "Corrupt"?*

"The American system is rooted in the assumption of political equality: 'one person, one vote.' But money, which candidates need to harvest votes, is not distributed equally. The substantial inequities of campaign financing have hindered the quest for political equality and have worried concerned Americans since the beginning of the twentieth century."[118] Republican and critical thinkers consider the political advantages of wealth to be just as corrupting as bribery: There is only a scholastic distinction between a $100,000 bribe to Senator Sludgepump and a $100,000 campaign contribution. Both "corrupt" the legislator's judgment in favor of wealthy special interests to the likely detriment of public-regarding deliberation and of poorer, probably more marginalized groups.[119] Liberals are generally less bothered by money in politics, so long as it does not take on qualities of bribery, because money signals the intensity of voter preferences on particular issues and can be used to fund political speech and other expression. Furthermore, liberals are extremely skeptical that regulation will solve the problems identified

---

[118]Herbert Alexander, *Financing Politics: Money, Elections, and Political Reform* 3 (4th ed. 1992). See also Joseph Cantor, *Campaign Financing* (1994); Frank Sorauf, *Inside Campaign Finance: Myths and Realities* (1992).

[119]See Owen Fiss, *Free Speech and Social Structure*, 71 Iowa L. Rev. 1405 (1986); Edward Foley, *Equal-Dollars-Per-Voter: A Constitutional Principle of Campaign Finance*, 94 Colum. L. Rev. 1204 (1994); John Rawls, *The Idea of Public Reason Revisited*, 64 U. Chi. L. Rev. 765 (1997); David Strauss, *Corruption, Equality, and Campaign Finance Reform*, 94 Colum. L. Rev. 1369 (1994).

by republicans.[120] The push-and-pull between thoughtful republican arguments for reform and persuasive liberal arguments demonstrating at the least the futility of reform is evident in the statutes regulating campaign finance and the court decisions evaluating them. The result is a mess.

Enacted in the wake of Watergate and abuses in the 1972 presidential campaign, the Federal Election Campaign Act Amendments of 1974[121] set limits on campaign contributions and expenditures in presidential and congressional campaigns. The Act also established the Federal Election Commission (FEC) to administer and enforce the law. In *Buckley v. Valeo*,[122] the Supreme Court addressed the federal law's constitutionality in light of the First Amendment's core commitment to free speech and political association. The Court famously ruled that money is a form of expression and therefore required the government to show a narrowly tailored and compelling state interest to justify the restrictions.

In its *contribution limits*, the Act prohibited individuals and most groups from contributing more than $1,000 per election to any single candidate; individuals cannot contribute more than a total of $25,000 per year. Certain "political committees" registered with the FEC can contribute up to $5,000 to any candidate for federal office. *Buckley* upheld these provisions, because their purpose of limiting "the actuality and appearance of corruption resulting from large . . . financial contributions" was a sufficiently compelling government interest. "To the extent that large contributions are given to secure a political *quid pro quo* from current and potential office holders, the integrity of our system of representative democracy is under-

---

[120]See Lillian BeVier, *Campaign Finance Reform: Specious Arguments, Intractable Dilemmas*, 94 Colum. L. Rev. 1258 (1994); Samuel Issacharoff & Pamela Karlan, *The Hydraulics of Campaign Finance Reform*, 77 Tex. L. Rev. 1705 (1999); Bradley Smith, *Faulty Assumptions and Undemocratic Consequences of Campaign Finance Reform*, 105 Yale L.J. 1049 (1996); Kathleen Sullivan, *Political Money and Freedom of Speech*, 30 U.C. Davis L. Rev. 663 (1997).

[121]88 Stat. 1263 (1974), codified (as amended) at 2 U.S.C. § 431 *et seq.*

[122]424 U.S. 1 (1976) (per curiam), excerpted and discussed in Eskridge & Frickey 208-18; Hetzel, Libonati & Williams 1062-67; Issacharoff, Karlan & Pildes 618-20; Lowenstein 407-16, 509-44; Mikva & Lane 452-76; Popkin 750-53.

mined. . . . Of almost equal concern as the danger of actual *quid pro quo* arrangements is the impact of the appearance of corruption stemming from public awareness of the opportunities for abuse inherent in a regime of large individual financial contributions."[123] Actual *quid pro quo* arrangements, and the appearance of such, remain the most widely accepted compelling state interests for the regulation of campaign speech and the expenditure of money in the political arena.

In its *expenditure limits*, the Act restricted expenditures by individuals and groups "relative to a clearly identified candidate during a calendar year" to $1,000. It also limited spending by candidates from their personal or family funds, as well as overall expenditures by candidates, to differing amounts depending upon the federal office sought. *Buckley* struck down these provisions. The expenditure limits restricted political expression more severely than the contribution limits because "[a] contribution serves as a general expression of support for the candidate and his views, but does not communicate the underlying basis for the support."[124] In contrast, expenditure limits directly restrict the expression of ideas by individuals; thus, the speech at issue is particularly valuable. On the other side of the balance, the state interest is less compelling with regard to expenditures made independently of a particular candidate because they do not implicate *quid pro quo* corruption or the appearance of such.

Quid pro quo corruption is distasteful to all theories of representation. Republicans make a further argument that might also appeal to critical thinkers: expenditure limitations can serve a government interest "in equalizing the relative ability of individuals and groups to influence the outcome of elections." The Court in *Buckley* rejected this egalitarian argument: "[T]he concept that government may restrict the speech of some elements of our society in order to enhance the relative voice of others is wholly foreign to the First Amendment, which was designed 'to secure "the widest possible dissemination of information from diverse and antagonistic sources,' " and 'to assure unfettered interchange of ideas for the

---

[123]424 U.S. at 26-27.

[124]*Id.* at 21.

bringing about of political and social changes desired by the people.' "[125]

Finally, *Buckley* upheld the Act's requirements that political committees report contributions and expenditures to the FEC and that individuals and non-PAC groups making contributions or expenditures exceeding $100 "other than by contribution to a political committee or candidate" file reports as well. Although compelled disclosure can implicate First Amendment freedoms, the Court held that the governmental interests in political openness and effective enforcement of the contribution limits outweigh possibilities of any generally alleged First Amendment chilling effects. In addition, disclosure denies *quid pro quo* arrangements the secrecy they need to flourish, and it reduces any public perception that such unseemly behavior is widespread.

The Court has retained *Buckley*'s analytical structure in subsequent cases,[126] although it has satisfied no one. For example, Justices from across the political spectrum have criticized the divergent treatment of contributions and independent expenditures, arguing that both implicate political speech and can be functional equivalents.[127] In particular, republican thinkers object that Congress has regulated too timidly and that the Court has discouraged even that low level of regulation. Theirs is a broad understanding of corruption: the legitimacy of government will erode as people perceive that big

---

[125]*Id.* at 48-49 (quoting *New York Times v. Sullivan*, 376 U.S. 254, 266 (1964), which in turn quotes *Associated Press v. United States*, 326 U.S. 1, 20 (1945)).

[126]See *Colorado Republican Fed. Campaign Comm. v. FEC*, 518 U.S. 604 (1996) (striking down regulations of expenditures by political parties); *FEC v. NCPAC*, 470 U.S. 480 (1985) (striking down a provision forbidding a PAC from spending more than $1,000 in support of any presidential or vice-presidential candidate receiving public funds); *California Med. Ass'n v. FEC*, 453 U.S. 182 (1981) (upholding contribution limitation of $5,000 per year from individuals and unincorporated associations to a PAC); *Republican Nat'l Comm. v. FEC*, 487 F. Supp. 280 (S.D.N.Y.) (three-judge court), *aff'd*, 616 F.2d 1 (2d Cir. 1980), *aff'd mem.*, 445 U.S. 955 (1980) (upholding the conditioning of federal funding of presidential campaign upon the candidate's acceptance of overall limitations on expenditures and private contributions).

[127]See *Colorado Republican Fed. Campaign Comm.*, 518 U.S. at 631 (Thomas, J., concurring in the judgment); *FEC v. NCPAC*, 470 U.S. 480, 518 (1984) (Marshall, J., dissenting).

money, especially corporate money, dominates politics. To redress the imbalance in political speech, the state must be allowed to "enhance" the voices of excluded groups or, at least, to tone down voices that dominate political discourse.[128]

Although *Buckley* rejected enhancement theory as a justification for general expenditure limits, in *Austin v. Michigan Chamber of Commerce*[129] the Court upheld a more limited state regulation of corporate expenditures on the ground that the limitation attacked "the corrosive and distorting effects of immense aggregations of wealth."[130] The *Austin* majority was careful to limit its egalitarian concern to corporate wealth, which does not necessarily reflect the political views of shareholders and is amassed with the help of state corporate laws. No subsequent opinion has read *Austin* more broadly, and its nod to the republican view that the state should work to reshape the political environment to equalize voices has been ignored even in subsequent separate opinions that consider "leveling the electoral playing field" a worthy state interest.[131]

Some liberal thinkers object that the Court has been overly lenient in upholding any campaign finance regulation other than disclosure. At the extreme, theirs can be a narrow understanding of corruption: the state must demonstrate an actual *quid pro quo*, and it cannot simply assert that giving money to a campaign assures legislator loyalty. Buttressing their position is a wealth of empirical data. The pervasiveness of money in politics from a variety of sources has diminished its purchasing power. Studies of legislative behavior

---

[128]See E. Joshua Rosenkranz, Buckley *Stops Here: The Report of the Twentieth Century Fund* (1998); Jeffrey Blum, *The Divisible First Amendment: A Critical Functionalist Approach to Freedom of Speech and Electoral Campaign Spending*, 58 N.Y.U. L. Rev. 1273 (1983). But see L.A. Powe, Jr., *Mass Speech & the Newer First Amendment*, 1982 Sup. Ct. Rev. 243 (vigorously criticizing enhancement theory).

[129]494 U.S. 652 (1990).

[130]*Id.* at 660. See also BeVier, *supra* note 120 (criticizing *Austin* for apparently adopting egalitarian justifications for restrictions on political speech); Julian Eule, *Promoting Speaker Diversity:* Austin *and* Metro Broadcasting, 1990 Sup. Ct. Rev. 105 (1990) (reading *Austin* for a broader enhancement principle).

[131]See, e.g., *Colorado Republican Fed. Campaign Comm.*, 518 U.S. at 648 (Stevens, J., dissenting).

suggest that contributions have minimal impact on legislator voting, which continues to correlate most closely with constituent preferences and political party.[132] Nor is there hard evidence that government legitimacy has eroded as a result of increased corporate and PAC spending to influence elections. Finally, liberals argue that money in politics, like water in a river, can only be displaced and rechanneled — it simply does not evaporate completely. Thus, limits on individual contributions will beget political action committees aggregating such contributions; regulation of fundraising and spending by candidates will beget fundraising and spending by parties; and so on.

An example of the hydraulic quality of money in politics was also the occasion for the Court's most recent struggle with *Buckley*'s unsatisfying theoretical framework. In *Colorado Republican Federal Campaign Committee v. FEC*,[133] the Court struck down the FEC's regulation of party expenditures that are not coordinated with a specific candidate. In a narrow opinion, three Justices (Breyer, O'Connor, Souter) rejected the FEC's conclusive presumption that party expenditures are always coordinated with specific candidates and therefore subject to a statutory limitation. Three Justices (Kennedy, Rehnquist, Scalia) believed the application invalid under *Buckley* because party spending is indistinguishable from expenditures made by a candidate, which *Buckley* held cannot be limited constitutionally.[134] Two Justices (Stevens, Ginsburg) accepted the traditional constitutional framework but believed the regulation constitutional because the contributions presented the appearance of *quid pro quo* corruption. Three Justices (Thomas, Rehnquist, Scalia) took a more radical stance and called into question the continuing

---

[132]See Larry Sabato, *PAC Power: Inside the World of Political Action Committees* (1984); Sorauf, *supra* note 118, at 163-74 (collecting sources). But cf. Daniel Lowenstein, *On Campaign Finance Reform: The Root of All Evil Is Deeply Rooted*, 18 Hofstra L. Rev. 301 (1989) (critically reviewing the studies).

[133]518 U.S. 604 (1996).

[134]On remand, the district court seemed to accept these Justices' rationale when it found that the FEC could not prohibit party expenditures on behalf of candidates. The Court also found that contributions by a political party to one of its candidates were inherently not corrupt; instead, they were desirable interactions between representatives and mediating institutions. See *FEC v. Colorado Republican Fed. Campaign Comm.*, 41 F. Supp. 2d 1197 (D. Colo. 1999).

vitality of *Buckley*'s framework. They equated political contributions with independent expenditures in terms of the First Amendment analysis; these Justices would require strict scrutiny for all campaign finance regulations. In an even more far-reaching repudiation, these Justices rejected any regulation except disclosure as required to combat *quid pro quo* corruption, particularly because federal bribery laws operate more effectively to combat corrupt conduct. *Buckley* may still stand, but on wobbly legs.

3

Theories of the Legislative Process

Representatives work within the larger context of the legislative process. The theories of representation that we explored in the preceding chapter form the foundation for understanding the environment in which representatives operate and the nature of the laws they produce. A sophisticated sense of this environment, as well as of the different ways theorists envision an ideal legislative process, will complete the theoretical framework that we will apply to concrete problems in the following chapters. Just as with the theories of representation, these theories of the legislative process and its products usually have both descriptive and normative dimensions. Even those theories that purport to be merely descriptive tend to have normative bite. For example, if you view lawmakers as pursuing only self-interested goals and the objectives of well-funded groups, you are apt to view the laws that they write with more skepticism than if you believe legislators are also motivated in more public-regarding ways.

Theories of the legislative process can be usefully divided into three groups, although, as before, any such categorization tends to de-emphasize the nuances in all the theories. Moreover, scholars and observers of the legislative process will often draw insights from several of the perspectives. None accurately describes the rich and complicated real world of legislatures, lawmakers, interest groups, and constituents, and thus their prescriptive force is limited by this divergence from actual experience and behavior. Nonetheless, the theories provide us with a way to organize the world, and each highlights important aspects of the legislative process for lawmakers, judges, and lawyers seeking to influence Congress and state legislatures. We will describe and discuss in this chapter *proceduralist theories*, which focus on the many procedures through which a bill is enacted; *interest group theories*, which emphasize the pivotal, and perhaps disproportionate, role of organized groups in the legislative process; and *institutional theories*, which center on the relationships among various political institutions and the effects of broad governmental structures on policy.

I. Proceduralist Theories[1]

The most salient aspect of the modern legislative process is that it is filled with a complex set of hurdles that proponents of a new policy must overcome before their bill becomes law. At each stage in the legislative process, a proposal can be changed or halted, new coalitions must be formed, and opportunities for logrolling, strategic behavior, and deliberation are presented. Because those who control each of these choke points have the ability to kill a proposal, some political scientists have termed them *vetogates*.[2] Vetogates emanate from a number of sources: some result from constitutional provisions, some from rules adopted formally by a legislative body, and some from norms or practices that are more informal.

A. *The Legislature as an Obstacle Path*

Given the different sources of rules establishing vetogates, it may be helpful to think of them as lying along a spectrum. Constitutional prohibitions are perhaps the strongest and the most durable because they can be changed only through the difficult process set forth in Article V. Under Article I, Section 7, a bill cannot become a law unless adopted in the same form by both chambers of Congress (the bicameralism requirement) and presented to the President for signature or veto (the presentment requirement). The Constitution also allows the legislature to take some actions only with a supermajority vote, such as overriding a presidential veto. Also, as we saw in *Powell v. McCormack* (Chapter 2), a house can expel a member only with a two-thirds vote. These provisions do not bar legislative actions, but they make legislating substantially more difficult.

Each house also has a series of formal rules that bind it until they are changed by a vote of that house. Like constitutional provisions, some of these rules prohibit certain actions; for example, Rule XXI prohibits the House of Representatives from considering any retroactive increase in the federal income tax rate. Other congressio-

---

[1]See Eskridge & Frickey 1-34, 44-48; Mikva & Lane 235-301; Hetzel, Libonati & Williams 256-297.

[2]See, e.g., McNollgast, *Legislative Intent: The Use of Positive Political Theory in Statutory Interpretation*, 57 Law & Contemp. Probs. 3 (1994).

nal rules impose supermajority voting requirements on certain congressional actions. The federal budget process rules (Chapter 5) require 60 Senators to vote to allow consideration of legislation that violates the caps placed on spending or of any proposals that might undermine the fiscal integrity of the Social Security trust fund. Or, more familiarly, 60 Senators must vote to cut off debate if a member engages in a *filibuster*, which is extended debate with the intention of killing a bill or forcing substantial changes in it. Another set of congressional rules merely articulates the regular procedure by which Congress considers legislative proposals, for example, by requiring in most cases that every bill be considered by a committee before it reaches the full house. All these vetogates are less durable than constitutional ones because they can be changed, in most cases, by a majority vote of the relevant house. Moreover, if the House or Senate violates the rules, there is often no effective enforcement mechanism to void its action. Courts have been loath to enforce congressional rules when they are ignored, holding instead that rulemaking and enforcement are committed by the Constitution to the discretion of each house.

The least durable vetogates are those that are matters of informal norms and practices, sometimes called the *folkways* of Congress.[3] For example, the informal norm of apprenticeship encourages more junior members to learn the ropes and develop skills and knowledge before taking high-profile roles in the body. Under the related seniority norm, which allocates power and position to members with long tenure, senior legislators and committee chairs can block bills they do not like, even when most of the chamber or committee favor the legislation. In recent years, these norms, along with norms of courtesy and bipartisanship, appear weaker, perhaps because of high turnover rates and an influx of junior members with relatively extreme ideologies.

Think for a moment of all the vetogates facing a legislative proposal. Once proponents convince a legislator to draft (or accept their draft of) a bill and to introduce it, they must make sure it survives the committee to which it is referred. In some cases,

---

[3]See Donald Matthews, *U.S. Senators and Their World* (1960) (coining the term "folkways").

legislation is referred to more than one committee, a process called a joint referral, and must be approved by all of them. Committees exert enormous influence over the congressional agenda. By ignoring a proposal entirely, a committee can effectively kill it; members' ability to discharge a bill without the committee's support is limited. In fact, no more than one in ten bills introduced becomes law; most bills die in committee.[4] Members of Congress seek increased power by expanding their committees' jurisdictions and thus obtaining control over the fate of more policies. Advocates of new laws work to convince the Speaker of the House or the presiding officer of the Senate, advised by the parliamentarians, to refer their bills to committees that will be sympathetic to their proposals.[5]

The committee structure of the House and Senate is chosen by members to serve instrumental purposes; committees and subcommittees are not required by the Constitution. Political scientists disagree about the objectives that lawmakers seek to pursue through the committee structure. Some argue that committees allow members to specialize and accumulate expertise in a substantive area. Other members defer to the specialists in an area, thereby avoiding the costly prospect of becoming experts in every matter raised for a vote.[6] This *informational role* suggests that committees are part of an efficient congressional organization, particularly necessary in an increasingly complex world. Members must monitor committees to ensure that they are faithful agents of the full body and that the information and recommendations they put forth are consistent with the wishes of the majority. As long as monitoring is less costly than developing expertise on all matters and allows members to detect any shirking by their agents, a committee structure is sensible.

---

[4] See Burdett Loomis, *The Contemporary Congress* 156 (1996).

[5] For one of the best analyses of congressional committees and their jurisdictions, see David King, *Turf Wars: How Congressional Committees Claim Jurisdiction* (1997). Professor King's approach is particularly interesting to lawyers because he argues that committee jurisdictions change over time in an incremental way similar to the development of common law principles, rather than as a result of abrupt and far-reaching reforms.

[6] See, e.g., Keith Krehbiel, *Information and Legislative Organization* (1991); Thomas Gilligan & Keith Krehbiel, *Organization of Informative Committees by a Rational Legislature*, 34 Am. J. Pol. Sci. 531 (1990).

A more beady-eyed theory maintains that committees are engines of *rent-seeking,* or the distribution of unjustified benefits to interest groups.[7] Members largely self-select their committee assignments,[8] so they all seek appointment to committees with jurisdiction over areas about which they and their constituents have particularly intense preferences. Accordingly, committees are typically composed of preference outliers. In most cases, they specialize in areas that allow them to send benefits back to their constituents or key special interests to improve their reelection chances. In other cases, they may seek committee assignments that allow them to capture personal benefits from interest groups (for example, the Senate Finance Committee, which has jurisdiction over the tax code) or that allow them to spend time on topics that interest them or propel them into the national limelight (for example, the Intelligence Committees). More concretely, Senators from farm states who want to channel public benefits to their farmer-constituents at the expense of other Senators' constituents actively seek membership on the Agriculture Committee. A member from a largely urban state will not be willing to specialize in agriculture issues because she has no particular interest in those policies. This explanation for committees is a disturbing one. Committees are not necessarily the faithful agents of the rest of the body because their preferences are outlying; the larger body must be constantly vigilant to ensure that extreme policies are not enacted. Committees pass policies that distribute public goods to small and active interest groups vital to their members' reelection at the expense of the greater public good.

Finally, a recent theory of committees posits that they are *tools of the majority party.*[9] Gary Cox and Mathew McCubbins argue that

---

[7]See, e.g., Kenneth Shepsle & Barry Weingast, *Legislative Politics and Budget Outcomes,* in *Federal Budget Policy in the 1980s* 343 (Gregory Mills & John Palmer eds., 1984); Barry Weingast & William Marshall, *The Industrial Organization of Congress; or, Why Legislatures, Like Firms, Are Not Organized as Markets,* 96 J. Pol. Econ. 132 (1988).

[8]See Richard Fenno, *Congressmen in Committees* 19-20 (1973).

[9]See Gary Cox & Mathew McCubbins, *Legislative Leviathan: Party Government in the House* (1993). But see Eric Schlicker & Andrew Rich, *Controlling the Floor: Parties as Procedural Coalitions in the House,* 41 Am. J. Pol. Sci. 1340 (1997) (critiquing the theory). See also Tim Groseclose & David

majority-party committee members exclude members of the other party from decisionmaking and cooperate to further the majority party's collective goals. Again, take the case of the Agriculture Committee. Most members of the majority party probably favor relatively modest subsidies to farmers, but a few members intensely prefer high subsidies and believe their reelection chances are linked to enacting such a national policy. Committees provide a structure for most members of the majority party to defer to the few with intense preferences and to ensure that the high-subsidy Senators return the deference on other issues in the future. This organization enables most majority-party members to be reelected and permits the party to remain in control of Congress, which allows its members more benefits in the future and the ability to shape policy.

If the congressional committee (or, in some cases, a subcommittee) decides to move forward on the bill, it may hold hearings and then meet to "mark up" the bill, a process in which members of the committee amend the original proposal before they send it to the floor. Once the committee has approved the bill, the staff prepares a report on the bill, along with a description of the details of the committee's consideration and dissenting views. Committee reports are circulated to other members and are often the only documents that legislators or their staffs read before a vote of the full house on a bill. In some cases, members bypass the often-lengthy committee reports in favor of more informal and concise descriptions prepared by the party leadership or the sponsors of the bill.

Passing the vetogate of the committee is only an early hurdle in a bill's tortuous journey to enactment. In the House, major legislation reaches the floor in one of two ways. Certain budget resolutions and laws have privileged status and can be brought up almost immediately upon their approval by the Budget Committee. Otherwise, the chairman of the committee with jurisdiction over a bill will ask the House Rules Committee for a rule that schedules floor consideration, structures the debate, and limits amendments. The Rules Committee can bar any amendments (a "closed" rule), allow only some amend-

---

King, *Committee Theories and Committee Institutions* (1997) (paper prepared for the American Political Science Association) (testing all three theories of committee organization and offering their own of *bicameral rivalry*).

ments (a "modified closed" rule), or allow any and all amendments (an "open" rule). Even most budget proposals come to the floor under special rules that limit amendments and waive procedural points of order. Thus, the Rules Committee provides opponents of the bill a vetogate either to kill the proposal or to structure its consideration so that it is effectively watered down or transformed.

The Senate is a much less rigidly controlled body than the House of Representatives. Only if the majority leader obtains a "unanimous consent" agreement can he provide a structure for deliberation in much the same way as a rule from the House Rules Committee. Otherwise, any Senator can delay in most cases by filibustering both the motion to proceed to consider a bill and the final vote. Only if 60 Senators vote to invoke cloture twice will the filibusters be terminated, and then only after an additional thirty hours of debate on each vote. In addition, Senators can offer any amendments they wish to a bill on the floor; the Senate generally has no germaneness requirement limiting amendments to the same subject matter as the underlying proposal. Indeed, this expansive ability to amend proposals is an effective way to circumvent the vetogate of a Senate committee. If a committee refuses to consider and discharge a bill, its sponsors can add the proposal to any legislation under consideration by the full body.

If the proposal negotiates its way successfully through one house, it must pass the vetogates of the other house. And, if the two versions that emerge are different, the House and Senate appoint a conference committee to iron out disagreements and draft a common bill that can be passed by both houses. The conference committee writes a report on the final version of the proposal that can be used by lawmakers to discover differences between the original versions and the final draft. At every stage in this path, vetogates allow opponents to block a bill or to wring concessions from its advocates. And, of course, once Congress has acted, the President may exercise his constitutional veto and stop the bill in its tracks; few vetoes (approximately seven percent) are overridden. The primary consequence of this arduous obstacle path facing legislative proposals is that a determined minority can block virtually any bill — at least for long enough to obtain concessions that make the change more palatable.

Scholars have observed that understanding the importance of vetogates and the structure of Congress provides useful information to statutory interpreters. As we will discuss in more detail in Chapter 8, interpreters often use legislative history to determine the meaning of vague or ambiguous statutory terms. How can you discern whether a statement in a congressional debate or a committee report is a credible signal of the intent of the lawmakers supporting the proposal? One way is to link the history with a vetogate because statements at these junctures of legislative consideration are crucial to the enactment of laws. For example, committee reports are typically given great weight by interpreters because they reflect the understanding of key gatekeepers. Moreover, they are representations about the meaning of statutory language on which lawmakers rely when they decide how to cast their votes. If non-committee members discover that committee reports contain inaccurate statements (perhaps because preference outliers dominate the drafting), then they will no longer give credence to committee members' assurances and will be less likely to defer to their expertise. To the extent that those who control vetogates are repeat players, they must maintain their reputations for honesty to assure their continuing influence.

As we will see, the keepers of the vetogates also have incentives to shade the truth, so relying on committee reports and statements by floor managers does not always provide accurate information. Take, for example, *Montana Wilderness Association v. United States Forest Service*.[10] The case involved the interpretation of a provision of the Alaska Lands Act, which clearly, and apparently exclusively, dealt with lands in Alaska. One provision arguably changed the rules concerning access to all nonfederally owned land within the boundaries of the National Forest System throughout the country, however — a result with serious environmental consequences. Although nothing in the Act specifically limited this provision to such land in Alaska, every other provision in the bill focused only on territory within Alaska. The question before the court was whether to limit the generally worded provision to National Forest System land in Alaska or to give it nationwide effect.

---

[10]No. 80-3374 (9th Cir. May 14, 1981), withdrawn and replaced by 655 F.2d 951 (9th Cir. 1981), excerpted and discussed in Eskridge & Frickey 797-813.

Turning to the legislative history for an indication of meaning, Judge Norris for the Ninth Circuit panel gave great weight to the remarks of Representative Udall, the chairman of the House committee with jurisdiction over the proposal. Contrary to the representations of other lawmakers, particularly those by the Senate author of the contested section, Representative Udall stated that, although the final version of the bill was "ambiguously drafted and not expressly limited to Alaskan lands, the House believes that, as with all other provisions of the bill, the language of the section applies only to lands within the State of Alaska."[11] Here Judge Norris found credible the statement of a repeat player who controlled a number of vetogates. Senator Melcher, the author of the provision, was also a key player, but his comments stating that the provision had nationwide application were delivered after Congress had passed the bill. Statutory interpreters often discount such subsequent legislative history in part because there is little sanction for distorting the meaning of the bill once it has been passed. In fact, very few lawmakers may even be paying attention to subsequent representations so that the possibility of discipline for misstatements is slim.

In short, one reading Judge Norris's seemingly sophisticated use of legislative history might be convinced that he understood the notion of vetogates, repeat players, and credible signals. He used the notion of proceduralism to tease meaning from an ambiguous and poorly drafted provision: notwithstanding its language, Congress meant it to apply only to lands in Alaska. But further reading of all the proceedings demonstrates that Judge Norris misread the signals and was duped by a wily congressional player.

The House had passed a version of the Alaska lands bill, which then was transmitted to the Senate. The Senate eventually passed a substitute bill that incorporated Senator Melcher's provision that seemed to have nationwide application. On October 2, 1980, Representative Udall proposed an amendment to the Senate version that would have limited the Melcher provision to Alaska, but that amendment was never adopted. Then, on November 12, 1980, the House simply passed the Senate version. (We realize that this is ancient history to contemporary law students, but try to figure out

---

[11]126 Cong. Rec. H10549 (daily ed. Nov. 12, 1980).

why at this point Representative Udall had good reason to give up any chance of amending the Senate version to make the bill more environmentally friendly). Representative Udall inserted into the record a long written discussion of the bill prefaced with the assertion that it was an "explanation of those aspects of the legislation that affect the National Park System as the official legislative history" of the Act.[12] Part of his written statement repeated the claim given determinative weight by Judge Norris in the opinion.[13]

In fact, Representative Udall's floor statement was misleading, probably purposively so. The Melcher provision had been part of the version adopted by the Senate committee and thus was the subject of a Senate report. Representative Udall's conscious attempt to craft legislative history sympathetic to the House's position was able to trump the language of the law itself, in part because the House was voting on the version already passed by the Senate. Thus, Udall's history could not be challenged by any Senator before final passage of the bill. When Senator Melcher realized what had happened, he stormed to the Senate floor and denounced the House's attempt to win in legislative history what it could not in negotiations. "[T]he House was unable to muster the necessary support to amend the Senate compromise Alaska lands bill; certainly their attempt to amend it with fine print in the [CONGRESSIONAL] RECORD will not stand."[14] But, it did stand, and in part because a judge attempted to read the signals provided at vetogates but was misled by the more experienced congressional gatekeepers themselves. Judge Norris later reversed his interpretation, but not on the basis of a more accurate reading of the legislative history of this Act.[15]

---

[12]*Id.* at H29265 (daily ed. Nov. 12, 1980).

[13]*Id.* at H29282 (daily ed. Nov. 12, 1980).

[14]*Id.* at S30370 (daily ed. Nov. 20, 1980).

[15]See *Montana Wilderness Association v. United States Forest Service,* 655 F.2d 951 (9th Cir. 1981), *cert. denied,* 455 U.S. 989 (1982) (reversing interpretation on the basis of legislative history in a subsequently passed bill that indicated that Udall now understood the provision to have nationwide application).

B. *Vetogates as a Method To Make Legislating Difficult and Infrequent*

Some liberal theory includes a strong preference for private ordering and a distaste for government intervention that reduces private autonomy or affects economic markets. Such theorists favor governmental organization that makes enacting legislation difficult; the vetogates that pervade the legislative process are consistent with that objective. For liberals, a system full of hurdles is normatively attractive, as well as descriptively accurate. Interestingly, the Framers of the Constitution shared the liberal goal of reducing the amount of legislation. In *Federalist* No. 73, Hamilton defended proceduralism because it provides a "an additional security against the [enactment] of improper laws."[16] He acknowledged that "the power of preventing bad laws includes that of preventing good ones; and may be used to the one purpose as well as to the other. . . . The injury that may possibly be done by defeating a few good laws will be amply compensated by the advantage of preventing a number of bad ones."[17]

It does not seem a fair reading of *The Federalist Papers*, however, to view them as hostile to all legislative intrusions into private ordering. As pervasive a theme as the negative power of proceduralism is the idea that the obstacles will moderate proposals and allow delay that may temper public passion and avoid the enactment of unwise legislation. Legislation is not inherently untrustworthy or always likely to produce more harm than good, but some proposals are hastily considered and should either be changed substantially or allowed to die. For example, in *Federalist* No. 62, the requirement of bicameralism is seen as an additional impediment to improper acts of legislation caused by "the propensity of all single and numerous assemblies to yield to the impulse of sudden and violent passions." [18]

The liberal distrust of legislation and preference for private ordering may be anachronistic. Since the New Deal, legal scholars and judges have come to see that common law ordering is not necessarily the natural order of things and is, instead, just another

---

[16]*The Federalist* No. 73, at 443 (A. Hamilton) (Clinton Rossiter ed., 1961).

[17]*Id.* at 443-44.

[18]*The Federalist* No. 62, at 379 (J. Madison).

regulatory regime.[19]   Under this view, new legislation is not the abrogation of a prepolitical state of liberty, but rather the substitution of one regulatory regime (statutory) for another (common law). Thus, to the extent that proceduralism entrenches one vision of government — a particular liberal vision — and handicaps other systems of regulation, it must be defended on that basis. In short, a preference for the status quo and against legislative change is not a neutral preference.

Proceduralism is also problematic because it is an over-inclusive solution to the problem of unwise or dangerous legislation.   A plethora of vetogates awaits all proposals; the system does not include a separate track with fewer procedural hurdles for thoughtful, public-regarding legislation. For example, bicameralism, the disproportion-ate voting power of the Southern states in the Senate, and a series of successful filibusters delayed civil rights legislation for over a decade.[20] Alexander Hamilton recognized this problematic aspect of proceduralism, but he argued that the loss of some good laws was a price worth paying to avoid passage of bad laws. That is surely an empirical question: What is the cost of delaying certain beneficial legislation or failing to enact it entirely? Is that cost less than the cost of private-regarding or oppressive legislation that would be passed under a more streamlined system but that is now halted by legislative procedures?

C. *The Effect of Proceduralism on Legislative Deliberation*

Republicans also lay claim to *The Federalist Papers* as their inspiration, in part because they see proceduralism as a tool to encourage public deliberation about legislative proposals.[21] Delibera-tion shapes and changes public preferences on issues; it allows lawmakers to modify, amend, or discard proposals on the basis of new thinking and information; and it facilitates the development of civic virtue in citizens. Deliberation thus is an end in itself, and it

---

[19]See Gary Peller, *The Metaphysics of American Law* , 73 Calif. L. Rev. 1151 (1985). See also Cass Sunstein, *After the Rights Revolution: Reconceiving the Regulatory State* 19-20 (1990).

[20]See Eskridge & Frickey 4-24.

[21]See *Symposium on Republicanism*, 97 Yale L.J. 1539 (1988).

serves the larger instrumental purpose of improving public policy. Indeed, the fact that Congress engages in a deliberative process before adopting a particular proposal may be sufficient evidence of the soundness of the law.

Certainly, some of the passages of *The Federalist Papers* link proceduralism to deliberation.[22] Often the delay inherent in proceduralism is defended as conducive to deliberation and informed decision-making. Madison justified the arguably duplicative role of the Senate as useful "to check the misguided career" of bills inspired by temporary passions or deception "and to suspend the blow meditated by the people against themselves, until reason, justice, and truth can regain their authority over the public mind[.]"[23] The Founders devised institutions and procedures to shape the content of that deliberation. The more accountable House of Representatives was frequently elected so that its members would have an "immediate dependence on, and an intimate sympathy with, the people."[24] The importance of the public's views in the process of deliberation is underscored by the constitutional requirement that revenue-raising bills originate in the house more closely tied to public sentiment. The Senate, a body that was not directly elected until the first part of this century and thus theoretically more removed from the passions of the people, would play a vital deliberative role in "refin[ing] and enlarg[ing] the public views."[25]

The effect of proceduralism on deliberation and, in turn, the effect of deliberation on legislative outcomes are difficult to understand completely. First, proceduralism does not guarantee that lawmakers will deliberate at all, or that when they do, their deliberation will be reasonable and intelligent. At the most, procedures allow the opportunity for deliberation and provide a means to slow a proposal down to make time for dialogue and investigation. A bill that passes through a vetogate may not necessarily have been the subject of any

---

[22]See Joseph Bessette, *The Mild Voice of Reason: Deliberative Democracy and American National Government* 13-39 (1994) (discussing the role of deliberation in the Framers' design).

[23]*The Federalist* No. 63, at 384 (Madison).

[24]*The Federalist* No. 52, at 327 (Madison).

[25]*The Federalist* No. 10, at 82 (Madison).

deliberation, however. Process only creates an environment that fosters robust deliberation of important issues — it shapes and strengthens the structure of deliberations — but it does not force elected officials to take advantage of this opportunity.

Moreover, proceduralism does not impose any particular requirements for acceptable deliberation. Even if theorists could agree on what counts as meaningful deliberative dialogue,[26] nothing in our system works to enforce a requirement that such dialogue occur and be considered by lawmakers in reaching decisions. Imagine a court looking at the quality and content of deliberation before deciding whether a particular law is legitimate.[27] First, in what records would the judge look? Often deliberation among policy-makers occurs behind closed doors or informally. Is such discussion irrelevant because it is not public? Or can these conversations usefully inform elected representatives? What if the judge determines that the public deliberation was not sincere? Instead, lawmakers mouthed platitudes and high-minded thoughts, but they actually cast their ballots on the basis of which interest group contributed the most money to their political coffers. Or does it matter whether the deliberators sincerely believe what they say? Perhaps the exercise of providing reasons and justifications, even if done strategically, will affect the way other lawmakers perceive the action or will change public preferences in a way that affects the behavior of elected representatives.

Even if deliberation occurs in public and the reasons discussed are sincerely offered and rebutted, it is unclear whether deliberation necessarily improves legislation. Some republicans do not defend deliberation in this instrumental way, arguing that the process of public dialogue results in better citizens full of more civic virtue. But

---

[26]For one of the classic statements of what constitutes acceptable public reason, see John Rawls, *Political Liberalism* 212-54 (1993). For a recent formulation of a principled framework for deliberation, see Amy Gutmann & Dennis Thompson, *Democracy and Disagreement* (1996).

[27]See *Fullilove v. Klutznick*, 448 U.S. 448, 546-51 (1980) (Stevens, J., dissenting) (analyzing the congressional deliberation surrounding a federal bill enacting minority set-asides and justifying this approach as required by due process in the context of legislation employing race-based classifications). See also Chapter 5, Part IIB, for a discussion of due process of lawmaking.

many link the process of deliberation to better substantive outcomes. Such a claim requires a metric to measure outcomes — what counts as a "better" law — and the metric is inevitably tied up with a normative vision of the public good.[28] Deliberation may allow individuals who have diverse knowledge and experience to share information and thus to reach better results. Unfortunately, it may also allow those who are more persuasive but who are not necessarily more committed to the public good to prevail, or it may result in lawmakers' sharing incorrect information that cannot provide a firm basis for optimal problem solving.

Proceduralism is only one characteristic of the modern political process; the presence of organized groups is another salient feature. The two features are crucially intertwined. As we will see, different interest groups have varying abilities to navigate through the legislative vetogates.

II. Interest Group Theories[29]

Observers of American life have long noted our tendency to form groups and to participate in society and politics as members of larger groups rather than as single individuals. Alexis de Tocqueville commented, "In no country in the world has the principle of association been more successfully used or applied to a greater multitude of objects than in America."[30] In *Federalist* No. 10, James Madison justified the institutional arrangements of the new Constitution in part as devices to control the mischievous effects of these inevitable factions. The Founders are not alone in their distrust of factions; much of the criticism leveled against government and politicians today centers on the disproportionate influence of special interests. Interestingly, the label "special interests" clearly carries negative connotations, even though we are all members of many groups, some of them organized and politically active.

---

[28]See Laurence Tribe, *The Puzzling Persistence of Process-Based Constitutional Theories*, 89 Yale L.J. 1063 (1980) (making a similar argument in the context of a critique of Ely's representation-reinforcing theories).

[29]See Eskridge & Frickey 49-61.

[30]1 Alexis de Tocqueville, *Democracy in America* 191 (P. Bradley ed. 1945).

As a initial matter, we should clearly define the crucial term for pluralist theories: What is an *interest group*? Madison defined faction as "a number of citizens, whether amounting to a majority or minority of the whole, who are united and actuated by some common impulse of passion, or of interest, adverse to the rights of the citizens, or to the permanent and aggregate interests of the community."[31] Thus, like the current popular use of the term, Madison included a normative element in his definition. Factions were motivated by thoughtless passion or self-interest, and they acted in ways contrary to the public good. Many modern interest group theorists attempt to provide a purely descriptive definition without a negative undercurrent. For example, David Truman defines an interest group as "any group that, on the basis of one or more shared attitudes, makes certain claims upon other groups in the society for the establishment, maintenance, or enhancement of forms of behavior that are implied by the shared attitudes."[32] Peter Schuck's definition is even broader: "special interests . . . include any group that pursues contested political or policy goals, and that is widely regarded by the public as being one contending interest among others."[33] Both Schuck and Truman view interest groups as forces for positive political change — at least in some cases — and thus fit into a scholarly tradition of *interest group liberalism*.

A. *Interest Group Liberalism: Pluralism as Positive Force in Politics*

Rather than fearing factions, we now rely on organized groups to play a large role in the political process. Political parties mediate between individuals and representatives, providing structures for governance and information for voters choosing among candidates for a particular office. Other institutionalized groups, such as churches and trade organizations, arise to facilitate their members' long-term social or economic interests and become involved in politics as a secondary matter. Still other, sometimes less permanent, groups form

---

[31]*The Federalist* No. 10, at 78.

[32]David Truman, *The Governmental Process* 33 (1951).

[33]Peter Schuck, *Against (and for) Madison: An Essay in Praise of Factions*, 15 Yale L. & Pol'y Rev. 553, 558 (1997).

as reactions to particular issues; they may view political activity as their primary objective. One group of pluralist theorists, called "interest group liberals" by Theodore Lowi, sees the prevalence, strength, and diversity of interest groups as a sign of political health. The ideal pluralist system is one where "[o]rganized interests emerge in every sector of our lives and adequately represent most of those sectors, so that one organized group can be found effectively answering and checking some other organized group as it seeks to prosecute its claim against society." For interest group liberals "the role of government is one of insuring access to the most effectively organized, and of ratifying agreements and adjustments worked out among the competing leaders."[34] Interest group liberalism not only allows a give-and-take among different points of view, but also allows constituents to signal the intensity of their preferences in a way voting under a one-person, one-vote rule cannot. Politicians can consider the information provided to them by interest groups and adopt policies that balance a myriad of interests appropriately.

The optimistic vision of interest groups portrays such activity as consistent with the larger public good in a number of ways. First, strong interest groups, many of which are private or voluntary organizations, are bulwarks against oppressive and tyrannical government. Power is dispersed among many competing interest groups.[35] In a way, a decentralized pluralist system expands the check on tyranny identified in *Federalist* No. 10; the ambition of one group checks the ambition of others and of governmental actors. For some, elected officials' role is merely to determine the result of interest group conflict and implement it; representatives have little independent importance, serving only as referees of the pluralist game. "The legislative vote on any issue tends to represent the composition of strength, i.e., the balance of power, among the contending groups at the time of voting. What may be called public policy is the equilibrium reached in this struggle at any given moment, and it represents

---

[34]Theodore Lowi, *The End of Liberalism: The Second Republic of the United States* 51 (2d ed. 1979).

[35]See Robert Dahl, *Pluralist Democracy in the United States: Conflict and Consent* 23 (1967).

a balance which the contending factions of groups constantly strive to weight in their favor."[36]

Second, these scholars argue that the result of a robustly pluralist system will be moderate and well-considered policies. In part, moderation results because of the connections among interest groups. All of us are members of multiple interest groups, and our overlapping memberships might provide an effective restraint on the extremism of any one group.[37] In addition, "[b]ecause constant negotiations among different centers of power are necessary in order to make decisions, citizens and leaders will perfect the precious art of dealing peacefully with their conflicts, and not merely to the benefit of one partisan but to the mutual benefit of all the parties to a conflict."[38] By operating on a variety of levels, interest groups provide a multi-layered structure for conflict.

Third, and important to republicans, interest groups represent the most meaningful possibility for real political participation by individual citizens. "[F]actions facilitate participation by providing fora and occasions for purposeful, discursive interaction among members in common undertakings. . . . Precisely because these groups' concerns are more partial and narrowly defined than those of the polity as a whole, they are more likely to engage the interests and energies of voters with severely limited attention spans, time, and political knowledge."[39] Thus, the activity of interest groups is likely not only to improve the policies adopted by the government, but also the involvement of individuals in groups will increase their civic virtue and their ability to participate intelligently in public deliberation about important issues.

Thus, interest group liberals view our pluralist system as a sort of marketplace of ideas, where perspectives are articulated forcefully and persuasively. The best ideas succeed, while the worst are discarded. This optimistic vision is accurate only if *all* views are represented ably by some group. Truman, for example, argues that

---

[36]Earl Latham, *The Group Basis of Politics* 36 (1952).

[37]See Truman, *supra* note 32, at 509-10.

[38]Dahl, *supra* note 35, at 24.

[39]Schuck, *supra* note 33, at 581.

groups will naturally arise around new problems, and that balanced group pressures will be the rule rather than the exception. A different group of theorists, however, is more concerned that some interests are not represented effectively, and sometimes not at all, in our political system. Such gaps in representation can lead to unfortunate policy outcomes that disserve the public interest. It is that group of pluralists that we describe next.

B. *Public Choice Theory: Interest Groups as Pernicious Political Influences*

Optimistic pluralists claimed to describe current political arrangements, but many observers of the political process questioned their confidence that all voices are heard and all interests articulated. Indeed, many critics noted systematic disparities of access to the political process. As E.E. Schattschneider put it: "The flaw in the pluralist heaven is that the heavenly chorus sings with a strong upper-class accent. Probably about 90 percent of the people cannot get into the pressure system."[40] He based his observation in part on his study of the Smoot-Hawley Tariff, which he found to have been enacted as the result of logrolling among well-heeled special interest groups rather than any systematic consideration of the public interest.[41] Kay Lehman Schlozman and John Tierney provided a stronger empirical basis for this observation, which seems at least intuitively plausible to any observer of politics. They found that "the pressure community [in Washington] is heavily weighted in favor of business organizations: 70 percent of all organizations having a Washington presence and 52 percent of those having their own offices represent business. The overrepresentation of business interests takes place at the

---

[40]Elmer Schattschneider, *The Semisovereign People: A Realist's View of Democracy in America* 34-35 (1960).

[41]Elmer Schattschneider, *Politics, Pressures and the Tariff: A Study of Free Private Enterprise in Pressure Politics as Shown in the 1929-1930 Revision of the Tariff* (1935). But see Raymond Bauer, Ithiel Pool & Lewis Dexter, *American Business and Public Policy: The Politics of Foreign Trade* (1963) (finding little interest group activity surrounding the enactment of tariffs between 1953 and 1962).

expense of two other kinds of organizations: groups representing broad public interests and groups representing the less advantaged."[42]

A number of political scientists and economists have tried to provide explanations for the pattern of interest group formation. Many of these scholars work from a perspective called public choice, a methodology that involves applying economic principles to political decisionmaking. All actors — lawmakers, candidates, and voters — are seen as rational entities intent on maximizing utility, just as some economists view people when they make decisions in the economic marketplace.[43] Moreover, theorists recognize that political activity is costly. In the case of providing funds to candidates for their campaigns, it is evidently costly, but the observation applies more broadly. Time spent lobbying a legislator is time unavailable for leisure, work, or activities with family and friends. Thus, rational actors will participate in politics only when they are willing to bear the costs, presumably because they expect to obtain some kind of valuable benefit.

Public choice and other economic theory provided the first systematic attempt to explain why some groups form and work to influence politics and why some do not. In *The Logic of Collective Action*, Mancur Olson argued that large groups representing diffuse interests typically will not form.[44] Legislation is a public good; once the state has decided to provide clean air for its citizens, all in society will benefit. Yet any individual effort to pass such a law will have only an infinitesimal effect on the probability of its enactment. Thus,

---

[42]Kay Lehman Schlozman & John Tierney, *Organized Interests and American Democracy* 68 (1986).

[43]See Dennis Mueller, *Public Choice* 1 (1979); Daniel Farber & Philip Frickey, *Law and Public Choice: A Critical Introduction* 1 (1991); Gary Becker, *A Theory of Competition Among Pressure Groups for Political Influence*, 98 Q.J. Econ. 371 (1983). Public choice theorists apply economic models to a variety of political questions, including those that do not involve interest groups. We will return to some of these theories in the succeeding chapters. For example, when we think about the regulation of elections, we will consider one of the classic works in public choice that studies voting. See Anthony Downs, *An Economic Theory of Democracy* (1957).

[44]Mancur Olson, *The Logic of Collective Action: Public Goods and the Theory of Groups* (1965).

a rational person will not participate in the political process of enactment at all, preferring instead to free-ride on the efforts of others. As long as the free-rider cannot be excluded from the legislative benefits, she will have no incentive to expend time and resources to obtain them. If all citizens are rational, then, none will work to influence her representative to pass legislation providing diffuse benefits to the public at large.

Olson's theory predicts, therefore, that the formation of large groups will be virtually impossible. Smaller groups will often form, however, for a number of reasons. First, in some groups, one entity may receive such a large fraction of the total benefit that it would work to obtain the legislative benefit even if it had to bear all the costs of political activity itself. A group may form around this entity for a number of reasons, but the activity would be undertaken by the individual alone. Second, a group may be small enough that members can detect and punish free-riders and thus force collective action. In short, small groups have the advantage over large ones because the former can work to receive targeted benefits at the expense of the diffuse and unorganized public. As Olson concludes, "[T]here is a surprising tendency for the 'exploitation' of the great by the small."[45]

Olson's work is crucial for understanding interest group activity in politics and the threat that organized minority factions pose to the public good. But his theory is an incomplete description of the political process in a number of respects. Most obviously, large groups do form and influence political outcomes. Under Olson's logic, these groups should remain latent, silently footing the bill for the rent-seeking legislation that small groups manage to enact.

Olson explained such groups in two ways. First, some may have formed for nonpolitical reasons and then turned to political activity as a byproduct. For these groups, the initial costs of organizing, often the greatest hurdle facing those seeking to influence governmental policies, are already defrayed when they turn some of their attention to lobbying the national government.

---

[45]*Id.* at 35 (emphasis omitted).

Large groups can also form if they offer desirable selective benefits only to their members. For example, the American Association of Retired Persons not only engages in political activity, but also provides its members with discounts on hotel bills and medical and life insurance. This explanation for the formation and maintenance of large groups seems rather unpersuasive, however. If people are joining the Sierra Club only for the calendar, why do we not observe another group that provides only a nature calendar for vastly lower dues forming to compete with the Sierra Club? The explanation for the existence of large organizations has to be more sophisticated and must relate to the political activity itself. Rational individuals must find it worthwhile to band together to work to influence public policy even when they will capture only a small amount of the public benefit. Some interest group theorists argue that participation in group activity provides members with purposive or solidary benefits that justify any costs they incur.[46] *Purposive benefits* accrue to members who seek ideological or issue-oriented goals and find pursuit of those objectives more meaningful as part of an organized group; *solidary benefits* provide members social rewards, including satisfaction of the desire to be politically involved.

Such benefits may also explain the existence of groups representing the interests of the poor or powerless in society. Those living in poverty, children, and other similarly situated people may not have the resources to lobby elected officials so they rely on others to make their case before the legislature. In many instances, their advocates are private individuals who receive purposive or solidary benefits from political activity on behalf of disempowered groups. In other cases, government officials see part of their role as protecting the rights of such groups and ensuring that their voices are heard. These efforts are often undertaken by intensely motivated individuals that political scientists term *policy entrepreneurs*. Policy entrepreneurs are people "in or out of government who, through adroit use of the

---

[46]See, e.g., Burdett Loomis & Allan Cigler, *Introduction: The Changing Nature of Interest Group Politics*, in *Interest Group Politics* 1 (Cigler & Loomis eds., 1991) (noting that selective benefits need not be material; they can also be solidary or expressive). See also Russell Hardin, *Collective Action* 31-32 (1982) (discussing byproduct theory and noting the "less obvious, but more important, forms that selective incentives can take").

media, can mobilize public support by appealing to widely shared values such as a concern about health, safety, or environmental preservation and by making opponents seem self-serving and careless of the public interest."[47] Critical scholars argue that groups that must rely on others to assert their interests face significant disadvantages in the political system: both they and their advocates will be unable to escape from disempowering ideologies.[48]

Finally, scholars have recently criticized Olson's work because of the evidence that legislators pay attention to issues that affect large numbers of people, even when those individuals have not formed an interest group or when their political activity pales in comparison to that of smaller groups. For example, Congress enacts environmental legislation, even though business groups may be more influential than the Sierra Club. And Congress is loath to pass a general tax increase even when it needs the money to send targeted benefits to organized and intensely motivated groups. R. Douglas Arnold explains why Congress sometimes responds to the interests of the diffuse public, which he terms the *inattentive public*, and does not solely spend its time legislating on behalf of the organized and *attentive public*.[49] Members of Congress want to be reelected, and they know that the inattentive public, many of whom will vote in the next election, can be roused into action on particular issues under certain conditions. Accordingly, legislators will consider the potential preferences of the inattentive public, and the likelihood that they will focus on those preferences at election time, when they are determining policy positions.

Arnold identifies several factors that affect the likelihood that a citizen will care about an issue when she votes. The magnitude of the cost or benefit affects the probability that a citizen will perceive it; the timing of the cost or benefit is important because voters can more easily trace direct effects of a policy back to a legislative action than effects farther down the causal chain; and the proximity of a citizen to others similarly affected will influence the probability that she will

---

[47]Schlozman & Tierney, *supra* note 42, at 84.

[48]See Richard Davies Parker, *The Past of Constitutional Theory — And Its Future*, 42 Ohio St. L.J. 223, 244 (1981).

[49]See R. Douglas Arnold, *The Logic of Congressional Action* 68-71 (1990).

notice the cost or benefit. Perhaps most crucially, the inattentive public is more likely to snap to attention when an instigator brings an issue forcefully to its attention at election time. The media, challengers in elections, and political parties can serve this vital role. Given the possibility that the unorganized mass of voters will care enough about a particular issue to use it as a basis for their votes, representatives must consider their preferences as well as the preferences of organized interest groups.

C. *Interest Group Theories and the Transactional Model of the Political Process: Explanation and Criticisms*

Despite their limitations, public choice theories of interest group activity can help explain why Congress passes some kinds of legislation more frequently than other kinds. For example, scholars have studied the behavior of those who demand legislation — interest groups — and under what circumstances the groups will work together to pass legislation or find themselves in conflict. Theodore Lowi argued that the political relationship among demanders of the legislative product is "determined by the type of policy at stake, so that for every type of policy there is likely to be a distinctive type of political relationship."[50] Although in the long-run, all policies are redistributive in nature because someone, either now or later, has to pay for them, in the short run, some government policies are not constrained by limited resources. With such *distributive* policies, all interests can be satisfied as omnibus bills are constructed handing out goodies to the constituents of a majority of lawmakers. Examples of distributive laws are tax bills that enact tax benefits for hundreds of interest groups, defense appropriations bills that send money for projects in hundreds of congressional districts, or tariff bills that promise protection to dozens of domestic businesses and labor unions. "They are policies in which the indulged and the deprived, the loser and the recipient, need never come into direct confrontation"[51] perhaps because they are funded by increasing the government's deficit, which passes the burden to future generations. Interest

---

[50]Theodore Lowi, *American Business, Public Policy, Case-Studies, and Political Theory*, 16 World Pol. 677, 688 (1964).

[51]*Id.* at 690.

groups will cooperate to pass distributive laws because they are non-zero-sum games — every participant is a winner.

By contrast, some laws force interest groups into conflictual behavior because they are zero-sum propositions. Lowi identified two different kinds of policies that cause interest groups to clash because the losers are clearly identified. *Regulatory policies* are "distinguishable from distributive in that in the short run the regulatory decision involved a direct choice as to who will be indulged and who deprived. Not all applicants for a single television channel or an overseas air route can be propitiated."[52] *Redistributive policies* are like regulatory policies, but "[t]he categories of impact are much broader, approaching social classes. They are, crudely speaking, haves and have-nots, bigness and smallness, bourgeoisie and proletariat."[53] Again, in both these cases, the issue produces interest group conflict, although the groups implicated in the redistributive arena may be sufficiently large to find collective action difficult.

Drawing on Lowi, Olson, and James Q. Wilson,[54] Michael Hayes has constructed a transactional model of legislation that provides a taxonomy of the demand for legislation and its supply.[55] The insight from Wilson that undergirds the model is that the degree and nature of interest group activity is determined by the perceived incidence of costs and benefits of a specified policy. Costs may be broadly distributed, such as through an across-the-board increase in tax rates, or they may be narrowly concentrated, such as an excise tax on a particular service or industry. Similarly, benefits may be broadly distributed, as in the case of national defense or environmental regulation, or they may be narrowly targeted, as in the case of wheat subsidies or tax benefits for the oil and gas industry. Wilson maintained, consistent with Olson's work, that laws enacting concentrated costs or benefits will generally stimulate more interest group activity than those enacting widely distributed costs or benefits. Furthermore, knowing that the attentive public of small, organized

---

[52]*Id.* at 690-91.

[53]*Id.* at 691.

[54]See James Q. Wilson, *Political Organizations* (1973).

[55]Michael Hayes, *Lobbyists and Legislators: A Theory of Political Markets* (1981).

groups is more likely to be active in the next reelection campaign, legislators will take account of these patterns of behavior in supplying the legislative product. Hayes combined these theories to develop the following model of the legislative process.

Majoritarian politics describes the situation of a proposal of distributed costs and distributed benefits. Such a proposal might be an environmental proposal funded through a general tax rate increase. We would expect there to be little interest group activity on either side, although we know that some large groups of citizens will weigh in both in favor of the benefits (e.g., Sierra Club and Greenpeace) and against the method of funding (e.g., Citizens for a Sound Economy). Without strong interest group activity, lawmakers may be unwilling to spend time on the issue or, at most, pass only a symbolic proposal that makes little real change. Of course, Arnold's work suggests that legislative action will occur when representatives believe that the potential preferences of the inattentive electorate will be triggered during a reelection campaign. Given the factors he identifies that may motivate voters, lawmakers may fear reprisals from a tax rate increase, an action with early-order effects that can be directly traced to the lawmaker's decision, more than they believe environmentalists will provide active electoral support. The phenomenon of loss aversion may result in a stronger negative reaction to a tax increase than a positive reaction to an improvement in the air quality. For all these reasons, Congress is not likely to pass substantial amounts of majoritarian legislation.

Another type of legislation produces distributed benefits and concentrated costs. For example, some environmental legislation requires businesses to comply with regulatory mandates and to bear the costs of compliance. Or, a tax reform bill reducing tax rates generally could be offset by increased taxes on particular industries or activities. Here we would expect organized groups to form or to mobilize in opposition to the proposal. In the conflict between these effective groups and any group representing the more diffuse interests of the public, the former is better situated to win. Nonetheless, such legislation is still proposed and passed, and the dynamics of this process fit the model of *entrepreneurial politics*. Representatives will be willing to risk the punishment of the groups bearing the costs of such laws when they are convinced by a policy entrepreneur that change is required and that the inattentive public will reward them at the polls.

The course of entrepreneurial legislation is tortuous; one lesson of proceduralism is that organized minority interest groups can block legislation at one of the many vetogates in the system. Moreover, legislators may seek to placate all participants in this arena either by passing symbolic legislation or by delegating the tough decisions to an agency. Lawmakers hope that the latter strategy will allow them to escape blame for any costs of the new law while gaining credit with voters for the overall policy. The regulated interests may accept this outcome, hoping that their superior organization will allow them to capture the regulating agency and subvert the policy.

Client politics corresponds to Lowi's distributive policies. Here, the benefits are concentrated, but the costs are widely distributed. A tax bill full of provisions allowing preferential treatment to particular groups and funded either through a general tax rate increase or deficit financing is a classic example of client politics. Interest groups strongly support the legislation and work together to ensure its passage. Logrolling will dominate congressional deliberations and may lead to the enactment of an omnibus bill full of goodies, aptly called a "Christmas tree bill." Any opposition is likely to be weakly organized, although lawmakers will consider the likelihood that voters will notice the costs imposed on them and hold their representatives accountable at the polls. We might suspect that the legislature will tend to overproduce this kind of legislation relative to the amount that would best serve the public interest, just as we might anticipate that laws in the majoritarian or entrepreneurial sectors will be underproduced.

Finally, some proposals produce concentrated benefits and concentrated costs. The bills in the arena of *interest group politics* correspond to Lowi's redistributive policies. Groups that benefit are clearly identified and well organized, and groups that will pay are clearly identified and perhaps even better organized. A good example of such a measure is a labor proposal that benefits unions at the expense of business and management. Given the insights of proceduralism and the relative ease with which groups can block a proposal at one of the many vetogates in the system, we would expect most of these proposals to fail. Indeed, Schlozman and Tierney discovered that interest groups are most influential when they seek to block legislation, rather than propose new policies, because of the many opportunities for an organized group to kill or delay new legislation.[56]

This taxonomy is helpful because it suggests tendencies in the legislative process based on the interest group activity surrounding a particular policy. It may also suggest reforms that are likely to improve the process because it helps to identify market failure. For example, if legislation in the majoritarian and entrepreneurial arenas tends to be more public-regarding but is underproduced because of interest group dynamics, reforms might emphasize empowering people whose interests are not well represented by organized groups. Alternatively, it might suggest that we should identify proxy groups with related interests who can serve as champions for the unorganized. Or, if we notice that rent-seeking legislation is less likely when interest group behavior is conflictual and not cooperative, we might seek to structure the legislative process to force interest groups to compete for limited resources. Legislation structured so that the losers are clearly identified is legislation that will be more difficult to enact.

Scholars from different parts of the ideological spectrum have attacked the transactional view of the legislative process because it treats legislators as ciphers. Legislators discern interest group preferences and implement whatever policy results from the interplay of the various organized entities participating in the political process. In this sense, the public choice lawmaker is more consistent with some liberal views of appropriate representation, rather than with republican ideals. The lawmaker is willing to act as the agent for interest groups because she is solely interested in reelection[57] and knows that satisfying those who care about legislative outcomes is the way to stay in power. Indeed, even in Arnold's world, the lawmaker works to ensure her reelection by ascertaining potential preferences of the normally inattentive public, not by constructing her own view of the public good or seeking to shape preferences in a particular way.

---

[56]See Schlozman & Tierney, *supra* note 42, at 314-15.

[57]See, e.g., David Mayhew, *Congress: The Electoral Connection* 16 (1974).

One of the more interesting criticisms of the view of the legislator in the transactional model has been leveled by Fred McChesney, a theorist in the public choice tradition. He notes that those expounding the economic theory of legislation and legal regulation largely ignore the ways that politicians benefit from their offices other than by sending benefits to interest groups. McChesney argues that "payments to politicians [campaign contributions, gifts, post-tenure employment] often are made, not for particular political favors, but to avoid particular political disfavor, that is, as part of a system of political extortion, or 'rent extraction.' . . . Because the state, quite legally, can (and does) take money and other forms of wealth from its citizens, politicians can extort from private parties payments *not* to expropriate private wealth. . . . In that sense, rent extraction — receiving payments not to take or destroy private wealth — is 'money for nothing,' in the words of the song."[58] Rent extraction is theoretically possible in any legislative realm, because legislators always have the ability to repeal existing beneficial legislation or to enact burdensome laws. Interest groups that do not want to be penalized by such actions will try to influence lawmakers not to harm them.

One of the conditions necessary for effective rent extraction is that the victim group must believe that the chances are great that Congress will overcome the hurdles to legislation and actually pass the harmful law. In other words, the threat of rent extraction must be credible. One arena of particularly credible threats is the tax legislative arena because Congress frequently passes new tax legislation decreasing some tax subsidies and increasing taxes on other groups. This behavior produces enough uncertainty that current beneficiaries of tax subsidies are regularly worried that their provisions will be scaled back or modified and are willing to pay protection money to lawmakers.

Rent extraction almost certainly explains some legislative behavior, but like other public choice theories, it assumes an inaccurate view of legislators as one-dimensional seekers of financial rewards from special interest groups. Although reelection and financial considerations are important to lawmakers, most are also

---

[58]Fred McChesney, *Money for Nothing: Politicians, Rent Extraction, and Political Extortion* 2-3 (1997).

motivated by the desire for status and reputation and the objective of affecting policy and the national agenda in ways consistent with their ideological commitments.[59] Empirical studies have found that a legislator's voting behavior is most related to her constituents' interests.[60] Although interest groups play prominent roles in the political process, those that exert the greatest influence on major legislative votes have agendas that reflect the interests of the law-maker's constituents. Contrary to popular belief, interest group benefits seem not to be the equivalent of payments to buy votes. Instead, interest group contributions flow to members who share the interest group's ideological perspective and who can therefore be expected to vote consistently with its interests even in the absence of benefits. Thus, the primary purpose of campaign contributions may be to elect sympathetic members in the first place and then to keep them sympathetic. Of course, interest groups may obtain access or other advantages, but they do not reach agreements among themselves and force lawmakers to implement them without input or change.

Perhaps in part because of the independent nature of lawmakers and the importance of constituent views, interest group clout varies across legislation and bills. Schlozman and Tierney found that interest group influence depends on context.[61] Not only are interest groups more successful at blocking than passing legislation, they are also more influential when the issue has low public visibility and their objectives are narrow and technical. These issues will escape the notice of the inattentive public, and they are unlikely to have strong ideological components. Coalitions are more successful than interest

---

[59]See Richard Fenno, *Congressmen in Committees* (1973) (reaching that conclusion on the basis of extensive interviews of members).

[60]See, e.g., Morris Fiorina, *Representatives, Roll Calls, and Constituencies* (1974); John Kingdon, *Congressmen's Voting Decisions* (1989). The consensus view is that legislators do not engage in substantial shirking from their constituents' preferences as measured by the salient votes evaluated by various rating organizations like the National Taxpayers Union and the Americans for Democratic Action. This certainly holds true as long as politicians know that voters can remove them from office in the next election, and apparently it still holds true even when the threat of electoral consequences is removed in the representative's last term. See Bruce Bender & John Lott, Jr., *Legislator Voting and Shirking: A Critical Review of the Literature*, 87 Pub. Choice 67 (1996).

[61]See Schlozman & Tierney, *supra* note 42, at 317.

groups working alone, and the support of the media or other policy entrepreneurs can improve the chance for success. Finally, an interest group is most successful when it lays the groundwork in a sympathetic decisional forum, perhaps by devoting substantial resources, such as time, information, and money, to cultivate bureaucrats and members of Congress with jurisdiction over relevant issues. Once interest groups have spent the time to become aligned with such policymakers, they become part of a cozy triangle so that they are consulted before policy is adopted and they have the opportunity to influence its direction at the early stages.

III. Institutional Theories[62]

While interest group theorists focus on the participants in the process — groups, lawmakers, policy entrepreneurs, constituents — a different group of theorists turns its attention to the institutions that shape the structure of the interactions. Again, these institutionalists claim the Madisonian tradition as their own. Like Madison, they emphasize the nature of institutionally generated incentives to shape individual behavior, and they explain outcomes in terms of "balance" or "equilibrium."[63] Perhaps the common claim of Madison as inspiration demonstrates that the three theories described in this chapter are complementary and must all be used to explain the political process fully. At the least, we must understand the new institutionalism for a complete picture of the theories that we will apply to the electoral process and the legislative process in following chapters.

A. *The Effect of Institutions on Decisionmaking*

Not all public choice scholars focus on interest groups; a different set of theorists in this tradition has applied economic principles to political decisionmaking. Drawing from the work of Kenneth Arrow, these social choice theorists suggest that political outcomes under majority-voting schemes inevitably will be incoherent, will not

---

[62]See Eskridge & Frickey 61-66.

[63]See Thomas Schwartz, *Publius and Public Choice*, in *The Federalist Papers and the New Institutionalism* 31, 35 (Bernard Grofman & Donald Wittman eds., 1989).

necessarily reflect the preferences of the majority, and hence will lack legitimacy.[64]   Arrow's objective was to determine the minimal conditions required to ensure that individual preferences are combined so that any decision improves social welfare by reflecting the aggregate preferences of members of society. He set forth five basic requirements for an acceptable method of aggregation:

Rationality: If society prefers outcome *A* to outcome *B* and outcome *B* to outcome *C*, the society prefers outcome *A* over outcome *C*.

The Pareto requirement: If one person prefers outcome *A* to outcome *B* and no one else cares, then society prefers outcome *A* over outcome *B*.

Non-dictatorship: The outcomes adopted by society are not dictated by one person's preferences.

Independence of Irrelevant Alternatives: If outcome *C* is not on the agenda, whether outcome *A* is preferred to outcome *B* should not depend on how either one compares to outcome *C*.

Citizens' Sovereignty: Citizens should be free to prefer any policy option at all and to rank options in any way that they want; no institution should have the power to declare certain choices or rankings off the table.

Arrow's Paradox asserts that majority-voting methods of preference aggregation cannot meet these conditions. The phenomenon of *majority vote cycling* is a simple illustration of his conclusion, which is supported by complicated mathematical proofs.[65] In some circumstances, majority rule may not resolve the choice among three or more mutually exclusive alternatives that are voted on in pairs. Take the following prosaic example: three people — Sarah, Rachel,

---

[64]See Kenneth Arrow, *Social Choice and Individual Values* (2d ed. 1963). The basic idea is associated first with the Marquis de Condorcet, who wrote in the eighteenth century. See Cheryl Block, *Truth and Probability — Ironies in the Evolution of Social Choice Theory*, 76 Wash. U.L.Q. 975 (1998).

[65]See Dennis Mueller, 2 *Public Choice* 384-99 (1989) (summarizing Arrow's Theorem and its proof); Maxwell Stearns, *Public Choice and Public Law: Readings and Commentary* 255-372 (1997) (providing critiques of social choice theory as applied to legal problems).

and Alexander — are deciding what kind of ice cream to buy. They decide that they will vote among the following choices: chocolate, vanilla, and cappuccino. Each person's order of ice cream preferences is as follows:

Sarah: chocolate, cappuccino, vanilla
Rachel: cappuccino, vanilla, chocolate
Alexander: vanilla, chocolate, cappuccino.

With these preferences and pairwise voting, majority voting cannot resolve their problem. A majority (Sarah and Alexander) will vote for chocolate rather than cappuccino; a majority (Sarah and Rachel) will vote for cappuccino rather than vanilla; and a majority (Rachel and Alexander) will vote for vanilla rather than chocolate. Absent any rules or other constraints, the voting will go on forever, and any decision will be immediately unsettled by a new vote. Accordingly, institutions are created that prevent cycling, perhaps by specifying an agenda in advance and limiting the number of votes. If the agenda first requires a vote between chocolate and cappuccino (chocolate wins), and then a final vote on chocolate versus vanilla (vanilla wins), the ice cream lovers will eat vanilla. Different ordering of votes or number of votes would yield a different dessert selection.

Knowing this, one of the voters may decide to vote strategically, rather than sincerely, to prevent the cycle and substantially satisfy her preferences. For example, assume that Sarah, who likes cappuccino almost as much as chocolate, knows the preferences of the other voters. For her the worst possible outcome is vanilla, which will win under the decisional rules described above. But, if she votes for cappuccino at first, setting up a battle with vanilla, she knows that cappuccino will win ultimately and she will be happier with the outcome than had she voted sincerely.

The prevalence of strategic voting as a response to cycling has led some public choice scholars to be very pessimistic about democratic outcomes. William Riker, for example, concluded from Arrow's work that all methods of aggregating preferences are prone to irrationality and chaos, and therefore meaningless, or that they will be manipulated by those in power, and therefore arbitrary and undemocratic.[66] Even under a less bleak view, Arrow's Theorem poses hard questions for democracy, because it suggests an inevitable trade-off between democracy (and attendant chaos) and stability (and attendant unfairness).[67] The crucial consideration is to identify the ways cycling is avoided and order is brought to a chaotic decisionmaking process. Often these mechanisms of stability are found in the institutional design that constrains decisionmakers. Thus, Arrow's work leads us to a focus on institutions and what some call "structure-induced equilibria."[68]

Theories of proceduralism have identified some of the primary mechanisms through which the legislative structure provides stability. Committees limit choices and shape how the choices are presented; the Rules Committee in the House determines the order of amendments and the choices presented to the full body; germaneness requirements and time limits further structure legislative choice. The Constitution provides many of these structures; other institutional arrangements fill gaps and provide additional constraints. Of course, decision structures may be determined in an arbitrary way, thereby undermining the legitimacy of the outcomes they produce. For example, critical theorists might well indict many of the institutions shaping legislative outcomes as controlled by powerful elites and insufficiently attentive to the voices of outsiders.

This kind of institutional perspective provides theoretical support for one aspect of the decision in *Powell v. McCormack* (Chapter 2). Remember that the Supreme Court declined to equate a two-thirds vote to exclude Representative Powell with a two-thirds vote to expel. Why? Understanding the order of the voting may illuminate the Court's decision. The Committee that investigated the allegations against Powell recommended that he be seated and censured. After debate, the House rejected a motion on previous question that would have forced an immediate vote. The resolution was amended so that

---

[66]See William Riker, *Liberalism Against Populism: A Confrontation Between the Theory of Democracy and the Theory of Public Choice* 137 (1982).

[67]See Jerry Mashaw, *Greed, Chaos, and Governance: Using Public Choice to Improve Public Law* 13 (1997).

[68]See Kenneth Shepsle & Barry Weingast, *Structure-Induced Equilibrium and Legislative Choice*, 37 Pub. Choice 503 (1981).

it required exclusion; that amendment passed by a simple majority of 248 to 176. The Chair ruled that the final vote required to exclude Powell was a simple majority; only expulsion required a two-thirds majority under the Constitution. On final passage of the resolution to exclude, 59 members who had opposed the amendment switched their votes to support passage. Why did they change their minds? Had they been convinced by stirring speeches offered by supporters of the resolution? Probably not. These members realized that the resolution of exclusion was going to pass because a simple majority had already voted in favor of it. Perhaps they thought some punishment appropriate, or perhaps they did not want their votes to become an issue in their next reelection campaigns. Had the final vote been one to expel Powell, which would have required two-thirds support, they might well have continued to oppose the resolution to force a compromise solution to the problem. In short, the Supreme Court was entirely right to refuse to equate the exclusion motion with a decision to expel, given the difference in the voting rule applied to each.

The importance of institutions to legislative outcomes may also influence statutory interpretation. Constitutional structures in particular are institutions chosen because of the way they are expected to shape legislation. The legitimacy of the decisions reached by Congress and their claim to coherence and meaning stem in part from the process through which they have been made. Accordingly, interpreters of statutes may be wary of relying on any legislative products, such as committee reports and other aspects of legislative history, that have not passed through the required procedures. They result from structures without the pedigree of constitutional institutions and thus lack the legitimacy of duly enacted laws. In this way insights from social choice theory may support formalist methods of interpretation such as textualism.[69]

Congressional institutions are also designed to provide the opportunity for deliberation, and the same process that shapes

---

[69]See Antonin Scalia, *A Matter of Interpretation: Federal Courts and the Law* 30-35 (1997). For an extended version of this argument, see John Manning, *Constitutional Structure and Statutory Formalism*, 66 U. Chi. L. Rev. 685 (1999). We consider textualism in Chapter 6, Part II. The constitutionally inspired textualist attack upon the use of legislative history in statutory interpretation is examined in Chapter 8, Part II.

preferences may also work to avoid the problems of cycling and legislative incoherence. As lawmakers discuss alternatives and justify their positions, preferences change, and consensus is formed. At the least, participants can isolate the arenas of disagreement and structure voting procedures and agendas to allow coherent resolution.[70] Just as the related interest group school of public choice, pessimistic social choice theorists may ignore the important role of lawmakers in ascertaining constituent preferences, molding those preferences, and finding innovative solutions to improve social welfare. The increasing body of work produced by scholars writing in the republican tradition may be relevant to our search to understand why a bleak view of legislative outcomes should be moderated.

B. *Positive Political Theory: Institutionalism and Game Theory*

Related institutional work growing out of the public choice tradition and influenced by game theory is known as *positive political theory* ("*PPT*"). PPT recognizes that political players understand that other political actors will influence the content and timing of policy. Because outcomes are dependent on the actions of several decision-makers, each party will anticipate the reactions of others and act strategically to ensure that the ultimate decision is as close to her preference as possible. PPT sees all political actors as goal-oriented, although it does not specify that the goals must be economic or self-interested. "The core assumption is that all relevant actors — elected politicians and judges — act rationally to bring policy as close as possible to their own preferred outcome."[71] Thus, when the chair of a House committee drafts legislation, she anticipates the reaction of her members, the Rules Committee, the full House, the Senate, the President, the bureaucracy that will administer the law, and the courts that will interpret it.

---

[70]See Richard Pildes & Elizabeth Anderson, *Slinging Arrows at Democracy: Social Choice Theory, Value Pluralism, and Democratic Politics*, 90 Colum. L. Rev. 2121 (1990) (providing a sustained critique of social choice theory from the perspective of democratic theory).

[71]McNollgast, *Politics and the Courts: A Positive Theory of Judicial Doctrine and the Rule of Law*, 68 S. Cal. L. Rev. 1631 (1995).

This *anticipated response* feature of PPT is integral to the theory, as is the awareness of the importance of the institutions in which such responses occur. Institutions provide the context for political interdependence and the environment in which actors pursue their goals. The structures of institutions — formal and informal — alter the ways in which they interact. PPT studies institutions in two ways. It describes, first, how the institutions that exist change behavior and, second, how the players structure institutions to help them reach their goals.[72] After all, institutions are the creations of humans, and they can be often be altered by those who work within them. Many institutions are relatively stable, but virtually none, not even constitutionally based structures, are immutable.

Although PPT brings to our attention features of the political landscape that we might otherwise overlook — the interdependence of actions, the role of non-legislative players in the formation of policy, the effect of anticipation on current behavior — it does not fully describe the political process. Like some of the other public choice literature, it accepts preferences as stable and unchanging, even though we know that deliberation and other institutions actually work to shape preferences over the course of political decision-making. Often, it assumes that players have full information about the preferences of other players in the political game, even though we know that information is costly and therefore incomplete and that players make mistakes in their predictions of subsequent actions.

To get a more concrete idea of the application of PPT to the political process, we will apply it to an actual legislative proposal to explain the behavior of the relevant parties. Institutional models are often presented in the form of a sequential anticipated response "game," in which each player's choice is determined not only by her preferences on a topic, but also by her place in the institutional structure and her understanding of the preferences of the other players who follow her. The institution that provides structure for this game is primarily the Constitution, although it also includes other legislative structures like committees and rules of debate. Professors

---

[72]See Terry Moe, *Political Institutions: The Neglected Side of the Story*, 6 J.L. Econ. & Org. 213 (1990).

William Eskridge and John Ferejohn call it "The Article I, Section 7 Game."[73]

C. *The Article I, Section 7 Game*

1. *Interactive, Sequential Lawmaking by Interrelated Actors*

Article I, Section 7 of the Constitution requires that, for a bill to become a federal law, it must pass both houses of Congress in identical form and be presented to the President, who may either sign it into law or veto it. Congress may override a Presidential veto by a vote of two-thirds of each house. Unless all this is accomplished, the legal status quo will remain undisturbed.

To model this "game" under the simplified assumptions described above, let us start with the following notations:

SQ = Existing policy (status quo), the default position if no legislation is enacted to deal with a social problem

H and S = Preferences of a median legislator in the two chambers of the bicameral Congress

P = Preferences of the President

x = Statutory policy resulting from the game

Suppose, first, that the status quo is objectionable to both the President and both houses of Congress, and that all three actors would like to change policy in the same direction. Assume further that the President's preferences are more extreme than those of either chamber of Congress. Figure 1 demonstrates these preferences:

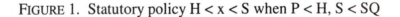

	x		
P	H	S	SQ

FIGURE 1. Statutory policy $H < x < S$ when $P < H$, $S < SQ$

---

[73]See William Eskridge, Jr. & John Ferejohn, *The Article I, Section 7 Game*, 80 Geo. L.J. 523 (1992).

On these simplified assumptions, there should be no problem enacting a statute because all three players prefer a range of policies to the status quo. The statute adopted should reflect a compromise between the positions of the House and Senate. The preferences of the President should have little effect on the final outcome, because the Congress acts first and because, based on this array of preferences, any presidential threat of a veto will not be credible.

Note how important it is in Figure 1 that the House and Senate both prefer change to the status quo. If SQ were between H and S in Figure 1, no statute would be enacted: H would prefer SQ to any point to the right of SQ, and S would prefer SQ to any point to the left of SQ. Thus, as procedural theories predict, the Framer's requirement of *bicameral* support for a change in the status quo reflects a strong bias in favor of limited or only moderate shifts from the status quo, promoting continuity in public policy and structurally inhibiting drastic shifts in law.

Even when both houses support a change in the status quo, however, the President may thwart their efforts if he or she prefers the status quo. In assessing the role of the President's veto power, let us add two more notations:

h and s = Preferences of the pivotal legislator in the House and Senate, whose vote is needed for the two-thirds majority needed to override a presidential veto

If the median legislators in the House and Senate prefer to change the status quo in the same direction, but the President prefers the status quo and has sufficient allies in at least one house to uphold a veto, then no statute will result. Consider Figure 2:

| h | P | SQ | H | s | S |

FIGURE 2. No statute when h < P < SQ < H, S.

The information in Figure 2 indicates that the majority of both houses would prefer to move the status quo to the right, at a point somewhere between H and S. Because the President prefers SQ to such a move,

LEGISLATION

the President should veto the bill. In Figure 2, there are enough votes in the Senate to override such a veto (s prefers a point between H and S to SQ), but the President has enough allies in the House to sustain the veto. As Figure 2 indicates, Article I, Section 7's bias in favor the status quo is enhanced by the presidential veto and requirement of a supermajority override in both houses.

Finally, consider the role that administrative agencies can play in this process. Returning the array of preferences identified in Figure 1, one would expect that Congress would adopt a statute at x, between H and S, and virtually ignore the preferences of the President. But suppose that Congress adopts a statute that fails to specify policy precisely at x, instead delegating authority to an administrative agency with the expectation that the agency will implement policy somewhere around x.[74] If the agency ("A") shares the same preferences as the President — as one would often expect for executive branch agencies — then the agency has the capacity to promulgate an interpretation shifting the policy substantially without fear of congressional amendment and override. Consider Figure 3:

	x'				x		
P	h	s	H		S	SQ	
A							

FIGURE 3. Statutory policy shifts from H < x < S to x' = h, if Congress delegates lawmaking authority to agency

As Figure 3 indicates, any effort by H or S to enact legislation returning the law to x will be vetoed by the President and cannot be overridden unless the new law is set at h. A clever agency, therefore, would set the policy at x' = h, assuming that only something left of h would bestir enough members of the House to support a veto override. Figure 3 demonstrates the dramatic shifts in policy that can arise from the delegation of lawmaking authority to administrative

---

[74]See Chapter 5, Part IIIC, for a discussion of the interaction between Congress and administrative agencies.

agencies — perhaps undermining the strong preference for the status quo the Framers built into Article I, Section 7.

Note, finally, the role of the courts in interpreting legislation. In Figure 3, assume that the statute did not delegate authority to an agency but also did not unequivocally specify policy. Assume further that the Supreme Court's policy preferences are the same as the President. The Court could interpret the statute to mean x', and that would be protected against congressional override by the presidential veto.

As we explained earlier, PPT is a useful tool for evaluating legislative processes, but it cannot capture the full dynamics. For example, in Figure 3, the head of the agency, the President, or the Supreme Court may feel compelled to follow legislative intent and keep policy somewhere around x. The practices of legal interpretation and the norms of public officials charged with interpretive responsibilities can greatly complicate the predictive power of any model of legal change. The manner and the extent to which legal theory and practice constrain strategic behavior are ubiquitous topics in law school. We address statutory interpretation in Chapters 6-9 of this book.

The value of PPT to law students may sometimes be obscured by all the abstractions involved in this analysis. To concretize this approach, consider the following case study.

2. The Proposed BTU Tax: A Case Study

In the first days of the Clinton administration, the President and his advisers began to work on their first budget proposal.[75] Under the federal budget laws, the President must submit his budget proposal to Congress on the first Monday in February. Although deficit reduction had not been a central theme of the Clinton-Gore campaign, members of the White House economic team had convinced the President that he needed to formulate a budget that made significant inroads on the nearly $200 billion annual budget deficit. Vice President Gore argued that some of the deficit reduction should come from revenue raised

---

[75]Some of this story concerning President Clinton's first budget submission is drawn from Bob Woodward, *The Agenda: Inside the Clinton White House* (1994).

by a tax that would also improve the environment. Gore supported a broad-based energy tax such as a tax levied on British Thermal Units, or BTUs, a basic measure of energy.

Accordingly, on February 17, 1993, the administration proposed a "broad-based tax on all types of energy, based on the content of the energy of the fuel (measured in [BTUs])."[76] The President provided very few details about his new tax, but he projected it would raise $50 billion over five years. He did indicate that some accommodation for coal interests would be made in the BTU tax, which probably represented a shift away from the preferences of Vice President Gore to take account of the political power of lawmakers from coal states. Using a PPT model to compare the proposal with the status quo, which would prevail in the absence of legislation, we would express the relationship as P < SQ:

[BTU]	[No Tax]
P	SQ

All tax bills must originate in the House, and House rules give the Ways and Means Committee jurisdiction over all such bills. The Ways and Means Committee was relatively liberal and strongly in the control of the Democratic Party. Nonetheless, as the Committee held hearings on the President's proposal, it became clear that members wanted to grant a series of exceptions and enact a number of changes to the President's proposal, mostly to benefit particular industries with influence in members' districts. In April, the Department of Treasury released a modified BTU tax proposal, adding thirteen exemptions, further lessening the tax burden on coal, and reducing the scope of the tax in a number of ways. Clearly, this modification was a response to the White House's increased understanding of lawmakers' preferences. Or, as we might express this in our model: P<W&M<SQ, where W&M is the preference of the median legislator on the Ways and Means Committee, or the legislator whose vote is required to pass the proposal through the Committee.

---

[76]A Vision of Change for America, Feb. 17, 1993, at 105.

[BTU]	[Modified BTU]	[No Tax]
P	W&M	SQ

As the Ways and Means Committee continued to consider the BTU tax proposal, and as the bill moved to the House floor, the Senate Finance Committee also began holding hearings on the proposal. This feature of the BTU tax saga demonstrates that players in the Article I, Section 7 game play both concurrently and consecutively, increasing the complexity of the game. At the time, the Senate was a less partisan body than the House and much less firmly controlled by the Democratic Party both because the Senate rules do not allow such tight control and because the Democrats had a slimmer majority. The composition of the Finance Committee meant that the defection of even one Democratic Senator would cause a bill to die in Committee, so its chairman had to craft a proposal that would garner the votes of all his co-partisans.

During the hearings, key Democratic Senators made long speeches signaling the House and the President of their concerns with the modified proposal. Senators from Louisiana and Oklahoma wanted concessions for independent oil and gas producers who were afraid they could not pass along the costs of the tax to consumers; the Senator from North Dakota asked for exemptions for farming interests. In informal discussions, these Senators indicated they were open to considering a different kind of energy tax, perhaps a much smaller tax on transportation fuels. As the full House prepared to vote on the bill, conservative Democratic Representatives indicated that they would oppose the BTU tax. Their position was no doubt strengthened by their understanding of the preferences of key Senators and the virtual certainty that the BTU tax would not survive the Senate. Indeed, the critical votes in the House were obtained only by the White House Chief of Staff's promise to key Representatives that the BTU tax would be jettisoned in the Senate. He argued that House Rules precluded the change before the House voted and that the conservative Democrats' support for the entire budget package was required to keep the process going forward. For social choice theorists, their votes represent the kind of strategic voting that makes the notion of legislative intent problematic.

Thus, the median Representative's preference was nearer the status quo than the Ways and Means committee, a situation that may often occur if committees consist of members with outlying preferences. Thus, P<W&M<H, SFC<SQ, where SFC is the preference of the median member of the Finance Committee and H is the preference of the median legislator in the House. Or,

[BTU]	[Modified BTU]	[Smaller Energy Tax]	[No Tax]
P	W&M	H, SFC	SQ

The Senate version of the budget bill rejected the BTU tax, but it contained a transportation fuels tax of an additional 4.3 cents on certain motor fuels, including gasoline. The new tax was projected to raise only $25 billion over five years, requiring the Senate to find other sources of revenue for deficit reduction. The bill barely passed the Committee, and it passed the full Senate only because Vice President Gore cast a vote in favor of the proposal to break a 49-49 tie. Because the tax provision was part of an Omnibus Budget Reconciliation Act, it was not subject to a filibuster in the Senate that would have required 60 votes to end. Had the bill been a regular piece of legislation susceptible to the threat of a filibuster, it would no doubt have been much closer to the status quo to attract the support of more Senators. Indeed, given the partisan makeup of the Senate and the Republicans' unwillingness to support any kind of energy tax, the status quo would doubtlessly have survived with the aid of the filibuster. Under our model, the preferences of the pivotal voter to break a filibuster (sf) would appear as follows: P<W&M<H, SFC, S<SQ(sf). (S represents the preferences of the median Senator.)

The conference committee submitted a bill to the full Congress that contained the transportation tax rather than the BTU tax. Our model suggests that even though the Ways and Means Committee majority played a large role in the conference committee, the BTU tax was unlikely to be resurrected at this juncture. Theoretically, the modified BTU tax was on the table during the conference committee meetings because it had survived the House floor. However, all the participants understood that it could not survive a vote in the Senate, and probably not in the House if the key Democrats voted sincerely this time. Ultimately, the Vice President had to break another tie just to get the transportation tax and other budget provisions past the Senate.

Thus, the bill reached the President's desk with a vastly different and smaller tax than he had proposed. Was he likely to veto the proposal? Of course not. He understood that the transportation tax was the most he was going to get from this Congress; it was certainly closer to his preferred policy than the status quo. Any veto probably would have been sustained; after all, nearly half of the Senate preferred the status quo to the transportation tax and thus would have voted to kill the bill by sustaining the President's veto. But the President was unlikely to do any better in any subsequent budget bill — assuming that Congress had the time left in the session to begin the process again. Or, to represent the pivotal voter in a veto override in the two chambers using h and s:

[BTU]	[Modified BTU]	[Transportation Tax]	[No Tax]
P	W&M	H, S, SFC	h, s, sf, SQ

3. Further Developments in the Game

As suggested earlier, an interesting twist to the Article I, Section 7 game appears if we add into the mix an administrative agency. Imagine that the Congress and the President had enacted a bill, delegating to the Internal Revenue Service the power to design some kind of broad-based energy tax that would raise $50 billion over five years, improve the environment, and be progressive in effect. (These were the original goals of the President when he released his initial BTU tax proposal in February.) Assuming that the IRS knew the preferences of all the players in the game, where would it locate the policy? The IRS is the President's agent, so presumably it would try to construct a policy as close to his preference as possible. The tax bureaucrats would know that Congress would probably have to pass another law to remove the delegated power or to repeal any regulation they promulgate. Perhaps, then, the IRS would adopt a modified BTU tax, the preference of Ways and Means, because the agency administrators would know that the Committee occupies a vetogate and could block any attempt to repeal the tax and replace it with something less radical. On the other hand, other committees in Congress, such as appropriations committees and the Senate Finance Committee, have power over the IRS though oversight and budget control. These powers can be used to punish the IRS if it uses its delegated power in ways consistent with the underlying law but inconsistent with the preferences of crucial congressional players.[77] So, perhaps, the IRS would adopt a less radical transportation tax that represents the preferences of more members of Congress, particularly if the members of Ways and Means have outlying preferences.

Of course, congressional preferences may shift with each election. The 103rd Congress considered Clinton's first budget proposal that included the BTU tax; in that Congress, Democrats controlled both the House and the Senate, although pivotal members were not as liberal as the President and his administration. The next Congress, the 104th, represented a partisan sea change and ushered in Republican control of both houses. Suppose the IRS drafted the tax under its delegated authority after 1994. A Republican Congress has vastly different preferences than a Democratic one. Where would the policy equilibrium lie? In part, it would depend on the extent of Republican control. In both houses, the Democrats maintained sufficient numbers to sustain any presidential veto of a bill either removing the delegated authority or repealing any regulation that implemented a broad-based energy tax. Or, to use a PPT model to locate the preferences of the new players:

[BTU]	[Modified BTU]	[Transportation Tax]	[No Tax]
P	h	s	W&M, SFC, H, S

The IRS could therefore adopt a tax close to the President's preferences, knowing that the Republicans would not have the votes to override a presidential veto of any bill that tried to return to a state

---

[77]See Chapter V, Part IIIC (discussing effect of legislative oversight on agency policies).

of no energy tax at all.[78] In fact, the preference of the pivotal voter in the House would probably be closer to the President's more radical BTU tax than any Republican response, so the IRS might well adopt something very much like Clinton's original proposal. Members of Congress have other ways to exert pressure on the agency, however; thus the policy equilibrium might lie somewhat to the right of the President's preference to take account of continuing influence of a more conservative political player.

In short, this kind of institutional analysis has proved beneficial for a sophisticated understanding of the legislative process. It clearly demonstrates the interdependence of the players, and it suggests that President Clinton might have done better to propose a transportation tax rather than his BTU tax at the outset of the game. Of course, in February 1993, Clinton may not have known the preferences of other key players, and thus he modified his proposal as he received better information. Moreover, he may have submitted a larger and more far-reaching tax than he expected to get in order to shape the terms of the negotiations. Had he proposed the more modest transportation tax first, perhaps the oil and gas state Senators would have demanded its elimination. By using the BTU as a starting place, the President was able to convince Congress to enact some kind of broad-based energy tax, and opposing Senators and Representatives were able to portray their compromise proposal as consistent with the interests of important constituencies, rather than as a sellout.[79] Finally, the model starkly demonstrates the different policy equilibria that result when Congress acts with great specificity and when it delegates to a bureaucracy headed by a player with preferences that diverge from legislative ones.

---

[78]Budget rules might also make it difficult for the Republicans to change the status quo (which would now include a law delegating power to the IRS). Such a bill would result in a revenue loss for the federal government, and current budget rules require Congress also to enact a provision offsetting the lost revenue. See Chapter 5, Part IIC, for a discussion of offset requirements in the federal budget process.

[79]See John Gilmour, *Strategic Disagreement: Stalemate in American Politics* (1995) (discussing difficulties lawmakers face in reaching compromise solutions and discussing various bargaining strategies).

One actor left out of the BTU tax game was the judicial branch, but judges have policy preferences that lawmakers also take into account.[80] After all, law implementation is left not only to agencies, but also to courts. Furthermore, when they interpret legislation, judges are aware that Congress will often have the ability to override their opinion, and thus they may tailor their holdings to eliminate the risk of subsequent congressional nullification.

---

[80]See William Eskridge, Jr. & Philip Frickey, *The Supreme Court, 1993 Term — Foreword: Law as Equilibrium*, 108 Harv. L. Rev. 26 (1994).

4

Electoral Structures

The previous chapters have provided you with a variety of theoretical frameworks with which you can approach and analyze problems that arise in the electoral and legislative processes. Chapters 4 and 5 will present detailed studies of several of the most pressing issues, ranging from ballot access laws and the regulation of political parties to the arcane but ubiquitous federal budget process laws. Federal and state statutes are drafted and passed by multi-member, bicameral legislatures (except in Nebraska, which has a unicameral legislature). How citizens select such representatives plays a crucial role in the legislative process and may be relevant to courts when interpreting statutes. If we assume that most lawmakers are interested in reelection, for example, the structure of the campaign finance system may determine which interests have the most influence in determining legislative priorities. If judges believe that lawmakers are unduly influenced by rent-seeking private interests, they may adopt interpretations of statutes that are more consistent with the public interest. Or courts may interpret statutes narrowly to deny interest groups more benefits than they bargained for. Thus, the discussions in this chapter and the next will be necessary for a sophisticated understanding of the methods of statutory interpretation addressed in the final four chapters of this book.

Chapter 2 discussed a variety of structural features — rules governing eligibility to serve as a legislator, limitations on the right to vote, reapportionment of seats and the problems of racial and political gerrymandering, regulation of political corruption and campaign contributions — in the context of theories of representation. From that discussion it should be apparent that electoral structures are enormously significant in a democracy. To take perhaps the most vivid example, the history of racial discrimination in voting is a history of the manipulation of structural barriers to representation. By the use of such devices as literacy tests, good-character requirements, grandfather clauses, and white primaries, African Americans were initially excluded from voting. In the Voting

Rights Act of 1965,[1] Congress adopted a dual strategy: to remove barriers to registration and voting by racial minorities and to protect them against further attempts to dilute their new voting power. Thus, for the states and localities covered by § 5 of the Act, the statute not only outlawed "tests and devices" as prerequisites to voting, it also provided that no change in voting qualifications, procedures, or structures could be implemented without the prior determination by either the Attorney General or the United States District Court for the District of Columbia (not the local federal district court) that the change did not have the purpose *and* would not have the effect of causing a retrogression in minority voting strength.

The case law implementing the Act has invalidated changes in a variety of electoral structures. For example, in a situation with racial bloc voting in which African Americans constitute a minority in a community and live in identifiable areas, the Act prevents officials from manipulating electoral structures to dilute minority voting power — from switching from ward elections to at-large elections by majority vote (thus destroying the ability of the minority community to elect officeholders of its choice from its own neighborhoods), from annexing suburbs to increase white voting power, and so on.[2] Since 1982, § 2 of the Act has also outlawed existing electoral structures, not merely changes in such structures, that dilute minority voting strength.[3]

In this chapter, we will analyze other relevant electoral structures: those that shape the ballot and the content of the electoral campaign; those that regulate political parties, which have both public and private roles in governance; and those that regulate campaign contributions and expenditures. Our cast of characters is large. Both federal and state laws contribute to the structuring of electoral institutions. In addition, although voters ultimately determine who represents them by casting individual ballots, interest groups and

---

[1]42 U.S.C. § 1973 *et seq.*

[2]See, e.g., *City of Rome v. United States*, 446 U.S. 156 (1980).

[3]See 42 U.S.C. § 1973, as interpreted in *Thornburg v. Gingles*, 478 U.S. 30 (1986). For consideration of the Voting Rights Act, see Eskridge & Frickey 146-52, 184-87; Issacharoff, Karlan & Pildes 264-545; Lane & Mikva 53-62, 235-301, 313-65, 936-84; Lowenstein 30-32, 143-257.

political parties are largely responsible for winnowing the possible candidates so that only a few — usually two — appear on the final ballot.

As you read the discussion of the public law issues structuring the electoral process, consider how the different theories of representation introduced in Chapter 2 animate calls for reform and for judicial review of electoral structures. Most of the discourse of reform and review is *liberal*, theoretically aspiring to enable voters to articulate their electoral choices meaningfully. Liberal theory would appear presumptively hostile to state regulation, except that much regulation is justified on the ground that it prevents voter confusion or minimizes secret corruption. The evidence for such propositions is typically unimpressive. *Republican* theorists focus on the way the state structures electoral choice and vigorously object when they believe the structures lock in the power of incumbents and established interests, especially monied ones. Republicans seek greater equality in meaningful access to electoral politics, an idea that liberals believe is unrealistic. *Critical* theorists emphasize the ways in which formal equality and even some forms of functional equality can preserve patterns of race-based political marginalization. They often support radical state or federal regulation of local electoral processes corrupted by longstanding practices with racial effects.

I. Regulating Ballot Access and Campaigns

Article I, Section 4 of the Constitution allows the states to regulate the "Times, Places and Manner of holding Elections for Senators and Representatives," although Congress can pass legislation to make or alter state electoral regulations. Most ballot regulations are therefore the creatures of state law, passed by lawmakers who understand that reelection campaigns will be shaped by the regulations. Furthermore, virtually all of these lawmakers are members of one of the two major political parties and view the party label as a valuable cue for incompletely informed voters. To understand ballot access regulations, then, we must understand how they affect the fortunes of incumbents and political parties. We will also canvass some of the regulations affecting the information provided to voters at election time. Again, this analysis relates to political parties generally because one of the strongest voting cues — and one of the few that appear on the ballot — is party affiliation.

A. *The Constitutional Issues Implicated by Ballot Access Laws*[4]

Before 1900, the study of ballot access restrictions was much simpler. There were no official ballots; instead, political parties provided voters with ballots listing only their candidates for offices. Because party ballots were printed in distinctive colors, secret balloting was difficult, and voters were often bribed or intimidated into voting in a particular way. Only at the end of the nineteenth century, with the adoption of the Australian ballot — the secret, uniform, and government-printed ballot — did the question of ballot access become important for policymakers and the courts.[5] Indeed, ballot access is so vital to political parties that Justice Stevens has observed that "the right to be on the election ballot is precisely what separates a political party from any other interest group."[6] Soon after the widespread adoption of the secret ballot, partisan legislators began to pass laws restricting the ability of independent candidates and candidates from minor parties to appear on the official ballot.

Although states have the constitutional power to regulate elections, their authority is not absolute. Ballot access restrictions implicate important constitutional guarantees because they fundamentally shape the electoral choices presented to voters. First, ballot access laws implicate the right to vote effectively. In addition, laws that substantially impair the right of minor party candidates to obtain a place on the ballot undermine the right to associate for political purposes. On the other hand, states have a legitimate interest in regulating elections to reduce disorder, voter confusion, and fraud. Thus, the Supreme Court has developed a flexible test to assess the

---

[4]See Eskridge & Frickey 350; Eskridge, Frickey & Garrett Supp. 20-21, 23-25; Issacharoff, Karlan & Pildes 193-212, 242-63, 711-12; Lowenstein 391-406; Mikva & Lane 438-46; Popkin 717-22.

[5]See, e.g., Paul Allen Beck & Frank Sorauf, *Party Politics in America* 305 (7th ed. 1992).

[6]*Timmons v. Twin Cities Area New Party*, 520 U.S. 351, 373 (1997) (Stevens, J., dissenting).

constitutionality of ballot access laws under the First and Fourteenth Amendments.

Regulations that impose severe burdens on rights — for example, those that essentially make it impossible for independent candidates to obtain ballot position — must be narrowly tailored and serve a compelling state interest. Laws requiring new political parties to obtain substantial numbers of signatures months before an election have been held unconstitutional because they virtually preclude such parties from qualifying for ballot access.[7] Less onerous burdens trigger less exacting judicial scrutiny, allowing legitimate state regulatory interests to support reasonable and nondiscriminatory burdens. In most cases, the courts use the less stringent test and are willing to uphold ballot access restrictions on the ground that "there must be a substantial regulation of elections if they are to be fair and honest and if some sort of order, rather than chaos, is to accompany the democratic processes."[8]

Several state interests have been identified to support ballot access restrictions. Perhaps the most frequently heard is the concern that listing many candidates and political parties on the ballot will confuse voters and undermine their ability to vote effectively. Interestingly, states seldom present empirical evidence that voters actually are confused by long ballots or other unusual ballot configurations. For example, in *Timmons v. Twin Cities Area New Party*,[9] the Court faced the question whether Minnesota could ban fusion candidacies. Fusion, or the nomination of the same candidate by more than one political party, allows minor parties to exert influence on the outcome of elections, thereby increasing their potential influence over policies adopted by representatives. Most states prohibit fusion candidacies, citing, among other factors, confusion when voters are faced by a multiple-party nomination.[10] As in other ballot access cases, however, claims of voter confusion were entirely

---

[7]See *Williams v. Rhodes*, 393 U.S. 23 (1968) (striking down requirement for signatures equaling 15% of number of ballots cast in last election coupled with early filing date).

[8]*Storer v. Brown*, 415 U.S. 724, 730 (1974).

[9]520 U.S. 351 (1997).

[10]See *id.* at 357 n.6, 364.

hypothetical. The only empirical data from a state with vibrant fusion politics, New York, revealed that "the parade of horribles [described by the majority] is fantastical."[11] Unfortunately for adherents of the New Party in *Timmons*, the Court continued its practice of not requiring empirical evidence of voter confusion;[12] instead, it deferred to the legislature's predictive judgment regarding deficiencies in the electoral process.

A related state concern involves protecting the integrity of the official ballot. The state in *Timmons* had articulated such a regulatory interest, and the Court worried that major party candidates could exploit fusion to associate themselves with popular slogans. For example, a Republican candidate could encourage a No New Taxes Party to form and endorse her on the ballot. "[S]uch maneuvering would undermine the ballot's purpose by transforming it from a means of choosing candidates to a billboard for political advertising."[13] Similarly, the Court has reasoned that a ballot full of candidates from minor parties who cannot hope to command significant support may increase voter alienation and dissatisfaction with the electoral process.[14]

Finally, and perhaps most controversially, the Court has been willing to consider state claims that regulation is required to promote political stability, to avoid splintered parties, and to restrain factionalism. This interest may be merely an interest in avoiding intraparty disputes by, for example, limiting the ability of people who have previously run in party primaries to appear on the ballot as independent candidates. Framed in this manner, the interest is not sufficient to support restrictions that are applied to independent candidates not recently associated with political parties.[15] Increasingly, courts are also willing to consider the state's interest in maintaining a stable, two-party electoral system, an interest that can be advanced to justify

---

[11]*Id.* at 375 n.3 (Stevens, J., dissenting).

[12]See, e.g., *Munro v. Socialist Workers Party*, 479 U.S. 189, 195-96 (1986).

[13]*Timmons*, 520 U.S. at 365.

[14]See, e.g., *Storer*, 415 U.S. at 732.

[15]See *Anderson v. Celebrezze*, 460 U.S. 780, 805 (1983). See also Bradley Smith, Note, *Judicial Protection of Ballot-Access Rights: Third Parties Need Not Apply*, 28 Harv. J. Legis. 167, 191 (1991).

broader ballot access provisions. Even though he dissented in *Timmons*, where the majority seriously entertained this state interest, Justice Souter agreed that "[i]f it could be shown that the disappearance of the two-party system would undermine"[16] the state's interest in preserving a political system capable of governing effectively, it might justify certain ballot access regulation.

The state interest in a stable two-party system has been limited, however. First, the state does not have an interest in promoting two particular parties — the Democratic and Republican parties — even if promotion of a two-party electoral system is legitimate. Of course, laws that promote a two-party system necessarily preserve the duopoly enjoyed by the two current major parties. Second, restrictions on minor parties and independent candidates cannot be so onerous as to eliminate competition entirely.[17] Whatever the Court's minor limitations, however, consider two more fundamental questions: How can the state rely on an effort to channel political association to defeat a First Amendment challenge? And how can such channeling be considered a compelling state interest?

Not only is the Court relatively deferential to the foregoing state interests, asserted either singly or in combination, but the Court also has a relatively limited notion of the rights being burdened. First, the right to vote effectively is considered in purely instrumental terms. For example, in *Burdick v. Takushi*,[18] the Court considered the constitutionality of Hawaii's ban on write-in voting in primary and general elections. The Court found the prohibition was only a minimal burden on voters' First Amendment rights because the function of the electoral process is " 'to winnow out and finally reject all but the chosen candidates.' "[19] It rejected the argument that the right to vote has an expressive component, permitting the voter to express her dissatisfaction, alienation, or pique by voting for a fringe

---

[16]520 U.S. at 384 (Souter, J., dissenting).

[17]See *Williams v. Rhodes*, 393 U.S. at 31-32 (also evidencing some distrust of the state's interest in preserving the two-party system).

[18]504 U.S. 428 (1992).

[19]*Id.* at 438 (quoting *Storer*, 415 U.S. at 735).

candidate, a relative, or her favorite cartoon character.[20] Republicans might reject the Court's narrow vision of voting, arguing instead that the act of voting is an expression of participation in the life of the polity and that this value should be considered in addition to the instrumental aspect of voting.[21]

Similarly, the Court has viewed the role of minor parties narrowly. In *Timmons*, the Court saw the ban on fusion candidacies as only a slight burden on the associational rights of political parties because members of minor parties can still nominate and vote for their own candidates. The majority characterized political parties as solely concerned with electing their own representatives. Of course, most minor parties can never hope to elect their nominees, certainly not to national or state offices. Instead, minor parties work to influence the policy agenda of the major parties, forcing them to address ignored or controversial issues that they have ducked or mishandled. Third parties in America have either popularized new and innovative ideas or served as political vehicles for citizens' discontent; with only a few exceptions, they have not elected their candidates to office.[22] Had the Court considered these objectives of minor parties, it might well have viewed the elimination of fusion candidacies as a substantial burden on the associational interests of members of third parties.

B. *Criticisms of the Court's Permissive Approach to Ballot Access Laws*

In part because of the way the Court has framed the balancing test and in part because judges tend to be deferential to legislative

---

[20]See Adam Winkler, Note, *Expressive Voting*, 68 N.Y.U. L. Rev. 330 (1993) (arguing for a broader conception of the right to vote that would include the expressive quality of protest voting).

[21]See also Donald Green & Ian Shapiro, *Pathologies of Rational Choice Theory* ch. 4 (1994) (countering the public choice literature on the paradox of voter turnout with evidence that people vote for expressive, norm-governed or habitual reasons).

[22]See Steven Rosenstone, Roy Behr & Edward Lazarus, *Third Parties in America: Citizen Response to Major Party Failure* 221-222 (2d ed. 1996). This has been the historical role of minor parties. See V.O. Key, *Politics, Parties, and Pressure Groups* 288 (1946).

decisions they see as inherently political, most ballot access provisions have survived constitutional attack. Restrictions at issue in the cases include fees, signature requirements, and filing deadlines designed to reduce the number of independent and minor party candidates. Courts have been much more likely to strike down filing fees than other regulations, particularly when the state does not provide an alternative method for ballot access such as gathering signatures on petitions.[23] Some commentators have argued that the reliance on the availability of the petition drive option reflects the Court's political naïveté.[24] Successful petition drives can also be enormously costly. For example, Ross Perot spent $18 million to qualify for the ballot in all the states and the District of Columbia.[25]

The Court's analysis in these cases might be questioned in another way: it tends to assess the challenged component of the electoral system in isolation rather than as part of a larger system, which may be designed to entrench the existing major parties by excluding new entrants in the political market. For example, the ban on write-in votes in Hawaii, which was upheld in *Takushi*, could have been analyzed as a part of a larger electoral scheme that operated to eliminate any competitive pressure on the dominant political party in the state, the Democratic Party.[26]

Increasingly, scholars have criticized the Court's deferential approach to ballot access provisions.[27] They argue that the Court should be particularly aggressive in its review of these laws because they are enacted by incumbents who are members of the established political parties. Professor Klarman cites ballot access laws as examples of legislative entrenchment that foreclose for voters the

---

[23]See, e.g., *Bullock v. Carter*, 405 U.S. 134 (1972); *Lubin v. Panish*, 415 U.S. 709 (1974).

[24]See Smith, *supra* note 15, at 201-02.

[25]See Rosenstone, Behr & Lazarus, *supra* note 22, at 260.

[26]See Samuel Issacharoff & Richard Pildes, *Politics as Markets: Partisan Lockups of the Democratic Process*, 50 Stan. L. Rev. 643, 670-72 (1998) (discussing the entire Hawaiian system as an example of a partisan lockup).

[27]See, e.g., *id.*; Richard Hasen, *Entrenching the Duopoly: Why the Supreme Court Should Not Allow the States To Protect the Democrats and Republicans from Political Competition*, 1997 Sup. Ct. Rev. 331 (1997).

option of expressing discontent with the major parties. Incumbents have little to lose by this strategy, he argues, because the laws operate to keep candidates who might change the system off the ballot.[28] Such scholars not only find the state interest of promoting the two-party system unpersuasive, they argue it should serve as a red flag to courts to view such restrictions with great skepticism.

These critics of the Court's ballot access jurisprudence attempt to assuage the concerns of those who fear that a system of many political parties is an unstable system of governance by pointing out that other structural features of our electoral process would ensure that the two-party system remained strong. Nonetheless, Professor Cain, among others, objects to this new *partisan lockup approach* to electoral laws because he sees no logical stopping place.[29] If ballot access provisions allow partisan lockup and are thus vulnerable to constitutional attack on that ground, what stops a successful challenge to first-past-the-post (plurality) elections or single-member districts? These electoral structures similarly promote a two-party system and reduce the vitality of upstart political parties.[30] While Cain agrees that courts should be careful to police attempts to lock voices out of the political

---

[28]Michael Klarman, *Majoritarian Judicial Review: The Entrenchment Problem*, 85 Geo. L.J. 491, 522 (1997).

[29]See Bruce Cain, *Garrett's Temptation*, 85 Va. L. Rev. ___ (1999).

[30]Anthony Downs, in *An Economic Theory of Democracy* 115-17 (1957), explained the pressure toward two centrist parties that is exerted by the predominant American electoral scheme. Drawing an analogy to economic markets, he envisioned the population of an electoral district as located along a line, dispersed from right to left along ideological grounds. "If there were two political parties, the population's views would be most 'efficiently' represented by each party posturing itself one-third of the way in from the respective poles. However, were one party to camp itself one-third of the way in from the left pole, for example, the other party would lay claim to the greatest number of potential voters by positioning itself only slightly to the right of the first party. The first party would be at a tremendous competitive disadvantage unless it were to move more toward the center." Issacharoff, Karlan, & Pildes 261-62. The process goes on until both parties are situated in the center of the ideological spectrum. Any third party that tries to compete and locates itself, say, to the right of center will merely divide voters with the major center-right party and, in a plurality vote, ensures that the center-left party will win the seat. The third party would only guarantee the victory of the party least compatible with its ideology, so it has a great incentive to join the center-right party and work for change from within the party structure.

process and exclude new parties entirely, they should not seek to overturn the legitimate decision of states to favor a two-party system over other forms of organization.

One could also criticize those who propose aggressive judicial review of laws facilitating partisan lockups from an institutional competence perspective. Are judges equipped to distinguish between regulations impermissibly favoring entrenched political players from those designed to ensure that elections run smoothly and fairly? Are notions of entrenchment and partisan lockup sufficiently well defined to allow courts to apply them without errors or arbitrariness? Should all ballot access regulations enacted by the legislature (the bastion of entrenched political interests) rather than by popular vote be subject to vigorous judicial review consistent with the strict scrutiny normally afforded to laws placing burdens on fundamental First Amendment freedoms?

C. Ballots, Voting Cues, and the Informed Voter

Political parties are vital components of the electoral process not only because they, along with state legislators, structure the mechanisms we use to select candidates, but also because the party label provides voters important information about the ideology of candidates. Given their limited attention to political matters, most people vote on the basis of certain *voting cues*, primarily incumbency or party affiliation.[31] Voters hope such shortcuts will allow them to vote in the same way that they would if they had full information about the candidates and their positions. In other words, they search for cues that will allow them to *vote competently* although they have only limited information.[32] Understanding voting cues and the shape of

---

[31]See W. Russell Neuman, *The Paradox of Mass Politics: Knowledge and Opinion in the American Electorate* 82 (1986) (noting that for unsophisticated voters, "political parties or the perceived ethnicity of the names of candidates" are the strongest voting cues); Bruce Cain, *The American Electoral System*, in *Developments in American Politics* 37, 43-45 (Gillian Peele, Christopher Bailey & Bruce Cain eds., 1992) (explaining role of incumbency cue).

[32]See Elisabeth Gerber & Arthur Lupia, *Voter Competence in Direct Legislation Elections*, in *Citizen Competence and Democratic Institutions* 147, 149 (Stephen Elkin and Karol Edward Soltan eds., 1999) (terming voters as competent if they cast the same votes that they would have had they possessed all the available

the information environment in which elections are conducted is vital to understanding how citizens exercise their right to vote.

Except for a minority of citizens who follow politics and campaigns closely because they enjoy it or because it is part of their jobs, most Americans will never allocate much of their limited attention to gathering and assessing information about politics, government, and candidates for public office. Professor Ortiz terms these politically disengaged voters "civic slackers."[33] Republican theorists might hope to convince such citizens to become more civically virtuous; liberals would be more likely to accept that many citizens prefer to spend their time in pursuits other than politics. Liberals might nonetheless seek reforms designed to increase the competence of voters so that their inattention to politics does not undermine their ability to vote in ways that comport with their preferences. For example, laws that require candidates to disclose the names of their contributors and the amount each contributes may increase voter competence significantly, particularly if the information is structured in a way that allows the media and political entrepreneurs easy and timely access. Provided with that data, voters can determine whether their interests are aligned with those of the candidate's major contributors and vote accordingly. Similarly, candidates work to supplement the voting cue of party affiliation with the development of a distinct political brand name so that voters are aware of their ideological commitments.[34] Voters cannot know at the time of the election which particular decisions a legislator will confront during her term of office. Knowing her overall ideology, however, can provide voters a way to predict generally how she will decide in the future.

The information environment surrounding elections is shaped in large part by the Court's jurisprudence. As we have seen, the voting cue of major party affiliation is especially salient to voters because it

---

knowledge about the policy consequences of the decisions).

[33]Daniel Ortiz, *The Democratic Paradox of Campaign Finance Reform*, 50 Stan. L. Rev. 893, 903 (1998).

[34]See John Lott, Jr., *Brand Names and Barriers to Entry in Political Markets*, 51 Pub. Choice 87 (1986) (explaining the concept of political brand name and why the need for it acts as a barrier to entry, thus favoring political incumbents).

appears on the ballot. The Court's relatively deferential stance toward ballot access regulations allows states to restrict the access of minor parties and independent candidates to this potent form of communication. States can also prohibit fusion candidacies, further limiting the ability of minor parties to provide voting cues. Similarly, the courts have struck down attempts by term limit activists to note on the ballot next to candidates' names whether they oppose term limits for federal lawmakers.[35] Had these so-called "informed voter ballot notations" been allowed, candidates who promised to support term limits proposals and then failed to do so would find next to their names the notation "DISREGARDED VOTERS' INSTRUCTION ON TERM LIMITS."

In two other contexts, the Supreme Court has been willing to limit the speech relevant to elections, and in both cases the limitations operate to disadvantage third parties and grassroots political movements relative to established political parties. First, under their authority to regulate the "Times, Places and Manner of holding Elections," the states have enacted various restrictions on partisan Election Day speech and conduct. The most frequently used restriction is the creation of zones around the polling place where particular kinds of activities are banned. All the states except Vermont have established these politics-free buffer zones, which usually either restrict access to voters and certain state officials or prohibit loitering or congregating within the zone.[36] A fractured Court upheld such a ban on electioneering within 100 feet of a polling place;[37] interestingly, the Tennessee law at issue in the case was not content-neutral, for it banned only the "solicitation of votes for or against any person or political party or position on a question" rather than all speech within the zone. Applying strict scrutiny but relying

---

[35]See Elizabeth Garrett, *The Law and Economics of Informed Voter Ballot Notations*, 85 Va. L. Rev. __ (1999). On term limits, see Chapter 2, Part IIA.

[36]See Robert Brett Dunham, Note, *Defoliating the Grassroots: Election Day Restrictions on Political Speech*, 77 Geo. L.J. 2137, 2143-45 (1989).

[37]See *Burson v. Freeman*, 504 U.S. 191 (1992). For an interesting contrast, see *Mills v. Alabama*, 384 U.S. 214 (1966) (striking down laws forbidding campaign-related newspaper stories on election days and rejecting state-asserted interest in eliminating voter confusion by decreasing the opportunity for dissemination of fraudulent charges at a time when no rebuttal was possible).

on the ballot access cases as well, the Court held that buffer zones serve the compelling state interest of combating voter intimidation and election fraud. In addition, the plurality and a concurring opinion noted that laws establishing buffer zones had a long tradition in this country, dating back to the late nineteenth century.

As in the ballot access context, the Court's willingness to accept the proffered state interest without any empirical evidence of voter confusion or fraud may be unfortunate. Before the adoption of the secret ballot, such buffer zones no doubt served the legitimate purpose of insulating voters from coercion from those who lined the route to the ballot box thrusting distinctive ballots into the hands of voters and who used their close proximity to the polls to monitor how people voted. It seems clear, however, that restricting political speech in areas outside polling places in modern times helps incumbents, who have established political brand names and overflowing coffers to pay for media campaigns, and the practice harms grassroots groups with limited financial resources. Grassroots groups might be able to send workers to the polls to provide last-minute information to voters, but the buffer zone laws eliminate this avenue of communication.

Similarly, the Supreme Court in *Arkansas Educational Television Commission v. Forbes*[38] allowed public television stations substantial discretion in their selection of candidates to participate in debates during an election. The Arkansas Educational Television Network, a state-owned public television broadcaster, sponsored a debate between the major party candidates for a congressional seat in 1992. The Commission, the state agency in charge of the network, refused to include Ralph Forbes, a perennial independent candidate who historically and currently commanded very little popular support. The Supreme Court acknowledged that candidate debates "are of exceptional significance in the electoral process."[39] Nevertheless, the Court held that the debate was a "nonpublic forum," a finding crucial to the First Amendment analysis because it allowed the Commission more leeway to exclude speakers, as long as it did so on a viewpoint-neutral basis and in a reasonable manner. There was no dispute that

---

[38]118 S.Ct. 1633 (1998). See also Jamin Raskin, *The Debate Gerrymander*, 77 Tex. L. Rev. 1943 (1999).

[39]118 S.Ct. at 1640.

Forbes' candidacy had elicited virtually no public interest, and this fact provided the basis for the exclusion. Indeed, the Court believed that a contrary decision — requiring the state actor to include all candidates on the ballot in the debate — would result in less speech, as public broadcasters would decline to hold debates or as debates with dozens of candidates proved chaotic and uninformative.

As in earlier cases, the Court's ruling in *Forbes* places burdens on independent and third-party candidates not faced by the nominees of the major parties. The Arkansas television authority automatically included the Republican and Democratic candidates, and it probably would have even if there was good reason to believe that the race was going to be a landslide in favor of one of them. Ross Perot mounted a similar challenge to the Commission on Presidential Debates' decision to exclude him from the 1996 debates. The Commission rested its decision on a finding that he did not have a "realistic chance of winning" the election.[40] Of course, his chance of success would have been greatly improved if he could have appeared in a nationally televised debate with the major party candidates. Arguably, one reason for Perot's strong showing in 1992 was his performance in the presidential debates, as well as the access to television that his wealth provided him. Certainly, the themes he sounded during his campaign shaped the political agenda pursued by the Clinton administration.

Furthermore, the Court's decision in *Forbes* moves away from several reform proposals that would require all candidates to participate in debates in order to provide more information to voters about the candidates' positions on issues.[41] Requiring participation in candidate debates raises a host of new constitutional issues because it forces candidates to speak when they may prefer not to and it reduces their control over the timing and content of their message. Such reforms tend to be supported by republicans who hope that, by requiring a particular kind of political engagement, the content of political discourse will improve and the voters will receive informa-

---

[40]*Perot v. FEC*, 97 F.3d 553, 556 (D.C. Cir. 1996) (denying injunctive relief to hear Perot's claim against the FEC or to force the FEC to hear Perot's claim quickly).

[41]See, e.g., Jeremy Paul, *Campaign Reform for the 21st Century: Putting Mouth Where the Money Is*, 30 Conn. L. Rev. 779 (1998).

tion more relevant to their electoral choices than is provided by candidate- and party-controlled advertisements.

The previous examples of state decisions that reduce the amount of political speech — whether through buffer zones or through the decision to limit participants in televised debates — are a bit unusual. Because political speech lies at the core of the First Amendment, the Court is typically most solicitous about protecting the right of candidates and others to speak freely about political matters. The Court's general approach in this area is demonstrated by its aggressive protection of anonymous political speech. In *McIntyre v. Ohio Elections Commission*,[42] Margaret McIntyre circulated leaflets opposing a school tax levy and signed "CONCERNED PARENTS AND TAXPAYERS." Ohio required that any such leaflet or publication regarding a candidate or a ballot issue contain the name of the person responsible for the publication. The state justified the regulation on the ground that it would help deter and punish those responsible for fraud and false statements. The Court resoundingly affirmed the right of citizens to engage in anonymous pamphleteering. "Anonymity is a shield from the tyranny of the majority. . . . It thus exemplifies the purpose behind the Bill of Rights, and of the First Amendment in particular: to protect unpopular individuals from retaliation — and their ideas from suppression — at the hand of an intolerant society."[43] The Court relied on *McIntyre* in a subsequent case, *Buckley v. American Constitutional Law Foundation*,[44] where it ruled that people circulating petitions for signatures to qualify an initiative proposal for the ballot did not have to wear nametags. The majority was particularly concerned about the forced identification at the time the circulator asked a passerby for her signature because it occurred "at the precise moment when the circulator's interest in anonymity is greatest."[45]

---

[42]514 U.S. 334 (1995).

[43]*Id*. at 357.

[44]119 S.Ct. 636 (1999).

[45]*Id*. at 646.

II. Regulation of Political Parties and their Selection of Candidates[46]

As the foregoing discussion makes clear, political parties play a vital role in the electoral process, providing important information to relatively uninformed voters searching for cues that will increase their competence and determining the choices that will face voters on the ballot. The relationship between political parties and electoral ballots, as well as other electoral structures such as party primaries, has served as the basis for some state regulation of the parties themselves. In fact, no other country regulates the internal operations of its political parties as aggressively as do the states in this country.[47]

The jurisprudence concerning the regulation of political parties — both as they operate to select candidates and in their internal operations — has been muddled because courts are uncertain how to characterize political parties. Are they private organizations whose members have rights of association and First Amendment rights to shape their message without interference from the government? Not really: a major political party is not just another interest group, because it exerts a different kind of influence on the political process by virtue of its official role in the electoral process. Are they therefore public organizations, and perhaps state actors, because they are so vitally involved in the selection of representatives and other elected policymakers? The latter characterization undergirds the venerated *White Primary Cases*.[48] In those cases, the Supreme Court ruled that the Texas Democratic Party could not exclude blacks from voting in its primary; it found that political parties were state actors when nominating candidates in primary elections.

The problem is that political parties have elements of both private entities and public organs. Leon Epstein has analogized political parties to public utilities. He argues that this label "suggests an agency performing a service in which the public has a special interest

---

[46]See Issacharoff, Karlan & Pildes 212-42; Lowenstein 297-390; Mikva & Lane 419-20; Popkin 722-24.

[47]See Beck & Sorauf, *supra* note 5, at 28.

[48]These cases include *Terry v. Adams*, 345 U.S. 461 (1953), and *Smith v. Allwright*, 321 U.S. 649 (1944).

sufficient to justify governmental regulatory control, along with the extension of legal privileges, but not governmental ownership or management of all the agency's activities."[49] The tension that the dual nature of political parties causes for the courts is evident in three areas: the regulation of primaries, laws affecting the internal operations of political parties, and laws limiting patronage in government employment decisions.

A. *State Regulation of Parties' Methods of Selecting Candidates*

Since the 1970s, the direct primary has become the mechanism by which parties select their candidates for office. Very few states continue to rely on caucuses or conventions, where party leaders can control the selection. Progressive reformers saw the primary as a way to democratize the nominating process, and many hoped that the ascendancy of the primary would weaken the major political parties. Thus, even at the beginning, state imposition of the direct primary was viewed as a threat to the strength and autonomy of party leaders.[50]

There are three basic types of primaries. In a closed primary, only voters who have declared their party affiliation can vote in the primary, where they choose among their copartisans for the nomination. In an open primary, a citizen votes in the primary without declaring any party preference, although she can participate in only one party's primary. Finally, in the blanket primary, not only do voters not declare any party affiliation, but they can also vote in the primary of more than one party. For example, a voter can choose among Democrats for Governor and among Republicans for Secretary of State.

In two opinions in the 1980s written by Justice Marshall, the Supreme Court appeared to signal that political parties have substantial ability to structure their primaries as they choose, without interference from states. The Court gave great weight to the associational interest of the political organizations, particularly at the point when they select their nominees. The Court viewed nomination as a

---

[49]Leon Epstein, *Political Parties in the American Mold* 157 (1986).

[50]See Beck & Sorauf, *supra* note 5, at 232-34.

critical juncture because the party is acting to translate its philosophy into concerted action and political power. In *Tashjian v. Republican Party of Connecticut*,[51] the Court struck down a state law requiring closed primaries in a challenge brought by the Republican Party, which sought to allow independent voters to vote in its primaries. Justice Marshall saw this decision by the party as part of its right to identify its membership and to broaden its base of support. He was unconvinced by the state's argument that the closed primary prevented party raiding and voter confusion and protected the integrity of party government. For example, he observed that independent voters who wished to "raid" the Republican Party, as the state described the possibility, could easily register as Republicans and vote in a closed primary.

In an interesting passage in *Tashjian*, Justice Marshall appeared to apply a partisan lockup analysis of the sort we discussed in the ballot access context. He noted that Connecticut defended its statute in part because it protected the integrity of the two-party system. The state contended that closed primaries increase the accountability of representatives to their constituents. Justice Marshall first noted the lack of consensus about the merits of closed versus open primaries. Perhaps the Republican Party selected the open primary so it could become more informed about the preferences of independent voters, surely important data for success in the general election. "In the present case, the state statute is defended on the ground that it protects the integrity of the Party against the Party itself. Under these circumstances, the views of the State, *which to some extent represent the views of the one political party transiently enjoying majority power*, as to the optimum methods for preserving party integrity lose much of their force."[52] In other words, the Democratic majority in the legislature might have been interfering in the internal operations of the Republican Party because the Republicans' open primary system would allow them to nominate candidates more likely to win in the general election. Perhaps the participation of independents would balance the more extreme views of party activists and allow a more moderate candidate to receive the party's nomination.

---

[51]479 U.S. 208 (1986).

[52]*Id.* at 224 (emphasis added).

Justice Scalia, in dissent, made a different kind of argument in support of the state's regulation, but his argument is similarly sophisticated in its awareness of political dynamics. He noted that the decision to open the primary to independent voters was not made by a democratic vote of Republican Party members; rather, the party leaders imposed this regime at a state convention. Party leaders may pursue objectives that systematically diverge from the interests of the party rank and file. Party leaders primarily want to elect their candidates so they can control state government. Thus, they may have changed their primary system to disempower rank and file members who were more committed to extreme ideologies and preferred to express those ideological commitments when they voted even if it meant choosing candidates who could not win in the general election. Justice Scalia observed: "I had always thought it was a major purpose of state-imposed party primary requirements to protect the general party membership against this sort of minority control."[53]

Two years later, in *Eu v. San Francisco County Democratic Central Committee*,[54] the Court was united in its decision to strike down a California law that prohibited party organizations from endorsing particular candidates in primary elections. Justice Marshall characterized this restriction on speech as burdensome because it affected speech during the primary, when free discussion of candidates and ideas is crucial. In rejecting the state's argument that its law promoted party stability, the Court pointed to the lack of evidence that stability had improved with the passage of the law and noted that virtually no other jurisdiction had imposed such a ban, despite similar legitimate concerns with party stability. Furthermore, state claims that the ban avoided intraparty disputes were unconvincing because the party is presumably in the best position to determine what promotes its own stability and power.

The Court may soon face a new challenge to party control of the nomination process in the context of blanket primaries in California.

---

[53]*Id.* at 236 (Scalia, J., dissenting).

[54]489 U.S. 214 (1989). See Daniel Lowenstein, *Associational Rights of Major Political Parties: A Skeptical Inquiry*, 71 Tex. L. Rev. 1741 (1993) (discussing both *Tashjian* and *Eu* and the difficult questions posed by state regulation of political parties).

In 1996, California voters enacted an initiative that replaced closed primaries with a blanket primary system. Recently, the Ninth Circuit upheld the blanket primary against an attack from a political party that wished to continue to use the closed primary method.[55] Unlike the Supreme Court in *Tashjian* and *Eu*, the circuit court found that the state interest in conducting elections outweighed the political party's associational rights. The judges even accepted the characterization of this burden on constitutional rights as serious, noting that the possibility of cross-over votes would affect the conduct of elections and representatives and could lead to a loss of party discipline and power. The court seemed to view this weakening of political parties as a positive development, however, noting that adoption of the blanket primary could be viewed as a continuation of the progressive agenda to enhance the democratic nature of the election process and to increase the accountability of elected officials to all voters. Not only will the blanket primary diminish the power of party loyalists, thereby increasing the power of independents and minority party voters, but it may also increase voter turnout. This judicial approach is fundamentally different from the Court's language in *Tashjian* and *Eu*, and even inconsistent with the Court's willingness in *Timmons* to entertain as a legitimate state interest the desire to strengthen and preserve the two-party system. Is one difference between these cases and California's blanket primary the fact that the latter is a popularly enacted reform, not one adopted by influential members of established political parties?

B. *Judicial Involvement in Parties' Internal Decisions*

Courts tend to protect political parties' decisions relating to their internal operation from state interference. For example, in *Eu*, the Court struck down California laws that attempted, among other things, to regulate the size and composition of party central committees, to set forth rules governing the selection and removal of committee members, to specify the time and place of committee meetings, and to require that the chair rotate between parts of California.[56] A political party has also been allowed to remove from

---

[55]See *California Democratic Party v. Jones*, 169 F.3d 646 (9th Cir. 1999).

[56]See *Eu*, 489 U.S. at 229-33.

the primary candidate list persons whom the party leaders agree do not reflect the principles and platform of the party.[57] Similarly, a political party has some ability to deny a group access to exhibit booths at its party convention if it determines that the objectives of the group are inconsistent with its platform. In the opinion allowing the Texas Republican Party the right to deny access to the Log Cabin Republicans, a group that supports gay and lesbian rights, the Texas Supreme Court concluded that the political party was not a state actor when it determined access to its convention because access was desired to influence the party platform, a document not integrally related to the electoral process.[58]

Disagreements about the proper characterization of a political party — as a state actor or a private organization — prompted a spirited separate opinion in the Texas case that noted the "symbiotic relationship . . . between the state and a major political party."[59] Perhaps because of the influence of the *White Primary Cases*, courts allow more state regulation of political parties when the laws are designed to combat racial discrimination and to protect the civil rights of racial minorities to participate fully in political parties.[60] Just as in the context of direct democracy, where courts seem more likely to strike down laws aimed at racial minorities than laws targeting sexual orientation minorities,[61] it seems questionable to limit concerns about unequal treatment of members of these quasi-public political entities to some minority groups and not others.

Political parties desire to exert such control over their own internal procedures because they hope to encourage and elect members of their party who are accountable to the party leaders and

---

[57]See *Duke v. Massey*, 87 F.3d 1226 (11th Cir. 1996) (allowing the Georgia Republican Party to remove white supremacist David Duke from its list of presidential candidates in the primary).

[58]See *Republican Party of Texas v. Dietz*, 940 S.W. 2d 86, 92-93 (Tex. 1997).

[59]*Id.* at 96 (Spector, J., concurring).

[60]See, e.g., *Morse v. Republican Party of Virginia*, 517 U.S. 186 (1996) (holding that the party's decision to require a registration fee for delegates to the state nominating convention was subject to § 5 of the Voting Rights Act and required preclearance from the Attorney General).

[61]See Chapter 2, Part IC.

its membership. It is more likely that their copartisans will enact policies that correspond to the party's ideological platform and that they will send other benefits to fellow party members. A significant part of those benefits is government jobs, and the proper role of patronage in government has provided the courts another arena of jurisprudence affecting political parties.

C. *Patronage: Corrupt Practice or Politics as Usual?*

The patronage system grew up as a response to the demands of the party machine. V.O. Key described it as a "method of financing party activity. The operation of a party organization requires the services of many men and women. . . . Much of this work is performed by unpaid volunteers, but their efforts are not adequate. In effect, a considerable part of party expenses is met by the public treasury, and the chief means of diverting public funds to party purposes is through the appointment of party workers to public office."[62]

Republican theorists have attacked patronage as inconsistent with the ideals of good government, where the metric for selecting bureaucrats and other elected officials should be merit and ability rather than partisan affiliation. The problem with this argument is that merit in a political system where policies have ideological components contains some element — potentially a large one — of political assessment. It is entirely rational for a member of Congress, for example, to prefer that her staff be members of her party and supporters of her campaign because she is more certain of their loyalty and their views. Andrew Jackson, an early proponent of the patronage system, defended it on a slightly different, more republican-sounding ground. He argued that patronage served the principle of rotation in office — the goal currently championed by supporters of term limits — because government officials would change with each change of government control. Those who stayed in government too long, he contended, "are apt to acquire a habit of looking with indifference upon the public interests."[63]

---

[62]Key, *supra* note 22, at 335.

[63]*Id.* at 335-36 (quoting President Jackson).

Nevertheless, the progressive attack on patronage as a corrupt political practice led to the enactment of civil service laws at the state and federal levels and to laws protecting federal employees from being forced to participate in political campaigns.[64] In some areas left unaffected by laws prohibiting patronage, the Court has stepped in and developed a line of cases that is hostile toward patronage. In *Elrod v. Burns*,[65] the Court held that the First Amendment prohibited politically motivated discharges because they amounted to the denial of government employment on the basis of an unconstitutional condition, the requirement that an employee compromise her freedom of association. The Court limited the government's ability to dismiss employees on purely political grounds to those employees who work in policymaking positions. In *Rutan v. Republican Party of Illinois*,[66] the Court expanded the rule in *Elrod* to apply to promotion, transfer, recall, and hiring decisions based on party affiliation. Again, it held that political considerations are appropriate only in employment decisions relating to high-level policymakers. Most recently, the Court held that the First Amendment protects independent contractors from termination of at-will government contracts on the basis of the contractor's political speech or affiliation.[67]

All the patronage cases spurred passionate dissents. In the recent cases, Justice Scalia mounted a defense of patronage as an important and longstanding tradition in our government. Patronage, he argued, has historically played a role in increasing political participation in civic life, strengthening political parties, and opening up government

---

[64]See, e.g., Hatch Political Activity Act, 5 U.S.C. §§ 1303, 3333, 7311, 7324, 7325 (1998), as amended by Hatch Act Reform Amendments of 1993 (codified as amended in scattered sections of 5 U.S.C.).

[65]427 U.S. 347 (1976).

[66]497 U.S. 62 (1990).

[67]See *Board of County Comm'rs, Wabaunsee County, Kan. v. Umbehr*, 518 U.S. 668 (1996). In a case decided the same day, *O'Hare Truck Serv., Inc. v. City of Northlake*, 518 U.S. 712 (1996), the Court extended constitutional protection to prohibit retaliation against a contractor for the exercise of rights of political association.

and the political process to excluded groups.[68] The latter argument resonates with critical scholars eager to increase the participation of minority groups in government. Critical theorists might cite the anti-patronage decisions of recent years for alarming hypocrisy. Patronage has long been one ladder by which immigrant groups ascend to self-sufficiency and political power in this country. Earlier immigrants have already climbed the patronage ladder and reached positions of influence; for example, Justice Brennan, the author of *Rutan*, may have benefitted from a political system in which ethnic and political affiliations, as well as merit, mattered. Now that these established groups no longer need the aid of patronage, they support efforts to eliminate it before it assists other groups to achieve similar prominence.

Justice Scalia's dissents rest primarily on liberal theory, however. He has noted that the democratic branches had paid great attention to the proper role of political considerations in decisions relating to government contracting. He thought it inappropriate for the Court to use the First Amendment to second-guess the decisions reached by the accountable branches, particularly when a decision to retain an element of patronage is one with such a long historical pedigree. There is no reason for the Court to use the Constitution to disallow patronage systems adopted by lawmakers; rather, it is up to legislators and elected officials, who are accountable to the people, to determine whether they will select and retain employees on the basis of merit or political affiliation.

III.   Campaign Finance Reform[69]

One important aspect of the electoral and political-party regulations we have canvassed in this chapter is their effect on political speech and activity. Another context that demonstrates the Court's

---

[68]See *Rutan*, 497 U.S. at 95-96 (Scalia, J., dissenting) (terming patronage as a "venerable and accepted tradition"). Justice Scalia's characterization of the benefits of patronage is not universally accepted. See, e.g., Cynthia Grant Bowman, *"We Don't Want Anybody Anybody Sent": The Death of Patronage Hiring in Chicago*, 86 Nw. U.L. Rev. 57, 75-95 (1991).

[69]See Eskridge & Frickey 206-37; Eskridge, Frickey & Garrett Supp. 25-31; Issacharoff, Karlan & Pildes 618-32, 658-64; Lowenstein 477-544, 581-797; Mikva & Lane 446-79; Popkin 725-28, 742-81.

broad protection for political speech is the realm of campaign finance regulation. The Court's decision that campaign spending is the equivalent of political speech has reduced the flexibility of Congress and state legislatures to regulate campaign contributions and expenditures. And, like the laws at issue in anonymous speech cases such as *McIntyre*, campaign finance laws include numerous disclosure provisions that may chill the willingness of unpopular people and groups to participate in the political process. Nonetheless, disclosure provisions are perhaps the least controversial campaign finance laws and receive support from a broad array of theorists.

In Chapter 2, Part III, we discussed the philosophies that animate various campaign finance regulation schemes, and we detailed the provisions limiting campaign contributions by individuals. The foundational, and much vilified, decision in *Buckley v. Valeo*[70] provides the constitutional framework; the Court's approach that equated spending money with political speech required it to strike down limitations on expenditures as unconstitutional infringements on free speech. In this chapter, we will first detail other aspects of the federal regulatory system. The system has a number of gaps in coverage, the most notable relating to soft money expenditures and issue advertisements. Such loopholes in the legal structure have prompted lawmakers to propose new solutions. Not only do these reform proposals seem unlikely to pass given the power of entrenched interests that benefit from the current structure, but if passed they may well serve only to channel money into new forms, rather than to eliminate it from the scene. We will also discuss state reform efforts, which have been largely the result of direct democracy but which may not surmount formidable judicial hurdles.

---

[70]424 U.S. 1 (1976) (per curiam).

A. *The Federal Election Campaign Act*[71]

Like some ballot access laws, the regulation of presidential elections found in the Federal Election Campaign Act[72] (FECA) favors major parties and reduces the role of minor parties. Unlike the rest of the federal system, presidential elections have an element of public funding. Major parties, whose candidates for President garnered 25% or more of the popular vote in the last election, receive matching funds collected through the $3 voluntary taxpayer check-off. In the 2000 election cycle, for example, as long as the candidate complies with certain spending limits, such as a $50,000 cap on the amount of her own money she can spend, the government will match money raised in the primary election up to nearly $40 million and provide a grant of more than $65 million for the general election. If a candidate does not accept federal funds, she can spend as much of her own money as she wishes (as Ross Perot did in 1992, as Steve Forbes did in 1996, and as George W. Bush may do in 2000), although she is still subject to the $1,000 contribution limit. In addition, the major parties will each receive over $12 million to help defray costs of their nominating conventions.

Contrast this arrangement with the public financing available to third parties. If a candidate abides by other spending limits (including the limit on her personal funds) and also meets a threshold of 5% of the popular vote in the general election, she is eligible for matching funds *after* the election. Such a candidate can try to raise money before the election on the strength of her probable electoral showing, but lenders are loath to rely on the vagaries of the popular vote for collateral. In subsequent elections, a party that received 5% or more of the popular vote may be eligible for general election funding before the election. The Court in *Buckley v. Valeo* upheld the public financing provisions of FECA against an equal protection attack, on the authority of the ballot access cases. It held that "the inability, if

---

[71]See Eskridge & Frickey 206-14; Hetzel, Libonati & Williams 1062-67; Issacharoff, Karlan & Pildes 616-20; Lowenstein 507-44; Mikva & Lane 450-55; Popkin 750-60. Perhaps the best book describing the legal landscape of federal campaign finance regulations is *Campaign Finance Reform: A Sourcebook* (Anthony Corrado et al. eds. 1997) [hereinafter cited as *Campaign Finance Reform: A Sourcebook*].

[72]2 U.S.C. § 441 *et seq.*

any, of minor-party candidates to wage effective campaigns will derive not from lack of public funding but from their inability to raise private contributions."[73] Moreover, Congress has a legitimate interest in not funding "hopeless candidacies with large sums of public money."[74]

Does the partisan lockup approach to ballot access laws suggest that the court was too deferential in its review of these provisions? As you consider current FECA provisions and the reforms proposed by federal lawmakers, keep in mind the insights provided by this theoretical approach because virtually all campaign finance laws are passed by incumbent legislators who are members of the major political parties. James Buckley, the plaintiff in *Buckley v. Valeo*, describes his fellow plaintiffs as a "group of political underdogs and independents; and although we spanned the ideological spectrum, we shared a deep concern that [FECA] would dramatically increase the difficulties already faced by those challenging incumbents and the political status quo."[75]

Buckley also upheld the disclosure provisions of FECA. First, political committees must disclose the source of every contribution over $100 and the payee and purpose of every expenditure over $100. In addition, individuals and groups making contributions or expenditures, other than contributions to political committees or candidates, must disclose them. The Court interpreted these provisions to require disclosure only when they relate to "expenditures for communications that in express terms advocate the election or defeat of a clearly identified candidate," not to all partisan discussions.[76] These disclosure provisions raise First Amendment concerns; compelled disclosure can infringe on the freedom of speech or association because people may not want to identify themselves as contributing to unpopular causes or despised people. Recall, for example, the Court's aggressive protection of anonymous political speech in *McIntyre*. The Court in *Buckley* identified three important state

---

[73]424 U.S. at 94-95.

[74]*Id.* at 96.

[75]James Buckley, *Campaign Finance: Why I Sued in 1974*, Wall St. J., Oct. 11, 1999, at A23.

[76]*Id.* at 44.

interests served by disclosure requirements: providing information to voters about the source and use of money; deterring *quid pro quo* corruption and the appearance of such; and providing state officials the information necessary for enforcement. These interests outweighed the possibility that speech or association might be chilled, particularly because the record contained no evidence of this kind of effect.

Powerful players in this complicated electoral environment are *political action committees* or *PACs*. Generally speaking, a PAC is a political committee, other than that of a political party, that receives contributions from more than fifty people and makes contributions to at least five candidates for federal office. Political action committees are not creatures of FECA; the first PAC was established in 1943 through the efforts of a national labor union. But various provisions of FECA have stimulated an explosion of PACs because of their comparative advantages relative to individuals and political parties. Individuals can contribute only $1,000 per candidate per election; PACs can contribute five times as much.[77] In addition, a PAC can contribute as much money to a House candidate as the candidate's party can,[78] a reality that has led to a shift of influence away from political parties and towards PACs. The effect of FECA on the prevalence of PACs is staggering. In 1974, the number of registered PACs stood at 608; ten years later, 4,009 were registered, and the number has remained at around 4,000 since then.[79] The largest category of PACs consists of corporate PACs — in 1996, 1,642 of 4,079 PACs were characterized as corporate — and corporate PACs

---

[77]The term "political action committee" is not used in FECA. Our definition of PAC is derived from the statute's definition of a "multicandidate political committee." Most PACs become multicandidate political committees because such organizations may contribute up to $5,000, rather than $1,000, to any candidate in any election. See 2 U.S.C. § 441a(a); Frank Sorauf, *Political Action Committees in American Politics: An Overview*, in *What Price PACs?*, Report of the Twentieth Century Fund Task Force on Political Action Committees 29-31 (1984).

[78]FECA limits a political party's direct contributions to $5,000 per congressional candidate, the same limit as for multicandidate political committees. See 2 U.S.C. § 441a(a)(2). Political parties can directly contribute up to $17,500 per senatorial candidate. See *id.* at § 441a(h).

[79]See Frank Sorauf, *Inside Campaign Finance: Myths and Realities* 15-16 (1992).

donated more money to campaigns than labor or membership organizations.[80]

Although PACs provide a way for individuals to increase their political influence by working collectively, they have also been described as pernicious influences on the electoral process. Making arguments similar to those of some interest group theorists discussed in Chapter 3, critics argue that corporate PACs exert disproportionate influence compared to labor PACs or public interest PACs like those supported by environmental groups. Indeed, one's view of PACs may depend significantly on the state and character of pluralism. If various and diverse interests use this type of political organization to wield electoral influence, to gain access to politicians, and to affect the policy agenda, then PACs can be seen as a positive political force. Reformers who propose to ban PACs reject this rosy vision, arguing that the voices of the well-to-do drown out other viewpoints and that PACs tend to contribute money only to incumbents, further entrenching the status quo.[81] Certainly, there are exceptions to the more pessimistic descriptions; for example, EMILY's List contributes money to female candidates and promotes a moderately feminist agenda. But this PAC and others like it are notable because they are so rare.

A related concern that reformers target is the practice of *bundling*, which has grown in importance as PACs have come under fire. In bundling, individual contributions are presented as a group to a candidate in a way that makes it clear the contributions were organized through a collective effort. Because the contributions are individual, the bundles of money do not count against the PAC contribution limit, although each check cannot exceed the $1,000 ceiling for individual contributions. In most cases, candidates are aware of the forces behind the bundling and the interests that the contributions seek to advance, but they are not disclosed to the voters.

---

[80]See Frank Sorauf, *Political Action Committees*, in *Campaign Finance Reform: A Sourcebook*, *supra* note 71, at 123, 140-41 (providing FEC data since 1974).

[81]See Malcolm Jewell & William Cassie, *Can the Legislative Campaign Finance System Be Reformed?*, in *Campaign Finance in State Legislative Elections* 209, 218-220 (Joel Thompson & Gary Moncrief eds. 1998) (discussing patterns of PAC contributions and implications for reform).

Some bundling is more public, but only because the organizers wish the publicity. For example, EMILY's List publicly encourages bundling by requiring its members to contribute at least $100 to two or more candidates that it endorses.[82]

B. *Current Federal Campaign Finance Reform Issues*[83]

The description of the major features of FECA suggests some of the problems targeted by reformers. For example, recent campaign finance reform proposals seek to ban or limit PACs and to prohibit bundling. Legislation aimed at reducing the growing influence of unregulated spending has also received serious consideration and substantial support in recent Congresses. But no bill is likely to be enacted, given the strong opposition by powerful lawmakers and interest groups and their ability to take advantage of procedural hurdles to stymie passage.

Even if Congress did act to regulate these aspects of the electoral system, many question the effectiveness of any reform other than more aggressive disclosure. For liberal theorists, the clearest lesson of the past decades of regulation is the futility of attempts to remove money from the political system.[84] Rules may channel money into particular forms, but they may not be able to eliminate it or even substantially reduce it. New restrictions may merely encourage more creative forms of spending. If that is true, the liberal would maintain that the only successful way to combat political corruption is detailed and timely disclosure so that voters, the media, and political entrepreneurs can learn the source and amount of money spent in elections. In contrast, many republicans and critical thinkers view disclosure as an insufficiently vigorous form of regulation and an unfortunate admission that money will rule American politics.

---

[82]See *Campaign Finance Reform: A Sourcebook, supra* note 71, at 152-53, 163 (discussing EMILY's List's activities as a PAC, a donor network, and a bundler).

[83]See Eskridge & Frickey 235-37; Eskridge, Frickey & Garrett Supp. 25-30; Issacharoff, Karlan & Pildes 662-64; Lowenstein 742-48; Mikva & Lane 478-79; Popkin 758-59.

[84]See, e.g., Samuel Issacharoff & Pamela Karlan, *The Hydraulics of Campaign Finance Reform*, 77 Tex. L. Rev. 1705 (1999).

In election law parlance, money spent in connection with federal candidates, and therefore regulated by FECA, is hard money. *Soft money*, then, is any money left unregulated by the federal act (although the Federal Election Commission requires limited disclosure of soft-money expenditures).[85] Soft money can be spent on organizing grassroots campaign efforts, such as voter registration drives, voter education programs, and get-out-the-vote efforts. Political parties can also use soft money to fund issue advertisements that do not expressly advocate the election or defeat of a particular candidate. Although soft money expenditures cannot be connected with a particular candidate, in fact they contribute significantly to the success of the parties' nominees and are often intertwined with candidates' campaigns. For example, federal candidates are actively involved in soliciting soft money. Videotapes of White House coffee meetings where President Clinton asked supporters to contribute soft money in sums larger than allowed for direct contributions provide only the most publicized example of widespread candidate involvement. In addition, the activities funded by soft money are timed to benefit particular candidates and to emphasize themes important in their campaigns. In some cases there is explicit coordination (although that is prohibited); in virtually all cases, the use of soft money is not meaningfully independent from candidates' campaigns.

The use of soft money to evade or escape federal restrictions, particularly in presidential elections where candidates must comply with expenditure limits to qualify for federal matching funds, has substantially increased in the last several elections. By the end of the 1995-96 election cycle, the two parties had raised $262 million in soft money. The Republican National Committee raised $138.2 million, a 178% increase over the amount raised in 1992; the Democrats raised over $123.9 million, up 242% from 1992.[86] The Democratic National Committee intends to raise $200 million in soft money for the 2000 presidential election, in large part because party leaders expect the Republican nominee to reject public financing and thus not

---

[85]See Anthony Corrado, *Party Soft Money*, in *Campaign Finance Reform: A Sourcebook, supra* note 71, at 174 (detailing FEC's 1990 rulemaking).

[86]See Note, *Soft Money: The Current Rules and the Case for Reform*, 111 Harv. L. Rev. 1323, 1333 (1998).

abide by spending limits.[87]   A study of the 1998 congressional elections revealed that soft money spent by party committees and raised from a few large donors also plays an important role in competitive congressional elections.[88] Soft money spending in the 1998 midterm election was more than double the spending in 1994, signaling a shift in the strategies of the two major parties. Interestingly, fundraisers reported that concerns about the influence of issue advertisements funded by special interest groups, an aspect of a related reform proposal, encouraged party supporters to give more generously to soft money accounts.

Notice one other interesting aspect of soft money: it is spent by political parties. Thus, the notion of corruption articulated by *Buckley v. Valeo* is attenuated here. If the problem of soft money is to be fit within the traditional judicial framework, then the parties must be seen as conduits of money that allow well-to-do donors the possibility of corrupt influence. Perhaps this possibility is sufficient to raise the appearance of corruption that has long served as a compelling state interest to justify campaign finance restrictions. On the other hand, influence exerted by political parties on their candidates hardly seems corrupt; rather, parties appropriately seek ways to influence and discipline their members in order to advance their ideological agendas. Moreover, using parties as mediating institutions between donors and candidates may actually decrease the former's influence over policy. If parties receive donations from a range of diverse interest groups, they may provide a forum of relatively robust pluralism where no one interest can dominate policy.

At the least, the relationship of political parties to campaign finance presents new and difficult questions for legislative reforms and for courts. The Supreme Court began to wrestle with some of these issues in *Colorado Republican Federal Campaign Committee v. FEC*,[89] when it held that party expenditures in a candidate election

---

[87]See Linda Feldmann, *Rise of the Small Contributor: A Record Number of Individual Donors Feed Political War Chests — Again Prompting Questions About Soft Money*, Christian Science Monitor, Aug. 2, 1999, at 1.

[88]See David Magleby & Marianne Holt, *Outside Money: Soft Money and Issue Ads in Competitive 1998 Congressional Elections* (1999).

[89]518 U.S. 604 (1996).

were not necessarily coordinated with the candidate's campaign. The lower court considering this case on remand rejected the argument that party pressure over candidates represented unacceptable corruption of the political process. "[A] political party functions to promote political ideas and policy objectives over time and through elected officials.... [A] political party's decision to support a candidate who adheres to the [party's] beliefs is not corruption. Conversely, a party's refusal to provide a candidate with electoral funds because the candidate's views are at odds with party positions is not an attempt to exert improper influence."[90] Indeed, those who advocate measures to strengthen the power of political parties over candidates and elected officials might view the increasing role of soft money as a positive political development.

Nonetheless, recent campaign finance reform proposals contain a number of provisions to limit party use of soft money.[91] Under most, the national committees of a political party could neither receive nor spend soft money. Local and state committees of political parties could not spend soft money on activities to benefit federal candidates, although they could still use soft money solely to influence state or local races. In the definition of "activities to benefit federal candidates," the proposals include voter registration drives 120 days before a federal election, voter identification and get-out-the-vote efforts during a campaign where a federal candidate appears on the ballot, and communications that refer to a clearly identified federal candidate for the purpose of influencing an election. Finally, the proposals attempt to prohibit federal candidate involvement in soft money fundraising. Federal officeseekers, officeholders, and their agents would be barred from raising or spending soft money.

Parties often spend soft money on issue advertisements. In addition, many interest groups work to influence the outcomes of elections through unregulated issue advocacy. Again, the rise of issue advertisements is an outgrowth of the *Buckley* framework that

---

[90]*Federal Election Comm'n v. Colorado Republican Fed. Campaign Comm.*, 41 F. Supp. 2d 1197, 1212 (D. Colo. 1999).

[91]See, e.g., Bipartisan Campaign Finance Reform Act of 1999, H.R. 417, 106th Cong., 1st Sess. See also Corrado, *supra* note 85, at 176-77 (summarizing recent reform bills).

allowed regulation of some political activity while protecting other kinds of political speech. In order to avoid constitutional problems, the Court in *Buckley* upheld limitations only on expenditures made in connection with a federal election that are used for communications that expressly advocate the election or defeat of a clearly identified candidate. The Court rejected any test for express advocacy that depended on the speaker's purpose or the audience's understanding because such a subjective test would significantly chill political speech. Rather, the Court adopted objective criteria to distinguish regulated communications from unfettered political speech because it did not want to discourage groups from engaging in substantive policy discussions. In a famous footnote, the Court indicated that the following terms would meet the "express advocacy" test: "vote for," "elect," "support," "cast your ballot for," "Smith for Congress," "vote against," "defeat," or "reject."[92] Although the Court subsequently stated that a communication "marginally less direct than 'Vote for Smith' does not change its essential nature,"[93] the phrases listed in *Buckley* have become known as the *magic words* distinguishing regulated communications from unregulated ones.

The absence of federal regulation has resulted in an explosion in the use of issue advocacy. The Annenberg Public Policy Center has estimated that political parties and various interest groups spent between $135 million and $150 million on issue ads in the 1996 election cycle.[94] Labor groups alone spent over $35 million on issue advertisements aimed at defeating 32 freshman House Republicans.[95] This trend shows no sign of abating: more issue ads were run in 1997-1998 than in 1995-1996, and the overall amount of money spent for such ads increased.[96] A study of the 1998 midterm elections revealed several instances of groups using the threat of issue

---

[92] 424 U.S. at 44 n.52.

[93] *Federal Election Comm'n v. Massachusetts Citizens for Life*, 479 U.S. 238, 249 (1986).

[94] See Deborah Beck, Paul Taylor, Jeffrey Stranger & Douglas Rivlin, *Issue Advocacy Advertising During the 1996 Campaign* (Issue Paper for Annenberg Public Policy Center) at 3 (1997) [hereinafter cited as Beck].

[95] See *id.* at 11, 13.

[96] See Magleby & Holt, *supra* note 88, at 23.

advocacy campaigns to pressure congressional candidates on particular issues.[97] For example, the president of U.S. Term Limits threatened to spend $100,000 for issue advertisements if Representative Merrill Cook of Utah did not sign a pledge to abide by term limits. Cook refused to accede to the demand, calling it political blackmail, and the interest group spent nearly $400,000 in direct mail, phone calls, and advertisements unsuccessfully opposing Cook's reelection.[98]

Although issue advertisements are supposedly designed only to further the discussion of particular issues rather than of specific candidates, the Annenberg Center found that nearly 87% mentioned a candidate by name and 59% pictured a candidate.[99] Accordingly, reform proposals seek to require disclosure of amounts spent for advocacy that may not meet the magic words test but which nonetheless relate to a particular candidate's election or defeat. A leading proposal would more broadly define the term "express advocacy" and subject a wider range of communications to regulation. It defines the term to mean, in addition to the magic words, a campaign communication that refers to a clearly identified candidate and is aired within 60 calendar days before an election, or any communication that expresses unmistakable and unambiguous support for or opposition to a clearly identified candidate when considered in the context of relevant external events, such as proximity to an election.[100]

This expansion of the scope of FECA to include some currently unregulated issue advocacy may not be constitutional. The courts of appeals have disagreed about what kinds of political communication can be considered express advocacy and thus subjected to regulation

---

[97]See *id.* at 24-25.

[98]See *id.*

[99]See Beck, *supra* note 94, at 8. See also Richard Briffault, *Issue Advocacy: Redrawing the Elections/Politics Line*, 77 Tex. L. Rev. 1751, 1760-61 (1999) (discussing study and other data).

[100]See H.R. 3526, 105th Cong., 2d Sess., § 201(b) (1998). In the 106th Congress, reformers deleted these provisions from their proposal, limiting reform to soft money, in an attempt to gain support. See Gebe Martinez & Carroll Doherty, *Narrower Campaign Finance Bill Still a Long Shot in Senate*, Cong. Q. Wkly., Sept. 18, 1999, at 2157.

such as source limitations that would prohibit the use of soft money for this purpose. The Ninth Circuit rejected the argument that express advocacy is limited to *Buckley*'s magic words and adopted a more comprehensive and flexible approach.[101] The court tried to avoid adopting a subjective standard, holding that express advocacy must include a message that is "unmistakable and unambiguous, suggestive of only one plausible meaning."[102] In addition, the communication must exhort the listeners to some concrete action regarding a candidate or incumbent, rather than merely informing them about political issues. In contrast, several other circuits have adopted a strict approach to express advocacy, requiring that the communication include one or more of the magic words before regulation is constitutional.[103] The drafters of the legislative proposal to regulate issue ads were guided by the Ninth Circuit's test. Similarly, the Federal Election Commission incorporated the Ninth Circuit's expansive test into its express advocacy regulation, but the First Circuit struck down the regulation.[104] The Supreme Court has so far declined to address this controversial First Amendment issue, leaving the constitutionality of the proposed reform in limbo.

C. *State Campaign Finance Reform Laws*[105]

Unlike the continuing stalemate in Washington, D.C., campaign finance reformers have been successful in a number of states, often using the tool of direct democracy to pass laws opposed by political parties, incumbents, and powerful special interest groups. Some reforms are driven by the liberal objective of increasing the amount of information available to the public about the source and amount of funding. For example, all the states except Nevada are investigating

---

[101] *Federal Election Comm. v. Furgatch*, 807 F.2d 857 (9th Cir.), *cert. denied*, 484 U.S. 850 (1987).

[102] *Id.* at 864.

[103] See, e.g., *Faucher v. FEC*, 928 F.2d 468 (1st Cir.), *cert. denied*, 502 U.S. 820 (1991); *Federal Election Comm. v. Christian Action Network*, 110 F.3d 1049 (4th Cir. 1997).

[104] See *Maine Right to Life Comm. v. FEC*, 98 F.3d 1 (1st Cir. 1996), *cert. denied*, 118 S.Ct. 52 (1997).

[105] See Eskridge, Frickey & Garrett Supp. 30-31; Issacharoff, Karlan & Pildes 662-64; Lowenstein 735-39, 782-97.

ways to compile and disseminate data about campaign spending via the Internet.[106] Other more far-reaching state laws are consistent with a more activist republican vision and might be justified by equality arguments as well as concerns about the reality and appearance of *quid pro quo* corruption. To the extent that they open the political system to challengers lacking the support of monied interests, these reforms may also be supported by critical theorists. Such laws include draconian limits on contributions and comprehensive systems of public financing for candidates who agree to abide by spending limits. The state efforts are notable because they often go much further than federal proposals. In addition, the legal challenges that tend to follow popular enactment of sweeping campaign finance reform may have implications for the continuing vitality of the *Buckley* framework.

Several grassroots organizations without substantial political war chests, such as Common Cause, the Public Interest Research Group (PIRG), and the League of Women Voters, have mounted successful ballot-initiative campaigns to enact comprehensive "Clean Election Acts."[107] Their success reveals the extent of popular support for reform, or perhaps the depth of public disgust with the current system, as well as the need to bypass state legislatures to pass these laws. Not surprisingly, legislators often block implementation of the laws, refusing, for example, to pass laws setting up the administrative apparatus necessary to administer public funding systems. In addition, opponents of the laws usually go to court to block implementation, arguing that the reforms violate the First Amendment and are inconsistent with *Buckley*.

Over 30 states impose limitations on individual contributions to candidates, nearly 40 prohibit or limit direct contributions by labor unions, and over 40 restrict direct corporate contributions.[108] Recent ballot initiatives have imposed very stringent restrictions on contribu-

---

[106]See Craig Holman & Robert Stern, *Campaign Money on the Information Highway: Electronic Filing and Disclosure of Campaign Finance Reports* (1998).

[107]See, e.g., PIRG, "Clean Money Campaign Reform," available at <http://www.publicampaign.org/cleanmoney.html>.

[108]See Anthony Corrado & Daniel Ortiz, *Recent Innovations*, in *Campaign Finance Reform: A Sourcebook, supra* note 71, at 337, 338.

tions. The courts have been hostile to such stingy caps on contributions, arguing that they are severe restrictions on political speech that cannot be justified by concerns about *quid pro quo* corruption. In 1995, the Eighth Circuit, following the lead of other circuits, struck down a Missouri statute, enacted by the people, that would have restricted individual contributions to $100 to $300, depending on the state office.[109] The court found that such low limits were not narrowly tailored to combat the kind of corruption described in *Buckley*. The stories of *quid pro quo* arrangements — or appearances of such — in the record concerned substantial contributions of hundreds of thousands of dollars by wealthy individuals or PACs. Contributions of a few hundred dollars do not appear to be corrupt, the court found. Moreover, a significant number of voters in Missouri had contributed sums in excess of the ceilings, decreasing the possibility that a candidate could be captured by one or a few well-heeled special interests if the caps were higher.

With the demise of its popularly enacted contribution limits, the law in Missouri reverted to the legislatively adopted restriction limiting contributions to candidates for governor or other statewide offices to $1,075, a figure that would be adjusted biennially for inflation. This limitation is nearly equivalent to the federal limitation of $1,000 (which is not adjusted for inflation), so legislators doubtlessly assumed this regulation comported with the Constitution. In November 1998, however, the Eighth Circuit struck down this contribution limit on First Amendment grounds; the Supreme Court has granted *certiorari* in this case, which implicates the continuing legality of FECA's contribution provisions.[110]

---

[109]See *Carver v. Nixon*, 72 F.3d 633 (8th Cir. 1995), *cert. denied*, 518 U.S. 1033 (1996). See also *California Prolife Council Political Action Comm. v. Scully*, 989 F. Supp. 1282 (E.D. Cal. 1998) (preliminarily enjoining the enforcement of California's Proposition 208, which limits campaign contributions to $500 for candidates in statewide races and to $100-250 in district-wide races, depending on the size of the district), *aff'd mem.*, 164 F.3d 1189 (9th Cir. 1999).

[110]See *Shrink Missouri Government PAC v. Adams*, 161 F.3d 519 (8th Cir. 1998), *cert. granted sub nom. Nixon v. Shrink Missouri Government PAC*, 119 S.Ct. 901 (1999). But see *Kentucky Right to Life v. Terry*, 108 F.3d 637 (6th Cir.), *cert. denied*, 522 U.S. 860 (1997) (upholding state contribution limit of $1,000).

The Eighth Circuit's opinion represents a departure from *Buckley* in several ways. First, although it acknowledged that the Court in *Buckley* upheld $1,000 limits, it noted that decision considered whether such a sum could present the appearance of corruption in 1974. In 1998, $1,075 is simply not a large enough sum to threaten the integrity of the electoral system. Instead, such a cap would have a severe impact on the political dialogue by both restricting candidates' abilities to accumulate sufficient resources to run for office and limiting voters' abilities to participate in politics. Congress did not provide for inflation adjustments to the contribution caps in FECA; thus, this case may well implicate whether FECA's limits remain constitutional.

Second, the Eighth Circuit opinion appears to tighten the corruption rationale that can support state regulation. Rejecting Missouri's argument that corruption and the appearance thereof are "inherent in political campaigns where large contributions are made," the court required "some demonstrable evidence that there were genuine problems that resulted from contributions in amounts greater than the limits in place."[111] The record in *Buckley* contained no such evidence; indeed, it is hard to imagine an example of improper influence being bought with a contribution of only $1,000 in today's expensive campaigns. Such low contribution limits seem much more compatible with egalitarian rationales because they tend to equalize citizen influence in politics. The historic judicial unwillingness to accept equality justifications discourages advocates from using them in court, notwithstanding their closer fit with the laws at issue. Moreover, if support for contribution caps reflects a desire to equalize the voices of the voters, they may not successfully reach this goal unless they are accompanied by restrictions on independent expenditures. Evidence from Oregon suggests that, after the people passed a measure imposing a cap of $100 in statewide races, independent expenditures increased sharply in the next election.[112]

The other innovative state reform, again largely a result of direct democracy and seemingly compelled more by egalitarian concerns

---

[111]161 F.3d at 521.

[112]See Eliza Newlin Carney, *Taking on the Fat Cats,* Nat'l J., Jan. 18, 1997, at 110.

than by fears of *quid pro quo* corruption, is public financing. Consistent with the presidential system upheld by the Supreme Court, state public financing systems are voluntary, providing public money to candidates who agree either not to accept any private money (Maine[113]) or to abide by strict spending limits (Vermont[114]). In Maine, candidates qualify for public funds by raising a small amount of seed money from voters making small contributions; this threshold requires that recipients demonstrate a level of popular support. Under some state systems, qualifying candidates receive additional funds if their competitors do not participate in the system and substantially outspend the publicly financed candidate.

Supporters advance arguments in favor of public financing that should resonate with republicans: reform should guarantee fairer and more equal representation of all citizens; reform should improve deliberation by reinvigorating public participation in democracy; and reform should enable all Americans, regardless of their wealth or connections, the opportunity to run for office. Many new public financing laws have been attacked in court, where opponents hope that shifts in judicial views since *Buckley* will cause courts to strike down public financing even if candidates can choose not to participate.

The states will continue to be the arenas for innovative campaign finance proposals given gridlock on Capitol Hill and voter demands for reform of the electoral process to decrease the perceived influence of special interests and money over policymakers. Interestingly, differences in state laws may allow scholars to discover the effects of various reform schemes on electoral outcomes, spending and contribution patterns, and the involvement of organized interests and individual citizens in campaigns. State experimentation may be abruptly halted, however, by the judiciary, and the outcome of the Missouri case in the Supreme Court may also transform the legal environment that shapes federal regulation of the electoral process.

---

[113]See Me. Rev. Stat. Ann. tit. 21-A, § 1121 *et seq.*

[114]See Vt. Stat. Ann. tit. 17, § 2801 *et seq.* (Supp. 1997). Vermont is unusual because its clean money statute was passed by the legislature, not by popular vote.

5

Legislative Structures

Once elected, state and federal legislators convene and produce the statutes that may later present challenging questions of interpretation for judges and attorneys. One reason citizens accept statutes as legitimate is that they represent the collective action of many diverse individuals selected through fair procedures to represent our interests. The integrity of the electoral process is inextricably linked to the rule of law and the willingness of those who disagree with a statute nonetheless to abide by it. Statutory legitimacy is also affected by the structures and rules that shape the process through which collective action occurs.[1] Procedures are not neutral; they profoundly influence the content as well as legitimacy of laws. As attorneys, you will be concerned with legislative process when you are faced with a difficult problem of statutory interpretation requiring you to distinguish credible from strategic legislation history. You may also work in a legislature and play a role in devising rules, or you may discover that a client needs you to negotiate the vetogates of the legislative process to solve a problem.

In this chapter, we will survey a few of the structures that shape the legislative environment, both at the federal and state levels. To begin with, we will set out the various immunities that protect lawmakers from lawsuits stemming from their official duties. At the federal level, the Constitution provides the only protection through the Speech or Debate Clause. We will next canvass a variety of rules that shape deliberation and drafting, such as single-subject rules and federal budget process rules. Finally, we will assess the relationship of the legislature to other private and public institutions — interest groups, the President and the executive branch — because the presence of so many players in the lawmaking game greatly influences the behavior of legislators.

Consider these materials in light of the various theories of representation offered in Chapter 2. Liberal and republican theories place great stock in procedure as a means of assuring the legitimacy

---

[1]See Jeremy Waldron, *Law and Disagreement* (1999).

of legislation. Theorists from both schools appreciate legislative structures assuring that a plurality of interests or viewpoints are heard and that authoritative decisions can be efficiently made on issues as to which there is disagreement. The rules governing the federal budgetary process are the most interesting recent development along these lines. Along other dimensions, liberals and republicans part company. Chief among them are their stances toward logrolling and compromise. Liberal thinkers emphasize the ways in which structures can facilitate bargaining among relevant legislative players to devise moderate policies that are acceptable to a broad array of interests. Republicans are less concerned that compromises be reached than that legislative structures encourage lawmaking that advances the public good. Some republican thought supports procedures that set limits on bargaining and logrolling in the legislature. Single-subject rules, line item vetoes, and bars to appropriations riders — all found in some state constitutions or laws — can serve these purposes.

Both liberals and republicans are also concerned that the legislative process have the *appearance* of fairness, and so both support requirements that lobbyists reveal their activities and that legislators not take bribes (Chapter 2). Critical thinkers lament that mere appearance is sometimes the only fair thing about the structure of legislative bodies in this country. Legislators are immunized from lawsuits as a matter of state or federal constitutional rule and are insulated as a practical matter from the concerns of their neediest constituents. If liberal interest group pluralism excludes or marginalizes the poor, people of color, those who don't speak English, single mothers, and sexual minorities, then seemingly transparent procedures will assure only that the interests of the "have" groups are satisfied. Critical thinkers would be especially scornful of civic republicans, whose aspiration for a truly public-regarding democracy is empty proceduralism unless it is accompanied by a substantive agenda of wealth redistribution.

I. Legislative Immunities[2]

Legislative immunities are found in both state and federal constitutions. They preserve the independence of legislators, a minimum condition for the process to work effectively, but at a possible cost in legislator accountability for irresponsible statements and even, in some cases, outright corruption. How these dueling concerns are balanced, against the backdrop of constitutional language and its history of interpretation and practice, forms the core of this Part. Note how the issues here relate back to those raised in Chapter 2, such as bribery.

A. *Speech or Debate Clause: The Sole Protection for Members of Congress*

Article I, Section 6, Clause 1 of the Constitution provides that "for any Speech or Debate in either House, [members of Congress] shall not be questioned in any other Place." The Framers saw inclusion of this protection in the Constitution as crucial for full and uncoerced deliberation; they were aware that the English monarchs in the sixteenth and seventeenth centuries, seeking to halt the move to parliamentary supremacy, had arrested and interrogated members of Parliament. The Speech or Debate Clause helps to ensure congressional independence because it reduces the ability of the executive branch to harass lawmakers. In addition, the Speech or Debate Clause relieves members of Congress of the burden of defending themselves in court and allows them to concentrate on their duties as representatives. The Speech or Debate Clause thus reduces the chance that the judicial branch can be used to interfere with the legislative branch.

The clause has not been interpreted literally; rather, courts construe it functionally and pragmatically to achieve its objective of preserving legislative independence. For example, it does not apply only to speech or debate. It extends to "things generally done in a session of the [Congress] by one of its members in relation to the business before it," including committee reports, resolutions, and the

---

[2]See Eskridge & Frickey 262-76, 282-87; Hetzel, Libonati & Williams 323-72; Mikva & Lane 714-29.

act of voting.[3] Furthermore, the immunity protects congressional aides with respect to conduct that would be protected if it were performed by a lawmaker. The Court's decision in *Gravel v. United States*[4] to immunize an aide when acting as the alter ego of a member grew out of the awareness that members must delegate many legislative tasks in order to work effectively in a complicated environment. Although *Gravel* involved a Senator's legislative assistant, presumably the alter ego rationale extends to any congressional employee acting at the direction of a member, even if the aide is not on the particular member's payroll. For example, lawyers, economists, and other policymaking staff in the Congressional Budget Office are not employed by particular lawmakers but often perform legislative activities on behalf of a member of Congress.

A different set of decisions relating to congressional staff reveals the difficulties inherent in distinguishing legislative from other activities. When does the Speech or Debate Clause prohibit judicial inquiry into the reasons for the termination of congressional employees? The Court of Appeals for the D.C. Circuit has been faced with several of these cases and has adopted a test that immunizes termination or other staffing decisions when they relate to employees with duties "directly related to the due functioning of the legislative process."[5] So, although lawmakers who fired the first African American to serve as Official Reporter of the House of Representatives were protected against a civil rights claim, a member of Congress could be sued by the manager of the House Restaurant System who claimed her discharge stemmed solely from her gender, not her performance.[6] Interestingly, the Congressional Accountability Act of 1995,[7] which allows congressional employees to sue their employing office for wrongful discharge, carefully avoids raising a Speech or Debate Clause issue. Members of Congress are not

---

[3] *Kilbourn v. Thompson*, 103 U.S. 168, 204 (1880).

[4] 408 U.S. 606 (1972).

[5] *Browning v. Clerk, U.S. House of Representatives*, 789 F.2d 923, 929 (D.C. Cir.), *cert. denied*, 479 U.S. 996 (1986).

[6] Compare *Browning* (Official Reporter of the House) with *Walker v. Jones*, 733 F.2d 923 (D.C. Cir.), *cert. denied*, 469 U.S. 1036 (1984) (restaurant manager).

[7] P.L. No. 104-1, 109 Stat. 3, codified at 2 U.S.C. § 1301 *et seq.*

personally liable for any damages; instead, awards are paid by a contingent fund of the United States. The Act specifically states that "[t]he authorization to bring judicial proceedings under [this Act] . . . shall not constitute a waiver . . . of the privileges" of any lawmaker under the Speech or Debate Clause.[8]

The functional approach to interpretation also limits the clause's coverage, so that some speech by members that literally falls within the ambit of the constitutional clause does not receive immunity. In *United States v. Rose*,[9] the D.C. Circuit confronted the case of Congressman Rose's testimony before the House Committee on Standards of Official Conduct relating to allegations that several of his financial transactions violated House rules. The court held that the Speech or Debate Clause did not immunize his testimony because it did not relate to legislative business, but rather to "his handling of various personal financial transactions. . . . In short, Congressman Rose was acting as a witness to facts relevant to a congressional investigation of his private conduct."[10] In response to the argument that his testimony would have been protected had it been given on the floor of the House because it would have come within the literal language of the clause, the court opined that speech in the House "wholly unrelated to legislative business" would not be protected. "We focus on what Congressman Rose said, not where he said it."[11]

Once a legislator's activities fall under the constitutional immunity, the lawmaker cannot be questioned about them, or the motives behind them, in any place other than the House or Senate. The protection afforded by the Speech or Debate Clause can therefore complicate the government's job in a criminal prosecution of a legislator accused of accepting bribes. In a series of cases, the Supreme Court has held that a federal legislator cannot be questioned either about any legislative act or about the reasons why the legislator acted, decided, or voted in a particular way, even in the face of

---

[8]P.L. No. 104-1, 2 U.S.C. § 1413.

[9]28 F.3d 181 (D.C. Cir. 1994).

[10]*Id.* at 188.

[11]*Id.*

allegations that the action was the result of a bribe.[12] Although evidence relating to a past legislative act is inadmissible, the promise by a member of Congress to perform a legislative act in the future is not immunized. As long as the prosecutor shows only the corrupt promise, without introducing evidence of any subsequent performance, the constitutional protection is not implicated.[13]

The line here is fuzzy. Inquiry into the lawmaker's decision to accept a bribe, which seems to be allowed, may well shed light on her motives in performing any subsequent and related legislative act. Furthermore, as Justice Stevens has pointed out,[14] the lawmaker may refer to past legislative acts to convince an individual to participate in a corrupt scheme. Are self-laudatory references excluded from evidence because they relate to past legislative acts? It would seem so, even though the accuracy of the statements is not necessarily relevant to the prosecution. The Court's difficulties in constructing a workable test for these cases lies in the tension between vindicating the separation-of-powers principles that undergird the clause and allowing successful prosecution of dishonest lawmakers. Some of the tension is reduced by the fact that the House or Senate itself can question a member of Congress about alleged corrupt legislative acts without violating the Constitution. The clause protects the member from questioning only "in any other Place," and therefore it places on the Congress the responsibility to discipline its members.

Many of these cases, including criminal prosecutions and civil actions relating to staffing decisions, raise the issue whether the immunity can be waived. The Supreme Court has avoided deciding whether a member can waive the protection individually, whether Congress as an institution can waive the immunity without the member's acquiescence, or whether both waivers are required. A purposive approach to this question indicates that both the member and the institution have important interests at stake, and so perhaps both must be involved. The clause is justified by separation-of-powers concerns to protect the legislative branch from executive branch intimidation; thus, allowing individual waiver in the absence

---

[12]See, e.g., *United States v. Brewster*, 408 U.S. 501 (1972).

[13]See *United States v. Helstoski*, 442 U.S. 477 (1979).

[14]See *id*. at 497-98 (Stevens, J., concurring in part and dissenting in part).

of congressional assent would be anomalous. On the other hand, the Court has noted that "Congress, as a body, should not be free to strip individual Members of the protection guaranteed by the Clause. . . . The controversy over the Alien and Sedition Acts reminds us how one political party in control of both the Legislative and the Executive Branches sought to use the courts to destroy political opponents."[15] Because the Court requires that any waiver be explicit and unequivocal, it avoids resolving these questions by finding that no waiver has occurred by either the member or the institution.

B. *Defining Legislative Acts: The Narrow Scope of the Speech or Debate Clause*

Courts have developed a definition of legislative acts falling within the protection of the Speech or Debate Clause that leaves a lawmaker unprotected with respect to a variety of official actions. In part the judiciary's approach may be explained by its unwillingness to depart too substantially from the text of the Constitution. The somewhat cramped notion of legislative activity may also stem from the courts' lack of familiarity with the day-to-day activities of the modern lawmaker. The latter explanation is not wholly satisfying because in some areas — most notably, the extension of immunity to the staff of lawmakers — the Court has adapted the doctrine to account for current realities.

One of the earliest Speech or Debate Clause cases, *Kilbourn v. Thompson*,[16] provides the first limitation we will discuss. Although a member's vote on a particular matter is protected, subsequent conduct to implement the legislative decision can be examined in court. Thus, the arrest of Hallett Kilbourn, although authorized by an immunized legislative vote holding him in contempt of Congress, could be challenged as unconstitutional, and those executing the order of the House could be forced to defend themselves in court. *Kilbourn* involved the activities of the House Sergeant-at-Arms rather than a member of Congress, but subsequent cases such as *Gravel* emphasize that the Speech or Debate Clause analysis is purely functional and does not turn on whether the activity is performed by a lawmaker or

---

[15]*Id.* at 492-93.

[16]103 U.S. 168 (1880).

an employee. Thus, presumably a lawmaker who wrongfully arrests an individual held in contempt of Congress is amenable to suit, just as the House aide was in *Kilbourn*.

Even more controversially, the Court has repeatedly held that the Speech or Debate Clause does not apply to efforts to educate the public about legislative matters. This limitation is best illustrated by *Hutchinson v. Proxmire*,[17] a case concerning Senator William Proxmire's infamous Golden Fleece Awards, which were given to agencies that the Senator believed were wasting the taxpayers' money. The National Science Foundation received a Golden Fleece award for its grant of nearly $500,000 to fund Ronald Hutchinson's research, which Proxmire characterized as a study of why monkeys clench their teeth. Hutchinson sued for defamation. Clearly, the Speech or Debate Clause immunized the Senator and his aide with respect to any claims stemming from speeches made on the floor of Congress and the preparation of such speeches. Proxmire also disseminated a press release publicizing this Golden Fleece award, and he reprinted his speech in a newsletter sent to his constituents. The Court did not extend Speech or Debate Clause protection to these publications because it found that they were not essential to the deliberative process or related to legislative activities.

Justice Brennan, driven by the more expansive view of deliberation adopted by many civic republicans, dissented in *Proxmire* and a similar holding in *Gravel*.[18] He argued that the *informing function* of members of Congress is as important to a healthy democracy as their legislating function. Legislators have an obligation to communicate with their constituents and to listen to their feedback; although the Congressional Record is available to the public, voters are more likely to receive information from the press or newsletters. A purposive approach to the Speech or Debate Clause, Justice Brennan reasoned, would protect legislative independence with respect to a broad range of informing activities vital to the deliberative process. Notwithstanding these arguments, the Court has not included within

---

[17]443 U.S. 111 (1979).

[18]See *Proxmire*, 443 U.S. at 136 (Brennan, J., dissenting); *Gravel*, 408 U.S. at 648 (Brennan, J., dissenting).

the constitutional protection the informing function of lawmakers if the communication is directed at people outside the legislative forum.

Similarly, the Court refuses to extend immunity to lawmakers who contact administrative agencies on behalf of constituents or who engage in similar kinds of casework. "Members of Congress are constantly in touch with the Executive Branch of the Government and with administrative agencies — they may cajole, and exhort with respect to the administration of a federal statute — but such conduct, though generally done, is not protected legislative activity."[19] The judicial unwillingness to protect legislators from suits arising from casework suggests that courts view casework as less valuable than legislating and deliberating on policy. Such a value judgment is questionable because lawmakers often have the most direct effect on constituents' lives when they help them resolve a problem with a bureaucrat or when they oversee execution of the laws. Scholars have noted that casework often takes up more of legislators' time than does legislating, and casework tends to produce a more positive voter response.[20]

The modern lawmaker certainly considers as integral to her responsibilities the duty to inform constituents of legislative matters and to represent their interests before various federal agencies. Yet, she soon discovers that the immunity accorded to federal legislators may be less robust than that given to high-level executive officials or judges, who sometimes have absolute immunity from common law tort actions as long as their activities are within their official duties. Perhaps one could justify the refusal to extend protection to a lawmaker's political activities like casework as consistent with good public policy as well as compatible with the constitutional text. Immunities work as incentives to increase the amount of the protected behavior, so a relatively narrow immunity might work to encourage lawmakers to engage in more legislative activity relative to casework.

---

[19]*Gravel*, 408 U.S. at 625. See also *Chastain v. Sundquist*, 833 F.2d 311 (D.C. Cir. 1987), *cert. denied*, 487 U.S. 1240 (1988) (allowing defamation suit against congressman relating to casework concerning the activities of attorneys in the Memphis Area Legal Services).

[20]See Robert Klonoff, *The Congressman as Mediator Between Citizens and Government Agencies: Problems and Prospects*, 16 Harv. J. Legis. 701 (1979).

This strategy might be a corrective for the incentives in the current system that cause lawmakers to prefer casework because they wish to avoid the greater controversy inherent in taking positions on legislation. Furthermore, legislators may intervene in administrative proceedings more often for wealthy special interests than for ordinary citizens, a charge heard often during the savings and loan crisis when members of Congress attempted to convince regulators not to close insolvent thrifts owned by influential campaign contributors. Speech or Debate Clause immunity would encourage more such interventions, thereby threatening the independence of the executive branch and implicating issues of distributive justice. Courts have not offered these explanations for their decision to interpret the Speech or Debate Clause to exclude casework, relying instead on assertions that the text should be read only to cover legislative acts. Because the clause's meaning has already been decoupled from the plain language of the Constitution, however, judges should provide better explanations for the lines that they draw.

C. *Immunities Accorded to State Lawmakers*[21]

The federal Speech or Debate Clause does not extend to state legislators, and the Supreme Court has refused to use the policy behind the clause to construct an evidentiary privilege for state legislators involved in federal criminal prosecutions. In *United States v. Gillock*,[22] the Court found that none of the purposes underlying the federal clause warrants its application to state lawmakers. No separation-of-powers concerns are implicated; instead, the Supremacy Clause requires that federal law prevail over state laws and actions. In addition, the Court held that enforcing criminal statutes is an important federal interest that outweighs any negative effect on federalism values. In the civil realm, on the other hand, the Court has provided state legislators with absolute immunity from suits stemming from alleged violations of the federal civil rights acts.[23] In that

---

[21]See Eskridge & Frickey 271-76; Hetzel, Libonati & Williams 369-72; Mikva & Lane 725-29.

[22]445 U.S. 360 (1980).

[23]See *Tenney v. Brandhove*, 341 U.S. 367 (1951). See also *Spallone v. United States*, 493 U.S. 265 (1990) (refusing to enforce a civil contempt order that fined city council members as individuals for refusing to pass ordinances required by a

context, the need to protect legislator independence and comity interests is sufficiently strong to justify a grant of common-law immunity. Indeed, the different treatment in the civil and criminal contexts is related. "[T]he cases . . . which have recognized an immunity from civil suit for state officials have presumed the existence of federal criminal liability as a restraining factor on the conduct of state officials."[24]

State constitutions contain clauses similar to the federal Constitution's Speech or Debate Clause. These state provisions provide immunity from civil or criminal suits based on state law. Many are virtually identical to the wording of the federal Speech or Debate Clause; others appear to be more narrowly phrased. For example, article 4, § 11 of the Michigan Constitution protects state legislators "from civil arrest and civil process during sessions of the legislature and for five days next before the commencement and after the termination thereof." The scope of these provisions, even those phrased differently from the federal provisions, is usually interpreted to be equivalent to the federal protection. Lawmakers are immunized with respect to their legislative activities, as that term has been interpreted by the Supreme Court in the federal context.

State courts have struggled, as have the federal courts, with the effect of such immunity on criminal prosecutions. For example, the Supreme Court of Kansas was faced with the scope of the state constitutional provision in a criminal prosecution of a lawmaker who threatened to blackmail another lawmaker by telling his wife that he had been caught in a compromising position with two female lobbyists.[25] The threat occurred immediately before a vote, when the two were talking on the floor of the legislature. The Kansas Constitution provides that "[f]or any speech, written document or debate in either house, the members shall not be questioned elsewhere."[26] Although the state supreme court found the defendant's behavior to be corrupt and reprehensible, it still held that evidence relating to discussions about a vote was inadmissible. It accepted, after a

---

consent decree to eliminate racial discrimination in public housing).

[24]*Gillock*, 445 U.S. at 372.

[25]See *Kansas v. Neufeld*, 926 P.2d 1325 (Kan. 1996).

[26]Kansas Const., art. 2, § 22.

lengthy analysis of the federal case law we detailed above, the defendant's argument that "legislators are frequently asked, under a great deal of pressure, to put aside their personal will and vote in a certain way on a bill. . . . [T]hese vote requests are often accompanied by threats that the wrong vote will result in a harsh editorial, letters to the editor, negative campaigning, loss of campaign support (financial or otherwise), or loss of a coveted chairmanship or committee assignment."[27] Just as lawmakers cannot be questioned about such hard bargaining tactics, so are they immunized from interrogation about less savory threats.

One difficulty posed by state formulations like that of Michigan, which provides immunity from arrest or process for a limited period, is measuring the time that protection is accorded to the lawmaker. In *Bishop v. Montante*,[28] the Michigan Supreme Court was asked to interpret the word "sessions" in its state speech or debate clause. It found that the immunity continued even during a legislative recess, when the legislature was formally in session because it had not adjourned. The court reasoned that legislators continue to perform legislative business such as "[c]onstituent contact, research, [and] committee assignments"[29] even when the body is not sitting. This holding is thus premised on an expansive view of legislative activity that has not similarly compelled courts to extend their notion of what sorts of actions constitute lawmaker activity that ought to be protected from judicial or executive interference. Somewhat paradoxically, Michigan courts rely on the federal precedents to determine what behavior falls within the zone of legislative activities protected by the state provision, and so the state immunity does not extend to casework or informing activities.[30]

II. Structures that Shape Legislative Deliberation

Optimistic pluralists suppose that legislation does and should serve to accommodate the needs of all relevant interest groups, and that all interests are adequately represented by some influential group.

---

[27]926 P.2d at 1335.

[28]237 N.W. 2d 465 (Mich. 1976).

[29]*Id.* at 467.

[30]See, e.g., *Wilkins v. Gagliardi*, 556 N.W. 2d 171 (Mich. App. 1996).

Today, most theories of the legislative process that include study of interest groups join in identifying and criticizing the pathologies of pluralism. Some liberals, particularly those in the public choice tradition, fear that interest groups engage in rent-seeking that undermines aggregate social wealth; they argue that politics should be structured to reduce such behavior or to channel it so that it better serves public welfare. Republicans have always maintained that government should be structured to encourage transparent deliberation in the interest of the public good. Critical theorists might add that the structures of deliberation should be crafted to amplify the voices of traditionally marginalized groups.

Judicial review and interpretation of statutes to assure their public-regarding purposes are two strategies for dealing with the problem of rent-seeking. Courts act as independent observers and monitor legislative activity. The problem is that the independence that enables judges to monitor effectively also undermines their authority to monitor frequently and aggressively. For that reason, the framers of state and federal constitutions and the authors of legislative rules and procedures have sought to control the vices of faction and rent-seeking by adopting particular structures for legislative deliberation. We will begin our study by looking at the single-subject rule, a part of nearly all state constitutions, as well as similar rules on the federal level. We will turn next to a discussion of the appropriate role of courts in enforcing rules that shape legislative deliberation, whether they are constitutional or passed in some less durable form, such as internal rules. Justice Linde described the appropriate judicial role as one to ensure "due process of lawmaking."[31] Finally, we will describe generally the most important procedural framework in the current U.S. Congress — the complex and evolving federal budget process system.

A. *Single-Subject Requirements*[32]

Nearly all state constitutions have requirements that limit substantive bills to one subject. The Illinois Constitution is typical.

---

[31]See Hans Linde, *Due Process of Lawmaking*, 55 Neb. L. Rev. 197 (1976).

[32]See Eskridge & Frickey 250-55; Hetzel, Libonati & Williams 737-45; Mikva & Lane 71-73, 115-18; Popkin 803-13.

Article IV, § 8(d) provides: "Bills, except bills for appropriations and for the codification, revision or rearrangement of laws, shall be confined to one subject. Appropriation bills shall be limited to the subject of appropriations." Many state constitutions also require that the subject be expressed in the title of the bill.

The single-subject requirement serves several objectives. The most frequently mentioned justification is to minimize logrolling, which one court pejoratively described as the "practice of jumbling together in one act inconsistent subjects in order to force a passage by uniting minorities with different interests when the particular provisions could not pass on their separate merits."[33] Logrolling can still occur through vote trades regarding separate bills but is less likely to be executed successfully, because the deals may unravel when performance must take place over time. The second bill may never be brought to a vote, or one of the bargainers may decide to defect once her program has been enacted. In state legislatures where members serve long terms and occupy vetogates for many years, reputational sanctions may work to enforce logrolls that occur across bills, but the vagaries of the legislative process will inevitably prevent lawmakers from keeping some promises relating to future performance.

Distaste for logrolling reflected in single-subject requirements goes further than the concern that programs without majority support may become law. Legislators who oppose a particular program may feel forced to vote for it when it is part of an otherwise popular omnibus (or "Christmas tree") bill. Or a governor may sign a bill even when he or she finds a provision unacceptable; as we will see, many governors can exercise a line item veto only in regard to appropriations bills. An Illinois state court vividly described this pressure in a case dealing with "An act in relation to public safety":

> This Act is a textbook case of the type of situation that [the single-subject requirement] was enacted to prevent — attaching an unpopular bill to a popular one to circumvent legislative input or scrutiny. Imagine the public rebuke that would be directed at a legislator who did not vote for a bill that sought to protect children from the horrid abuses at the hand of sex offenders. At the same

---

[33]*State ex rel. Martin v. Zimmerman*, 289 N.W. 662, 664 (Wis. 1940).

time these legislators are drafting in a measure in that very same Act that would allow employers to, in effect, eavesdrop on their own workforce. It is a reprehensible measure to ride a potentially unpassable piece of legislation on the backs of abused children.[34]

This passage suggests why republican theorists might support a single-subject requirement: it may improve deliberation. Most obviously, rules that reduce the number of omnibus bills and require the title to reflect all the contents of the proposal increase the chance that lawmakers will know what they are voting on.

Again, the Illinois case provides an enlightening example of this republican concern. The bill at issue in the case began as an eight-page act proposing changes to prisoners' reimbursements to the Department of Corrections for the expenses incurred during their incarceration. Soon, the bill was renamed "An act in relation to crime" because lawmakers had amended it to include subjects ranging from student expulsion for bringing a weapon to school to implementation of the Police Corps to changing penalties for the manufacture and possession of cannabis. By the end of the second conference committee, the title had become the very generic "An act relating to public safety" because it now included fees for motor fuels and underground storage facilities as well as the challenged exemption for certain corporations from the wiretapping statute. The bill had grown to 243 pages. The increasingly broad title of this bill reflected the legislature's rather feeble attempt to meet the single-subject requirement while constructing a wide-ranging omnibus bill. (One difficult question in the enforcement of the requirement is the level of abstractness that is allowed in defining the single subject.) On the same day that the conference committee was named and the final bill on public safety drafted, it was submitted for a vote of both houses of the state legislature. The court concluded: "Not only had the single subject [requirement] been violated, the legislature trampled upon the spirit of the Constitution by stopping the public and the press from knowing about what they were doing until it was a *fait accompli*."[35]

---

[34]*Johnson v. Edgar*, No. 95 CH 12004, mem. op. (Cir. Ct. of Cook County, IL, May 7, 1996), *aff'd*, 680 N.E.2d 1372 (Ill. 1997).

[35]*Id.*

The federal legislature, although subject to the same problems, is not required to meet single-subject rules. However, internal House and Senate rules are designed to reduce the number of extraneous matters included in a single bill. The House of Representatives requires that all amendments to legislation be germane and that "no motion or proposition on a subject different from that under consideration shall be admitted under color of amendment."[36] The Senate Rules do not include germaneness requirements (except in the context of some budget bills which we will discuss below), but both houses have rules that prohibit placing substantive legislation on appropriations bills. Again, the justification for the latter prohibitions stems from the greater element of coercion inherent in appropriations bills. If they are not passed, the government must shut down and vital services to citizens halted, so lawmakers are apt to vote for legislation containing amendments they would otherwise find repugnant. Furthermore, the President has no line item veto and may be unwilling to veto an entire appropriations bill on account of a few programs.

Because the federal requirements are internal congressional rules, they can be waived by the body. Courts will consider any bill passed that seems to violate these rules as implicitly waiving the requirements; at the most, they will narrowly construe substantive riders on appropriations bills because such provisions often are not accompanied by full deliberation and vigorous debate.[37] The absence of any robust single-subject requirement may be responsible in part for the rise of omnibus bills in Congress as the preferred legislative vehicle. Whether this trend is negative is not clear. Most liberals believe that logrolling is necessary for interest group pluralism to flourish, and it provides the normative advantage of enabling each group to satisfy its most intensely held preferences. Critical theorists can appreciate this argument as well because minority legislators can sometimes obtain government benefits for marginalized groups by logrolling with a faction of the majority. In a real sense, logrolling and "Christmas tree" bills that give a little present to everyone are the glue that holds

---

[36]House Rule XVI, § 7.

[37]See *TVA v. Hill*, 437 U.S. 153, 190-91 (1978) (discussing the canon of construction that appropriations riders should be narrowly construed).

legislative deals together, allowing a greater number of proposals to be enacted.

In contrast to the federal rules, state single-subject requirements are constitutional provisions, so courts more often enforce them. Even so, few laws are struck down because they encompass more than a single subject; instead, judges tend to defer to the legislature's judgment on both the content of the bill and the accuracy of the title. In most cases, the only remedy for a single-subject rule violation is for the court to invalidate the entire act. It is difficult to sever one part and declare it void because the judge cannot be certain which part of the act, if any, could have been passed by itself. If the title mentions only one subject, some courts will allow the provisions relating to that subject to take effect. Other courts attempt to determine whether one of the subjects "is of greater dignity or is the dominant subject so that it can be concluded that the legislature wished that subject to be law over the others or that the other subjects furnished no special inducement for the passage of the act."[38] If a court's only option is to declare the entire act void, the court will often strain to avoid this outcome. For example, the Illinois courts, which had begun to wield the single-subject rule aggressively to strike down state laws, backed away from the implications of the doctrine in a case that would have required the invalidation of the implementing legislation for one fiscal year's budget.[39]

Single-subject rules can also apply to laws passed through direct democracy, and they are increasingly used as weapons by the opponents of ballot initiatives to invalidate them after passage or to deny them ballot access in the first place. The rule's objectives in the context of direct democracy include the traditional goals of avoiding logrolling (here, among groups seeking to enact laws through popular votes) and reducing the pressure on voters to enact provisions they find distasteful in order to pass programs they support. In addition, a single-subject requirement may decrease voter confusion in an arena

---

[38]Millard Ruud, *"No Law Shall Embrace More than One Subject,"* 42 Minn. L. Rev. 389, 399 (1958).

[39]See *Arangold Corp. v. Zehnder*, 1999 WL 482301 (Ill. 1999) (holding that a provision enacting a tobacco tax act was part of the single subject of an act implementing the state budget for fiscal year 1996).

where electors are often uncertain about the meaning and effect of ballot propositions. Some state constitutions also require that each amendment to the constitution submitted to the people be voted on separately.[40] Related requirements that ballot proposition titles and summaries fairly reflect their content also serve to combat voter confusion.[41] Some proponents of direct democracy complain that courts apply the single-subject requirement more rigorously to direct legislation than to traditional laws, in part because of the general judicial hostility toward initiatives.[42] Furthermore, they argue that state officials who enforce single-subject requirements and approve titles for ballot questions attempt to thwart objectives of proponents and undermine the people's lawmaking power.[43]

The judiciary's role in enforcing procedural restrictions on deliberation and the legislative process has been problematic. Often, cases that reach the court look political, and judges work diligently to display the passive virtues of resisting the temptation to enter into the political fray. But the courts may serve a valuable function if they assiduously enforce legislative procedures that are designed to improve deliberation or to restrain the ill effects of interest group activity. The notion that courts should be guided by a *due process of lawmaking* principle is one relevant to a host of rules, including single-subject requirements.

---

[40]See, e.g., Mont. Const. art. XIV, § 11.

[41]See Daniel Lowenstein, *California Initiatives and the Single-Subject Rule*, 30 UCLA L. Rev. 936 (1983) (discussing justifications and tests).

[42]Only one state, Florida, has explicitly adopted a more rigorous test for initiatives than for statutes passed by the legislature. See Caroline Tolbert, Daniel Lowenstein & Todd Donovan, *Election Law and Rules for Using Initiatives*, in *Citizens as Legislators: Direct Democracy in the United States* 27, 43 (Shaun Bowler, Todd Donovan & Caroline Tolbert eds., 1998).

[43]Cf. *Campbell v. Buckley*, 11 F. Supp. 2d 1260 (D. Colo. 1998), *appeal pending* (holding against those challenging single-subject requirements and concluding that the test was equivalent to the test for legislatively enacted bills).

B. *Due Process of Lawmaking: A Concept for Courts and Legislatures*[44]

Due process of lawmaking encompasses a variety of approaches to the legislative process, many of which resonate with republican theorists, who believe that laws derive legitimacy in part from the quality of the deliberation accompanying their enactment. Furthermore, if particular legislative structures or judicial strategies work to highlight the concerns of the disempowered, they can serve a representation-reinforcing role that appeals to critical theorists. One aspect of due process of lawmaking concerns how particular decisions should be allocated among various political institutions. Institutional theories emphasize differences in competence among the branches of government. Legislatures, which allow for deliberation and broad fact-finding and which comprise accountable elected representatives, are the institutions best suited for resolving important and controversial policy problems. Professor Tribe terms this approach *structural due process* because it focuses not on the substance of the policy or the procedures for enforcing rights, but on the "structures through which policies are both formed and applied."[45]

Perhaps the best example of this aspect of due process of lawmaking is *Hampton v. Mow Sun Wong.*[46] Five resident aliens had been denied jobs by the federal government because of a Civil Service Commission rule that barred all noncitizens from federal civil service employment. The Commission justified the exclusion primarily on foreign policy grounds (for example, it facilitated the President's treaty power because he could waive the exclusion in return for concessions). The aliens sued, alleging that the denial of employment violated the Due Process Clause of the Fifth Amendment. Rather than decide the merits of the constitutional claim, the

---

[44]See Eskridge & Frickey 485-506; Lane & Mikva 118-38. Cf. Hetzel, Libonati & Williams chap. 5, entitled "Due Process of Lawmaking" to call attention "to the extent to which legislatures are designed to be rule-bound and rule-oriented institutions of governance," *id.* at 729.

[45]Laurence Tribe, *Structural Due Process*, 10 Harv. C.R.-C.L. L. Rev. 269, 269 (1975) (emphasis omitted).

[46]426 U.S. 88 (1976). See also *Kent v. Dulles*, 357 U.S. 116 (1958) (similar approach taken in case where Secretary of State withheld passports from "subversives"), discussed in Chapter 9, Part IIA.

Court held that the Civil Service Commission could not adopt such a rule on any basis other than promoting efficiency in the civil service. Decisions made by the Commission are legitimate in part because they involve expertise; the Commission has no special expertise in foreign affairs. Although there are sensitive government jobs that should be open only to loyal citizens, the Commission had not proved that a blanket exclusion was necessary or that its benefits outweighed the loss of a pool of qualified applicants for nonsensitive positions. The Court concluded that "due process requires that the decision to impose [the] deprivation of an important liberty be made either [by the Congress or the President] or, if it is to be permitted to be made by the Civil Service Commission, that it be justified by reasons which are properly the concern of that agency."[47] Note that the Court did not rule out the decision to exclude aliens from all civil service jobs; in essence, it remanded that decision to a different institution.

The idea behind *Mow Sun Wong* — that certain important decisions affecting substantive rights must be made by particular government entities that have the capacity to deliberate and consider all the relevant factors — is potentially far-reaching. For example, it casts doubt on the legitimacy of direct democracy because the initiative process is not conducive to reasoned deliberation, compromise, or the articulation of reasons to support decisions.[48] Justice Stevens, the author of *Mow Sun Wong*, made a similar kind of argument for judicial deference to administrative agencies in *Chevron v. NRDC*,[49] a case we will discuss in Chapter 8. Such deference seems strange. After all, courts are experts in statutory interpretation. Why should judges defer to bureaucrats whose expertise lies in a substantive policy area? Justice Stevens' response was that agencies have a stronger democratic pedigree than courts. Statutory interpretation of regulatory laws rests often on policy determinations, and those should be made by the more accountable entity. In addition, agencies

---

[47]*Mow Sun Wong*, 426 U.S. at 116.

[48]See Lawrence Sager, *Insular Majorities Unabated:* Warth v. Seldin *and* City of Eastlake v. Forest City Enterprises, Inc., 91 Harv. L. Rev. 1373 (1978) (applying due process of lawmaking concepts to draw into question the legitimacy of direct democracy).

[49]467 U.S. 837 (1984).

can more easily modify statutory interpretation over time to account for new information, economic and social developments, and scientific advances. Regulatory laws must often be updated, but legislatures are busy and sometimes fail to amend them to accommodate changed circumstances. Agencies are institutionally suited to undertake that role.[50]

Due process of lawmaking may support more than a decision to locate the resolution of a particular issue in a particular institution; it may also justify judicial inquiry into the decisionmaking process of that institution. Justice Linde, who coined the phrase "due process of lawmaking," maintains that the central function of judicial review should be "to guarantee the democratic legitimacy of political decisions by establishing essential rules for the political process."[51] In other words, courts should aggressively enforce the kinds of rules we have studied in Chapters 4 and 5 — those relating to the composition of legislatures and the selection of representatives and those structuring the deliberative process, such as the single-subject rule. Some courts have gone further than this, adopting judicial strategies designed to encourage, or even require, a certain kind of deliberation. This aspect of due process of lawmaking is more intrusive than merely enforcing rules that the legislature imposes on itself, although it is less intrusive than a decision striking down the law on substantive grounds.

Two examples of such a judicial approach will make due process of lawmaking a less abstract concept. First, courts can use *appropriate-deliberation tests* to help determine a statute's constitutionality.[52] For example, *Fullilove v. Klutznick*[53] upheld the constitu-

---

[50]See *id.* at 863-66. Academics have elaborated on Justice Stevens' point in, e.g., William Eskridge, Jr., *Dynamic Statutory Interpretation* 161-73 (1994); Mark Seidenfeld, *A Civic Republican Justification for the Bureaucratic State*, 105 Harv. L. Rev. 1511 (1992). See also Cass Sunstein, *One Case at a Time: Judicial Minimalism on the Supreme Court* 227-31 (1999).

[51]Linde, *supra* note 31, at 251.

[52]See Richard Fallon, *The Supreme Court, 1996 Term — Foreword: Implementing the Constitution*, 111 Harv. L. Rev. 54, 70 (1997).

[53]448 U.S. 448 (1980). But see *Adarand Constructors, Inc. v. Pena*, 515 U.S. 200 (1995) (striking down a similar set-aside program and overruling *Fullilove* to the extent necessary to do so).

tionality of a provision in a public works bill that required that 10% of the federal funds be used to purchase goods or services from minority owned businesses. Justice Stevens, the author of *Mow Sun Wong* (and later *Chevron*), used a due process of lawmaking rationale to justify his vote in dissent from the holding. He argued that the Due Process Clause imposed "a special obligation to scrutinize any governmental decisionmaking process that draws nationwide distinctions between citizens on the basis of their race."[54] He was unimpressed by the amount and content of congressional debate on the set-aside provision. Stevens found no justification in the public records of congressional deliberation for the 10% figure or for the decision to include various groups, including blacks, Spanish-speaking Americans, Asians, Indians, Eskimos, and Aleuts, in the group eligible for preferential treatment. Furthermore, Congress had not considered alternative and less burdensome remedies for the problem of racial and ethnic discrimination. In short, Congress had failed "to follow procedures that guarantee the kind of deliberation that a fundamental constitutional issue of this kind obviously merits."[55]

Interestingly, Justice Stevens never acknowledged that some deliberation, perhaps on these issues, doubtlessly occurred in nonpublic forums. Nor did he justify his decision to consider only public debate. Perhaps he was unwilling to countenance private discussions because due process of lawmaking requires transparency so that the public can understand and assess the reasons for laws that make racial distinctions. On the other hand, if some element of private negotiation is required for lawmakers to reach agreements and a judicially crafted doctrine of due process of lawmaking can be satisfied only by public discussions, Justice Stevens' approach might produce net harm to the lawmaking process. Moreover, judges, who often have little knowledge of the dynamics of the legislative process, may be ill-suited to determine what kinds of deliberation should occur in public and what can remain behind closed doors without impairing the legitimacy of the laws that result.

---

[54]*Fullilove*, 448 U.S. at 548 (Stevens, J., dissenting).

[55]*Id.* at 552.

Stevens' approach in *Fullilove* is unusual; very few Justices, let alone majority opinions, have adopted an appropriate-deliberation test to vindicate constitutional rights. Quasi-constitutional *clear statement rules of statutory construction*, however, can be viewed as close relatives and are also supported by the idea of due process of lawmaking. Clear statement rules, which are discussed in more detail in Chapter 9, are canons of construction that require explicit and targeted textual instructions to cause a deviation from the status quo. For example, the Court requires a clear textual statement before it will hold that Congress intended to intrude on state governmental functions or that Congress intended a law to apply extraterritorially.[56] Courts tend to rely on strong clear statement rules to vindicate *underenforced constitutional norms*[57] like the structural norm of federalism, rather than to protect those values by invalidating statutes that threaten them.

Requiring a clear textual statement not only makes it more difficult for Congress to pass laws impinging on such norms, but the judicial tactic also indirectly works to influence the kind of congressional deliberation that accompanies such laws. These methods of statutory interpretation provide Congress with incentives to deliberate transparently about important values, to provide satisfactory reasons for decisions, and to set forth clearly articulated laws on these subjects. Due process of lawmaking ideals may also support a more generalized method of statutory interpretation — textualism — which attempts to improve the quality of legislative drafting as well as the conditions of deliberation. We will describe textualism more fully in Chapter 6; at this juncture, it is important to understand that several currently popular methods of interpretation can be justified in part by a due process of lawmaking rationale.

If due process of lawmaking is intended to improve legislative decisionmaking, why should we rely on the relatively indirect

---

[56]See *Gregory v. Ashcroft*, 501 U.S. 452 (1991); *Equal Employment Opportunity Comm'n v. Arabian Am. Oil Co.*, 499 U.S. 244 (1991). See generally William Eskridge, Jr. & Philip Frickey, *Quasi-Constitutional Law: Clear Statement Rules as Constitutional Lawmaking*, 45 Vand. L. Rev. 593 (1992).

[57]See Lawrence Sager, *Fair Measure: The Legal Status of Underenforced Constitutional Norms*, 91 Harv. L. Rev. 1212 (1978).

mechanism of judicial review? Congress may not be aware of the judicial techniques and thus not respond to the incentives they embody — or members may forget them in the rush of last-minute lawmaking. Legislators who know about the judicial posture may nonetheless ignore its implications in the hope that a particular law will never face a judicial challenge or will be considered by a judge who does not use the particular canon. Why not approach the problems of deliberation and decisionmaking more directly through the use of internal legislative rules and procedures designed to foster full and transparent deliberation? A framework that affects a substantial amount of congressional business may be more salient to lawmakers and the public than the occasional judicial pronouncement.

Congress has recently adopted several procedures and structures designed to protect underenforced constitutional norms like federalism or to reduce the negative effects of interest group activity. We will consider in some detail the most ubiquitous of these frameworks, the federal budget process. But it is not unique. For example, the Unfunded Mandates Reform Act of 1995[58] provides Congress with detailed information about the direct costs to state and local governments of implementing federal mandates. This information is disseminated before the House or Senate votes on proposals that contain significant intergovernmental mandates. Moreover, any member of Congress can object to the consideration of a bill that does not provide state or local governments with funding to defray the expenses of such mandates. Although such objections can be waived and the bills passed despite the lack of funding, the procedure enables interested legislators to turn congressional attention to certain constitutional norms. Process is used to create an environment conducive to robust deliberation of important issues — to shape and strengthen the structure of deliberation. Thus, due process of lawmaking, traditionally limited to the judicial realm, can be invoked to support and justify various congressional rules and procedures,

---

[58]Pub. L. No. 104-4, 109 Stat. 48 (codified in scattered sections of 2 U.S.C.). See Elizabeth Garrett, *Enhancing the Political Safeguards of Federalism? The Unfunded Mandates Reform Act of 1995*, 45 Kan. L. Rev. 1113, 1174-1177 (1997) (discussing relationship of congressional procedures to due process of lawmaking and to judicial clear statement rules).

perhaps as a complement to judicial strategies or as a substitute for them.

C. *The Federal Budget Process*[59]

No federal lawmaker can act without considering the effect of the budget process; it is a ubiquitous element of any complete due process of lawmaking analysis. The federal government's budget decisions inevitably involve balancing the demands of some groups against those of others. Congressionally established budget rules set forth in a series of federal laws define the scope of tradeoffs. They help determine which issues are most salient to lawmakers, and they can make budget outcomes and the decisionmaking process more transparent to the electorate. Congress began to construct the procedural framework that guides modern budget decisions when federal budgeting became an especially acrimonious and partisan process in the late 1960s and early 1970s.[60] Conflicts among those competing for federal benefits resulted in greater and more apparent political strife as the crisis of the ballooning federal budget deficit, combined with several years of slow economic growth and the reduction in revenue caused by the indexation of tax benefits and entitlement programs, brought pressure to bear on budget decisions. The budget framework established incrementally over the following 25 years, a period typified by large cash-flow deficits, continues to shape most important allocative decisions, even as the country enters a prolonged era of budget surpluses. Indeed, it has been estimated that over 40% of the Senate's work occurs in the context of some sort

---

[59]The following discussion is largely drawn from Elizabeth Garrett, *Harnessing Politics: The Dynamics of Offset Requirements in the Tax Legislative Process*, 65 U. Chi. L. Rev. 501 (1998), and Elizabeth Garrett, *Rethinking the Structures of Decisionmaking in the Federal Budget Process*, 35 Harv. J. Legis. 387 (1998).

[60]For a clear discussion of the federal budget process, see Allen Schick, *The Federal Budget: Politics, Policy, Process* (1995). The major congressional budget acts include the Congressional Budget and Impoundment Act of 1974, the Gramm-Rudman-Hollings Balanced Budget and Emergency Deficit Control Act of 1985, the Budget Enforcement Act of 1990, and the Balanced Budget Enforcement Act of 1997.

of budget legislation,[61] and virtually all legislation may trigger particular budget rules in one or both houses.

Unlike the Unfunded Mandates Reform Act, a procedural framework that works to protect underenforced constitutional norms, the budget process laws attempt to solve collective action problems, channel and harness interest group activity, and structure fiscal decisions into manageable parts. To the extent the budget process implicates constitutional values, they are the structural ones relevant to the largely unwritten *fiscal constitution*. Understanding the effect of the budget process on legislative activity requires that we understand the objectives it was designed to serve.

First, designing a budget, and allocating scarce resources, is a daunting task for humans with *bounded rationality* and limited cognitive abilities. In theory, to reach rational and comprehensive decisions, lawmakers must pit all parts of the budget against all others at the same time to direct funds to the uses that promise the greatest return to the public. Realistically, however, budget decisions have to be structured, and arenas of conflict limited in scope, to allow lawmakers to make decisions in a timely fashion.

Second, those devising a congressional budget framework hope to *coordinate* the unwieldy legislative process so that Congress can better respond to executive branch proposals. For decades, Congress had developed its budget in a highly decentralized fashion so that lawmakers and voters had difficulty both developing an accurate picture of the magnitude of spending that resulted and controlling individual decisions so that they accorded with larger spending objectives. For example, the appropriations committees were fragmented into various subcommittees that were at best weakly controlled by a central authority. Different substantive committees oversaw the financing decisions for entitlement programs or the tax legislation required to fund them all. The pressures of the budget deficit, which required coordinated collective action to meet spending reduction targets, required a new organization.

---

[61]See Catherine Fisk & Erwin Chemerinsky, *The Filibuster*, 49 Stan. L. Rev. 181, 216 n.191 (1997).

Lawmakers have adopted a budget process that divides decisions into very large arenas of conflict. Policymakers set macrobudgetary spending or revenue goals within these packages and then make tradeoffs among the programs within each budget package. The budget is split primarily into two arenas: discretionary spending programs that receive periodic, usually annual, appropriations, and entitlement programs[62] and tax provisions that typically remain in effect until repealed. Most budget scholars would place Social Security into a separate third package because it is extraordinarily protected by budget process rules. Social Security is technically off-budget, although all the figures for budget deficits and surpluses that are used by politicians and the media include the Social Security trust fund, which currently runs large cash-flow surpluses. Other congressional rules also protect Social Security from congressional raiding.[63] In the House of Representatives, a proposal to increase benefits or cut the payroll tax must include benefit or tax changes sufficient to leave the trust fund's long-term actuarial balance unchanged. The Senate protects the program through a congressional single-subject rule: no legislation proposing changes to Social Security can be part of a large omnibus budget bill but must instead be considered on its own. This rule is important not only because it prohibits logrolling within any bill amending Social Security, but it also allows for a filibuster, unlike some budget legislation that is immune to a filibuster under current Senate rules.

Discretionary spending is controlled by statutory spending caps that have often been decreased in real terms (and sometimes in nominal terms as well). If spending exceeds the statutory limit, the executive branch is required to enforce the cap by implementing a sequester, an across-the-board cut of funding for most programs within the package. Funding that is characterized as emergency

---

[62]In budget process terminology, these are called *direct spending programs*. Entitlement spending is actually a subset of direct spending, although it is the most important for purposes of PAYGO (discussed below). Direct spending is any spending pursuant to a binding legal obligation to pay, including, for example, interest on the national debt.

[63]See Edward Davis, *Points of Order Under the Congressional Budget Act of 1974*, CRS Publication 91-347 GOV, April 12, 1991 (listing these and other budget rules empowering members to raise points of order).

spending, a purely political determination made by Congress and the President jointly, is unconstrained by the discipline of the caps.[64] For congressional budgeting purposes, the discretionary package also has subdivisions that correspond to the jurisdiction of the thirteen appropriations subcommittees. If an appropriations bill violates its allocation of money, a lawmaker can prevent its consideration by raising an objection, a process called raising a point of order. The powerful Rules Committee in the House typically waives budget points of order in the rule that structures floor consideration of a bill. In the Senate this point of order can be waived, but only by a vote of 60 Senators. Notice what this elaborate system of spending caps and allocations means for funding decisions. New programs receive funding only if they can fit within predetermined limits. They can succeed legislatively only if some previously funded programs receive fewer funds or no money at all. Because of these de facto offset requirements, those seeking federal funds must also adopt the role of funding predator, finding weakly supported programs to eliminate or cut back.

The other large budget package consists of revenue provisions and non-Social Security entitlement programs. Decisions in this package are enforced not through spending caps, but through an explicit offset requirement called the pay-as-you-go (PAYGO) provision. PAYGO requires that any entitlement spending or revenue bill that increases the deficit in any fiscal year must be offset by legislation reducing spending or increasing revenues so that the net deficit is not increased. PAYGO is enforced through a sequester of nonexempt entitlement programs, a procedure similar to the enforcement tool in the discretionary context. Most entitlement programs, most notably Social Security, are exempt from the threat of a PAYGO sequester.

---

[64]In the past several years, many have argued that Congress has increasingly used the emergency spending loophole solely to evade the spending caps rather than to respond to unforeseen crises. See Congressional Budget Office, *Emergency Spending Under the Budget Enforcement Act* (Dec. 1998) (noting that the 105th Congress approved $21.4 billion in emergency spending, the highest level in the 1990s, excluding funding for the Persian Gulf war); Stanley Collender, *The Guide to the Federal Budget: Fiscal 2000*, at 87-88 (1999) (discussing political nature of determination and questioning its use in fiscal year 1999).

While both sides of the budget are affected by offset require-ments, the nature of the competition engendered by the PAYGO requirement is different from the conflict that characterizes the discretionary side of the budget. In most cases of discretionary spending, the offset process occurs within the jurisdiction of the relevant appropriations subcommittee, which often places the competition within a subset of programs related loosely by subject matter. For example, the Senate Appropriations Subcommittee on Agriculture, Rural Development, and Other Related Agencies oversees many, but not all, of the programs affecting agriculture. Thus, committee members, as well as representatives of interest groups, are experts on agriculture policy and are more likely to make intelligent tradeoffs among competing uses of funds allocated to this government activity. In contrast, groups proposing a new tax subsidy are not limited to finding offsets in a universe of programs that serve largely the same general governmental objective or benefit similar groups. Instead, such proponents can meet PAYGO requirements by eliminating any current tax benefit or entitlement spending. For example, advocates of a new tax deduction for the oil and gas industry compete against all other beneficiaries of tax proposals and entitlements, not only against others seeking funds for the develop-ment of energy resources. Such diverse combatants may allow for the kind of robust pluralism of many competing interests that reduces the threat that policymakers will be captured by the groups they regulate. The appropriators in the agriculture subcommittee receive a substan-tial portion of their campaign contributions from agricultural interests, while the lawmakers that work in the PAYGO arena receive support and information from many strong, and often competing, groups. The latter configuration of interest groups may result in policies that more often serve the public good, rather than the objectives of a narrow segment of the economy with targeted clout.[65]

A framework like the budget process profoundly affects the deliberation surrounding appropriations bills and other budget laws, as well as the eventual budgetary outcomes. The structure can be accurately thought of as Madisonian in that it is constructed not

---

[65]See Edward Zelinsky, *James Madison and Public Choice at Gucci Gulch: A Procedural Defense of Tax Expenditures and Tax Institutions*, 102 Yale L.J. 1165 (1993).

necessarily to serve efficiency concerns but to prevent the abuse of power. Supermajority voting requirements to waive points of order make particular actions more difficult for lawmakers. Although such requirements can be changed by majority vote because they are merely internal rules of procedures, the political cost of actions that appear fiscally irresponsible to voters can be substantial. Legislative structures also determine what issues are salient and thus will tend to dominate the debate. For example, the current system requires Congress to set out aggregate spending and revenue goals first and then allocate resources among programs within that context. Accordingly, the macrobudgetary issues remain at the forefront of all subsequent congressional debates. The discussion regarding the fiscal year 2000 budget, when significant cash-flow surpluses have been projected, emphasized the effect of the stingy discretionary spending caps established several years earlier during a period of preoccupation with budget deficits. Without such a framework, Congress would find it considerably easier to dissipate the surplus through tax cuts or new spending programs.

The congressional structure also affects interest group behavior. To return to a theme from Chapter 3, a structure that incorporates offset requirements as an enforcement mechanism changes the legislative environment from a distributive one, where all participants receive governmental benefits, to a zero-sum one with identifiable winners and losers. Or, to use Michael Hayes' terminology from his transactional model of legislation,[66] offset requirements move us from the arena of client politics to the more contentious arena of interest group politics. In the latter arena, potential losers that have clout can often block enactment of new spending programs. Of course, predators seeking new programs realize the ramifications of this shift to a more competitive environment and thus may target diffuse and less-well-organized groups. Again, the structure of the conflict will determine whether such targeting is possible; for example, can the well-organized oil and gas lobby pay for their new benefits by repealing programs that help the poor? Or are they forced by the boundaries of budget packages to pick on groups of equal power and influence?

---

[66]See Chapter 3, Part IIC.

Legislative rules can also structure interest group conflict so that it produces a helpful byproduct for legislators: free information about federal programs. As predators seek offsets, they generate information not only about their own programs but also about the programs they propose to repeal or scale back. Although they may target programs on the basis of interest group clout, choosing relatively weak and unorganized beneficiary groups, they will phrase their arguments differently in public, discussing the relative merits of the programs. In this way, the conflict engendered by offset requirements produces information that lawmakers can use to make allocative decisions, along with the information generated by government agencies and experts. The scope of interest group conflict affects the quality of the information. A structure such as PAYGO that pits groups from different industries or subject matters against one another might lead to lower-quality information than one that packages related groups together. In the latter framework, groups might have more knowledge and understanding of the federal programs that could serve as offsets, and thus they could disclose better and more helpful information.

Finally, and not surprisingly given our understanding of the influence of procedures on legislative outcomes, legislative rules play a large role in determining the content of the bills that Congress enacts. If the interest group dynamics vary depending on the budget package, groups may draft their programs with the objective of falling into a particular package. For example, if very tight spending caps limit the ability of Congress to appropriate money to discretionary programs, hopeful beneficiaries will seek goodies in the form of tax subsidies or entitlement programs. If funding predators identify more programs that benefit weak interest groups in a particular budget package, they may work to fit into this package with the more susceptible prey. The current budget process works to achieve cash-flow balance and to avoid cash-flow deficits; thus, programs are drafted so that most of the spending occurs in future years. The success of such timing gimmicks can be reduced by requiring budget balance for several years into the future, but the time line cannot be infinite. Accounting games are common throughout the federal budget arena: pay dates shift from one year to another; changes in estimated tax provisions speed up the receipt of money so that it falls within the budget window; and sales of capital assets provide money for new spending programs. The now famous Roth IRA and related legislation, enacted in 1997, were heavily back-loaded; they were estimated to lose only $1.8 billion during the five-year PAYGO window, but would lose more than $20.2 billion over ten years.[67]

This discussion gives you a sense of the complexity of the budget process, a framework that shapes virtually all congressional decisions because allocating resources lies at the heart of governing. Any vision of due process of lawmaking would be incomplete without an awareness of these internal structures that affect deliberation, collective action, and interest group dynamics. One cannot make sense of legislative outcomes without understanding the environment in which they were crafted. Moreover, legislators increasingly are adopting similar frameworks to shape or generate information, channel activity, and tip the balance in favor of predetermined objectives. Not only has Congress recently enacted the Unfunded Mandates Reform Act, with its framework for the consideration of some intergovernmental mandates, but it also imposed a Tax Simplicity Analysis on committee consideration of all significant tax proposals in an effort to increase the salience of tax complexity for legislative drafters.[68] Congress is considering various proposals to impose procedural frameworks on the consideration of most regulatory bills. Rather than moving to eliminate non-constitutional vetogates and streamline the legislative process, the modern Congress has appeared to embrace proceduralism. The explanation for this trend is no doubt complicated: perhaps Congress hopes to improve deliberation in the republican tradition; perhaps lawmakers seek to reduce their ability to pass laws at all, consistent with some liberal theory; or perhaps they are responding to voter demands for action (such as to improve fiscal accountability) when substantive decisions are politically difficult.

---

[67]See Joint Committee on Taxation, *Estimated Budget Effects of the Conference Agreement on the Revenue Provisions of H.R. 2014, the "Taxpayer Relief Act of 1997," Fiscal Years 1997-2007* JCX-39-97 (July 30, 1997).

[68]See Internal Revenue Service Restructuring and Reform Act of 1998, § 4021, Pub. L. No. 105-206, 112 Stat. 685 (1998).

III.   The Effect of Outside Forces on the Legislative Process

Legislator behavior is shaped not only through the rules that afford particular kinds of legislative activity more protection than other political activities and through the rules that structure the drafting, deliberating, and enacting of bills. It is also profoundly influenced by groups that interact regularly with lawmakers, playing a role in policy formation and affecting whether lawmakers can achieve their objectives. Indeed, perhaps the most important insight of institutional theory is that each institution is shaped by other institutions with which it comes into contact. In this chapter, we will look at three such institutions: lobbyists who represent interest groups, the chief executive and the role he or she plays in enacting laws, and the administrative bureaucracy and the role it plays in implementing laws. Our analysis will give you only a flavor of the complex and varied interactions because the policymaking game is one that can go on indefinitely — there are very few players who have the last word in a matter.

A. *The Regulation of Lobbying: Relying on Disclosure To Combat Corruption*[69]

A system of representative democracy contemplates that communication from the people to their representatives will influence legislative behavior. Republicans argue that lawmakers should deliberate about the public good in a process that considers constituent views but is not entirely driven by them. Republicans may be concerned that efforts to influence lawmakers can be so pervasive that they distract legislators from their deliberative duties; if certain interests are more successful than others in gaining access or presenting their case, legislative outcomes will reflect that bias. Optimistic pluralists are less concerned about outside influence on lawmakers and thus advocate less regulation of lobbying. Viewing lawmakers as the accommodators of interest group pressures, who must assess the strength of the conflicting interests and reach an appropriate policy compromise, these liberal theorists consider the effort to influence lawmakers a vital part of the process itself.

---

[69]See Eskridge & Frickey 292-323; Eskridge, Frickey & Garrett 1998 Supp. 56-66; Hetzel, Libonati & Williams 1039-1117; Mikva & Lane 521-92.

Regardless of these differences, all the visions of good government depend on the public's taking advantage of the constitutional right to petition the government for the redress of grievances and to speak freely and fully about significant political issues.

If citizens want to maximize their influence, they will often organize into groups that seek to sway lawmaker and public opinion, and they may hire professionals with expertise in the policymaking process to guide them through the procedural hurdles of the legislature. Whether singly or as a group, whether advised by a professional or not, citizens who seek to influence legislative decisions are *lobbying* the government. John Wright provides a comprehensive definition of lobbying, which includes "efforts at cultivating and maintaining good working relationships with legislators; engaging in public relations and advertising campaigns; organizing and mobilizing constituents at the grassroots; making campaign contributions; researching policy issues; gathering information about legislators' voting intentions and the legislative agenda; testifying before congressional committees; and communicating directly with legislators, their personal staff, or committee staff."[70]

At its heart, lobbying is an informational process. Lobbyists inform lawmakers about constituent preferences and interests; they inform legislators about the effects of particular policies and problems that demand government solutions; they inform lawmakers about the preferences of other lawmakers so that proponents of policy change can successfully negotiate the vetogates of Congress; and they inform the public about lawmakers' views and efforts regarding policies. Armed with current information, lobbyists seek access to lawmakers, both to gather additional data and to use the information they have to influence legislative outcomes in their favor. Obtaining access includes a variety of activities. Lobbyists certainly seek private, face-to-face meetings with lawmakers and important staff, but they also spend a great deal of time seeking access to more public forums. As Jeffrey Berry points out: "Contrary to the image of lobbyists as back-room operators, much of their time is taken up in trying to be visible. They spend valuable time at congressional

---

[70]John Wright, *Interest Groups and Congress: Lobbying, Contributions, and Influence* 75 (1996).

hearings even though nothing of great consequence is likely to happen there — it's a chance to touch base with other lobbyists and congressional staffers. . . . They are constantly reminding legislators, staffers, and other lobbyists that they are around and that their views ought to be considered when policy decisions are being hammered out."[71]

Lobbyists can use a variety of strategies to impart information and exert influence, and technology has expanded the number of these strategies. Often they form coalitions, usually ad hoc groups to respond to a particular issue, in order to maximize their clout and resources. Increasingly, they use state-of-the-art telecommunications technology to mobilize substantial grassroots support. *Grassroots lobbying*, or efforts designed to encourage constituents to contact their representatives, is hardly new. Lobbyists have long exhorted members of groups to "Write your Congressmember!" and used ads and editorials to create public outcry. The modern difference is in the method of communication: constituents can now instantly email and fax lawmakers' offices. Lobbying firms can contact people identified through computer-generated lists of individuals whose profiles suggest sympathy with a particular issue and then arrange for those people to call legislators free of charge.

Although this technology may result in a deluge of information, it is not inherently corrupt to provide more information, more quickly, to lawmakers and constituents. The concern with lobbying that has prompted cries for regulation stems from three other factors.

First, it appears that all this information and activity may leave representatives little time for reflection or calm discussion. Scholars have identified an advocacy explosion in the lobbying realm. Professor Loomis notes that in 1977 there were around 4,000 Washington-based interest representatives; in 1991, there were more than 14,500. He estimates that in 1994, 91,000 people earned their living from Washington-based attempts to influence public policy.[72] Lobbying resulted in expenditures of over $1.4 billion in 1998, a 13% over the year before and a total that works out to $2.7 million per

---

[71]Jeffrey Berry, *The Interest Group Society* 96-97 (3d ed. 1997).

[72]See Burdett Loomis, *The Contemporary Congress* 35 (1996).

lawmaker.[73] This level of expenditures suggests a related concern about lobbying: it absorbs substantial financial and human resources that might be deployed in more efficient ways, particularly when the government responses to lobbying do not further the public good.

Second, as in the arena of campaign finance regulation, the well-funded are better able to manipulate the tools of lobbying than are the unorganized or less wealthy. This political environment is not different from others we have discussed — it is not robustly pluralistic but rather reflects some interests at the expense of others. Even grassroots movements, which require a significant amount of popular support, are expensive to run effectively, so only groups that can pay the price of admission can take advantage of technology to generate a flood of coordinated constituent communications.

Finally, many worry that the information produced by lobbyists is not accurate, or at least not complete. Some misrepresentation may be deliberate, although a professional lobbyist must be careful to avoid being caught in a lie because a reputation for accuracy and truth is one of her most valuable assets. On the other hand, a lobbyist seldom reveals everything she knows. Instead, she provides information selectively and may not indicate fully the extent and intensity of the grassroots support for a policy. In some cases, lobbying will occur on all sides of an issue, providing legislators complete and accurate information through the interchange among interest groups. As Professors Lupia and McCubbins observe in a discussion about the benefits of institutional design aimed at increasing competition among groups, "[T]he presence of a verifier creates competition in information provision, since the first information provider is aware that the effectiveness of any statement he makes could be affected by the verifier's statement. Thus, in legislatures where the likelihood that there will be informed adversaries is high, so is the probability of verification."[74] Legislators also have staffs to check and generate information, and Congress has established a number of organizations, such as the Library of Congress, the General Accounting Office, and

---

[73]See Allan Shuldiner, *Influence: The Bottom Line on Washington Lobbying* 3 (1999).

[74]Arthur Lupia & Mathew McCubbins, *Who Controls? Information and the Structure of Legislative Decision Making*, 19 Legis. Studs. Q. 361, 370 (1994).

the Congressional Budget Office, to provide additional data and to verify third-party information. However, these avenues of verification do not work perfectly, and the possibility that policy will be based on incomplete or inaccurate information is real.

Recognizing these problems but also acknowledging the importance of communication between policymakers and interested constituents, Congress has passed two major laws regulating lobbying. In 1946, Congress enacted the poorly drafted Federal Regulation of Lobbying Act.[75] The Act was motivated by a liberal concern about the accuracy of information provided by lobbyists "who do not visit the Capitol but initiate propaganda from all over the country in the form of letters and telegrams, many of which have been based entirely upon misinformation as to facts" and lobbyists "who are employed to come to the Capitol under the false impression that they exert some powerful influence over Members of Congress."[76] Accordingly, the law required disclosure from persons receiving contributions or spending money to influence legislation. It also mandated that paid lobbyists register with Congress and disclose their activities. The law was enforced through criminal penalties of fines and imprisonment.

The 1946 Act was attacked on First Amendment grounds, because it placed burdens on political expression, and on due process grounds, because it allegedly was too vague to give fair notice of the behavior it prohibited. In *United States v. Harriss*,[77] the Court construed the Act in a convoluted fashion so that it survived the challenge. It held that the Act applied only to persons who solicited, collected, or received contributions, and not to those who solely spent money to influence legislation. In addition, the Court required that one of the main purposes of the collection of contributions must be to influence the passage or defeat of legislation through direct communication with members of Congress. Only the requirement that the money be

---

[75]60 Stat. 839, originally codified at 2 U.S.C. §§ 261-264, 266-267, 269, repealed by Lobbying Disclosure Act of 1995, 109 Stat. 691, 2 U.S.C. §§ 1601-07.

[76]S. Rep. No. 1400, 79th Cong., 2d Sess. 27 (1946).

[77]347 U.S. 612 (1954). The Court justified its strained interpretation through use of the canon counseling that courts should avoid deciding serious constitutional questions. For a discussion of this canon, see Chapter 9, Part IIA.

intended to influence legislation can be found easily in text of the Act; the other aspects of the Court's interpretation are, at best, strained or, more accurately, invented to evade any constitutional doubts about the statute.

By narrowing the scope of the legislation so severely, the Court rendered the Act a dead letter. The Justice Department ceased to enforce the Act, and many who worked to influence the legislative process ignored the Act's disclosure and registration requirements. Yet the presence of a lobbying regulation act reduced the pressure on Congress to enact a law that would have a meaningful effect. When constituents complained about the advocacy explosion and demanded solutions, members could point to the Federal Regulation of Lobbying Act as a vehicle to provide information about lobbying activities.

Finally, in 1995, the public outcry grew loud enough to convince lawmakers to pass more comprehensive legislation. The Lobbying Disclosure Act of 1995[78] continues the older law's emphasis on disclosure and registration, but it identifies new objectives in addition to correcting inaccurate or misleading information. The Act includes findings that will resonate with republican theorists, specifically that "responsible representative Government requires public awareness of the efforts of paid lobbyists to influence the public decisionmaking process" and that increased disclosure of lobbying "will increase public confidence in the integrity of Government."[79] It does not include other possible legislative purposes, such as providing information about political connections between special interests and lawmakers in order to improve voter competence. Nor are any egalitarian concerns cited as a justification for regulation. Equality concerns might provide a basis for more aggressive regulation than disclosure and registration, although in the related context of campaign finance reform, the courts have been unwilling to limit political speech for this reason.

The Act requires that lobbyists register with Congress and file semiannual reports disclosing their clients, the issues on which they

---

[78]Pub. L. No. 104-65, 109 Stat. 691, codified at 2 U.S.C. §§ 1601-07.

[79]2 U.S.C. § 1601(1), (3).

lobbied, and the amount of money paid for lobbying activities.[80] Although the data can be somewhat general, for example, estimates can be rounded to the nearest $20,000, the information is much more extensive than that demanded by the 1946 law. Those who refuse to comply are given time to remedy the situation or face the possibility of a civil fine calibrated to account for the gravity of the violation.[81]

Most of the Act consists of definitions, delineating the people it covers and the activities that must be disclosed.[82] A *lobbyist* is any individual retained for compensation for services that include more than one lobbying contact. The Act exempts from coverage such an individual whose lobbying activities consist of less than 20% of the services rendered for the client during a six month period. A *client* need not be a third party; it can be a company with employees who act as lobbyists on behalf of the company, or it can be a coalition of organizations. The Act does not directly require a client to disclose any information or register with Congress. The duty of disclosure falls on the hired lobbyist, whose report will reveal clients and interests.

The Act defines *lobbying contact* broadly, and primarily through a series of exceptions. A lobbying contact is any "oral or written communication (including an electronic communication) to a covered executive branch official or a covered legislative branch official that is made on behalf of a client" with regard to a range of government activities, including legislative matters, administrative activities, or the nomination or confirmation of an executive branch official. This definition is much more inclusive than the previous one, which was limited to attempts to influence the passage or defeat of a particular bill through direct communication with legislators. The exceptions fall into four general categories: (1) ministerial or de minimis activities (e.g., a request for a meeting as long as there is no attempt to influence a covered officials); (2) information that other laws require people to disclose (e.g., disclosure pursuant to the Foreign Agents Registration Act[83]); (3) contacts that are required by other law

---

[80]See *id.* §§ 1603-04.

[81]See *id.* § 1606.

[82]All definitions appear in *id.* § 1602.

[83]22 U.S.C. §§ 611 *et seq.*

or court order; (4) and hardship cases (e.g., disclosure protected under the Whistleblower Protection Act[84]). If the lobbyist has performed more than one lobbying contact for a client, she must disclose the fees relating to all *lobbying activities*, which include preparation and planning, research, and other background work that is intended to be used in lobbying contacts. Interestingly, some lobbyists do not interpret that term to include *strategic counseling* or the service of providing advice to clients about how Congress is likely to deal with a particular issue or how the client itself can lobby the government.

The Act thus plugs many of the loopholes of the old law and requires disclosure that is more extensive and helpful to lawmakers and voters. The information is available in media reports and via the Internet. Before the Act went into effect, only 6,000 individuals and organizations had registered with Congress. Within six months, that number had nearly doubled. At this writing, over 20,000 individuals are registered.[85]

Perhaps the largest remaining loophole is also the fastest growing segment of the lobbying industry — grassroots lobbying. Public interest groups, labor unions, and business interests combined in their opposition to disclosing information about grassroots lobbying; thus, removing grassroots lobbying from its scope was necessary to assemble majority support for the law. Lawmakers offered somewhat strained First Amendment justifications for their decision. Although disclosure is certainly a burden on the right to petition, one can imagine several compelling state interests that might justify some regulation of grassroots lobbying. Certainly, grassroots campaigns depend on mass popular support, but the technology required to make them effective is available only to well-funded interests, often those that also exercise clout through traditional means.[86] Moreover, even if the citizens mobilized by phone banks and grassroots strategies articulate sincere positions on an issue, professional tactics often create an intensity of interest that did not exist before the lobbying campaign. Thus, an interest in accuracy could support a law that

---

[84]5 U.S.C. §§ 1211 *et seq.*

[85]Current information is available on the website of the Center for Responsive Politics: <http://www.opensecrets.org>.

[86]See Richard Davis, *The Web of Politics* 81-82 (1999).

requires disclosure of the money spent to amplify constituents' voices.

B. *The Line Item Veto Power*[87]

The influence that outside institutions can have on Congress is related to the tools such institutions can deploy in the political game. Lobbyists are influential because they provide lawmakers with information, represent interests whose members will vote on the basis of the legislator's record, and control campaign contributions made by large groups of individuals through PACs or bundling. Similarly, the President or governor plays a substantial role in the legislative process. For example, the President is the chief initiator of legislative proposals by virtue of his national stature, his control over a bureaucracy filled with experts and legislative drafters, and the advantages inherent in his unitary office relative to a collective body. The chief executive also has tools that can be used at the end of the legislative process, such as the veto and, in most states but not the federal government, the line item veto. Legislators are aware that the executive branch has the last word, subject to their ability to override a veto with a supermajority vote. Positive political theory and other institutional theories teach that this awareness will have profound influence on the legislative process and the dynamics of bargaining and deliberation.[88] To see how this works in practice, let us look more closely at the line item veto.

The constitutions in 43 states grant governors a line item veto power. All but one of these states limit the governor's use to appropriations bills.[89] Most of the states require the governor to disapprove of an item in its entirety; only 10 governors have the

---

[87]See Eskridge & Frickey 256-61; Eskridge, Frickey & Garrett Supp. 36-55; Hetzel, Libonati & Williams 1178-80, 1183-93; Mikva & Lane 669-99, 702-09; Popkin 881-96, 907-13.

[88]See William Eskridge, Jr. & John Ferejohn, *The Article I, Section 7 Game,* 80 Geo. L.J. 523 (1992).

[89]See Richard Briffault, *The Item Veto in State Courts,* 66 Temple L. Rev. 1171, 1175 (1993).

power to reduce items as well as eliminate them.[90] All states allow the state legislature to override a line item veto, usually through a supermajority vote.[91] Although constitutions establish the line item veto power, the breadth of the governor's power depends on the state courts' interpretation of the term *item* in the constitutional provisions. Wisconsin courts allow the governor to veto words and phrases, and perhaps even letters from words and digits from numbers as long as the resulting law makes sense.[92] No other state court has adopted an approach that so substantially strengthens the hand of the governor. In fact, some state courts defer entirely to the legislature's decision of how to package provisions, thereby allowing the legislative branch to insulate provisions from the line item veto by including them as part of a popular provision that the governor dare not cancel. For example, the Oklahoma legislature appropriated over $285,000 for the state university and then directed how the money should be spent. The governor used his item veto to disapprove only some of the directions, with corresponding apportionments; he allowed over two-thirds of the money to be spent. The state court invalidated the governor's act, reasoning that the aggregate number was the item, and the Constitution required the governor to eliminate an item entirely. The apportionment of that money for specific purposes did not result in separate items; the provisions were merely directions about how the lump sum should be spent.[93] Other courts have allowed governors to veto such provisions, adopting less deferential tests to determine what parts of a law are separate items.[94] Thus, for a clear sense of the extent of a governor's power, one must consult both the state constitution, which is typically rather general, and the relevant court decisions.

---

[90]See Ray Brown, *The Line Item Veto: How Well Does It Work?*, 36 Gov't Acct. J., Winter 1987-88, at 19-20.

[91]See Briffault, *supra* note 89, at 1176.

[92]See *State ex rel. Wisconsin Senate v. Thompson*, 424 N.W. 2d 385 (Wis. 1988).

[93]See *Regents of State Univ. v. Trapp*, 113 P. 910 (Okla. 1911).

[94]For an excellent discussion of the various judicial tests, see Briffault, *supra* note 89.

The line item veto is justified through arguments very much like those supporting the single-subject requirement. A line item veto reduces the pressure on a chief executive to accept provisions she finds repugnant in order to enact the bulk of a law she supports. Unlike the traditional veto, a line item veto is a targeted weapon. The line item veto also reduces logrolling, supporters of the procedure claim, because the governor can unravel deals by vetoing only one part of the bargain. In virtually all state constitutions, it is targeted at appropriations bills because these are especially susceptible to rent-seeking and logrolling. Most state constitutions also have balanced budget requirements, and the line item veto power is viewed as a way for the governor to enforce that requirement. State legislators face the same collective action problems that we discussed in the context of the federal budget process. If they favor reduced government spending but worry that members will defect from that strategy to send pork back to their home districts, they can solve their problem by allowing a third party with different electoral incentives — here, the governor — to enforce their larger objective. Supporters of the line item veto as a tool to control spending argue that the governor has a statewide constituency and, in most states, faces term limits, so she may be more willing to eliminate wasteful programs.

The federal Line Item Veto Act,[95] recently found to be unconstitutional by the Supreme Court,[96] was intended to combat the same sorts of problems. The cancellation power that it delegated by statute to the President was limited to spending programs, which included not only programs in appropriations bills but also tax provisions that are equivalent to spending programs. Again, it seems clear that the drafters of the federal Line Item Veto Act wanted to restrain federal spending through proceduralism, that is, by erecting new hurdles in the legislative process.

Given the agreement among supporters of the state item vetoes and the similar federal statutory power about the purposes the tool serves, it seems appropriate to explore whether the line item veto can achieve these objectives. The most obvious limitation is that the line

---

[95]Pub. L. No. 104-130, 110 Stat. 1200, codified at 2 U.S.C. §§ 691-692 (Supp. II 1996).

[96]See *Clinton v. City of New York*, 118 S.Ct. 2091 (1998).

item veto does not threaten programs that the chief executive supports. Only those programs added by the legislature to the governor's budget submission are likely targets that will need supermajority support to become effective. Furthermore, the programs that the governor supports may become easier to enact, and therefore more plentiful, because the governor's bargaining position with the legislature is stronger when she wields the additional weapon of the line item veto. Of course, gubernatorial support for spending programs is valuable even in states without the line item veto. The chief executive's budget can often serve as a starting point for legislative drafters, and the governor is a potent lobbyist, particularly in states with part-time, largely amateur legislators.

The line item veto significantly enhances the value of the governor's support for a program because she does more than set the budget agenda by laying out a comprehensive plan at the beginning of the process. She has a credible way to threaten to unravel deals struck in the legislature. Without the line item veto, groups that cannot obtain the governor's support can lobby the legislature for funds and be relatively certain that once they are included in the appropriations bill, they will receive their benefits. It is very unlikely that a governor will veto an entire spending bill, providing money for many of her priorities, in order to deny funding to a few programs she opposes. The line item veto makes it less difficult for the governor to cancel particular programs, because she does not face an all-or-nothing choice with each spending bill; interest groups and legislators thus know that she is more likely to exercise her power. If she decides to allow projects that she does not support to receive funding, the line item veto allows her to extract a price for her forbearance. It changes the dynamics of bargaining, making the governor a more vital force in the legislative negotiations.

Note that the line item veto does not necessarily mean that overall spending will be lower in states with the procedure than in states without it. Although some governors might use the threat of cancellation to extract lower spending from the legislature, it seems more likely that governors will use the power to shift spending toward their priorities.[97] Governors are ambitious politicians who hope to develop a reputation that will allow them to move to higher elected office. A few may hope to develop a reputation for fiscal austerity, but most seek to establish new programs that are popular with the voters and symbolize their policy agenda. In fact, absent a balanced budget requirement or some sort of global spending limit, we might predict higher levels of spending in states with the line item veto. The governor is transformed into a powerful player whose support must be assured, along with a majority of lawmakers. That support might be obtained by eliminating proposals the governor cannot support, but it can also be bought by enacting programs she favors. Moreover, she may be willing to enact some proposals she finds distasteful if the legislature agrees to fund even more of her policies. In this plausible scenario, the line item veto would only add programs to an appropriations bill, rather than eliminate a substantial portion of the funding.[98]

Professor Stearns draws on the transactional model of legislation that we studied in Chapter 3 to develop a dynamic model that captures the effect of the line item veto on legislative bargains.[99] Take, for example, a general interest bill that produces widely distributed benefits by imposing widely distributed costs. To assemble majority support for such a proposal, legislative advocates may reach deals with the representatives of minority interests that are adversely affected by the bill to reduce the cost to them. For example, provisions lessening the effect of an environmental bill on coal producers is such a *substantive bargain*. Other votes will be obtained by lengthening the bill to include additional riders that provide narrowly distributed benefits to an interest group. Such a *length bargain* in the context of our environmental bill might be to add a provision establishing a tax credit for the independent oil and

---

[97]Compare Glenn Abney & Thomas Leuth, *The Line-Item Veto in the States: An Instrument for Fiscal Restraint or an Instrument for Partisanship?*, 45 Pub. Admin. Rev. 372 (1985) (usually the latter), with James Alm & Mark Evers, *The Item Veto and State Government Expenditures*, 68 Pub. Choice 1 (1991) (item veto can reduce state spending when governor and legislature are of different parties).

[98]See Daniel Shaviro, *Do Deficits Matter?* 291-92 (1997).

[99]See Maxwell Stearns, *The Public Choice Case Against the Item Veto*, 49 Wash. & Lee L. Rev. 385 (1992)

gas industry in return for their support of a bill that otherwise imposes negative effects on their businesses.

According to Stearns' model, how does the line item veto disrupt bargaining? In most states, legislators can still make substantive bargains because such deals will seldom result in a new provision that will meet the definition of item. Instead, the bargains can be embodied in conditions or provisos embedded in legislative provisions. The length bargaining relating to riders (and substantive bargains that can only be drafted as separate items under state case law) may change, because these provisions are threatened by gubernatorial cancellation. Will such deals disappear? Absolutely not. The relevant bargainer is now the governor, or her legislative agents, who can credibly promise to withhold her item veto and allow the rider to be added safely. Her promise will not be free, however, for she will extract some benefit that she values. Stearns' model of the effect of the line item veto is consistent with the state experience. Studies of the line item veto reveal that its use has altered the mix of spending programs rather than the level of spending. The tool allows the governor more influence over the shape of the budget, and it plays a greater role when the two branches are controlled by different political parties.[100]

Thus, a sophisticated understanding of institutional relationships and of the preemptive responses to expected actions by other players in the future reveals that the line item veto does not eliminate logrolling or porkbarrel legislation. It merely improves the hand of one of the players, the chief executive. Given this scenario, we should see very few exercises of the item veto power once all the players understand the bargaining dynamics that it entails. Proponents of new spending programs, who understand the rules of the game, pursue one of several options. They sometimes determine that the benefit they seek is not worth enough to justify meeting the additional costs imposed by the presence of a line item veto, and thus they drop out of the legislative arena. They may work to draft provisions that are not susceptible to the power because they do not

---

[100]See Elizabeth Garrett, *Accountability and Restraint: The Federal Budget Process and the Line Item Veto Act*, 20 Cardozo L. Rev. 871, 916 & n.183 (1998) (collecting studies).

meet the definition of an item. Or they may convince the governor not to eliminate their program, either at the outset of the budget cycle when her staff prepares her submission or at a later stage in the negotiations. Just as occurs with other changes in legislative procedures, legislative actors also understand the game's dynamics and adjust their behavior accordingly. Of course, we will observe occasional use of the item veto power in cases where parties have been misinformed, when the governor uses the power for symbolic reasons, or when the legislature sets up a line item veto on a politically charged issue with the hope it will affect the next election. Again, this prediction is borne out in practice; governors use the item veto power primarily for partisan and policy reasons.[101]

C. *Congressional Interaction with the Executive Branch: The Legislative Veto and Oversight*[102]

Just as the President's veto power affects the content of legislation and the dynamics of bargaining, congressional expectations relating to the implementation of its directions influence legislative drafting and the extent of legislative oversight. A legislature inevitably faces an agency problem: it must rely on others to execute its policy directives. The agency problem is particularly tricky because the bureaucrats who implement the laws are more directly the agents of the President, who often has very different policy preferences from the legislature. Two types of solutions are possible: a legislature can pick trustworthy agents who will not shirk from its instructions, or it can learn enough to monitor agents and discipline them. Congress uses a mixed strategy, employing both techniques to seek fidelity from its agents. We will focus here on two examples of monitoring — the legislative veto and congressional oversight — but it is worth mentioning a few examples of congressional attempts to ensure that administrators have close allegiances to the legislative branch and will therefore require less monitoring.

---

[101]See, e.g., James Dearden & Thomas Husted, *Do Governors Get What They Want?: An Alternative Explanation of the Line-Item Veto*, 77 Pub. Choice 707, 718-19 (1993); Douglas Holtz-Eakin, *The Line Item Veto and Public Sector Budgets*, 36 J. Pub. Econ. 269, 291 (1988).

[102]See Eskridge & Frickey 909-52; Hetzel, Libonati & Williams 817-30, 1308; Mikva & Lane 637-49; Popkin 913-27.

Since the beginning of the modern administrative state early in this century,[103] Congress has created some agencies that are relatively independent from the President. As with other high-level executive branch officials, the administrators of these agencies must receive the advice and consent of the Senate to be appointed. Heads of independent agencies, unlike heads of executive branch departments, cannot be removed from office by the President except for reasons listed in the statute.[104] Usually, the enumerated reasons are limited to disability, inefficiency, neglect of duty, malfeasance, or criminal activity. In short, the President probably cannot remove the head of an independent agency on the basis of a policy disagreement. By restricting the President's removal power, Congress hopes that commissioners will be less faithful to his agenda and perhaps more interested in following the wishes of Congress, particularly given the legislature's ability to use oversight and appropriations to discipline wayward agents.

The need for monitoring would also be reduced if Congress could draft narrow and precise statutes that afforded agencies minimal discretion. Open-textured language allows a wider range of policy choices that will comport with the congressional instructions and therefore survive judicial scrutiny. For example, the Food and Drug Administration (FDA) has more latitude in setting policy when it is instructed to ensure that drugs, broadly defined, are "safe and effective,"[105] than when Congress spells out more particularly which drugs can be regulated and to what standards of safety they will be held. More concretely, the general language would seem to allow the FDA to regulate cigarettes, which are "intended to affect the structure

---

[103]See Robert Rabin, *Federal Regulation in Historical Perspective*, 38 Stan. L. Rev. 1189 (1986).

[104]See *Humphrey's Executor v. United States*, 295 U.S. 602 (1935). The other edge of this sword, from Congress' point of view, is that the Court has forbidden Congress itself from exerting removal or appointment authority. See, e.g., *Metropolitan Washington Airports Auth. v. Citizens for the Abatement of Aircraft Noise*, 501 U.S. 252 (1991); *Buckley v. Valeo*, 424 U.S. 1 (1976) (per curiam).

[105]21 U.S.C. § 393(b)(2)(B).

or any function of the body of man or other animals,"[106] even though no one believes that the Congress that enacted the Food and Drug Act in 1938 expected that the agency's jurisdiction would expand to include such tobacco products.[107] General language empowers Congress' agent to act consistently with the statutory text but in ways very different from the principal's expectations. Unfortunately for lawmakers, however, their ability to avoid general directives is limited. Often Congress cannot assemble majority support for precisely worded statutes, and in many cases general language is required to allow for necessary regulatory flexibility and updating.

In short, the devices available to restrain agency discretion *ex ante*, control over appointments and textual specificity, are imperfect and sometimes undesirable if they also reduce beneficial exercises of discretion. Thus, legislators must monitor agency implementation and discipline unfaithful agents. If agency heads know that Congress has this power and will use it, they are more likely to act consistently with congressional wishes in order to avoid punishment.

To monitor effectively, Congress must first develop accurate information regarding its agents' actions.[108] Members can develop their own expertise, either personally or through their staff. For example, lawmakers on substantive committees possess some element of expertise and use it to monitor agencies when they seek additional statutory authority or appropriations. In addition, members can obtain information from outside sources. One such source is the agent itself, and recent legislative proposals have been designed to increase the amount of information provided by the regulators. For instance, the proposed Regulatory Right-to-Know Act of 1999 would require the President to submit along with his budget an "accounting

---

[106]Under the Act, "drugs" are "articles (other than food) intended to affect the structure or any function of the body of man or other animals." 21 U.S.C. § 321(g)(1)(C).

[107]See *Brown & Williamson Tobacco Corp. v. FDA*, 153 F.3d 155 (4th Cir. 1998) (holding FDA regulations of cigarettes to be inconsistent with the statutory directives, notwithstanding the broad language), *cert. granted*, 119 S.Ct. 1495 (1999).

[108]See Lupia & McCubbins, *supra* note 74.

statement and associated report containing an estimate of the total annual costs and benefits of Federal regulatory programs."[109]

Congress recognizes that the agency may not be fully forthcoming in response to inquiries or in testimony before committees; thus, it has established various governmental third parties to monitor agency implementation of statutes. The General Accounting Office, for example, was established in 1921 to perform audits of the administrative branch and to modernize budgeting and accounting methods. Now it helps Congress in its oversight responsibilities by providing information and recommendations to improve performance and management. Congressional committees themselves hold oversight hearings, soliciting input from the agency, entities like the GAO, and people and businesses affected by the regulation. They hope that a robustly pluralistic system, full of competing interests, will provide them the data necessary for effective monitoring.

Unfortunately, congressional oversight is not always conducive to learning. Often, as we have seen vividly in recent years, Congress uses oversight purely for political purposes, not to gather accurate information and devise new policy. Legislative enthusiasm for oversight activities occurs only episodically and usually only in arenas that promise high visibility for lawmakers, who face substantial opportunity costs with respect to the time they spend in oversight. Public choice theory also presents a bleak assessment of congressional oversight. Assuming that the only goal of legislators is to be re-elected (a simplistic assumption but accurate at least as an intermediate goal necessary to accomplish other objectives), David Mayhew argues that oversight will be characterized by two negative features.[110] Oversight will manifest *particularism*, or focus on narrow issues that will yield concentrated benefits for people or institutions that the legislator wants to help, perhaps because they have financial and political clout. On issues of general concern, oversight will result in only *inaction or symbolic action* that will pacify the masses but result in little real change. This prediction is premised in part on the transactional model of legislation we discussed in Chapter 3, which can be used to explain a variety of legislative activities.

---

[109]H.R. 1074, § 4(a), 106th Cong., 1st Sess. (1999).

[110]See David Mayhew, *Congress: The Electoral Connection* 134-40 (1974).

Collecting information may change agency behavior slightly once it is publicized, but to control its agents most effectively, legislators must be able to discipline recalcitrant bureaucrats. Congress can always pass legislation abolishing the agency, transferring its powers, or narrowing its statutory powers. This course of action is difficult, because agency supporters can block the legislation at one of the procedural hurdles and the President, whose policy preferences may align with the agency's, can veto the legislation and force a super-majority vote. More important, Congress can also use its power of the purse to encourage agencies to move in a particular direction, perhaps by enacting appropriations riders that refuse funding to disfavored activities.

The relationship between Congress and the Internal Revenue Service is a good example of this sort of legislative enforcement. In 1970, the IRS ruled that schools with racially discriminatory policies could no longer be considered "charitable" institutions entitled to tax exemption and to receive donations that are tax-deductible. Although opponents of this policy could not convince Congress to overturn it, a rider was added to the Treasury, Postal Service, and General Government Appropriations Act of 1980 to deny the IRS funds to enforce this new policy aggressively.[111] Many reasons could explain the opponents' ability to pass a rider on an omnibus appropriations bill but not to enact a separate bill nullifying the IRS policy. Our discussion of federal rules similar to the single-subject rule suggested that the deliberation of appropriations riders may be less searching and that small pieces of a funding bill can be overlooked in the rush to keep the government up and running. In a more recent example of congressional oversight, significantly reduced appropriations to the IRS in the late 1990s, along with the appointment of a bipartisan commission on Restructuring the IRS and a series of high-profile hearings in Congress on IRS abuses, prompted an overhaul of the tax agency and the nomination of an IRS Commissioner with a back-ground in business and technology, rather than in tax administration. As a result of the oversight hearings, Congress passed legislation implementing some of the recommendations of the bipartisan

---

[111]See discussion of this episode in *Bob Jones Univ. v. United States*, 461 U.S. 574 (1983), excerpted and discussed in Eskridge & Frickey 815-28; Popkin 541-43.

commission to establish various new controls over the IRS,[112] but much of the legislative pressure on the agency was exerted in less direct ways.[113]

In view of the difficulty in passing legislation to discipline agencies, legislatures devised a different sort of enforcement technique. A *legislative veto* is a statutory mechanism that renders the implementation of agency decisions subject to some further form of legislative review or control, usually for a specified time. So, for example, a vote of one house of the legislature or even one committee would be sufficient to nullify the agency's action. Or, in the case of a positive legislative veto, the agency action would not be effective unless some part of the legislature, often the substantive committees, had approved.

The federal legislative veto made its first appearance in the Reorganization Act of 1932, which delegated to the President very broad powers to reorganize the executive branch. Congress was willing to delegate broadly but only with the assurance that it could retain some measure of continuing control that did not require presidential approval. The use of this tactic accelerated in the 1960s and 1970s as Congress delegated substantial power to administrative agencies; one scholar puts the number of legislative vetoes at nearly 300 by 1982, with 78 enacted between 1979 and 1982.[114]

Although Congress continues to enact legislative vetoes, the Supreme Court struck down this enforcement tool in *INS v. Chadha*.[115] Using a formalistic approach to the separation of powers, the Court invalidated a legislative veto that allowed one house to nullify the Attorney General's decision to allow a deportable alien to remain in the country. The legislative veto, a legislative action changing a federal policy, was unconstitutional because it violated the

---

[112]See Internal Revenue Service Restructuring and Reform Act of 1998, P.L. No. 105-206, 112 Stat. 685.

[113]See, e.g., National Commission on Restructuring the Internal Revenue Service, *A Vision for the New Internal Revenue Service* (1997).

[114]See Joseph Cooper, *The Legislative Veto in the 1980s*, in *Congress Reconsidered* 364, 367 (Lawrence Dodd & Bruce Oppenheimer eds., 3d ed. 1985).

[115]462 U.S. 919 (1983), excerpted and discussed in Eskridge & Frickey 921-35; Hetzel, Libonati & Williams 817-30; Mikva & Lane 639-48; Popkin 915-22.

bicameralism and presentment provisions of the Constitution. The legislative veto was the equivalent of passing a law to discipline the agency and thus was required to meet the procedural requirements for enacting laws. Many state courts have used similar reasoning to invalidate state legislative vetoes, although this result is not uniform.[116]

An excellent empirical study of the effect of the legislative veto suggests that its invalidation may not significantly affect Congress' ability to discipline wayward agencies, and that *Chadha* will almost certainly not increase the pressure on Congress to draft statutes delegating authority to agencies more narrowly. Jessica Korn concluded, after a series of case studies of the use of the legislative veto, that the practice was never a particularly important weapon in the arsenal of congressional oversight. "Members did not need the legislative veto shortcut to force executive branch officials to attend to congressional concerns, because the most useful sources of congressional oversight power — the power to make laws, and the power to require that executive branch and independent agency officials report [to committees] proposed actions before implementation — are well nestled in the authorities granted to members by Article I of the Constitution."[117] Of fourteen potential oversight mechanisms, the legislative veto ranked last in terms of frequency of use and ninth in terms of effectiveness.[118] Members preferred to incur the costs to enact new legislation in cases of politically visible problems, or to consult informally with agency administrators on the basis of information often required by law to be disclosed to Congress.

Although the invalidation of the legislative veto slightly reduced Congress' power to discipline its agents *ex post*, other forces, some of which we discussed in Chapter 3, continue to discourage legislators from using precise and detailed statutory directives to reduce

---

[116]See, e.g., *Mead v. Arnell*, 791 P.2d 410 (Ida. 1990) (upholding a state legislative veto).

[117]Jessica Korn, *The Power of Separation: American Constitutionalism and the Myth of the Legislative Veto* 116 (1996).

[118]See Joel Aberbach, *Keeping a Watchful Eye: The Politics of Congressional Oversight* 132 (Table 6-1), 135 (Table 6-2) (1990).

agency discretion *ex ante*. Lawmakers may be able to avoid negative reactions from organized interests who would be harmed by more pellucid directives but who can take advantage of vague or ambiguous statutes to influence captured regulators and avoid the imposition of costs. Nonetheless, the behavior of legislators here, as elsewhere, will be profoundly influenced by their ability to pick faithful agents, to learn of any deviations from congressional wishes, and to reorient policies so they are consistent with current congressional intentions.

6

Theories of Statutory Interpretation

For most lawyers the biggest payoff of the study of legislation is what it teaches about the theory and practice of statutory interpretation, which is the main topic in most courses.[1] This chapter will introduce the leading theories of statutory interpretation, and the next three chapters will explore the doctrines linked to each general theory. As we did in Chapters 2 and 3, we shall focus on *prescriptive* theories that tell citizens, agencies, and judges how they ought to interpret statutes. Three basic approaches will be considered: statutory meaning should be governed by legislative intent, or by textual meaning, or by a more dynamic, pragmatic assessment of institutional, textual, and contextual factors.

Before addressing these theories in detail, it might be useful to distinguish between the overall *goal* of interpretation prescribed by such theories and the admissible *sources* the interpreter may consider in attempting to achieve that goal. For example, intentionalist theories agree that the goal of interpretation ought to be figuring out legislative intent, but intentionalist theories have reached no consensus concerning what constitutes the appropriate evidence of that intent. For many intentionalists, legislative history — the documentary materials produced at the various stages of legislative consideration and passage — serves as a useful source for illuminating the meaning of statutory text. Contrarily, other intentionalists contend that statutory text, perhaps as read against the general background of enactment, provides a far more reliable indicator of legislative intent than the multifaceted, potentially manipulable, and often unfocused and even contradictory pieces of legislative history.[2] Thus, it is

---

[1] Two of the four current casebooks devote most of their coverage to statutory interpretation (Eskridge & Frickey 66-106, 383-481, 513-905; Popkin 180-700), and the other two devote considerable space to the topic (Hetzel, Libonati & Williams 387-727; Mikva & Lane 321-65, 755-1050). All of the casebooks devote special attention to the main theoretical debates that are discussed in this chapter, and two (Eskridge & Frickey 513-632; Mikva & Lane 755-803) devote whole chapters to introducing students to the theories of statutory interpretation.

[2] On the debate over the use of legislative history, see Chapter 8, Part II.

important to understand that the debate over interpretive methodology concerns not only broad conflicts among the three basic approaches, but lines of disagreement about how each approach should be undertaken.

Just as theories of representation rest on theories of state legitimacy,[3] so might prescriptive theories of statutory interpretation. Three different kinds of norms are potentially at work: *the rule of law idea* that statutory meaning should be relatively predictable and accessible to the citizenry and should be neutrally applied to everyone; *the democratic legitimacy idea* that interpreters ought to defer to decisions made by the popularly elected legislators who enact statutes; and *the pragmatic idea* that interpreters have an obligation to contribute productively to the statutory scheme and, perhaps ultimately, to the common good. Different theories of statutory interpretation — intentionalist, textual, and dynamic — might be tested against their ability to contribute to the rule of law, to democratic legitimacy, and to productive statutory schemes.

In addition to the prescriptive theories, we shall discuss *descriptive* theories that tell us what citizens, agencies, and courts actually do when they interpret statutes. Our own descriptive theory, drawn from Supreme Court practice in the post-World War II era, is pragmatic as to both goals and sources. That is, problem-solving judges in the real world are guided by several different goals when they construe statutes, and they consider a variety of sources for meaning. Pragmatic theory would describe at least some of the state court systems differently, especially as to sources considered. One insight of pragmatism is that different theories of interpretation will usually reach the same results. For example, should a municipal ordinance prohibiting "vehicles in the park" apply to a tricycle? The answer is probably no: the operative term, *vehicle*, does not ordinarily include tricycles; the goal and specific understanding of the legislators was to regulate cars and other dangerous machines, and not little ones like tricycles; it would be unreasonable and perhaps absurd to give the gendarmerie discretion to harass children on their harmless tricycles. This is an *easy case* because the major theories of statutory interpretation all lead to the same result.

---

[3]See Chapter 2.

Many issues that you will encounter in your career are easy ones, theoretically at least. Law professors are more interested in *hard cases*. Throughout this chapter, we explore the different approaches in light of their application to two very hard cases that have received extensive scrutiny from scholars of legislation.

In *Church of the Holy Trinity v. United States*,[4] the Supreme Court interpreted an 1885 statute criminally prohibiting anyone from contracting with an "alien" to pay his transportation to the United States "to perform labor or service of any kind." The Court's 1892 decision held the law inapplicable to a church's importation of a pastor from England. Almost 100 years later, the Court in *United Steelworkers v. Weber*[5] construed Title VII's rule that employers and unions cannot "discriminate against any individual" because of "race" to be inapplicable to an affirmative action training program designed to remedy a gross underrepresentation of minority craft workers. What methodology should the Court have followed in each case? Are the decisions justifiable under criteria other than those emphasized by the Court? What should have been the results?

I. Intentionalist Theories

Anglo-American theories of statutory interpretation have traditionally emphasized *legislative intent* as the object or goal of statutory interpretation.[6] A key reason why statutes ought to be

---

[4]143 U.S. 457 (1892), excerpted in Eskridge & Frickey 518-24; Mikva & Lane 828-35; Popkin 230-35. Our analysis of *Holy Trinity* draws from Carol Chomsky, *The True History of the* Holy Trinity *(Case)*, 100 Colum. L. Rev. ___ (2000) (forthcoming); William Eskridge, Jr., *Textualism, The Unknown Ideal?*, 96 Mich. L. Rev. 1509 (1998); Adrian Vermeule, *Legislative History and the Limits of Judicial Competence: The Untold Story of* Holy Trinity Church, 50 Stan. L. Rev. 1833 (1998).

[5]443 U.S. 193 (1979), excerpted and discussed in Eskridge & Frickey 71-99; Hetzel, Libonati & Williams 456-82; Mikva & Lane 835-55; Popkin 472-76. Our analysis of *Weber* is a distillation of William Eskridge, Jr., *Dynamic Statutory Interpretation* 14-31, 35-44 (1994).

[6]See, e.g., *Commissioner v. Engle*, 464 U.S. 206, 214 (1984); 2A Sutherland, *Statutes and Statutory Construction* § 45.05 (1984 ed.); Richard Posner, *The Federal Courts: Crisis and Reform* 286-93 (1985); Learned Hand, *How Far Is a Judge Free in Rendering a Decision?*, in *The Spirit of Liberty* 103, 105-10 (3d ed. 1960). The earliest expanded treatment was in *A Discourse Upon the Exposicion*

obeyed is that they are directives from the legislature that We the People have elected and that our Constitution has charged with issuing such directives. Citizens, agencies, and judges should therefore also apply those directives in a manner consistent with the expectations of their authors. This seems defensible and simple. But it's not simple and may not be defensible.[7]

The trouble starts when you try to determine what is meant by legislative intent: Is it the *specific intent* of the legislators, how they actually decided a particular issue of statutory scope or application? An *imaginative reconstruction* of what the legislators would have decided had they thought about the issue? Or the legislature's *general intent*, its *purpose* in enacting the law? The most legitimate basis for statutory interpretation under an intentionalist theory would be actual specific intent, but that is typically hard to discover, and it is completely unknowable when interpreters face new problems unanticipated by drafters. As the inquiry becomes steadily more abstracted from specific intent, however, not only does its democratic legitimacy fade, but the inquiry becomes less determinate and perhaps more driven by nonlegislator value choices, hence in tension with the rule of law. Finally, intentionalist theories do a poor job of explaining the results in leading cases such as *Holy Trinity* and *Weber*. Are such cases wrong? Or are the theories wrong?

A. *Specific Intent*

Critics of *Holy Trinity* and *Weber* maintain that those decisions were contrary to the specific intent of the Congresses that enacted the Alien Contract Labor Law of 1885 and the Civil Rights Act of 1964, respectively. Pointing to Congress' concern with a deluge of manual laborers from abroad who were assertedly driving down wages in this country, the Court in *Holy Trinity* reasoned that § 1 of the contract labor statute, which excluded aliens imported "for labor or service of

---

& *Understandinge of Statutes With Sir Thomas Egerton's Additions*, a sixteenth century manuscript published in 1942 by Samuel Thorne.

[7]For views of philosophers on this issue, compare Andrei Marmor, *Interpretation and Legal Theory* (1992) (arguing that legislative intent should be the goal of statutory interpretation), with Jeremy Waldron, *Law and Disagreement* (1999) (arguing against legislative intent as the goal of statutory interpretation).

any kind," was not meant to exclude "brain toilers," and certainly not Christian ministers. The Court might be criticized, however, for invoking legislative intent and then ignoring most of the actual legislative deliberations. In the Senate, an opponent of the legislation lampooned the bill for specifically exempting artists and lecturers, but not other professionals, like lawyers and sculptors; this was arbitrary, he argued. The Senate floor manager seemed to agree: "If that class of people are liable to become the subject-matter of such importation, then the bill applies to them. Perhaps the bill ought to be further amended."[8] Further amendment never occurred even though, contrary to the Court's implication, there was opportunity for revision. This exchange could be viewed as the proverbial "smoking gun" evidence of a specific legislative intent that importing *any* alien from abroad for labor or service in the United States violated § 1 of the statute, unless the alien fell within an exemption, such as § 5's exclusion of lecturers and the like.

Similarly, in his *Weber* dissent, then-Justice Rehnquist exhaustively reviewed the legislative history of Title VII and found smoking guns galore: statements by Senate sponsors who repeatedly reassured the chamber that the statutory anti-discrimination rule meant that there could be no hiring or firing based on race whatsoever — thus precluding employers from considering the race of employees even when the desire was to create a more racially balanced work-force rather than to exclude anyone based on racial animus.[9] Nonetheless, the majority relied in part on the touchstone of legislative intent in approving the remedial affirmative action program.

Under these analyses, the Church in *Holy Trinity* and the Steel-workers Union and Kaiser (the employer) in *Weber* were seeking to escape from directives aimed at prohibiting their conduct, and the judiciary was derelict in enforcing those directives. Not only does it seem undemocratic for these private bodies and their supporters on the Court to ignore legislative intent, but it also seems lawless. Indeed, if this happened often in our system, Congress might have less enthusiasm for cutting the deals needed to get legislation through

---

[8] 16 Cong. Rec. 1633 (1885) (exchange between Sens. Morgan [opponent] and Blair [sponsor]), discussed in Vermeule, *supra* note 4, at 1849-50.

[9] *Weber*, 443 U.S. at 238-39 (Rehnquist, J., dissenting).

the many vetogates described in Chapter 3, because such deals would not reliably be judicially enforced. Furthermore, disrespect for the rule of law might allow people to believe they can get away with more shirking of their lawful responsibilities.

These conclusions assume that the Court in *Holy Trinity* and *Weber* violated the statutory deal and betrayed the clear intent of Congress. To reach that conclusion is not easy, though, and the difficulties reveal both theoretical and practical limitations of specific intent as a lodestar for interpretation.

Any "legislative intent" is not only a collective intent, but under Article I, Section 7 of the Constitution must be a coincidence of at least two different collective intents, that of the Senate and the House. Thus there are problems of *aggregation*: Did a majority of the Senate that voted on the alien contract labor bill agree with the sponsor's concession? The full House? President Harrison, who signed the alien contract labor bill into law? Because none of these people spoke to the issue, the only way to solve the aggregation problem is by invoking legislative conventions — for example, committee reports and statements of sponsors may be deemed to represent the enacting coalition, much as the leading Federalists are taken to represent the coalition seeking ratification of the Constitution.

Unfortunately, this attempted solution to the problems of aggregation leads to problems of *attribution*. Invocation of conventional or constructed intent immediately sacrifices some of the normative appeal of intentionalism's professed goal, which is to implement the *actual* intent of the enacting Congress. And it may place too much weight on reports subject to manipulation and statements made in the course of heated, phony, or strategic debates. Much as a used car salesman can engage in a lot of *cheap talk* (this car will last a lifetime!) without legal responsibility, so might legislators (this is not a quota bill!). Perhaps, as positive political theorists say, the intentionalist inquiry ought to focus on the preferences of the *pivotal* legislators, those participants in the enactment process whose support was critical in helping a bill go through the various vetogates that can kill legislation.[10] Of course, it's not always

---

[10]See McNollgast, *Positive Canons: The Role of Legislative Bargains in Statutory Interpretation*, 80 Geo. L.J. 705 (1992).

easy to figure out who were the pivotal legislators and what were their sincere preferences, which are bound to be conflicting and hard to aggregate.[11]

Finally, the evidence of actual intent might itself be subject to varying interpretations. Consider a possible smoking gun in *Holy Trinity*. A diehard opponent accused the bill of arbitrary exemptions, favoring lecturers but not lawyers (a defensible distinction, perhaps). The flustered, and frankly rather dim, floor manager said that the bill only applied to "the importation of such people under *contract to labor*" (so maybe did not include lawyers to start with?) and then said this: "If that class of people [under contract to *labor*] are liable to become the subject-matter of such importation, then the bill applies to them. Perhaps the bill ought to be further amended." The opponent promised an amendment exempting all professionals. Neither senator actually introduced such an amendment, and no one else mentioned the colloquy after that. An even more general statement was made in the House. In neither chamber was there a single mention that ministers might be objects of the bill. This gun may have produced little smoke.[12]

Note that *Holy Trinity* involved a statute that was fresh when the Court construed it. A more typical case is *Weber*, where some time elapsed between the statute and its application. Justice Rehnquist's dissent made much of sponsor statements that employers "would not be obliged or indeed permitted — to fire whites in order to hire Negroes, or to prefer Negroes for future vacancies," even if the

---

[11]For an example, consider Judge Norris's travails in the *Montana Wilderness* case discussed in Chapter 3, Part IA.

[12]Vermeule notes that when a later Congress was alerted to the Christian minister scenario, in response to the prosecution of Holy Trinity Church, it created an explicit exemption for ministers and professionals, Act of Mar. 3, 1891, § 5, 26 Stat. 1084, 1085, but made the exemption inapplicable to pending prosecutions, *id.* § 12. See Vermeule, *supra* note 4, at 1841. This is an astute point but fails to provide evidence from the legislative deliberations to suggest that a single member of the original (1885) or the later (1891) Congress intended any church to be prosecuted for bringing over a minister from abroad. The likely reason for the effective date of § 12 was constitutional or policy-based doubt that Congress should try to affect a pending judicial proceeding.

employer had an all-white workforce when Title VII took effect.[13] This seems more like a smoking gun than the *Holy Trinity* quotation, albeit subject to the aggregation and attribution problems noted above. It is also subject to the problem of changed circumstances. When the Steelworkers and Kaiser, the employer, created the affirmative action program for craft employees in 1974, the craft force in Gramercy, Louisiana, where Weber worked, was 98.2% white in a 39% black labor pool — fishy numbers ten years after Title VII had prohibited race discrimination and three years after the Supreme Court had ruled that employers could be sued for imposing qualifications that had a racially discriminatory effect.[14] The legislative record contains no statements that affirmative action could not be used to remedy fishy post-1964 employment practices, and § 706(g) of the statute explicitly allows courts to impose "affirmative action" as a remedy for violations such as this kind of potential disparate impact claim. This undermines Justice Rehnquist's specific intent argument: it is not clear that Congress considered affirmative action in the context of Weber's case. Furthermore, it reveals a primary difficulty with the search for specific intent: How specific must the legislative evidence be? Is a discussion about lawyers in the debate on the Alien Contract Labor Act a close enough fit to provide an answer for ministers?

B. *Imaginative Reconstruction*

Because of the foregoing problems with specific intent, intentionalism is pressed toward a more generalized version of the theory, *imaginative reconstruction*. The interpreter tries to discover "what the law-maker meant by assuming his position, in the surroundings in which he acted, and endeavoring to gather from the mischiefs he had to meet and the remedy by which he sought to meet them, his

---

[13] 110 Cong. Rec. 7213 (1964) (explanatory memorandum by managers of Title VII), quoted in *Weber*, 443 U.S. at 240 (Rehnquist, J., dissenting). Justice Rehnquist's use of this statement was misleading, for the managers were discussing § 703(h), which says Title VII will not affect existing seniority rights, and not § 703(a) and (d), the nondiscrimination provisions construed in *Weber*.

[14] See *Griggs v. Duke Power Co.*, 401 U.S. 424 (1971).

intention with respect to the particular point in controversy."[15] Imaginative reconstruction provides the best way to read the *Weber* dissent: the sponsors (eastern liberals) and the pivotal voters (midwestern conservatives) agreed to prohibit racial quotas to enact the Civil Rights Act over determined southern opposition, and their consensus included at least an implicit concession to the conservatives that quotas would be neither required nor allowed under the statute. Professor Chomsky engages in a similar historical archaeology for *Holy Trinity*: everyone in the legislature wanted to do something about the flood of alien laborers, which was the only focus of discussion. Given the religious values of the nation and its respect for free exercise of religion, no one would have seriously intended the law to bar recruitment of a minister![16]

It is not clear that imaginative reconstruction can avoid the aggregation and attribution problems of specific intent theory, however. Whose intent should the interpreter reconstruct? For example, who was the pivotal voter for the civil rights bill in the Senate — the 51st senator, needed to pass the bill, or the 67th, needed to break the southern filibuster? What is the fairest way to frame the question? How, then, would the pivotal voter respond? Justice Rehnquist seemed to pose the issue in *Weber* by focusing on the midwestern conservatives and asking them, "Do you want to allow voluntary quotas in hiring?" He then argued from smoking guns and their conservative values that they would have answered, "No, I want to eliminate all racial categories from employment decisions." Justice Brennan's majority opinion focused more on the liberals who were the dynamos behind the bill and asked a different question: "Would you allow voluntary preferences if it could be shown that after ten years an employer had less than 2% blacks in its craft force, and that the disparity is probably the result of the continuing effects of past discrimination?" Many of the midwestern conservatives probably would have answered *yes* to this form of the question, even if they had answered *no* to Justice Rehnquist's question.

---

[15]Roscoe Pound, *Spurious Interpretation*, 7 Colum. L. Rev. 379, 381 (1907). This approach was perfected by Judge Learned Hand, see, e.g., *Fishgold v. Sullivan Drydock & Repair Corp.*, 154 F.2d 785 (2d Cir.), *aff'd*, 328 U.S. 275 (1946), and was once espoused by Judge Posner, see Posner, *supra* note 6.

[16]See Chomsky, *supra* note 4.

Which of these questions is the more accurate reconstruction? Even if the pivotal lawmakers would have answered *no* to both questions, they might have answered *yes* to the following: "Do you think that businesses ought to have flexibility to comply with the law in various practical ways, including the hiring of blacks in order to avoid possible liability?"[17] Midwestern Republicans' core constituency, other than farmers, was small businesses fearful of government intrusion into their affairs. Such Republicans also favored a stable pluralistic system where people of color were part of the American mainstream. Given these values, they might have been tolerant of affirmative action, especially when deployed, as in *Weber*, to avoid litigation or government pressure.

This extended exercise suggests how imaginative reconstruction may be more *imaginative* than *reconstructive*, and how hard it is for intentionalists to maintain their promised link between their methodology and democratic values. The rhetorical force of intentionalism rests upon its ability to link a current interpretation to past legislative majorities. In the hard cases, however, an intentionalist often cannot prove — through rigorous vote-counting, or through conventional sources, or even through credible imaginative reconstruction — that her interpretation is the one actually intended by most legislators. All that the intentionalist can persuasively claim is that if she had asked her chosen pivotal legislator a loaded interpretive question, the legislator would, arguably, have answered in a certain way.

C. *Purposivism*

Perhaps mindful of the difficulties in showing specific or reconstructed intent, the Supreme Court majority in *Weber* justified its allowance of affirmative action by relying on Congress' *general intent*, or its *purpose* in enacting Title VII. Justice Brennan's opinion reasoned as follows: the purpose of the statute announced by its sponsors was to bring blacks into the workforce; programs such as the Steelworkers-Kaiser one employed blacks in jobs that had remained

---

[17]This form of imaginative reconstruction would be consistent with the "arguable violation" approach taken by Judge Wisdom in his dissent in the Court of Appeals and embraced by Justice Blackmun in his concurring opinion in the Supreme Court. See Part IIIB, *infra*.

closed to them even after the act went into effect; the statute should be construed, if possible, to advance the workforce-integration purpose, which the program admirably did.

This kind of reasoning has a distinguished pedigree. Purposive interpretation of statutes was a conceptual hallmark of the New Deal, classically articulated in the Hart and Sacks legal process materials,[18] and it was reflected in Anglo-American jurisprudence going back to the sixteenth century. Indeed, a leading purposivist authority is *Holy Trinity,* which invoked the "spirit" of the Alien Contract Labor Law (its purpose to prevent employers from driving down wages by bringing in manual laborers from abroad) to support its holding. *Weber* relied on *Holy Trinity* as authority for the idea that courts should construe statutes in light of their "spirit."

Purposivism attempts to achieve the democratic legitimacy of other intentionalist theories in a way that renders statutory interpretation adaptable to new circumstances. Purposivism sets the originalist inquiry at a higher level of generality. It asks, "What was the statute's goal?" rather than "What did the drafters specifically intend?" Thus, purposivism asks questions about which there may have been greater consensus in the legislative deliberations and deploys a tool that more nimbly addresses new or unforeseen circumstances. Potentially, this kind of theory reconciles democracy, the rule of law, and practical efficacy. As with other kinds of intentionalist approaches, however, general intent theory is subject to great difficulties.

A key problem is the complexity of statutory purpose itself. In *Weber*, the Court's evidence for the workforce-integration purposes (mainly statements by liberal senators) was subject to the same aggregation and attribution objections as above, as well as the objection that Congress was surely unwilling to achieve that laudable purpose at any price. (For example, § 703(h) of the statute allowed seniority arrangements to remain in place even if they had a disparate

---

[18]See Henry Hart, Jr. & Albert Sacks, *The Legal Process: Basic Problems in the Making and Application of Law* 1374-80 (William Eskridge, Jr. & Philip Frickey publication editors, 1994) (from the 1958 "tentative edition"); see also Eskridge & Frickey, *An Historical and Critical Introduction to* The Legal Process, in *id.* at lxvii-lxviii, xc-xcii, cv-cvi, cxxviii-cxxxi (background and subsequent influence of Hart and Sacks' purposivist theory of statutory interpretation).

racial impact.) Most important, the Court oversimplified the statute's purpose and suppressed a possibly competing purpose. For the more conservative supporters of the legislation, the central purpose was to make employment decisions colorblind; the ultimate goal was equality of opportunity, not equality of results. That goal was not so supportive of the color-conscious Steelworkers/Kaiser program, a point the dissent emphasized.[19] Purposivism does not yield determinate answers when there is no neutral way to arbitrate among different purposes.

Even if there were agreement as to which purpose should be attributed to a statute, the analysis in the hard cases might still be indeterminate. Often an attributed policy purpose is too general and malleable to yield interpretive closure in specific cases, because its application will depend heavily upon context and the interpreter's perspective. Not only are such judgments difficult, but they implicate political and policy considerations better suited to the branches that are more democratically accountable than the judiciary.

For example, even if Justice Rehnquist were right that Title VII's purpose was equality of opportunity, *Weber* might be rightly decided, as a remedy for unequal opportunities for workers of color under Kaiser's requirement of prior craft experience. If structural impediments to equal job opportunities for people of color remain in place, it is hardly fair to say that there is genuine equality of opportunity. On the other hand, even if Justice Brennan were right that Title VII's purpose was equality of results, Justice Rehnquist's result might be preferable. Affirmative action programs might be counterproductive in the longer term. They might exacerbate race-based prejudice or encourage stereotyping. Moreover, under a *Weber* regime, companies such as Kaiser may have an incentive not to locate their plants in areas where blacks constitute a large percentage of the workforce. Also, by reintroducing race-based hiring and promotion, affirmative action perhaps threatens to marginalize and even demoralize African Americans in the workplace, stigmatizing them as "special hires," in contrast to others hired "on the merits."

---

[19]See *Weber*, 443 U.S. at 254 (Rehnquist, J., dissenting).

II. Textualist Theories

The sponginess of intentionalist theories might suggest that interpreters should lower their sights and just apply the *plain meaning* of the statutory text — either as the best evidence of legislative intent or as the only authoritative basis for interpretation. Descriptively, the plain meaning rule will solve most statutory puzzles, and the large majority of agency and judicial constructions of statutes, almost always in the easy cases and often in the hard ones, will either be consistent with plain meaning or not contrary to it. Prescriptively, plain meaning might be the best guide for applying a statute, because plain meaning is the most obvious and perhaps the most objective focal point for all of us to know what the rule of law requires of us and our neighbors; it is probably what our elected representatives intended or would have intended the law to mean; and it is likely to provide an acceptable resolution of the controversy. One might say that the default rule in statutory interpretation is plain meaning, and that such a practice is easily defensible.

Notwithstanding these boons, the plain meaning rule has proved to be a flaccid one in the hard cases that law professors like to teach and jurists enjoy debating. A unanimous Court in *Holy Trinity* conceded (perhaps too willingly) that its interpretation was at odds with the law's plain meaning, and a majority in *Weber* invoked an exceedingly weak textual basis for its decision. In the last century, the plain meaning rule has accumulated various loopholes, which a generation of *new textualists* is trying to plug. The new textualism views the goal of interpretation to be discerning the text's meaning and strongly urges rejecting sources like legislative history. The new textualists' disdain for intentionalist sources and their claims of determinacy are also subject to critique, however.

A. *The Soft Plain Meaning Rule*

Justice Rehnquist's *Weber* dissent opened with the argument that allowing race-based affirmative action violates the plain statutory command that employers and unions cannot "discriminate against any individual because of his race."[20] He swiftly moved to consider the legislative history, however, from which he made his intentionalist case, and ultimately stated that "[o]ur task in this case, like any other case involving the construction of a statute, is to give effect to the intent of Congress."[21] This reflects the Court's practice in this century: a plain meaning can be overcome by compelling evidence of a contrary legislative intent, and so the interpreter must always check plain meaning against legislative background.[22]

Justice Brennan's majority opinion conceded the "force" of Weber's plain meaning argument but immediately trumped it with Holy Trinity's " 'familiar rule, that a thing may be within the letter of the statute, and yet not within the statute, because not within its spirit, nor within the intention of its makers.' "[23] Justice Brennan claimed that his spiritual argument was "reinforced" by § 703(j). That subsection directs that Title VII cannot be interpreted to require unions and employers with racially imbalanced workforces to grant preferential treatment to racial minorities. Justice Brennan found it significant that the subsection did not also say the statute cannot be interpreted to permit such preferences. Because the statute included the one prohibitory rule, it implicitly excluded others and left employers and unions free to follow their own policies. Justice Rehnquist found that an outrageous argument in light of affirmative action pressure that the federal government was placing on companies, like Kaiser, who had government contracts, and he traded legislative history references and insults with Justice Brennan.

Weber illustrates several interesting quandaries about what we call the soft plain meaning rule. All of the Justices operated under the assumption that the existence of an apparent plain meaning is not

---

[20]Civil Rights Act of 1964, § 703(a)(1), (d), 42 U.S.C. § 2000e-2(a)(1), (d). Justice Rehnquist also invoked § 703(a)(2), which is an even broader ban on using race to "deprive any individual of employment opportunities." Section 703(a)(2) had not been pleaded in Weber's complaint as a ground for his Title VII claim, perhaps because it was the apparent statutory basis for Griggs, discussed in text at note 14, supra.

[21]443 U.S. at 253 (Rehnquist, J., dissenting).

[22]See, e.g., Griffin v. Oceanic Contractors, Inc., 458 U.S. 564 (1982).

[23]Weber, 443 U.S. at 201, quoting Holy Trinity, 143 U.S. at 459.

dispositive, because something deeper is going on when statutes are interpreted. If I tell you, "Drop everything and come here immediately!," you do not have an obligation to "drop everything," such as the baby you are carrying, and you should not come to me "immediately" if the baby is submerged in the bathtub. The soft plain meaning rule might well be a tacit admission that the *goal* of the inquiry is intentionalist, and plain meaning is just one important *source* of information about legislative intent or purpose. Or it might be a concession to normative complexity. If the rule of law requires interpreters to apply statutes to the letter, then sometimes the cost of "lawfulness" will be too great. If the legislature tells the Titanic to follow a course that will lead it into an iceberg, the captain is justified in departing from its plain meaning — not because he has no moral or political obligation to follow it, but because other moral or political obligations are more important under the circumstances. Finally, the soft plain meaning rule might be a statement about plain meaning itself: you cannot be sure the meaning is so *plain* unless you consider the legislative deliberations and the practical consequences. Ultimately, these concerns raise significant doubts about whether one may equate an interpreter's obligation of faithfulness to the lawgiver and to the enterprise of governing a complex society with simple adherence to the apparent meaning of statutory text.[24]

All these possibilities depend on the maxim that meaning depends on context, but this is a maxim that may destabilize the plain meaning rule altogether. Does Title VII have a plain meaning governing the issue of voluntary affirmative action? This is both less clear and more clear than Justice Rehnquist recognized. His dissent assumed, as many dictionaries say, that an employer *discriminates* on the basis of race if it makes any race-based *differentiation*. In a dictionary sense, it is a correct use of the term to say "I discriminate against peaches," if I prefer pears to peaches. But that is not the way we usually use the word *discriminate*, which connotes an *invidious* differentiation.[25] It is, therefore, not so clear that § 703(a) has a plain

---

[24]See Philip Frickey, *Faithful Interpretation*, 73 Wash. U. L.Q. 1085 (1995).

[25]Indeed, one of us teaches *Weber* by reading dueling definitions of "discriminate" — one concerning disadvantaging someone because of partiality or prejudice, the other concerning drawing a clear distinction — out of his desk dictionary, which was published in 1968, just four years after Congress enacted Title VII. In

meaning favoring Weber's claim, and perhaps that is why Justice Rehnquist looked at the legislative history. Maybe the text was plain only after reading what the sponsors said about balance-the-workforce preferences and what the pivotal voters thought the purpose of the law was.

The text of the statute might also lend some support to the Steelworkers/Kaiser view, though not for the reason Justice Brennan invoked. Title VII cannot be read, literally, for the proposition that race-based preferences are never allowed, because § 706(g) allows courts to remedy violations of the law, including disparate impact violations such as those Kaiser and the Steelworkers arguably committed, with "affirmative action" and other positive remedies. Section 706(g) therefore cuts against Justice Rehnquist's assertions about statutory plain meaning. But even in connection with § 703(j), which Justice Brennan unpersuasively invoked,[26] § 706(g) hardly creates a plain meaning for Justice Brennan's position. Although unmentioned by Justice Rehnquist, the structure of § 703 supports his position: subsections (a)-(d) set forth a sweeping rule against workplace "discrimination" by employers and unions; subsections (e)-(i) carefully craft exceptions to the general rule for the regulated

---

this dictionary, the "prejudice" meaning is the first definition given. One of his colleagues does the same thing with his newer desk dictionary, in which the "clear distinction" meaning is the first definition given. In addition to showing the potential drift in meaning of the word over time — which might explain why contemporary law students tend to think the word means "distinction" rather than "prejudiced disadvantage" — this example demonstrates the inherent difficulty of locating "plain meaning" in a source external to the judge. Should the older dictionary be preferred, because it was essentially contemporaneous with the adoption of the statute? Should the newer dictionary be preferred, because it might more accurately represent contemporary usage? Should neither dictionary control because each acknowledges both dueling definitions? How can the process be controlled so that advocates and judges don't merely cite the dictionary that supports them and ignore the others?

[26]Justice Brennan argued by negative implication: because § 703(j) did not include voluntary with mandated preferences in its prohibition, it implicitly permitted them. This is an unreliable form of argument. See Chapter 7, Part IC. If Mother tells Sally, "Don't bite, kick, or hit your sister Anne," that does not implicitly authorize Sally to choke Anne. That children quickly learn to interpret parental directives through this manipulative process of negative implication is probably not a good reason for judges to follow their lead.

entities; and subsection (j) contains a no-preference directive for the EEOC and other government organs. This structure supports the broader (denotative) reading of "discriminate," with the exceptions serving narrowing functions. And the structure suggests a particular hostility to race-based classifications. Not only can they not be forced on employers by the government, but race alone cannot ever be a *bona fide* occupational qualification, according to § 703(e).[27]

B. *The New Textualism*

In his judicial opinions and the Tanner Lectures at Princeton University, Justice Scalia has defended a hard-hitting "new textualism" as the best, and perhaps only legitimate, approach to statutory interpretation.[28] Stiffening up the old soft plain meaning

---

[27]These structural arguments are explained in Eskridge, *supra* note 5, at 42-44.

Part of the difficulty in *Weber* is that so many provisions of Title VII arguably apply. Section 703(a)(1) makes it unlawful "to fail or refuse to hire or to discharge any individual with respect to . . . privileges of employment, because of such individual's race . . . ." Section 703(d) makes it unlawful for "any employer, labor organization, or joint labor-management committee controlling apprenticeship or other training or retraining, including on-the-job-training programs to discriminate against any individual because of his race . . . in admission to, or employment in, any program established to provide apprenticeship or other training." As between these provisions, § 703(d), as the more specific one concerning apprenticeship, the program at issue in *Weber*, should arguably control. It probably makes no difference, though, because both provisions use the loaded term "discriminate against," and, as we have seen, "discriminate" is arguably ambiguous. But what about § 703(a)(2)? It forbids any employer "to limit, segregate, or classify his employees or applicants for employment in any way which would deprive or tend to deprive any individual or employment opportunities or otherwise adversely affect his status as an employee, because of such individual's race . . ." Because this provision lacks the term "discriminate," it may make a major difference whether it applies in *Weber* or whether the interpreter chooses to understand the claim as arising under the provision most squarely on point, § 703(d). How "plain" is the meaning of all this?

[28]See Antonin Scalia, *A Matter of Interpretation: Federal Courts and the Law* (1997) (published version of Tanner Lectures); *Bank One Chicago v. Midwest Bank & Trust Co.*, 516 U.S. 264, 279 (1996) (Scalia, J., concurring in part); *Chisom v. Roemer*, 501 U.S. 380, 404 (1991) (Scalia, J., dissenting); *Green v. Bock Laundry Mach. Co.*, 490 U.S. 504, 527 (1989) (Scalia, J., concurring in the judgment). See generally William Eskridge, Jr., *The New Textualism*, 37 UCLA L. Rev. 621 (1990).

rule, the new textualism holds that the only object of statutory interpretation is to determine the meaning of the text and that the only legitimate sources for this inquiry are text-based or -linked sources. Thus, the meaning an ordinary speaker of the English language would draw from the statutory text is the alpha and the omega of statutory interpretation. When the text is relatively clear, interpreters should not even consider other evidence of specific legislative intent or general purpose. Justice Scalia is insistent that judges should almost never consult, and never rely on, the legislative history of a statute. That approach does not mean the judge should not consider context. The new textualist is willing to consider various sources to provide context: dictionaries, especially those contemporaneous with the statute; other provisions of the statute and how competing interpretations fit with them; how similar provisions in related or borrowed statutes have been interpreted; and so forth. Justice Scalia's theory cut its teeth on the chestnuts we have been roasting: his Tanner Lectures heartily condemn *Holy Trinity*'s anti-textualist result and methodology, and a vehement dissent arguing for overruling *Weber* is one of his most noted opinions.[29]

Justice Scalia argues that the new textualism and its disregard of legislative materials is required by the rule in Article I, Section 7 of the Constitution that a bill does not become a statute unless it has been accepted in the same textual form by both Houses of Congress and presented to the President. Because the only thing that actually becomes law is the statutory text, any unwritten intentions of one House or of one committee or of one member are not law — nor should they be used as evidence of law. Committee reports (the most-invoked evidence of legislative intent) are not only an unreliable basis for reasoning about even one chamber's intent, but they are constitutionally inadmissible sources for statutory meaning. Judicial practice of relying on committee reports violates Article I, Section 7 for the same reason the legislative veto did: it amounts to lawmaking

---

[29]See Scalia, *supra* note 28, at 18-23; *Johnson v. Transportation Agency, Santa Clara County*, 480 U.S. 616, 657-77 (1987) (Scalia, J., dissenting) (a dissent particularly noteworthy for its fascinating last substantive paragraph).

by congressional subgroups, which the Court found unconstitutional in *INS v. Chadha*.[30]

The new textualism is also, according to Justice Scalia, the methodology most consistent with the rule of law and the separation of judicial from legislative powers in our system. *Holy Trinity* and *Weber* send unfortunate signals to the public: people need not obey the letter of the law because the softies in the judiciary will bend the law and create exceptions. The rule of law requires a law of rules that are predictably applied to everyone. The worst sin of *Holy Trinity* and *Weber*, however, is the way they corrupt the judiciary, inviting willful judges to substitute their political preferences for those legitimately adopted by the legislature. This corruption relates strongly to the increased deployment of legislative history, which "is extensive, [with] something for everybody. As Judge Harold Leventhal used to say, the trick is to look over the heads of the crowd and pick out your friends."[31]

One of us suggested a pragmatic argument for the new textualism, which Justice Scalia has readily endorsed.[32] If a majority of the Supreme Court decisively adopted the new textualist methodology and rejected the use of legislative history, as the United Kingdom used to do, not only would judges be saved a lot of bother, but attorneys and their clients would save substantial amounts of time and money (respectively) that is spent on unconstitutional and unproductive research. It appears that Justice Brewer, the author of *Holy Trinity*, did not make up his mind based on the legislative history, but relied instead on a purposive approach and his firm vision of the appropriate outcome in a "Christian Nation." But his invocation of legislative history stimulated a cottage industry of junior associates, law clerks, and lobbyists whose main job is to find or plant smoking

---

[30]462 U.S. 919 (1983) (invalidating the legislative veto). The argument is made in *Bank One Chicago v. Midwest Bank & Trust Co.*, 516 U.S. 264, 279 (1996) (Scalia, J., concurring). See also *INS v. Cardoza-Fonseca*, 480 U.S. 421, 452-53 (1987) (Scalia, J., concurring in the judgment); *Thompson v. Thompson*, 484 U.S. 174, 191-92 (1988) (Scalia, J., concurring in the judgment).

[31]Scalia, *supra* note 28, at 36.

[32]Eskridge, *supra* note 28, at 669, 684-85, drawing from Reed Dickerson, *The Interpretation and Application of Statutes* 150-51 (1975); see Scalia, *supra* note 28, at 36-37; Vermeule, *supra* note 4.

guns in the legislative history. Such guns provide costly ornaments for contemporary opinions driven by other reasons, as in *Weber*. If the Court rejected the relevance of the enterprise, not only would everyone save a lot of time and money, but congressional deliberations could return to normal, unaffected by strategic plants of smoking guns that lobbyists hope to use in later interpretive battles. Note, however, that legislative history would still be generated and perhaps manipulated, because it would still influence other lawmakers during deliberations and administrative agencies during implementation.

C. *Critiques of the New Textualism*

Justice Scalia's hard-hitting attack on current practice has generated a large literature, some of it appreciative of his attack, much of it critical, and an increasing amount of it both.[33] One point of agreement that has emerged from the critical literature is that neither citizens nor judges should consider legislative history to be *authoritative* in the same way the statutory text is authoritative: the latter is and has the force of *law;* the former is, at best, evidence of what the law means. A renewed emphasis on the text as the primary source of meaning may have salutary effects for courts, legislators, and citizens. Consider some problems with Justice Scalia's other arguments, however.

---

[33]Leading critiques include Stephen Breyer, *On the Uses of Legislative History in Interpreting Statutes,* 65 S. Cal. L. Rev. 845 (1992); Daniel Farber & Philip Frickey, *Legislative Intent and Public Choice*, 74 Va. L. Rev. 423 (1988); Thomas Merrill, *Textualism and the Future of the* Chevron *Doctrine*, 72 Wash. U. L.Q. 351 (1994); Stephen Ross, *Reaganist Realism Comes to Detroit*, 1989 U. Ill. L. Rev. 399; Patricia Wald, *The Sizzling Sleeper: The Use of Legislative History in Construing Statutes in the 1988-89 Term of the United States Supreme Court*, 39 Am. U.L. Rev. 277 (1990); Nicholas Zeppos, *Justice Scalia's Textualism: The "New" New Legal Process,* 12 Cardozo L. Rev. 1597 (1991). Leading appreciations include John Manning, *Textualism as a Nondelegation Doctrine*, 97 Colum. L. Rev. 673 (1997); Jerry Mashaw, *Textualism, Constitutionalism, and the Interpretation of Federal Statutes*, 32 Wm. & Mary L. Rev. 827 (1991); Frederick Schauer, *Statutory Construction and the Coordinating Function of Plain Meaning*, 1990 Sup. Ct. Rev. 231; Vermeule, *supra* note 4. Something of both is Eskridge, *supra* note 4.

Few have found much force in Justice Scalia's Article I, Section 7 argument. *Chadha* held that the bicameralism and presentment requirements are formally applicable when "actions taken by either House . . . 'contain matter which is properly to be regarded as legislative in its character and effect,' " namely, to alter legal rights and duties.[34] As a formal matter, committee reports consulted to explain the meaning of the statute do not themselves seek to alter legal rights and duties; consulting them does not violate bicameralism or presentment any more than would consulting a dictionary. *Chadha* emphasized that bicameralism and presentment were only limitations on Congress' actions (the requirements are in Article I), and not on the actions of branches of government regulated by Articles II and III. Bicameralism is formally and technically irrelevant as a limitation on subsequent implementation and interpretation of legislation. Moreover, the purpose of the bicameralism requirement is to "assure[] that the legislative power would be exercised only after opportunity for full study and debate in separate settings."[35] The Constitution's contemplation of deliberative discussion in the legislature suggests an implicit tolerance for reviewing those deliberations on the part of those charged with interpreting and implementing the legislation. To the extent that committee reports and other legislative history shed light on the "study and debate" that Congress is supposed to engage in, the constitutional procedures of legislation would seem to support some consultation of legislative history.[36]

Nor does separation of powers necessarily support Justice Scalia's theory. One reason for separating the enactment of statutes from their interpretation is the Framers' belief in the positive consequence of common law, equitable interpretation. In *Federalist* No. 78, Alexander Hamilton maintained that courts should not only interpret statutes equitably, but might also respond to "unjust and partial laws"

---

[34]*Chadha*, 462 U.S. at 952 (quoting S. Rep. No. 1335, 54th Cong., 2d Sess. 8 (1897)).

[35]*Id.* at 951.

[36]See Eskridge, *supra* note 28; Peter Strauss, *The Courts and the Congress: Should Judges Disdain Political History?*, 98 Colum. L. Rev. 242 (1998) (accordingly, terming legislative history as political history because it provides the context from which interpreters can discern purpose).

by "mitigating the severity, and confining the operation of such laws."[37] Hamilton's reasoning was that the possibility of interpretive curtailment of unjust laws would force the legislature to qualify the severity of statutes it enacted and thereby to control more directly the scope of the statutes. *Federalist* No. 78 also warned against "the substitution of their [judges'] pleasure to that of the legislative body," but that warning was sounded in connection with Hamilton's discussion of judicial review and not of statutory interpretation. Hamilton's discussion of the limits on judicial discretion does not mention the plain meaning of statutory texts but instead stresses the judiciary's adherence to "strict rules and precedents" and its dependence on other branches for the force and will to carry out its directives.[38]

Even if one accepts Justice Scalia's premise that courts are supposed to play a neutral, nondiscretionary, and perhaps even mechanical role in statutory policy implementation, it is not clear that his new textualism advances that goal. It is mildly counterintuitive that an approach asking a court to consider materials generated by the legislative process, in addition to statutory text (also generated by the legislative process), canons of construction (generated by the judicial process), and statutory precedents (also generated by the judicial process), leaves the court with *more* discretion than an approach that just considers the latter three sources. Justice Scalia's response is that legislative history is particularly soft and manipulable, while textual evidence is harder and more determinate. If you gave 100 judges the statute in *Holy Trinity* and told them to apply a pure textualist approach, they would all agree with Justice Scalia that the church was guilty of the statutory crime. Letting the judges look at legislative history will allow some of them to bail out of the right answer. Query: Is the text in *Holy Trinity* as clear as Justice Scalia makes it out to be? Consider textualist evidence that Justice Scalia did not discuss in his Tanner Lectures: dictionaries of the period, the structure of the statute, and longstanding rules of textual construction.

---

[37]*The Federalist* No. 78, at 470 (Alexander Hamilton) (Clinton Rossiter ed. 1961); see David Epstein, *Political Theory of "The Federalist"* 188-90 (1984) (Framers generally endorsed an equity-based approach to statutory interpretation).

[38]*The Federalist* No. 78, at 471; see also *id.* at 465.

The first definition of *labor* listed in the 1879 and 1886 editions of *Webster's Dictionary* was "Physical toil or bodily exertion ... hard muscular effort directed to some useful end."[39] The first, and preferred, definition lends some support to Justice Brewer's intuition that brain toilers were not targeted by the statute. The second definition, "[i]ntellectual exertion, mental effort," was broad enough to include brain as well as manual toilers. In the 1880s, however, judges interpreting the laws and treaties excluding Chinese *labor* held that the term should be read in its primary popular sense, to mean "physical labor for another for wages," and therefore refused to include actors, for example.[40] *Webster's* first, and only relevant, definition of *service* was "The act of serving; the occupation of a servant; the performance of labor for the benefit of another, or at another's command; the attendance of an inferior, or hired helper or slave, etc., on a superior employer, master, and the like."[41] Is it 100% clear that a minister is performing "labor or service of any kind"?

The criminal prohibition is found in § 1 of the 1885 statute. Section 4 of the statute enforces § 1's prohibition by holding criminally accountable the master of a ship "who shall knowingly bring within the United States . . . any alien *laborer, mechanic or artisan*" who had contracted to perform "labor or service in the United States." Section 4 appears to be *in pari materia* with § 1 (they regulate the same class of "aliens"), and plainly regulates just manual workers (the italicized occupations). Unless there is reason to separate the coverage of the two provisions, § 4's narrow ambit might inform the ambiguous ambit of § 1. (Of course, one can imagine some reasons for limiting the liability of transporters relative to the liability of employers, so the two sections may not be *in pari materia*. The legislative history, however, suggests that they were supposed to cover the same class of aliens. Is it admissible to look at legislative history for this purpose?)

---

[39]Noah Webster, *An American Dictionary of the English Language* 875 (1879 rev. ed.). See also Henry Campbell Black, *A Dictionary of Law* 682 (1891) ("exertion of the more onerous and inferior kind").

[40]See *In re Ho King*, 14 Fed. Rep. 724 (D. Or. 1883).

[41]Webster, *supra* note 39, at 1206; see Black, *supra* note 39, at 1083 ("being employed to serve another"). See generally Vermeule, *supra* note 4, at 1853 n.87 (other dictionary definitions of "service," some of which are broader).

On the other hand, § 5 is a specific list of exemptions from the statutory exclusion, for actors, artists, lecturers, singers, and domestic servants. By specifically listing those exempted, the statute might be read as signifying that all other occupations are included. Note that § 5 equally well applies to § 4; none of the classes exempted under § 5 would have been included under § 4.

Canons of statutory construction cut various ways. The whole act rule suggests that the prohibitions in §§ 1 and 4 be read to the same effect: § 1 defines the general prohibition, and § 4 defines a mechanism (but not the only mechanism) for enforcing § 1's rule. The rule of lenity suggests that any ambiguities in this criminal statute be read against the government, and in favor of the Church's reading of the law to allow ministers, at least, to be brought into the country by contract. On the other hand, the maxim *inclusio unius est exclusio alterius* (inclusion of one thing implies exclusion of all others), which is discussed in Chapter 7, Part IC, suggests that the listed exemptions in § 5 comprise a complete list. Although the *inclusio unius* argument was a lame one in *Weber*, it is much more plausible in *Holy Trinity*, because § 5's list was vigorously debated and even amended.[42]

Does Justice Scalia's textualist methodology demonstrate, objectively and clearly, that the importation of the pastor was "within the statute: end of case," as he asserted in the Tanner Lectures?[43] That the Court in *Holy Trinity*, therefore, got the result as well as the reasoning 100% wrong? Does this sort of textualist methodology narrow the options of Justice Scalia's *bête noire*, the willful judge? Or can the willful judge "look over the heads of the crowd and pick out [her] friends" among the various textual and canonical sources? Is there no admissible role for examining the legislative record in this

---

[42]Any attempt to read "lecturer" (one of the classifications exempted in § 5) to include "minister" would be countered, in part, by invoking the canon *noscitur a sociis* (a word is known by its associates). See Chapter 7, Part IB. At least some others exempted in § 5 (actors, artists) may be short-term itinerants, suggesting that "lecturer" includes those who give a series of lectures and then leave the United States, not those who give a weekly sermon as a small part of their many ministerial duties and have potentially indefinite employment.

[43]Scalia, *supra* note 28, at 20.

enterprise?[44] Most fundamentally, is this exercise in dictionary-shopping and statute-parsing all we should be doing in statutory interpretation? Does it threaten to reduce a complex normative art to a shell game or an exercise in cleverness?

A final question is one that Professor Vermeule has raised with us: Does textualism have a robust theory of political authority?[45] If the goal of statutory interpretation is discovery of the text's meaning and the sources are limited to text- and precedent-based sources (i.e., no legislative history), do we risk creating a "law without mind"?[46] A danger of a thoroughgoing textualism is that it may sever the connection between democracy and the rule of law in ways that we should find alarming. Shouldn't it make a normative difference that a statute was enacted by legislators seeking to solve a social problem in the face of disagreement, and not by a drunken mob of legislators with no apparent purpose or who had agreed to adopt any bill chosen by a throw of the dice?

An interpreter who wishes to avoid the "law without mind" problem by maintaining a link between democratic legitimacy and statutory meaning has a variety of options, and not all of them include unlimited reliance upon legislative history. For example, if you believe that the use of legislative history causes more harm than good

---

[44]For example, the legislative record reveals that §§ 1 and 4 were aimed at the same class of contracts; that § 5 was vigorously debated and amended; and that the term *labor* was the one legislators focused on, almost always referring to manual labor when using that term. See Chomsky, *supra* note 4; Eskridge, *supra* note 4, at 1537-39.

[45]Waldron, *supra* note 7, maintains that textualism is the only approach consistent with law's authority. Waldron, a philosopher, rejects strong linkages between democracy and legislation's authority and rests the legitimacy of statutes instead with their formality: deliberation about conflicting proposals by a diverse assembly of many legislators who resolve the issue by up-or-down voting that shows respect for the differing viewpoints. See also Jeremy Waldron, *Legislators' Intentions and Unintentional Legislation*, in *Law and Interpretation: Essays in Legal Philosophy* 329-56 (Andrei Marmor ed. 1995). Waldron's theory may make unrealistic assumptions about the legislative process and about textualism, however. See William Eskridge, Jr., *The Circumstances of Interpretation and the Application of Statutes*, 100 Colum. L. Rev. ___ (2000).

[46]See generally Steven Smith, *Law Without Mind*, 88 Mich. L. Rev. 104 (1989).

in ascertaining the legislative intent associated with a statute or the best organizing purpose to attribute to it, you could simply exclude legislative history from the sources available for supporting arguments about legislative intent or statutory purpose. Such an approach is based on a pragmatic, not formalistic, argument for jettisoning consideration of legislative history. Alternatively, if you want to avoid all-or-nothing approaches but minimize the role of legislative history, you might consider the suggestion of Hart and Sacks: use the other tools of interpretation to generate the plausible organizing purposes that one should consider attributing to the statute, then consult the legislative history only to ascertain whether it suggests a plausible purpose that you missed the first time around or whether it helps resolve doubts about which of several plausible purposes should be preferred. For them, "[e]vidence in the internal legislative history of a statute concerning a particular application envisaged by individual legislators should be given weight only to the extent that the application envisaged fits rationally with other indicia of general purpose," an approach that they contended "should go a long way to take care of" the problem of legislators' manipulation of legislative history to skew judicial interpretation.[47] Again, this approach is based on a pragmatic concern about the costs and benefits of the use of legislative history in the interpretive calculus.

III.   Dynamic Theories

Democracy and rule of law values do not support intentionalist and textual theories of statutory interpretation as much as their fans insist they do. Not only do they have few conclusive implications for deciding the hard cases like *Holy Trinity* and *Weber*, they do not accurately describe the decisionmaking process in those cases. Instead, normative rather than formal or historical arguments were arguably decisive in both cases. Justice Brewer's opinion in *Holy Trinity* concluded with an overall substantive point: because the United States, in its traditions and even in its Constitution, is a religious nation, it would require a more targeted statement than § 1 of the Alien Contract Labor Law provided to criminalize a church's importation of a minister. Under this reading, Justice Brewer has

---

[47]Hart & Sacks, *supra* note 18, at 1254.

imposed a requirement of clear statement when Congress wishes to unsettle longstanding traditions and understandings woven deeply into the fabric of society. Critics of *Weber* believe and sometimes openly charge that the Court's result was driven more by public values than by attention to the legal sources. An increasing number of statutory theories defend this kind of dynamic and flexible approach.

Such theories properly start with Professor Fuller's observation that when we retell a story we are consciously or unconsciously guided by our "notion of the story *as it ought to be*." The theories are therefore normative: when interpreters apply statutes, they are making value choices. They are also dynamic. A statute as it is applied over time is, like Fuller's story, "not something that is, but something that becomes; it is not a hard chunk of reality, but a fluid process, which is as much directed by men's creative impulses, by their conception of the story as it ought to be, as it is by the original event which unlocked those impulses."[48] Dynamic theories have proliferated in the last 20 years, mainly in academe. They may explain the cases, but judges are reluctant to endorse such theories without more evidence that they are sufficiently *constraining* on judges or agencies interpreting statutes or, relatedly, offer sufficient *guidance* to the citizenry.[49]

A. *Best Answer Theories*

Some theories of statutory interpretation emphasize what we, simplistically, call *best answers*. Natural law theories maintain that statutory texts should be read to reflect the underlying moral reality inherent in those words or in the evolving statutory policy.[50] Thus, there is a morally real meaning of *labor or service* in *Holy Trinity*, and of *discriminate* in *Weber*. As we pointed out above, there are a number of different conventional ways these terms have been used.

---

[48]Lon Fuller, *The Law in Quest of Itself* 8-9 (1940). For strikingly similar language, see Ronald Dworkin, *Law's Empire* 348 (1986).

[49]Judges are more willing to endorse dynamic interpretations when they are accomplished by agencies, a point developed in Chapter 8, Part III.

[50]See Heidi Hurd, *Challenging Authority*, 100 Yale L.J. 1611 (1991); Michael Moore, *A Natural Law Theory of Interpretation*, 58 S. Cal. L. Rev. 277 (1985).

Upon what basis can we say that one of them is morally more natural than the others? Professor Hurd says that statutes should be construed to produce an "optimal state of affairs," which can be found by construing them "in light of the purposes that they may best be made to serve," rather than "the intentions which legislators had in drafting them."[51] This formulation may add little to what Professors Fuller, Hart, and Sacks have introduced into statutory theory, yet it articulates their ideas in a way certain to raise rule of law and democracy concerns.

Perhaps complementing natural law theorizing is something more openly conventional: theories based on *coherence*. Legal process theories, such as that of Professors Hart and Sacks, are classic articulations of this kind of approach: statutory text should be construed not only in light of statutory purpose, but also statutory precedents and the principles and policies followed by the polity.[52] Justice Brewer was making this kind of argument in *Holy Trinity*: the Court should be loath to construe a statute beyond its original purpose when such construction is strikingly inconsistent with traditions of religious liberty. *Weber* can be defended upon like reasoning: *Griggs* properly recognized that the integrative goals of Title VII were potentially undermined by structures of exclusion that were persisting and thus that more aggressive measures were called for.

A number of questions can be raised about this kind of approach to statutory interpretation. Does it adequately tell citizens what the law demands of them? Is it predictable? One way of thinking about rule of law and democratic constraints is the concept of *equilibrium*.[53] For some moral or policy issues, our political and legal culture reaches a consensus over time. If the consensus is unshakable in the short term, the policy can be said to be in equilibrium, and anyone who "knows" the political and legal lay of the land "knows" what the

---

[51]Heidi Hurd, *Sovereignty in Silence*, 99 Yale L.J. 945, 1028 & n.177 (1990).

[52]Dworkin, *supra* note 48, works from Fuller's idea about the evolving story and Hart and Sacks' idea of construing law in light of principles and policies and develops a theory seeking to construe statutes to make the overall story the *best it can be*.

[53]See William Eskridge, Jr. & Philip Frickey, *The Supreme Court, 1993 Term — Foreword: Law as Equilibrium*, 108 Harv. L. Rev. 26 (1994).

equilibrium is. Thus, most citizens obey the law not by looking it up in the codes or by reading committee reports, but simply by observing the way things are done and occasionally asking an authority (e.g., an IRS agent) what is expected. Justice Brewer was relying on such an equilibrium in *Holy Trinity* when he announced the Court would not construe the law contrary to the nation's religious traditions. Few citizens were surprised by the decision, and no one in Congress was at all concerned that the Court was usurping its lawmaking prerogative. Justice Brewer was simply saying what most everyone else already thought.

Justice Brennan was appealing to a similar equilibrium in *Weber*: workforce integration. An equilibrium argument does not work nearly as well for him because the polity was unsettled as to the issue of affirmative action. In fact, Justice Brennan's ratification of an open quota program was at odds with the Court's emerging constitutional jurisprudence, which rejected racial quotas. A more cautious defense of *Weber* is that later suggested by Justice O'Connor, who sought coherence between Title VII and the Court's constitutional allowance of affirmative action only for remedial purposes.[54] Even her defense, of course, is linked to a policy that remains controversial and may become increasingly so as more time passes since the civil rights revolution under the Warren Court.

Weber is troubling for another reason *Holy Trinity* may not be: Justice Brennan's treatment of the original congressional deliberations may strike many as disrespectful as well as undemocratic. Justice Brennan's response in a later case was that the Congresses of the 1970s, which were aware of the persistence of workplace segregation whose possibility the 1964 Congress suppressed, acquiesced in the *Weber* policy, even after 1980, when Republicans controlled the Senate.[55] Note, however, that the political theories from Chapter 3, especially procedural and public choice theories, suggest that Congress would not and could not override such a controversial decision supported by organized and effective interest groups.

---

[54]*Johnson*, 480 U.S. at 647-57 (O'Connor, J., concurring in the judgment).

[55]See *id.* at 629 n.7 (Brennan, J., for the Court).

B. *Pragmatic Theory*

An overall problem with the big theories of statutory interpretation is that they are based on a single foundation (text or specific intent or general intent). This ignores the pragmatic insight that our intellectual framework is not single-minded, but consists of a "web of beliefs," interconnected but reflecting different understandings and values. As a consequence, human decisionmaking tends to be polycentric, spiral, and inductive, not unidimensional, linear, and deductive. We consider several values, and the strength of each in the context at hand, before reaching a decision. Problem-solving ought to "trust rather to the multitude and variety of its arguments than to the conclusiveness of any one. Its reasoning should not form a chain which is no stronger than its weakest link, but a cable whose fibers may be ever so slender, provided they are sufficiently numerous and intimately connected."[56] Thus, the goals of statutory interpretation may be multiple and the sources may be various.

Pragmatism can support different theories of statutory interpretation. Justice Scalia, for example, makes a pragmatic argument for insisting that courts not consider legislative history: it is a waste of resources and poses more risks than benefits. Professor Vermeule makes a different pragmatic argument for a textualist source rule: courts are not institutionally competent, on average, to handle legislative history with as much sophistication and predictability as they handle statutory texts. Most pragmatic theories, however, look to multiple goals for statutory interpretation and insist on considering multiple sources. Along these lines, consider the diagram on the next page, which two of us developed to show how statutory interpretation has customarily been done in this century by the U.S. Supreme Court.[57]

---

[56]5 Charles Peirce, *Collected Papers* ¶ 264 (Hartshorne & Weiss eds. 1960).

[57]On this diagram, see William Eskridge, Jr. & Philip Frickey, *Statutory Interpretation as Practical Reasoning*, 42 Stan. L. Rev. 321, 345-62 (1990). For documentation that the diagram accurately represents the interpretive practices of the U.S. Supreme Court, see Nicholas Zeppos, *The Use of Authority in Statutory Interpretation: An Empirical Analysis*, 70 Tex. L. Rev. 1073 (1992).

The Frickey and Eskridge Funnel of Abstraction

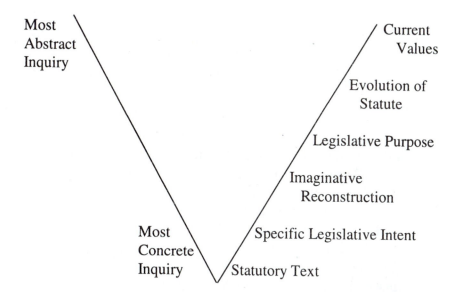

Most
Abstract
Inquiry

Current
Values

Evolution of
Statute

Legislative Purpose

Imaginative
Reconstruction

Most
Concrete
Inquiry

Specific Legislative Intent

Statutory Text

Our "funnel" reflects both the multiplicity of considerations and the conventional hierarchy ranking them against one another. For example, because statutory text is the most accessible and formally the most authoritative basis for knowing what statutes require, it is the weightiest evidence. Note also how the most concrete considerations, like text, outweigh more abstract ones, like best answer. This model also suggests the interactive process by which a practical interpreter will think about the various sources of statutory meaning: she will slide up and down the funnel, considering the strengths of various considerations, rethinking each in light of the others, and weighing them against one another using conventional criteria.

Justice Brewer structured his opinion in *Holy Trinity* along the lines of the funnel of abstraction. He conceded (candidly but perhaps prematurely) that the statutory text might support the prosecution but reconsidered that conclusion in light of the other funnel evidence: specific indication in a committee report that members did not want the law applied as broadly as the text might suggest; the narrower statutory goal of preventing employers from driving down wage rates by importing lots of manual workers from abroad; and America's tradition as a Christian Nation. Like a good pragmatist, Justice Brewer not only refused to anchor his result on just one factor, but wove together the various arguments like threads in a cable (not like links in a chain!). In the so-called *easy cases*, all the factors will either be neutral or will point toward the same answer; the mutual confirmation fortifies the interpreter's confidence that she has the right answer. Even when one factor cuts against the others in *hard cases*, thoughtful study of the factors singly and together will often lead the interpreter to a confident result.

Many supporters of the result in *Weber* believe that Justice Rehnquist's dissent deployed this pragmatic approach more effectively than Justice Brennan's majority opinion. The best pragmatic defense of the majority is one derived from Judge Wisdom's dissent in the lower court and Justice Blackmun's concurring opinion on appeal. These judges candidly acknowledged that textual and imaginative reconstruction evidence lent support to Justice Rehnquist's conclusion, although perhaps not providing such firm support as Justice Rehnquist claimed. Yet for them the integrative purpose of Title VII, as construed in *Griggs*, the evolution of the statute, and the best answer, in light of the country's sorry record of pushing people of color to the bottom, all supported the majority's result. As the most authoritative evidence supported Justice Rehnquist's position, it might be the better result — but for a changed circumstance created by *Griggs* itself. Because Kaiser and the Steelworkers had "arguably" perpetuated practices having an unlawful disparate impact on workers of color and wanted to rectify that error through voluntary preferences rather than through litigation, it made sense to allow affirmative action, at least of a remedial nature. The *Griggs*-induced dilemma not only suggested the relevance of § 706(g), the remedial provision explicitly authorizing "affirmative action," but it also suggested a less dogmatic reading of "discriminate" in § 703(a) and of the sponsors' comments suggesting that businesses should neither disfavor nor prefer blacks for positions under the law.

Textualist and intentionalist theorists can object that this multifaceted construction of *Weber* is too loose a reading of the text or legislative history to pass muster as "law," but recall that the textual and intentionalist approaches may not be significantly more determinate or predictable. Pragmatism claims the advantage of candor: the pragmatic judge must not, like Justices Brennan and Rehnquist, present a hard case as an easy one or suppress interpretive considerations that are pertinent. There is another way of criticizing this kind of pragmatic theory, however, and it is from a critical rather than conventional point of view.

C. *Critical Theories*

Critical theory has not often found its way into the statutory interpretation literature,[58] and critical scholars are carefully screened from judicial positions, but it is not hard to imagine what critical theories of statutory interpretation would look like. Critical theory is typically deconstructive but can be reconstructive as well.

Deconstruction, loosely put, opens up interpretive possibilities in statutory texts, the opposite agenda of textualist theories. Justice Brennan's deployment of § 703(j), which says the government cannot *require* race-based preferences to offset workforce imbalances, was playfully ironic, as it showed how the gaps in an anti-preference provision could support affirmative action under Title VII. The playfulness was exercised with a serious undertone of critique, however: Why should a provision put in to satisfy objectives of white conservatives not be *read* from the perspective of people of color? Justice Brennan could, even more effectively, have made the same move with *discriminate*: What does the word mean to the Gramercy blacks who had been trying for a generation to break into the craft jobs?[59]

---

[58]By critical theory, we mean work that deconstructs statutory texts, typically in order to show how particular readings are ideologically rather than objectively grounded. See, e.g., J.M. Balkin, *Deconstructive Practice and Legal Theory*, 96 Yale L.J. 743 (1987); William Eskridge, Jr. & Gary Peller, *The New Public Law Movement: Moderation as a Postmodern Cultural Form*, 89 Mich. L. Rev. 707 (1991); Peter Schanck, *Understanding Postmodern Thought and Its Implications for Statutory Interpretation*, 65 S. Cal. L. Rev. 2505 (1992).

[59]Consider Justice Brennan's argument in *Weber* that "[i]t would be ironic indeed if a law triggered by a Nation's concern over centuries of racial injustice and intended to improve the lot of those who had 'been excluded from the American dream for so long,' 110 Cong. Rec. 6552 (1964) (remarks of Sen.

Indeed, Weber, the white claimant, was making a deconstructive move, showing how the subjects benefitting from centuries of slavery and apartheid could now claim to be objects of *reverse discrimination* when remediation for continuing segregation was adopted. This analysis was particularly ironic in Weber's case, for he would not even have been eligible for a craft position if it were not for the affirmative action training program, which bypassed the older requirement of prior craft experience. Of course, the playful seriousness of Justice Brennan's arguments and the irony of Weber's position were lost on Justice Rehnquist, who cast Weber as a victim and accused Justice Brennan of Orwellian doublethink.[60] Like Justice Rehnquist in *Weber*, Justice Brewer in *Holy Trinity* was incapable of irony or deconstruction (he can be said to have trumped the law with God, a premodernist move), but his opinion can be defended by showing how chaotic the statutory text was[61] and, more deeply, how language could not capture what the sponsors of the bill were concerned with regulating.

By revealing multiple possibilities, this method deconstructs the rule of law itself. The common idea that the rule of law is a law of rules assumes a hierarchy whereby the subject (interpreter) retrieves the answer from the object (text) to which she pays homage. But if interpretation depends critically on the perspective of the interpreter even more than on what the text says, then the hierarchy is flipped: the seemingly subordinate subject actually controls the meaning of the supposedly superior object. All the foregoing theories of statutory interpretation — textualist, specific intent, imaginative reconstruction, purposivist, best answer, and even pragmatic — deny or suppress this way the rule of law flips in cases like *Weber* and *Holy*

Humphrey), constituted the first legislative prohibition of all voluntary, private, race-conscious efforts to abolish traditional patterns of racial segregation and hierarchy." 443 U.S. at 204.

[60]See *Weber*, 443 U.S. at 219-20 (Rehnquist, J., dissenting); see also *Johnson*, 480 U.S. at 676-77 (Scalia, J., dissenting) (Justice Scalia's ode to blue collar white guys, situating Paul Johnson as an "impotent" victim of a liberal coalition of big business, unions, and civil rights groups).

[61]For examples, the tension between the narrow ambit of § 4 and the seemingly broader ambit of § 1; the bizarre relationship of § 5 to either of the provisions; the wacky idea of making these contracts criminal.

Trinity. Everybody knows this goes on, and they all stonewall it. Do not expect Justices Scalia, Rehnquist, Brennan, or even Blackmun to confess, as Justice Cardozo did several generations ago, that the hard work of judging is creative, for it happens when the conventional sources fail to provide interpretive closure.[62] The strategy of the people in power whose work can be deconstructed is to ignore the critique or, if it cannot be ignored, to denounce it in eschatological terms as nihilist, or fascist, or even illiberal.[63]

Critical theory can also be reconstructive, suggesting positive moves that interpreters could take in the face of pervasive indeterminacy. The statutory interpreter, especially judges given some degree of academic luxury by their life tenure, might become, perhaps episodically, a *counterhegemonic* force in our polity, insisting that unspoken voices be considered.[64] A critical approach to *Weber* would, with Justice Blackmun, candidly admit the play within the text of Title VII and the assumption of the enacting Congress that colorblind employment decisions would lead to workforce integration. But rather than looking at the *Weber* dilemma only from the perspective of the displaced white employees (Justice Rehnquist) or of the politically powerful unions and employers (Justice Blackmun), the critic might have thought about the issue from the perspective of the people of color who, rather than Weber, received the opportunity to train for craft positions because of the Steelworkers/Kaiser program. Was it discrimination to help them? Was their lack of qualification — that they had less seniority than Weber — a function of prior race-based policies? What doors did the training program

---

[62]See Benjamin Cardozo, *The Nature of the Judicial Process* 166 (1921) (judicial decisionmaking "in its highest reaches is not discovery, but creation").

[63]The response in the text can, naturally, be deconstructed. People in power dichotomize the issue as, If you don't accept our deterministic theory, the alternative is chaos. But their theory is not deterministic, except in a self-serving way; accepting a fair amount of honest indeterminacy can lead to less chaos than a great deal of hypocritical determinacy; public chaos might be better than state-legitimated injustice, which is a privatized form of chaos. And so on. See Gary Peller, *The Metaphysics of American Law*, 73 Cal. L. Rev. 1151 (1985).

[64]Cf. Eskridge, *supra* note 5, at 151-54, 199-203 (republican and pragmatic theories require statutory interpreters to take a more critical stance and interpret ambiguous statutes to give voice to underrepresented concerns).

open up for them? Was there disabling resentment against them by people who felt the Webers were cheated out of their rightful spots?

Holy Trinity looks even more different when viewed critically. Justice Brewer's soliloquy about the United States as a Christian Nation was obviously very important to his resolution of the case, yet that norm seems more exclusionary than visionary today. The statute itself had more than a whiff of xenophobia and racism about it, patterned as it was on earlier Chinese exclusionary laws. Justice Brewer's opinion can be defended as a narrowing construction of a broadly sweeping, somewhat hysterical piece of legislation. Curtailing such laws is traditionally something judges have done, often to their great credit, in this country. But Justice Brewer's resolution also created a new injustice in the statute: the upper class, professional, brain-toiling imported alien can enter the country, and only the working-class manual laborers and servants (unless they were domestic servants of the upper crust, for such were exempted by § 5) were found to be excluded by the law. By carving out a theoretically big exception for professionals, *Holy Trinity* made a morally questionable statute more squalid (by adding a new class-based discrimination) and more palatable to the political culture (by exempting acceptable aliens from the prohibition). A counterhegemonic approach to the case would have given less emphasis to the Christian Nation, and more to the Equal Nation.

Such an aggressively counterhegemonic judiciary can readily be criticized, not only for undermining the rule of law and disrespecting the democratic process, but also for kamikaze normative arrogance. Unhappily, judges are neither well trained in moral philosophy nor particularly virtuous people themselves, raising questions whether Alexander Hamilton was right to call their office the "least dangerous branch."[65] How can we expect such state functionaries, first, to transcend their own prejudices and privileged station and empathize with the poor or the outcast; second, to translate that empathy to concrete statutory interpretations that have real-world bite; and, third, to pursue truly other-regarding moral theory in the face of political

---

[65]*The Federalist* No. 78 (A. Hamilton).

criticism and threats to the judicial office?[66] On the other hand, pragmatists and even more formal theorists might be inspired by critical thinkers to shake up the status quo and tip some sacred cows more often — in short, to take a few calculated risks to do the right thing for the dispossessed of our society.

---

[66]Taken as a whole, the judiciary's history has perhaps been as hegemonic, e.g., *Dred Scott v. Sandford*, 60 U.S. 393 (1857), as counterhegemonic, e.g., *Brown v. Board of Education*, 347 U.S. 483 (1954). Most typically, Court has been cautious even when being (at least mildly) counterhegemonic. See, e.g., *Brown v. Board of Education (Brown II)*, 349 U.S. 294 (1955).

7

The Role of Text and Precedent in Statutory Interpretation

All of the theories of statutory interpretation discussed in Chapter 6 consider, and most start with and privilege, textual and precedential rules and sources. *Textual* reasoning and rules ask what the statutory text typically means to an ordinary speaker of the language, as well as how well different possible meanings fit with the statute (or even the code) as a whole. *Precedential* rules tell us what terms or provisions mean based upon their interpretation in prior judicial precedents and determine whether prior interpretations are binding on the court or merely persuasive authority. Many of these rules parade themselves in the lists of *canons of statutory construction* that are popular with judges and law students. We refer to text-based canons throughout this chapter and discuss canons more generally in Chapter 9. Textual sources include dictionaries, grammar books, surveys of linguistic practice, and, traditionally most important, the interpreter's own sense of ordinary usage. Precedential sources, of course, are judicial opinions, including those of other courts as well as the court of last resort in the jurisdiction whose statute is being construed.[1]

The rich array of rules and sources might enable textualist theories to provide particularly determinate answers to statutory puzzles, as adherents of the plain meaning rule maintain. Their position is most defensible in the easy cases. Textual sources resolve almost all easy issues. If the statute says, "No vehicles in the park," interpreters from almost any perspective will agree that the statute covers automobiles, motorcycles, tractors, trucks, limousines, and buses. As for other modes of locomotion, such as tricycles, the statute may not be so textually clear, but many of these harder cases are rendered clear because they are covered by precedent (or even just practice).

In the hard cases, however, the wide array of textual sources and rules might enable clever advocates to devise a variety of arguments

---

[1]The next chapter discusses administrative precedents.

about plain meaning, which could defeat the idea of plain meaning altogether![2] Analyzing two celebrated cases, Chapter 6 introduced you to this theoretical debate, and we shall return to those cases from time to time in this chapter. But we shall focus on *Babbitt v. Sweet Home Chapter of Communities for a Great Oregon*,[3] where the Supreme Court grappled with most of the important textualist canons as the Justices debated the meaning of the Endangered Species Act of 1973 (ESA). Section 9(a)(1)(B) of the statute makes it unlawful for anyone to "take" any endangered species of fish or wildlife, and § 3(19) defines *take* to mean "harass, harm, pursue, hunt, shoot, wound, kill, trap, capture, or collect," or to attempt any such conduct. Although ESA does not define the specific terms in § 3(19), the Interior Department, charged with enforcing the law, has defined *harm* to mean any act which "actually kills or injures wildlife," including "significant habitat modification or degradation." Sweet Home objected to this regulation and, specifically, to its protection of the habitats of the red-cockaded woodpecker and the spotted owl. The Court of Appeals for the D.C. Circuit ruled that the department's definition was broader than the statute allowed. Reversing, the Supreme Court ruled that the administrative definition was allowable; three Justices vehemently dissented.

Not only does *Sweet Home* show many of the text-based rules at work, it shows them in conflict. Some rules point toward one interpretation, others in the opposite direction, and at least one of them points in both directions. A broader point emerges from our examination: although the textual rules are supposed to make statutory interpretation appear relatively objective, even mechanical,

---

[2]This was the argument of Karl Llewellyn, *Remarks on the Theory of Appellate Decision and the Rules or Canons About How Statutes Are To Be Construed*, 3 Vand. L. Rev. 395 (1950), excerpted and discussed in Eskridge & Frickey 705-13; Hetzel, Libonati & Williams 691-99; Mikva & Lane 770-75. Llewellyn argued that, for every *canon* that supports a particular result in a statutory interpretation case, there is a *counter-canon* that would support the opposite result.

[3]515 U.S. 687 (1995), *rev'g* 17 F.3d 1463 (D.C. Cir. 1994). The Supreme Court opinion is excerpted and analyzed in Eskridge, Frickey & Garrett Supp. 105-15, 137-38, and the court of appeals opinions are excerpted and analyzed in Mikva & Lane 1029-49. (Mikva was a judge on the D.C. Circuit who participated in the lower court proceedings. His view of the case was largely confirmed by the Supreme Court majority.)

the rules operate against the backdrop of normative baselines that are hidden in the ordinary easy case, but that are dramatically apparent in hard cases such as *Sweet Home*.

I. Sources for Discerning Statutory "Plain Meaning"

Figuring out whether the ESA's anti-take rule can be read to prohibit landowners from using their land in ways that injures the habitat of endangered species is not an easy enterprise. But it is an enterprise that can be pursued in an orderly way. Start with this inquiry: What is the *plain meaning* of § 9(a)(1)(B)? Some of the directions for thought or research are contained in the popular canons of textual interpretation discussed below.

A. *Ordinary Meaning Canons*

In a leading case, *Nix v. Heddon*,[4] the Supreme Court was asked to determine whether tomatoes are a "fruit" or a "vegetable" for purposes of the Tariff Act of 1883, which imposed duties on vegetables but not on fruits. "There being no evidence that the words 'fruit' and 'vegetable' have acquired any special meaning in trade or commerce, they must receive their ordinary meaning,"[5] the Court said. Dictionary definitions were admissible, "not as evidence, but only as aids to the memory and understanding of the court."[6] Conceding that tomatoes are, technically, the fruit of a vine, the Justices nonetheless concluded that "in the common language of the people"[7] tomatoes are vegetables as that term is typically used. This is a sensible conclusion, but the modern reader is left with this question: Why were fruits exempt from the tariff? Is there a sensible substantive reason for the different treatment, or does the answer lie in the interest group dynamics that surrounded the tariff enactment? Does the reason for their exemption bear on the question of how tomatoes should be characterized?

---

[4]149 U.S. 304 (1893), excerpted and discussed in Eskridge & Frickey 635-37; Hetzel, Libonati & Williams 641-43; Popkin 189-91.

[5]149 U.S. at 306.

[6]*Id*. at 307.

[7]*Id*.

Unlike the Tariff Act of 1883, the ESA defined *take*, as quoted above. Nonetheless, the Justices engaged in a lively debate about the ordinary meaning of the words in the definition. Quoting *Webster's Third New International Dictionary*, Justice Stevens' opinion for the Court argued that the ordinary meaning of *harm* (one of the verbs in the statutory definition of *take*) — "to cause hurt or damage to: injure" — readily supported the department's interpretation. If you destroy the spotted owl's habitat, you have *harmed* the owl, as a matter of ordinary usage. Nonetheless, Justice Scalia disagreed. His dissenting opinion focused more on the ordinary meaning of *take*, a word drawn from the common law of property and used in the animal context to mean reducing an animal to human control. Accordingly, he argued, *harm* should be understood more narrowly, to include only affirmative conduct deliberately targeting particular animals.

An interesting feature of this exchange is the role of dictionaries. Expanding on the idea in *Nix v. Heddon* and driven by the rise of the new textualism, the Supreme Court has increasingly relied on dictionaries in discerning ordinary meaning.[8] As in *Nix v. Heddon*, the Court usually deploys dictionaries as "aids to the memory and understanding of the court,"[9] but this deployment has created a junior cottage industry of dictionary shopping by counsel. A new jurisprudence of dictionaries is tentatively emerging. For example, Justice Scalia, who frequently cites dictionaries, objects to reliance on *Webster's Third*, which he (and some grammarians) consider too colloquial a dictionary to be authoritative for judges.[10] Is that a valid objection if the inquiry is finding out the "ordinary" usage of words?

---

[8]See, e.g., Ellen Aprill, *The Law of the Word: Dictionary Shopping in the Supreme Court*, 30 Ariz. St. L.J. 275 (1998); Lawrence Solan, *When Judges Use the Dictionary*, 68 Am. Speech 1 (1993); Note, *Looking It Up: Dictionaries and Statutory Interpretation*, 107 Harv. L. Rev. 1437 (1994).

[9]*Nix*, 149 U.S. at 307.

[10]Justice Scalia's objection is that *Webster's Third* accepts too much slang or colloquial usages as "proper." See *MCI v. AT&T*, 512 U.S. 218, 228 n.3 (1994), excerpted and discussed in Eskridge, Frickey & Garrett Supp. 132-38. Unlike its revered predecessor *Webster's Second*, the *Third* is a descriptive dictionary, chronicling actual usage, not a prescriptive dictionary. For a discussion of the outcry greeting the publication of the *Third*, see James Sledd & Wilma Ebbitt, *Dictionaries and That Dictionary* (1962).

Or should words be understood in their more formal sense when they appear in a legal document like a statute?

You might pause at this point: Should the focus be on *take* or on *harm*? (Both?) Does the ordinary meaning of the statute's terminology support the department's broad reading of the statutory anti-take rule? Is there a specialized meaning that should control instead, and how does that cut?

B. *Canons of Word Association (*Noscitur a Sociis *and* Ejusdem Generis)

The lower court majority and the Supreme Court dissenters relied on the canon *noscitur a sociis*, "a thing shall be known by its associates." This canon presumes that "when two or more words are grouped together, and ordinarily have a similar meaning, but are not equally comprehensive, the general word will be limited and qualified by the special word."[11] Section 3(19) includes ten activities in its definition of *take* — harm, plus nine other actions that are directed immediately and intentionally against a particular animal. Following Judge Williams' opinion for the lower court, Justice Scalia argued that *harm* should be read in light of its associates, and therefore more narrowly than the department was reading it.[12]

The Solicitor of the Fish and Wildlife Service had in 1981 construed the statute narrowly for this reason, but under the canon *ejusdem generis*, "of the same kind."[13] The leading treatise summarizes this rule as follows: "Where general words follow specific words in a statutory enumeration, the general words are construed to embrace only objects similar in nature to those objects enumerated by

---

[11]2A Sutherland, *Statutes and Statutory Construction* § 47.16, at 183 (5th ed. 1992, Norman Singer ed.). A leading case is *Jarecki v. G.D. Searle & Co.*, 367 U.S. 303 (1961), where the Court construed a tax statute allowing reallocation of income resulting from "exploration, discovery or prospecting" to be inapplicable to income from a patented item. *Discovery*, the Court held, should be limited to the finding of minerals, as suggested by its association with exploration and prospecting.

[12]*Sweet Home*, 515 U.S. at 719-20 (Scalia, J., dissenting), following 17 F.3d at 1464-66 (Williams, J.).

[13]Memorandum of Apr. 17, 1981, 46 Fed. Reg. 29,490, 29,491 (1981).

the preceding specific words."[14] Section 3(19) is not a good example of *ejusdem generis*. If the statute had defined *take* to mean "to harass, pursue, hunt, shoot, wound, kill, trap, capture, collect, or otherwise harm," *ejusdem generis* could be invoked to presume that *otherwise harm* was restricted to the sort of affirmative, targeted conduct as the listed items.[15] Because the key term was just another specific item in a list and not a general term surrounded by specific items, *noscitur a sociis* was the appropriate canon, but either canon works to the same effect. Both canons capture our intuitions about legislators' linguistic decisions, namely, that people use lists to link similar concepts and to illustrate coherent patterns. More deeply, *noscitur a sociis* reflects a similar normative baseline as *ejusdem generis*: for most statutes, both canons presume that broad regulatory duties or deregulatory exemptions should not be inferred without a relatively clear indication from the legislature. A majority of the Court rejected both

---

[14]2A Sutherland, *supra* note 11, § 47.17, at 188; see *Cleveland v. United States*, 329 U.S. 14, 18 (1946), discussed in Popkin 204; *Short v. State*, 122 N.E.2d 82, 85-86 (Ind. 1954), excerpted and discussed in Hetzel, Libonati & Williams 629-31.

[15]For example, consider a statute that provides:

> No person shall have in his actual or constructive possession any punch board, seal card, slot gambling machine or other implements, apparatus or materials of any form of gambling, and no person shall solicit, obtain or offer to obtain orders for the sale or delivery of any punch board, seal card, slot gambling machine or other implements, apparatus or material of gambling.

If a person possesses betting slips (pieces of paper recording bets on sports events), has she violated this statute? See *State v. Ferris*, 284 A.2d 288, 290 (Me. 1971), invoking ejusdem generis:

> Here, the enumeration of devices specifically prohibited — "punch board, seal card, slot gambling machine" — indicates that in adding the words "other implements, apparatus or materials of any form of gambling" the Legislature intended to include only other articles which also have a per se relationship to the determination of the outcome of wagers recognizable from common experience. . . . Betting slips and records of betting do not constitute such gambling devices as the Legislature has outlawed. Records of such things as amounts wagered, the point spreads, the odds, and the successes and failures of athletic teams or race horses in prior events are aids to the memory of the gambler but not in themselves devices which determine the outcome of the wager.

noscitur a sociis and a libertarian baseline in *Sweet Home*, because it found a broad regulatory intent on the part of Congress.

C. *Canons of Negative Implication (e.g.,* Inclusio Unius)

Justice Scalia maintained that the Court's willingness to read a "don't destroy the habitat" prohibition in § 9(a)(1)(B) must be contrasted with § 7(a)(2), which prohibits federal programs which "result in the destruction or adverse modification of habitat." This is an argument from negative implication. "[W]here Congress includes particular language in one section of a statute but omits it in another . . . , it is generally presumed that Congress acts intentionally and purposely in the disparate inclusion or exclusion."[16] By imposing a specific obligation on federal agencies (§ 7) but not on other entities or persons (§ 9) not to adversely affect endangered species' habitat, Congress *implicitly* allowed the other entities or persons to adversely affect habitat. This form of argument is close cousin to the hoary canon, *inclusio [expressio] unius est exclusio alterius,* "the inclusion [expression] of one thing suggests the exclusion of all others." This rule of thumb rests on the supposition that directives normally allow what they don't prohibit.[17]

Although frequently invoked by judges of all political persuasions,[18] *inclusio unius* is, in our opinion, an unreliable canon, and the reasons for its unreliability apply to other negative implication canons as well. *Inclusio unius* is sometimes a sensible inference. If Mother

---

[16]*Keene Corp. v. United States,* 508 U.S. 200, 208 (1993) (quoted in Justice Scalia's *Sweet Home* dissent).

[17]Traditionally, *inclusio unius* has been considered a libertarian canon, preserving spheres of private decisionmaking by narrow constructions of statutory regulations. This understanding is undercut if *inclusio unius* is applied to statutory deregulations or exemptions, as it seems to be. See, e.g., *Hishon v. King & Spalding,* 467 U.S. 69, 77-78 (1984).

[18]Including liberal Justice Brennan in the *Weber* case analyzed in Chapter 6 and Justice Scalia in cases like *Chan v. Korean Air Lines, Ltd.,* 490 U.S. 122 (1989) (over Brennan's heated objections). There have been judicial critics as well, ranging from liberals like Judge Skelly Wright, *National Petroleum Refiners Ass'n v. FTC,* 482 F.2d 672 (D.C. Cir. 1973), to conservatives like Judge Frank Easterbrook, *In re American Reserve Corp.,* 840 F.2d 487 (7th Cir. 1988), and centrists like Judge Richard Posner, *The Federal Courts: Crisis and Reform* 282 (1985).

tells Sally, "You can have one cookie and one brownie," Sally is not allowed to have a candy bar, because the instruction reflects a background rule of "no sweets unless authorized." But if Mother tells Sally, "Don't hit, choke, or kick your sister Anne," and Sally immediately pinches and pushes her sister, Sally cannot legitimately argue that pinching and pushing were implicitly authorized because they were omitted from the prohibition, notwithstanding *inclusio unius*. By "including" some forms of harm to sister, Mother is not "excluding" others from the prohibition, because the normative baseline from which Mother is clearly operating is to prohibit Sally from doing *harm* to her sister. For the same reason, the fact that Mother had earlier told Sally's older sister Martha, "Don't hit, choke, kick, pinch, or push your sister Anne," would add nothing much to the cogency of Sally's negative implication argument. Descriptively, people do not necessarily intend their lists of directed activities to be comprehensive ones or even think through all the permutations to which their directives might be applied.

The often chaotic Congress not only shares this cognitive failing but sometimes finds that it must suppress language as part of the compromise process needed to enact bills into law (Chapter 3). Normatively, the key issue is not whether a term has been left out, but what the presumption should be for filling in statutory gaps. In *Sweet Home*, Justice Stevens relied on repeated congressional signals and statements urging a broad application of the ESA, while Justice Scalia relied on general libertarian presumptions. Note, however, that the judicial approach might change if courts consistently and uniformly applied a set of canons of construction — like *noscitur a sociis* and *inclusio unius* — as default rules to fill all statutory gaps. In that case, would it then be appropriate for courts to adopt Justice Stevens' method? We will return to this question in Chapter 9.

D. *Grammar and Punctuation Rules (e.g., the Rule of the Last Antecedent)*

The debate in *Sweet Home* focused on the meaning of the verb *take*; there was no disagreement among the Justices about the grammar and syntax of the command in § 9(a)(1)(B). In other cases, rules of grammar can make a difference. Courts presume that the legislature expects its statutes to be read according to the ordinary rules of grammar and punctuation.[19]   Consider this tough example. Section 8, paragraph 4 of the Clayton Act prohibits anyone from serving as a director in "any two or more corporations . . . other than banks" that compete against one another.   Paragraph 1 prohibits anyone from being a director in more than one bank.   The rule assumes that interlocking directorates will tend to have anticompetitive effects and so prohibits them prophylactically.   Does the law prohibit serving as a director of a bank and an insurance company that competes with banks?   In *BankAmerica Corp. v. United States*,[20] the Supreme Court held that it did not.   Chief Justice Burger's opinion for the Court found this an easy matter of grammar: paragraph 1 does not prohibit the interlock because it is not with two banks, and paragraph 4 does not prohibit it because the "most natural reading" of "two or more corporations . . . other than banks" is that all the corporations have to be nonbanks.[21]

The dissenting Justices objected that the statutory language is genuinely ambiguous and must be construed in light of the statute's structure and purpose.   For example, suppose that a law prohibits anyone from owning "two or more automobiles, other than Fords."[22] According to the Court, the law would not prohibit people from owning one Chevy and one Ford, but it is nonsense to say that with certainty without considering the statutory purpose.   Because § 8 sought to head off anticompetitive activity by prohibiting interlocking directorates among competing companies, ambiguous paragraph 4 should be construed to reach bank-nonbank interlocks when the companies are admittedly competitors.   Is the law grammatically

---

[19]You might think that this is obvious and simple, but you would be wrong. For examples of deviations from standard grammar rules in regulatory contexts, and keen linguistic-legal insights generally, see Lawrence Solan, *The Language of Judges* ch. 2 (1993).

[20]462 U.S. 122 (1983), excerpted and discussed in Eskridge & Frickey 775-89.

[21]The Chief Justice also had an internal consistency argument.   The government conceded that paragraph 4, which also prohibited interlocks between "two or more corporations . . . other than . . . common carriers," only applied to interlocks where no corporation was a common carrier.   Section 10 of the statute prohibits interlocks among common carriers and between a common carrier and certain noncarrier but competing companies.

[22]See *BankAmerica*, 462 U.S. at 141 (White, J., dissenting).

ambiguous? Is the purpose argument persuasive? What if you think, as many economists do, that § 8's prophylactic rule is regulatory nonsense, imposing unnecessary costs on firms without really heading off anticompetitive conspiracies?

One grammar rule that is often invoked is the *rule of the last antecedent*: referential and qualifying words refer only to the last antecedent, unless contrary to the statute's punctuation or policy. A neat example is *Commonwealth v. Kelly*,[23] which construed a law prohibiting the sale of alcohol between eleven at night "and six in the morning; or during the Lord's day, except that [an innholder] may supply such liquor to guests." The innholder argued that it could sell liquor between midnight and 6 a.m. as well as on Sunday, but the court disagreed. The rule of the last antecedent suggested that the proviso only modified "during the Lord's day." Sometimes courts will relax the rule when the proviso is set off from a series of items by a comma, but the comma-trumping exception was itself trumped in this case by the semi-colon separating the two items. That the legislature had specifically amended the statute to replace a comma with the semicolon was evidence strongly confirming the applicability of the rule of the last antecedent, the court ruled. (The court also might have been influenced by the canon that provisos should be narrowly construed.) May the innkeeper sell liquor between midnight and 6 a.m. on Sundays?

For most of Anglo-American legal history, the role of punctuation in statutory interpretation has been uncertain. The English rule was to ignore it, but the modern practice, reflected in *Kelly*, is to consider it for what it is worth, but not when it would yield an absurd result or undercut the statutory goal.[24] Other grammatical chestnuts are treated similarly, including the *and/or rule* and the *may/shall rule*.[25] The legislature usually deploys "and" to connect items in a series and "or"

---

[23]58 N.E. 691 (Mass. 1900), discussed in Hetzel, Libonati & Williams 646. See also Eskridge & Frickey 640-42.

[24]See *United States v. Ron Pair Enters., Inc.*, 489 U.S. 235 (1989); Raymond Marcin, *Punctuation and the Interpretation of Statutes*, 9 Conn. L. Rev. 227 (1977); Eskridge & Frickey 640; Hetzel, Libonati & Williams 643-46; Popkin 210-14.

[25]See Eskridge & Frickey 641-42; Hetzel, Libonati & Williams 632-43.

to treat them separately or in the alternative. It usually uses "may" to allow greater discretion to the law implementer than when it uses "shall." Like the other grammar rules, however, these are only presumptions, and purpose-based exceptions abound. And, like other textual canons, these depend on careful legislative drafters who worry about punctuation and antecedents, often a daunting task in the chaos of the legislative process.

E. *Exceptions to Ordinary Grammar Rules (Man Includes Woman, Singular Includes Plural)*

Some grammar rules are generally *not* followed. Although the need for reconstruction has declined as legislatures revise the old gendered provisions of their codes, statutes referring to men are regularly construed to apply to women as well. Similarly, statutes written in the singular are often applied in plural situations.[26] What is most interesting about these exceptions to ordinary grammar rules is that so many jurisdictions have codified them. States like Pennsylvania and Minnesota have rather extensive codified rules of statutory construction that are virtually identical to the judicially constructed doctrines surveyed in this chapter and the next two.[27] Virtually all the states, the District of Columbia, and the U.S. Code have at least a few general statutory provisions setting out interpretive guides, usually stipulating that references to men include women and vice-versa. In most states with such a statutory provision, laws authorize marriages between a "man and a woman" who are at or above the age of consent, are not closely related, and are not married to anyone else. Can those provisions be interpreted to authorize the marriage of a "woman and a woman"? Does your answer change if the state has just recodified all its laws, rewriting then in gender-neutral terms but retaining the requirement that marriages be between a man and a woman?

---

[26] See Eskridge & Frickey 642-43.

[27] See Minn. Stat. ch. 645; 1 Pa. Cons. Stat. §§ 1921-1928 (reprinted in Hetzel, Libonati & Williams 540-42).

F. *Avoiding Absurd Results and Correcting Scriveners' Errors*

Assuming that the legislature does not intend irrational or incoherent directives, courts will read — or even rewrite — statutes to avoid *absurd results*. *Holy Trinity*, discussed in Chapter 6, illustrates this rule: given the constitutional protection of religion as well as the cultural assumption that this is a "Christian Nation," evangelical Justice Brewer thought it inconceivable that Congress in 1885 would have intended to exclude Christian ministers from this country. Note once again the importance of the normative baseline: to accept the argument, you must agree that this country is, as a matter of public law as well as culture, a Christian Nation. No less religiously devout than Justice Brewer, Justice Scalia has rejected that public law baseline and insisted, further, that general state laws may be applied to burden religious free exercise.[28] He considers *Holy Trinity* an abuse of the absurd-result canon.[29] Neither he nor Justice Stevens thought the canon applicable in *Sweet Home*.

What, then, is the difference between an *absurd* result (i.e., one the legislature certainly did not contemplate) and merely an *unreasonable* one (i.e., one the judge disagrees with and truly believes right-thinking people would find unreasonable)? A possible line is suggested by *Green v. Bock Laundry Machine Co.*[30] Federal Rule of Evidence 609(a)(1) then allowed a witness' credibility to be attacked by a prior criminal conviction, "but only if" the crime was a serious one *and* "the court determines that the probative value of admitting this evidence outweighs its prejudicial effect to the defendant." The asymmetrical rule is defensible in criminal cases, where defendants receive a lot of special procedural protections, but not in civil cases, where it would exclude many convictions by tort and contract defendants while admitting all such convictions of plaintiffs. All nine Justices agreed that a literal reading of the law was absurd, and a majority of the Court rewrote Rule 609(a)(1)'s balancing test to apply

---

[28]See *Employment Div., Dep't of Natural Resources v. Smith*, 494 U.S. 872 (1990) (Scalia, J., for the Court).

[29]See Antonin Scalia, *A Matter of Interpretation* 20-23 (1997) (scathing denunciation of the Court's approach and result in *Holy Trinity*).

[30]490 U.S. 504 (1989), excerpted and discussed in Eskridge & Frickey 589-603; Popkin 275-76.

only when a criminal defendant's credibility is attacked and to admit prior convictions of other witnesses.

Bock Laundry is probably the classic example of the absurd-results canon: not only would a literal application of the statute distinguish between civil plaintiffs and defendants without ascertainable reason, but the literal reading would probably have been unconstitutional.[31]   Furthermore, there was evidence from the legislative history of the rule suggesting that the textual oddity was a *scrivener's error* not attributable to any legislative deliberation on the issue or conscious policy decision.[32]   The Justices' willingness to rewrite the statute in *Bock Laundry* may have been contingent upon their belief that the absurd result was caused by a scrivener's error. Where an odd result is not the consequence of such an error, correction by the judiciary might be much less defensible under democratic premises.

The absurd-result canon produces complications, especially for textualists. In *Bock Laundry*, Justice Scalia agreed that the canon applied and contended that it should be implemented by reformulating the statute in the way that "does least violence to the text."[33] This

---

[31]For more on the line between an absurd result and a merely unreasonable one, consider Justice Kennedy's suggestion in his separate opinion in *Public Citizen v. United States Dep't of Justice*, 491 U.S. 440, 470-71 (1989), excerpted and discussed in Eskridge & Frickey 548-50, Popkin 235-41. Justice Kennedy asserted that the absurd-result exception "remains a legitimate tool of the Judiciary . . . only as long as the Court acts with self-discipline by limiting the exception to situations where the result of applying the plain language would be, in a genuine sense, absurd, *i.e.*, where it is quite impossible that Congress could have intended the result, and where the alleged absurdity is so clear as to be obvious to most anyone." For an even more restrictive statement of the absurd-result canon, see *Crooks v. Harrelson*, 282 U.S. 55, 60 (1930).

[32]See generally Henry Hart, Jr. & Albert Sacks, *The Legal Process: Basic Problems in the Making and Application of Law* 1375 (William Eskridge, Jr. & Philip Frickey publication editors, 1994) (from the 1958 "tentative edition"); 2A Sutherland, *supra* note 11, §§ 47.35-.38. Other apparent examples of scrivener's error cases include *United States Nat'l Bank of Oregon v. Independent Ins. Agents of Am.*, 508 U.S. 439 (1993), excerpted and discussed in Popkin 210-14; *United States v. Locke*, 471 U.S. 84 (1985), excerpted and discussed in Eskridge & Frickey 550-52; Popkin 247-50; *Shine v. Shine*, 802 F.2d 583 (1st Cir. 1986), excerpted and discussed in Eskridge & Frickey 543-48.

[33]See *Bock Laundry*, 490 U.S. at 529 (Scalia, J., concurring in the judgment).

approach seems puzzling, for at least three reasons. First, why should a textualist ever rewrite a statute? If law simply consists of text, the point of interpretation is to give the text its plain meaning. If that produces an absurdity, then the textualist judge should strike the statute down as unconstitutional for lacking a rational basis rather than, in effect, amend its text by judicial construction. Second, it seems odd to say that the text is simultaneously contaminated by absurdity — thereby liberating the judge to rewrite it — and yet sufficiently sacrosanct that the rewriting must do the "least violence" to it. One would think that either the text deserves respect or it doesn't. Third, how much "violence" to the text would be inflicted by alternative rewrites strikes us as a question beyond precise judicial calibration, undercutting the goals of predictability and certainty that support textualism.[34]

Even for nontextualists, however, the appropriateness of reformulating statutes to avoid absurd results is debatable. In *Bock Laundry*, the majority recrafted the rule of evidence to limit its application to criminal defendants, based on legislative history suggesting that Congress was only thinking about criminal cases when it considered the rule. Justice Blackmun, in dissent, contended that the legislative history was sparse and confused, and he concluded that the balancing test should apply to any party in civil cases, as well as criminal defendants, because that rewrite would best serve the purpose of the rule, which was to avoid the potential that prejudice would effect the

---

[34]The rule stated that evidence of a prior criminal conviction was admissible only if the crime was a serious one "and the court determines that the probative value of admitting this evidence outweighs its prejudicial effect to the defendant." Justice Scalia, concurring in the judgment that the rule should apply only to criminal defendants, thought his rewrite could be accomplished merely by inserting the adjective "criminal" before the noun "defendant," while the dissent's approach of applying the rule to all parties would require giving "defendant" a meaning it will not bear ("party"). This rewrite would not be the way that a skilled drafter would amend the rule, however. The rule applies in civil as well as criminal cases. Justice Scalia's rewrite would make the rule nonsensical in civil cases — what criminal defendant? To achieve Justice Scalia's result, the skilled drafter might well amend the rule to state: "and, *in a criminal case*, the court determines . . . ." In contrast, the drafter might achieve the other result simply by substituting "party" for "defendant." Which does less violence to the text: the addition of four words or the substitution of one word? Of course, there are surely other ways to do either rewrite, lending further subjectivity to the inquiry.

outcome of a trial.[35] Of course, neither the majority, nor Justice Scalia, nor Justice Blackmun could actually change the words of the rule on the books; they could only affect the meaning attributed to those words in court. Thus, interpreting statutes to avoid absurd results may create traps for the unwary. An attorney might consult the Federal Rules of Evidence and confidently allow her client, a civil defendant, to take the stand, confident that the judge will find that he cannot be impeached by prejudicial evidence of his prior felony conviction, only to be shocked when the judge automatically admits the evidence because, through the looking glass of precedent, "defendant" means only "criminal defendant." The ordinary citizenry is, of course, much more likely than attorneys to be misled in this fashion by judicial transfigurations of statutes, perhaps undercutting the very legitimacy of the rule of law itself. Should the Court in *Bock Laundry* have simply held that the rule was unconstitutional, thereby forcing Congress to redraft it?

II. Whole Act Rule and Holistic Textual Sources

The U.S. Supreme Court has frequently reasoned from the premise that "[s]tatutory construction . . . is a holistic endeavor. A provision that may seem ambiguous in isolation is often clarified by the remainder of the statutory scheme."[36] This *whole act rule* is universally followed — in state as well as federal courts, in civil law as well as common law countries. The rule clearly reveals a convention upon which text-based sources typically rest, namely, the assumption that the legislature writing a statute is a single-minded and omniscient author. Thus, it is presumed that Congress uses terms consistently, intends that each provision add something to the statutory scheme, and does not want one provision to be applied in ways that undercut other provisions. The assumption of a single-minded and omniscient legislature is strongly at odds with actual legislative practice, where terms are inserted willy-nilly into the law, duplication occurs for reasons of emphasis or even just oversight, and compromises may yield provisions that are in tension with one

---

[35]See 490 U.S. at 532-33 (Blackmun, J., dissenting).

[36]*United Savings Ass'n of Texas v. Timbers of Inwood Forest Assocs.*, 484 U.S. 365, 371 (1988). See generally 2A Sutherland, *supra* note 11, § 47.02; Eskridge & Frickey 643-52; Hetzel, Libonati & Williams 622-48; Popkin 198-214.

another. Does this disconnect between rule and reality negate the holistic canons?

This concern suggests that the normative justification for whole act canons is narrower than that supporting the plain meaning canons. Plain meaning rules can be defended on intentionalist as well as rule of law grounds: the meaning suggested by ordinary rules of grammar and word use is not only the most objective basis for everyone to know what the rule of law requires, it is also probably the meaning intended by the legislature as it focused on the particular provisions it was enacting. In contrast, because the legislature is incapable of comprehending the entire statutory scheme into which new provisions are being inserted, much less fine-tune the latter in light of the former, intentionalism provides little justification for the holistic canons. Probably the best defense for whole act rules is simply on rule of law grounds: the meaning suggested by considering other statutory provisions and structures might be the most objective basis to use in determining what the rule of law requires. This justification works better for *intra*textual arguments (the preferred meaning of a provision is the one consistent with the rest of the statute and statutory scheme) than for *inter*textual arguments (the preferred meaning of a provision is the one consistent with the rest of the code). Perhaps both kinds of arguments are justified on legitimacy grounds. A polity whose law knits together into a seamless fabric is one whose law enjoys greater authority than a polity whose statutory law appears largely random. Even if the U.S. Code falls somewhere between these two poles, there might be greater legal legitimacy, as well as an aesthetic advantage, if courts presume coherence among statutes as well as within statutes.

Notwithstanding these concerns, state high courts as well as the U.S. Supreme Court pay careful attention to the whole act rule. In *Sweet Home*, for example, both the majority and dissenting opinions relied heavily on holistic arguments, including intertextual ones.

A. *Presumption of Statutory Consistency*

A word or clause that is ambiguous at first glance might be clarified if "the same terminology is used elsewhere in a context that makes its meaning clear."[37] Justice Scalia in *Sweet Home* observed that § 3(19)'s definition of *take* was applicable throughout the statute, and that the ESA used the term in ways that were inconsistent with an understanding of *harm* that included indirect harm through destruction of habitat. For example, § 11(e)(4)(B) ordered forfeiture of "[a]ll guns, traps, nets, and other equipment . . . used to aid the taking, possessing, selling, [etc.]" of endangered animals. This seems to assume that *take* just has its ordinary meaning of taking control of an animal. If Congress had understood *take* to include indirect harm through habitat modification, it would have included plows, bulldozers, backhoes, and the like. "[I]f the Act is to be interpreted as a symmetrical and coherent regulatory scheme, one in which the operative words have a consistent meaning throughout,"[38] the department's (and the Court's) broad understanding of *take* must be wrong. Justice Scalia also argued that his narrow view of *take* better comported with the rest of § 9, which not only makes it illegal to take an endangered species, but also to import or export them, to transport or ship a taken species, or to sell them in interstate commerce. The overall policy in which § 9(a)(1)(B) is embedded is to prohibit actions directly aimed at reducing rare animals to human control and profit. The indirect-effect approach of the department was deeply inconsistent with this policy.

Coherence arguments like these may be invoked, perhaps more tentatively, across as well as within statutes. Thus, Justice Scalia not only cited the use of *take* elsewhere in the ESA, but also elsewhere in the U.S. Code and in treaties the United States has ratified. He found it significant that the Agreement on the Conservation of Polar Bears defines "taking" as "hunting, killing, and capturing" animals.[39] Because this obscure provision was the only example Justice Scalia offered of another treaty or statute actually defining *take* the way he thought the ESA should define it, the argument is a weak one in *Sweet Home*. Still, although the principle that courts should presume that the legislature uses a term consistently over time should probably

---

[37]*United Savings Ass'n*, 484 U.S. at 371.

[38]*Gustafson v. Alloyd Co.*, 513 U.S. 561, 569 (1995) (quoted in Justice Scalia's dissent).

[39]27 U.S.T. 3918, 3921, T.I.A.S. No. 8409.

be a weaker one than the principle of internal linguistic coherence, it is one that has been occasionally invoked by the Court, and persuasively so.[40]

At times, the Court will embrace this approach across the entire United States Code. Consider *West Virginia University Hospitals v. Casey*.[41] The question was whether a prevailing plaintiff in a civil rights action, who is entitled to "a reasonable attorney's fee" under 42 U.S.C. § 1988, may recover fees for services rendered to their attorneys by experts. Justice Scalia's majority opinion denied recovery because many fee-shifting provisions in other federal statutes, such as environmental statutes, explicitly shift expert witness fees as well as attorney's fees. For example, the Toxic Substances Control Act provides that a prevailing plaintiff may recover "the costs of suit and reasonable fees for attorneys and expert witnesses."[42] These statutes referring to attorney's fees and expert fees separately would be "an inexplicable exercise in redundancy" if attorney's fees were held to include expert fees. In dissent, Justice Stevens argued that allowing recovery would much better serve the purposes of § 1988 and would be more consistent with the legislative history. Justice Stevens asserted that Congress cannot be expected to use precise terminology perfectly across the whole Code and that the meaning of a statutory provision should be gleaned primarily from its text, legislative history, purpose, and the judicial constructions of it, not from more extraneous sources. Is intertextual argumentation persuasive in this context? Recall the normative qualms suggested in the introduction to this Part.

B. *The Rule Against Surplusage*

An additional response Justice Stevens had to the dissenters' *noscitur a sociis* argument in *Sweet Home* rested upon the *rule against surplusage*, the presumption that every statutory term adds something to a law's regulatory impact. "[U]nless the statutory term 'harm' encompasses indirect as well as direct injuries, the word has

---

[40]See, e.g., *Pierce v. Underwood*, 487 U.S. 552, 564-65 (1988) (interpreting the phrase "substantially justified" in a fee-shifting provision).

[41]499 U.S. 83 (1991), excerpted in Eskridge & Frickey 622-24; Popkin 676-81.

[42]15 U.S.C. §§ 2618(d), 2619(c)(2).

no meaning that does not duplicate the meaning of other words that § 3 uses to define 'take.' "[43] Justice Scalia responded that this argument "underestimates the ingenuity of our own species in a way that Congress did not. To feed an animal poison, to spray it with mace, to chop down the very tree in which it is nesting, or even to destroy its entire habitat in order to take it (as by draining a pond to get at a turtle), might neither wound nor kill, but would directly and intentionally harm."[44] In addition, the majority's reasoning ignored the possibility that Congress included some verbs for emphasis rather than to extend the Act's scope. Perhaps most important, there is surplusage even under the majority's theory. Because every wound "harms," § 3(19)'s inclusion of *wound* is unnecessary. (The majority's answer is that its interpretation reduces surplusage, even if it does not eliminate it.)

Justice Scalia himself invoked the rule against surplusage, in the context of the whole statute and not just the definitional provision. The Court's broad reading of § 9(a)(1)(B), he argued, rendered § 7(a)(2) essentially duplicative. Section 7(a)(2), as noted above, directs federal agencies to insure that actions and programs they authorize, supervise, or fund do not "jeopardize the continued existence of any endangered species . . . or result in the destruction or adverse modification of habitat of such species." If § 9(a)(1)(B) already prohibited anyone — including federal officials — from hurting animals by destroying or adversely modifying their habitat, then what did § 7(a)(2) add to the statute? To preserve a distinctive role for § 7(a)(2) would be an independent reason to read § 9(a)(1)(B) to adhere to what Justice Scalia contended was its ordinary meaning in any event.

Although this is an accepted form of textual argumentation in general, there may be answers to Justice Scalia's concerns in *Sweet Home* itself. The Supreme Court sometimes refuses to apply statutes against federal officials unless Congress has specifically named them in the law, and § 7 might have reflected attention to such a clear statement rule. Also, § 7 adds duties that § 9 does not clearly entail: the former makes federal agencies responsible for destructive actions

---

[43]*Sweet Home*, 515 U.S. at 697-98 (Stevens, J.).

[44]*Id.* at 721 (Scalia, J., dissenting).

carried out, often by other people or institutions, under their authority, funding, or supervision. Section 7 therefore imposes an extra monitoring duty on federal agencies not necessarily imposed by § 9 on individuals and private entities. Before deciding on the cogency of these reasons, consider a broader holistic rule.

C. *Statutory Amendment and Evolution*

The Interior Department had broadly construed the term *harm* since 1975, and landowners had complained that it worked unjustified hardships on them. Apparently responding to these complaints, Congress amended the ESA in 1982 to allow the department to permit a taking prohibited under § 9 so long as it was "incidental to" a "lawful activity."[45] The permit process requires the applicant to file a plan which shows how it will "minimize and mitigate" the impact of the lawful activity on the endangered species.[46] The statute as amended, Justice Stevens argued in *Sweet Home*, assumes that many takings will be indirect and the result of lawful developmental activities. New § 10, therefore, confirms the broad definition adopted by the department. Justice Stevens thought the permit provision would be absurd if *take* were limited to the dissent's understanding, for the department would not be expected to grant permits for intentional seizure of an endangered animal. Justice Scalia responded that there are many examples of conventional takings that could be exempted, as when fishing for unprotected fish has the result of taking endangered fish as well.

Statutory amendments can create new textual meaning as an indirect as well as a direct result of the new text they add to the law. *Sweet Home* may be an example of this: the new section added in 1982 not only changed the statute by creating a new procedure to ameliorate the anti-take provision, but may have broadened the anti-take provision itself, by ratifying the department's broad definition of *take*. (This is related to the reenactment rule treated below.) A clearer example of this phenomenon can be found in *Franklin v. Gwinnett County Public Schools*.[47] In 1979, the Supreme Court

---

[45]ESA § 10(a)(1)(B), 16 U.S.C. § 1539(a)(1)(B).

[46]16 U.S.C. § 1539(a)(2)(A)(ii).

[47]503 U.S. 60 (1992), excerpted in Eskridge & Frickey 902-03.

recognized an implied private right of action to enforce Title IX of the Education Amendments of 1972, which prohibits sex discrimination in many schools.[48] In *Franklin* a majority of the Court applied the earlier precedent to assure Title IX plaintiffs of damages, and not just injunctive relief. The Court found damages appropriate not only because they are consistent with ordinary principles of remedies, but also because 1986 and 1987 amendments to the statute assumed the existence of damages as well as injunctive relief to private parties.[49] Justice Scalia objected to any extension of the original (and in his view erroneous) precedent, but he concurred in the judgment on the ground that the 1986 amendment legislatively validated the precedent and was "an implicit acknowledgment that damages are available."[50]

D. *Statutory Structure*

The classic holistic argument is that one interpretation better fits the *structure* of the statute than another. The dissenting opinion in *Weber* (the affirmative action case discussed in Chapter 6) could have argued that its broad construction of *discriminate because of race* (to mean any race-based differentiation in workplace decisionmaking, including affirmative action) is more consistent with the structure of Title VII, as amended through 1979, than the majority's narrower construction (to mean only invidious differentiation).[51] Section 703(a)-(d) of the statute sets forth broad and sweeping antidiscrimination rules for employers and unions, and the most obvious policy is to make race, ethnicity, sex, and religion irrelevant criteria for workplace decisions. To the extent that such criteria might conceiv-

---

[48]See *Cannon v. University of Chicago*, 441 U.S. 677 (1979).

[49]See 42 U.S.C. § 2000d-7, enacted in 1986, which abrogated state immunity and provided that "remedies (including remedies both at law [i.e., damages] and in equity [i.e., injunctions]) are available . . . to the same extent" as against other defendants.

[50]*Franklin*, 503 U.S. at 78 (Scalia, J., concurring in the judgment).

[51]Not only did Justice Rehnquist's *Weber* dissent fail to make the argument in text, but Justice Scalia also ignored this kind of argument when he urged the overruling of *Weber* in *Johnson v. Transportation Agency, Santa Clara County*, 480 U.S. 616 (1987). The argument in text is developed in William Eskridge, Jr., *Dynamic Statutory Interpretation* 42-43 (1994), which also presents arguments in the other direction, *id.* at 43-44.

ably be relevant to valid decisions, Congress provided specific exceptions to that broad duty in § 703(e)-(i). The exceptions themselves are illuminating. Section 703(e)'s exception for cases where sex and religion are *bona fide occupational qualifications* does not allow a defense when the qualification is based on race. Section 703(i) allows employers near Indian reservations to prefer Native Americans for jobs; this is significant because it was Congress' only allowance of something arguably akin to race-based affirmative action and because the provision might have been unnecessary (surplusage) under the *Weber* majority's narrower view of *discriminate*. Section 703(j), the last 703 subsection in the original statute, applied a special rule to the government itself: it could not require employers and unions to establish racially preferential policies.

A structure-of-the-statute argument shows how a statute can be read holistically. Not only does each provision play a role in constructing a coherent policy, but the role played by each provision helps us see more precisely what role to assign the ambiguous provision. Justice Scalia's *Sweet Home* dissent is an extended exercise in this kind of argument. Recall his earlier points: a reading of *take* limited to actions targeting specific animals is more consistent with the idea suggested by the ten verbs in the definitional section, with § 9(a)(1)'s overall attention to conduct directly controlling and exploiting specific animals, with § 7(a)(2)'s particular habitat-protecting duties of federal agencies, and with one final but critical piece of structural evidence. It was obvious to Congress that endangered species are just as threatened by destruction of their habitat as by capture or hunt. According to Justice Scalia, the ESA dealt with each kind of threat, but in different provisions: § 9 regulated the latter by prohibiting people from taking animals, and § 5 regulated the former by authorizing the federal government to acquire private land in order to protect natural habitats.

But the dissenters have to answer this question: Is § 5 the *exclusive* remedy for threats to habitats? This is not apparent from the face of the statute but may be supportable in one of several ways. Judge Williams' opinion for the lower court found evidence in the legislative history that this was the deal, and Justice Scalia (who ordinarily hates this kind of evidence) smuggled it into his opinion as a response to the majority's rather generalized legislative history argument. The House floor manager explained the statutory scheme this way:

> [T]he principal threat to animals stems from destruction of their habitat. . . . *[The bill] will meet this problem by providing funds for acquisition of critical habitat.* . . . It will also enable the Department of Agriculture to cooperate with willing landowners who desire to assist in the protection of endangered species, *but who are understandably unwilling to do so at excessive cost to themselves.*
>
> Another hazard to endangered species arises from those who would *capture or kill them for pleasure or profit.* There is no way that the Congress can make it less pleasurable for a person to take an animal, but we can certainly make it less profitable for them to do so.[52]

Note that this passage might also be persuasive evidence as to linguistic usage: when legislators used the word *take* they were speaking of physical capture or hunting and killing of specific animals.

Another response would be more openly normative: The public law baseline — and probably one legislators would have recognized or at least paid lip service to — is that owners of private property should be able to use their land as they please, unless they tangibly harm their neighbors. Just as the government cannot impress our bodies into state service without paying us, so it cannot impress our land into state service without compensating us. Justice Scalia's evocative use of the word "conscripted" when describing what the government's act did to the land of "the simplest farmer" taps into this constitutional principle.[53] This background norm would suggest that Congress needed to be much clearer if it wanted to prohibit citizens from using their land in ways that adversely affected the habitats of endangered species.

---

[52]119 Cong. Rec. 30,162 (Rep. Sullivan), quoted in both 17 F.3d at 1466 (Williams, J.), and 515 U.S. at 728 (Scalia, J., dissenting). The emphasis is that added by Justice Scalia.

[53]See 515 U.S. at 714 (Scalia, J., dissenting).

E. *Other Parts of the Statute: Preambles, Titles, Provisos*

Does the whole act rule require the interpreter to consider everything that is part of the statute enacted into law? For example, should titles and preambles be considered when construing laws? On the one hand, titles and preambles are, literally, part of the bill that is engrossed after adoption by the legislature and presented to the chief executive. Hence, they bear the same formal and democratic legitimacy as other parts of the statute. On the other hand, the preamble and title are not directive in ways that the substantive parts of a statute are. Preambles setting forth the problems that gave rise to statutes and titles helping organize statutory provisions categorically might be viewed as background materials rather than authoritative in the same way that statutory directives are.

Black letter law seems to follow these intuitions. Thus, "the preamble cannot control the enacting part of the statute in cases where the enacting part is expressed in clear, unambiguous terms" but "may be resorted to to help discover the intention of the law maker."[54] For example, the Supreme Court ruled in *Sutton v. United Air Lines*[55] that the Americans with Disabilities Act does not protect people with correctable disabilities (such as poor eyesight), in part because the preamble noted that 43 million Americans were disabled, less than half the number who need glasses to correct poor eyesight. Increasingly, Congress includes findings within the enacting part of the statute to increase their authoritativeness and also to ensure that textualist judges will consider them.

Similarly, the leading treatise opines that "the title cannot control the plain words of the statute," but "[i]n case of ambiguity the court may consider the title to resolve uncertainty in the purview [body] of the act or for the correction of obvious errors."[56] Yet in *Holy Trinity* a unanimous Court relied, in part, on the title of the Alien Contract Labor Act of 1885 to avoid what the Court all but conceded was the

---

[54]2A Sutherland, *supra* note 11, § 47.04, at 146.

[55]119 S.Ct. 2139 (1999).

[56]2A Sutherland, *supra* note 11, § 47.03, at 140.

plain meaning of the statutory language.[57] Ought preambles as well as titles be used to create rather than resolve textual ambiguities?

Unlike preambles and titles, *provisos* are authoritative commands, typically restricting or creating exceptions to primary commands. There is no dispute that they should be given legal effect, but the traditional rule is that provisos should be narrowly construed.[58] We consider this rule as hard to apply across the board as *inclusio unius*. Father tells Sally, "You may accompany your sister Martha to the movies tonight, *provided that* you do not associate with ruffians." Just as there is no sensible reason to apply *inclusio unius* to think that the limited proviso allows Sally to engage in other risky behavior, such as taking drugs or having unsafe sex with a tony rather than roughneck crowd, so there is no sensible reason to privilege the libertarian policy of the main clause and subordinate the regulatory policy of the proviso. Section 9(a)(1) of the ESA says no one can take an endangered species "[e]xcept as provided" in § 10, the permit program. That the permit program appears as a proviso strikes us as no persuasive reason for a court to be stingy in delineating the department's authority to operate the program.

F. *Statutory Conflicts (No Repeals by Implication; Last Enacted Rule; Specific over General)*

As numerous and various as they are in our polity, statutes are bound to collide. Some rules of thumb seek to avoid unnecessary collisions. Chief among these is the *rule that repeals by implication are not favored.* In a leading case, *Morton v. Mancari*,[59] the issue was whether Title VII, which after 1972 applied to government work-places, overrode the 1934 Indian Reorganization Act's policy of preferring Native Americans for jobs with the Bureau of Indian Affairs. Relying in part on the presumption against repeals by

---

[57]See *Church of the Holy Trinity v. United States*, 143 U.S. 457, 462-63 (1892), discussed in Chapter 6, where the argument is made that the statutory text was in fact ambiguous.

[58]2A Sutherland, *supra* note 11, § 47.08, at 156.

[59]417 U.S. 535 (1974), excerpted and discussed in Eskridge & Frickey 847-54; see *Watt v. Alaska*, 451 U.S. 259 (1981), excerpted and discussed in Popkin 656-59. See also Hetzel, Libonati & Williams 609-11.

implication, the Court held the Indian preference to have been unaffected by the subsequent statute. *Mancari* was a relatively easy case for the application of this canon for several reasons. There was no evidence that Congress was aware of the possible inconsistency in 1972; the Indian preference was not only a longstanding one explicitly authorized by statute but had been considered implicitly exempted from pre-1972 executive orders prohibiting racial discrimination in federal employment; and the issue of "remedial" or "benign" preferences was itself a vexing one that the Court was able to duck in *Mancari* (and only provisionally resolved in *Weber*).

It is not apparent to us that the rule against implied repeals is a reliable guide to cases that pose harder challenges, however. Where a partial or even total repeal of an earlier law is evident from the plain meaning of a subsequent statute, the Supreme Court has declined to apply the rule against implied repeals and, instead, has invoked the *primacy of the last enacted statute.*[60] So long as it follows the Article I, Section 7 procedures, each Congress not only can enact statutes, but can amend or repeal statutes adopted by earlier Congresses. This idea could also justify the Court's dynamic interpretation of federal statutes in both *Sweet Home* and *Franklin*, where subsequent amendments arguably changed the proper interpretation of provisions that were not formally amended.[61]

In this regard, consider *Preiser v. Rodriguez.*[62] Plaintiffs were state prisoners alleging that their constitutional rights had been

---

[60]See, e.g., *Sorenson v. Secretary of the Treasury*, 475 U.S. 851 (1986) (see Justice Stevens' dissent), excerpted and discussed in Eskridge & Frickey 651-52; Popkin 652-56; *Smith v. Robinson*, 468 U.S. 992 (1984) (see Justice Brennan's dissent).

[61]Such an interpretation of *Sweet Home* and *Franklin* strikes us as inconsistent with the rule against implied repeals. The decisions might be reconciled with the rule against implied repeals by understanding the subsequent statutes as clearly, even if implicitly, ratifying earlier statutory interpretations that might have otherwise been questioned. Under this reading, the rule against implied repeals should be limited to cases where the earlier statute had a relatively clear and longstanding meaning and the later statute is ambiguous enough to give a neutral interpreter pause.

[62]411 U.S. 475 (1973), excerpted and discussed in Hetzel, Libonati & Williams 606-09.

violated and seeking early release from confinement. They sued under the Civil Rights Act of 1871 (42 U.S.C. § 1983), which provides relief against state actors for violations of federal law, and the habeas corpus statute, an older law providing a federal forum for challenges to state detention. The habeas law was amended in 1948 to require exhaustion of state remedies; § 1983 has no such requirement. The issue was whether plaintiffs could proceed in their § 1983 lawsuit without exhausting state remedies, as required before they could proceed in their habeas lawsuit. Although § 1983's "broad language" seemed to provide a remedy for the prisoners, the Court held that the habeas corpus statute is the exclusive remedy for prisoners seeking release or a shorter term of confinement. *Preiser* can be supported by the last enactment rule, as the Court held that allowing a terms-of-confinement lawsuit to proceed under § 1983 would frustrate the important federalism goal adopted by Congress in the 1948 amendments to the habeas law.

Yet we doubt that the Court would have decided the case differently if the habeas law had been amended in 1848 rather than 1948. *Preiser* might better rest on the *rule that the specific statute controls the general.* Because Congress focused on the precise issue of exhaustion of prisoner claims in the habeas statute and not in the civil rights statute, it might behoove the Court to give primacy to the more focused attention. This rule of construction is justified on republican grounds; the focused language suggests that Congress probably deliberated on the issue and developed a specific intent. Yet the *Preiser* Court did not invoke this well-established canon per se. Indeed, the Court's opinion ultimately rested upon a value judgment: the policy underlying the habeas exhaustion requirement is not only one Congress insisted upon, but one supported and perhaps even compelled by quasi-constitutional concepts of federal-state comity.[63] *Preiser* illustrates our thesis that the most classic citations for text-based canons of construction are not just mechanical applications of textual conventions, but they also, and often predominantly, involve normative judgments.

---

[63]See *id.* at 491-93. The dissenting Justices sharply disagreed with this value judgment, emphasizing the quasi-constitutional policy underlying the broad scope of § 1983 relief and the reasons why exhaustion of state remedies is not required in such lawsuits. See *id.* at 513-24 (Brennan, J., dissenting).

III.   Precedent and Statutory Meaning

Although statutory interpretation is different in many respects from common law decisionmaking, precedents are highly relevant to both. Once a statute has been authoritatively construed by the highest court in the jurisdiction, that precedent affects subsequent interpretations of the statute, and sometimes other statutes as well. Justice Stevens' *Sweet Home* opinion relied on the Court's leading interpretation of the ESA, *TVA v. Hill*.[64] In *Hill*, the Court enforced the plain meaning of ESA § 7 to protect the habitat of the endangered snail darter, even though such strict enforcement would halt construction of a multimillion dollar dam that had been repeatedly funded by Congress notwithstanding its knowledge that the dam would destroy the darter's habitat.[65] Although § 9 was not at issue in *Hill,* the Court's decision in that case rested in part on Congress' goal of preserving endangered species without much regard to monetary costs and noted, in approving dictum, the department's broad interpretation of § 9 to prohibit private interference with habitats of protected species. The dissenters in *Sweet Home* found this argument unpersuasive, as the doctrine of stare decisis does not consider dicta binding in subsequent cases. Furthermore, the passages from *Hill* invoked by the majority were too general to have much bite for the precise issue in *Sweet Home.*

Nonetheless, statutory precedents are critically important in many cases. Indeed, we treat such precedents in this chapter on textual sources, in part because these are among the most important sources for interpreting statutes, and in part because there are logical and historical connections between text and precedent. For decades,

---

[64]437 U.S. 153 (1978), an important plain meaning case, excerpted and discussed in Eskridge & Frickey 565-66, 575-76; Hetzel, Libonati & Williams 1263-77; Mikva & Lane 806-20; Popkin 663-65.

[65]Chief Justice Burger's opinion for the Court in *Hill* invoked the *Mancari* rule against repeals by implication to conclude that subsequent appropriations statutes should not be read to dilute the ESA's species-protective policy. This rule applies with particular "vigor when . . . the subsequent legislation is an *appropriations* measure." 437 U.S. at 190. See Popkin 659-65. Accord, *Robertson v. Seattle Audobon Soc'y*, 503 U.S. 429 (1992), excerpted in Eskridge & Frickey 948-50; Hetzel, Libonati & Williams 1277-80. See Chapter 5, Part I (discussing the justifications for this canon relating to appropriations rules).

judicial constructions of statutes were considered "part of the warp and the woof of legislation," virtual amendments to statutes which only Congress itself could change.[66] Although this is no longer an accepted justification for taking judicial constructions as seriously as the statutory text itself, the metaphor is consistent with the more defensible idea that a judicial construction is like a dictionary definition.[67] Both are conventional sources telling us how particular terms, clauses, and sentences are to be understood in particular contexts. The idea of a statutory precedent as creating a term of art resonates with other quasi-textual canons, such as the reenactment, borrowed statute, and *in pari materia* rules, which we analyze later in this chapter.

A. *The Super-Strong Presumption of Correctness for Statutory Precedents*

Once the Supreme Court has authoritatively construed a federal statute, that precedent is not only entitled to the usual presumption of correctness suggested by the common law doctrine of stare decisis, but it is supposed to be given a heightened stare decisis effect. Although the modern Court does not insist that statutory precedents are part of the "warp and woof" of statutes themselves, the Court does say that Congress is the more appropriate body for correcting erroneous constructions of statutes. Classically illustrating this super-strong presumption of correctness is *Flood v. Kuhn*.[68] The issue in the case was whether professional baseball is exempt from the Sherman Antitrust Act. Although nothing in the statute suggested such an exemption, the Court in 1922 ruled baseball exempt on the ground that it was not then an activity in "interstate commerce" (a requirement of the Sherman Act). In 1953 the Court reaffirmed that

---

[66]*Francis v. Southern Pac. Co.*, 333 U.S. 445, 450 (1948); see Frank Horack, Jr., *Congressional Silence: A Tool of Judicial Supremacy*, 25 Tex. L. Rev. 247, 250-51 (1947).

[67]Indeed, *Black's Law Dictionary*, a uniquely authoritative source of legal definitions, relies most heavily, and for many words exclusively, on judicial precedents.

[68]407 U.S. 258 (1972), excerpted and discussed in Eskridge & Frickey 425-38; Popkin 543-44, 548. Other references to the same effect include *Illinois Brick Co. v. Illinois*, 431 U.S. 720 (1977); *Cleveland v. United States*, 329 U.S. 14 (1945).

precedent, even though baseball by then was surely a vigorous participant in interstate commerce.[69]　When the Supreme Court decided Curt Flood's case in 1972, there was no factual doubt that professional baseball was an enterprise in interstate commerce.　All the Justices would have found baseball within the statute if the issue were one of first impression, and it is likely that the precedents would have been overruled had they been mere common law decisions.[70] Yet the Court reaffirmed the precedents.

All but the most devoted baseball fans have trouble swallowing Justice Blackmun's *Flood* opinion.　Critical scholars in particular indict the majority's insensitivity to Curt Flood's predicament.　As a black man, he was profoundly offended by the reserve clause, which resembled slavery in some ways and would result in his forced move to a less tolerant community.　*Flood*'s weaknesses exemplify both the strong academic consensus against giving statutory precedents such strong stare decisis effect[71] and the judiciary's (rhetorical) loyalty to the super-strong presumption.　Justice Blackmun's main argument for declining to revisit the precedents was that Congress is the more appropriate institution to do so.　This core argument has more facets than is apparent from the opinion itself.　To begin with, Justice Blackmun emphasized that Congress had indeed focused on the issue and signaled its acquiescence in baseball's exemption.　After 1953, Congress considered dozens of bills dealing with antitrust exemptions

---

[69]*Toolson v. New York Yankees, Inc.*, 346 U.S. 356 (1953), reaffirming *Federal Baseball Club v. National League*, 259 U.S. 200 (1922).

[70]One justification for this speculation is that the Court had repeatedly refused to expand *Federal Baseball*'s antitrust immunity to other sports, including football, boxing, and basketball.　A common law precedent isolated the way *Federal Baseball* was would not likely have survived challenge.　Compare *Moragne v. States Marine Lines, Inc.*, 398 U.S. 375 (1970), excerpted and discussed in Eskridge & Frickey 398-411.

[71]See, e.g., Hart & Sacks, *supra* note 32, at 1313-36; William O. Douglas, *Stare Decisis*, 49 Colum. L. Rev. 735 (1949); William Eskridge, Jr., *Overruling Statutory Precedents*, 76 Geo. L.J. 1361 (1988); Earl Maltz, *The Nature of Precedent*, 66 N.C. L. Rev. 367 (1988); J.W. Moore & R.S. Oglebay, *The Supreme Court, Stare Decisis, and the Law of the Case*, 21 Tex. L. Rev. 514 (1943).　But see Lawrence Marshall, *"Let Congress Do It": The Case for an Absolute Rule of Statutory Stare Decisis*, 88 Mich. L. Rev. 177 (1989), which argues for a rule against ever overruling statutory precedents.

for professional sports yet never adopted legislation affecting the judicially crafted baseball exemption. All but a few of the bills, in fact, would have confirmed baseball's exemption and expanded it to other sports. "Congress, by its positive inaction, has allowed those decisions to stand for so long and, far beyond mere inference and implication, has clearly evinced a desire not to disapprove them legislatively."[72]

The operation of the legislative process (Chapter 3) undermines this kind of argument. Given the many vetogates in Congress, it is perilous to divine much meaning from legislative failure to override Supreme Court decisions. Although Congress devotes significant resources to considering attacks on the Court's interpretation of federal statutes and each Congress overrides several statutory precedents, the burden of inertia makes it exceedingly difficult to do so.[73] And, as the transactional model of legislation suggests, it is virtually impossible to override a precedent unless powerful interest groups support the override. Baseball owners (and owners in other sports wanting an exemption) are the classic example of a small, homogeneous, and wealthy group that is best able to overcome free-rider problems and organize politically, while ticket buyers (the fans) are equally classic in our inability to organize, as we are a large, diffuse group of people, each one of which has little stake in the costs of the antitrust exemption. Although baseball players could provide an opposing force, Justice Marshall argued in dissent that in the early 1970s they had much less clout than wealthy owners. Moreover, we know from Chapter 3 that the owners were in a stronger position because they needed only to block legislation removing baseball's antitrust exemption rather than to enact reform.

Justice Blackmun also expressed concern with the "confusion and the retroactivity problems" that would accompany an overruling of the long-established precedents.[74] Although delphic at first glance, these factors point toward a better argument for not overruling the prior decisions than the contention about the supposed "positive

---

[72]*Flood*, 407 U.S. at 283-84.

[73]See William Eskridge, Jr., *Overriding Supreme Court Statutory Interpretation Decisions*, 101 Yale L.J. 331 (1991); Eskridge, *supra* note 71.

[74]*Flood*, 407 U.S. at 283.

inaction" of Congress. Because the baseball leagues had evolved for half a century under the umbrella of the antitrust exemption, they had reliance interests in the status quo that would be necessarily sacrificed by a retroactive judicial overruling. One reason Congress might have been the better forum for correcting the obsolescent precedents is that Congress would do so prospectively, and probably with a transition period and tailored exceptions to ameliorate the fairness problems that arise from exposing an established enterprise to new forms of regulation. Professor Ross, a leading commentator on *Flood*, believes the Court was concerned that antitrust principles do not generally fit well with professional athletics and thought that only Congress could tailor the antitrust laws to the special needs of baseball.[75] Finally, the owners' brief argued that the particular issue raised in Curt Flood's case — namely, the reserve clause, allowing owners to trade players without their consent — was best handled through arbitration rather than adjudication.[76] Do these kinds of arguments concerning institutional competence rehabilitate Justice Blackmun's disposition in *Flood*? How about this precept: You only get one pitch at overruling a statutory precedent, and the Court whiffed on that in 1953.

Whatever your views about *Flood*, the Supreme Court continues to say that statutory precedents should receive heightened stare decisis effect,[77] and state courts follow at least as strong a presumption. Of course, that does not mean courts always follow such precedents. The dissenting Justices in *Preiser*, for example, main-

---

[75]Stephen Ross, *Reconsidering* Flood v. Kuhn, 12 U. Miami Ent. & Sports L. Rev. 169 (1995). Ross believes those concerns are misplaced and argues that *Flood* and the prior precedents should still be overruled. (Law professors are never going to give up on this issue.)

[76]In the Andy Messersmith arbitration, the arbitrator overturned the reserve clause and was sustained in the courts. *Kansas City Royals Baseball Corp. v. Major League Baseball Players Ass'n*, 409 F. Supp. 233 (W.D. Mo.), *aff'd*, 532 F.2d 615 (8th Cir. 1976). After that, the owners and players have relied upon collective bargaining to establish the limits to which a player may be bound to play for a team.

[77]See *Neal v. United States*, 516 U.S. 284 (1996); *Patterson v. McLean Credit Union*, 491 U.S. 164 (1989); *Johnson v. Transportation Agency, Santa Clara County*, 480 U.S. 616 (1987) (especially strong statements in concurring opinions by Justices Stevens and O'Connor).

tained that the Court was bound by an earlier decision holding that § 1983 provides a remedy for prisoners without the exhaustion required by the habeas statute.[78] In good common law fashion, the *Preiser* majority distinguished the earlier decision on the ground that it dealt with conditions, rather than terms, of confinement and therefore did not present a square conflict between the civil rights and habeas laws. As experience with the common law teaches us, the relevance and importance of precedent do not assure its determinacy or dispositiveness. In the last generation, the Supreme Court has explicitly overruled about one statutory precedent each Term, implicitly overruled about one precedent per Term, and disavowed reasoning in statutory precedents at roughly the same rate that the Chicago Cubs lose baseball games.[79]

B. *The Reenactment Rule*

Recall that, in *Sweet Home*, the department had broadly construed the term *harm* since 1975. If Congress had reenacted the ESA and left §§ 3 and 9 unchanged, there would have been a plausible argument for the proposition that Congress "ratified" the department's established view of the statute. The Supreme Court has repeatedly held that "the reenactment by Congress, without change, of a statute, which had previously received long continued executive [or judicial] construction, is an adoption by Congress of such construction."[80] The reenactment rule is like heightened stare decisis in that it creates a strong presumption that authoritative constructions of a statute become tightly bonded to the text and ought not be overruled by the Court. It is narrower than heightened stare decisis

---

[78]See *Preiser*, 411 U.S. at 500-01 (Brennan, J., dissenting), relying on *Wilwording v. Swenson*, 404 U.S. 249 (1971).

[79]See Eskridge, *supra* note 51, at 316-22 (listing Supreme Court decisions in each category, 1962-92).

[80]*United States v. Cerecedo Hermanos y Compañía*, 209 U.S. 337, 339 (1908); see *Pierce v. Underwood*, 487 U.S. 552 (1988); *United States v. Board of Comm'rs of Sheffield, Ala.*, 435 U.S. 110 (1978); William Eskridge, Jr., *Interpreting Legislative Inaction*, 87 Mich. L. Rev. 67, 78-84, 129-31 (1988) (listing and discussing the reenactment precedents).

in that Congress must actually reenact the law,[81] and it is broader than heightened stare decisis because it is not limited to interpretations by the Supreme Court and can apply to agency or consensus lower court interpretations.

Like the other "rules," this one is not always followed. The issue in *Girouard v. United States*[82] was whether, under the Nationality Act of 1940, a noncitizen qualified for naturalization if he was willing to take the oath promising to defend the Constitution and laws of the United States against all enemies but, because of religious scruples, was willing to serve in the armed forces only as a noncombatant. In a series of cases, the Supreme Court had construed the prior law[83] containing this oath as requiring such noncitizens to agree to bear arms to qualify for citizenship. Even though in the 1940 statute Congress had retained the same wording for the oath, a majority in *Girouard* declined to interpret the new statute as precluding naturalization for noncitizens like Girouard. " 'It would require very persuasive circumstances enveloping Congressional silence to debar this Court from reexamining its own doctrines,' " the Court reasoned. "It is at best treacherous to find in congressional silence alone the adoption of a controlling rule of law."[84] As before, the Court's failure to follow the traditional presumption owed much to normative considerations. The Court in 1946 may have been less likely to penalize noncitizens for pacifist tendencies. More important, Congress had concretely adopted such a stance when it amended the law in 1942 to expedite citizenship applications by noncitizens who had served in the armed forces, including in noncombatant roles because of pacifist views, and who were subject to the same oath requirement. The Court will also refuse to apply the reenactment rule

---

[81]The old *acquiescence rule*, stipulating that congressional failure to override implicitly ratifies a conclusive judicial or administrative statutory interpretation, finds support in cases like *Flood v. Kuhn* and *Johnson v. Transportation Agency, Santa Clara County*, 480 U.S. 616 (1987), see also Eskridge, *supra* note 80, at 71-78, 125-28, but has been universally criticized, see *id.* at 68 n.9, and is no longer often invoked by the Court. For a recent invocation, however, see *Faragher v. City of Boca Raton*, 118 S.Ct. 2275, 2291 n.4 (1998).

[82]328 U.S. 61 (1946), excerpted and discussed in Popkin 549-50.

[83]The Naturalization Act of 1906, § 4, 34 Stat. 596.

[84]*Id.* at 69, quoting *Helvering v. Hallock*, 309 U.S. 106, 119 (1940).

when the prior interpretation was not authoritative or was clearly inconsistent with the new statute and its purposes.[85]

C. *Judicial Constructions of Similar Statutes*

In *Sweet Home*, Justice Scalia argued that *take* in the ESA should be read the same way *take* had been defined in another statute. Related to this idea is the rule that judicial interpretations of one statute can be informed by interpretations of similar statutes. In drafting statutes, legislatures frequently borrow terminology and phrasing from other statutes in the same jurisdiction or from other jurisdictions, a practice Professor Horack called *stare de statute.*[86] "Congress is presumed to be aware of an administrative or judicial interpretation of a statute and to adopt that interpretation when it re-enacts a statute without change," pursuant to the reenactment rule. "So too, where, as here, Congress adopts a new law incorporating sections of a prior law, Congress normally can be presumed to have had knowledge of the interpretation given to the incorporated law, at least insofar as it affects the new statute."[87] This presumption rests upon a legal fiction about what Congress "had knowledge of," but that fiction is similar to the fiction that Congress had knowledge of dictionary meanings of terms that it has chosen or of prior interpretations of statutes it is reenacting. All serve the rule of law by seeking objective bases for construing statutes, and they put the legislature on notice that it should expect its statutes to be interpreted along the lines of these precepts, at least if the principles are uniformly applied.

The presumption is variously called the *borrowed statute rule* or the *in pari materia rule*, depending on the jurisdiction and the context, but the idea is the same. The rule is particularly robust at the state level. Because many important state statutes are adaptations of Uniform Laws and because uniformity as to basic matters is an important federalism value, state high courts are particularly likely to

---

[85]See, e.g., *Aaron v. SEC*, 446 U.S. 680, 692-94 (1980); *Leary v. United States*, 395 U.S. 6 (1969).

[86]See Frank Horack, Jr., *The Common Law of Legislation*, 23 Iowa L. Rev. 41 (1937).

[87]*Lorillard v. Pons*, 434 U.S. 575, 580-81 (1978), a leading statement of both the reenactment and the borrowed statute rules.

follow this rule.[88] For example, in *Van Horn v. William Blanchard Co.*,[89] the New Jersey Supreme Court construed its Comparative Negligence Act. The law explicitly adopted a "modified comparative negligence" approach, whereby plaintiff could recover so long as her negligence was "not greater than the negligence of the person against whom recovery is sought." Can a plaintiff who is 50% negligent recover against two defendants who are 30% and 20% negligent? The plaintiff's fault is "not greater" than the fault of the defendants if aggregated but is "greater" than the defendants' fault if they are treated individually. Justice Clifford's opinion for the court concluded that the statutory text supported the individual-comparison approach. It also stressed that New Jersey had copied the statute verbatim from Wisconsin's comparative negligence law and that the Wisconsin Supreme Court (both before New Jersey's adoption and after it) construed the statute to follow the individual-comparison rule.

Justice Handler vigorously dissented in *Van Horn*. He first argued that the statutory text was not as clear as Justice Clifford assumed. Because New Jersey has a statutory rule that terms in the singular include the plural, the comparative negligence law could be read as adopting the aggregation approach, because *person against whom recovery is sought* can be read as *persons against whom recovery is sought* when there are two defendants, as in *Van Horn*. As to the borrowed statute argument, Justice Handler observed that statutory precedents from other jurisdictions are not binding as a matter of stare decisis, that the rule at most sets a presumption, and that where the policy of the adopting jurisdiction is different from that of the original jurisdiction the presumption is rebutted. He objected that "no compelling argument is made why the decisions of the Wisconsin Supreme Court should be clamped around this State's comparative negligence law like an iron girdle."[90] Moreover, the sponsors of the law invoked nine states (Wisconsin and eight others)

---

[88]The best illustration of this point is Hetzel, Libonati & Williams 589-600; see 2B Sutherland, *supra* note 11, § 52.02. Other casebooks emphasize federal cases, which less often follow the rule. See Eskridge & Frickey 832-47; Popkin 671-86.

[89]438 A.2d 552 (N.J. 1981), excerpted and discussed in Hetzel, Libonati & Williams 596-600.

[90]*Id.* at 560 (Handler, J., dissenting).

that had a similar law. At least one of the states (Arkansas) followed the aggregate rather than individual approach at the time of New Jersey's adoption, and one other adopted that interpretation afterwards. Should your view of the best policy affect your judgment in the case? Justice Handler openly admitted that it affected his vote and suggested that it affected the majority as well. The legislature shared Justice Handler's views and promptly overrode *Van Horn*. Does that vindicate the dissenting position?

Although Justice Handler's view was the minority in *Van Horn*, it is often the prevailing position, because judges conclude that the public policy of their state is sufficiently different from that of the originating jurisdiction[91] or because the statutory language has been borrowed from a different kind of statutory regime.[92] Moreover, legislative drafters often tinker with borrowed statutory language and cut and paste from different statutes. Does the rule have any bearing in those cases? In *Lorillard v. Pons*,[93] the U.S. Supreme Court held that it does. The issue was whether the Age Discrimination in Employment Act of 1967 (ADEA) carried with it a jury trial right. Avoiding the constitutional issue through the use of the borrowed language rule, Justice Marshall's opinion for the Court interpreted the ADEA to provide plaintiffs a right to jury trials. The case was not an easy one, because some language in the ADEA had been taken from Title VII, which lower courts had interpreted as not having a jury trial right, and other language from the Fair Labor Standards Act (FLSA), which did carry a jury trial right. Justice Marshall ruled that the procedural and enforcement sections of the ADEA were more closely patterned on the FLSA; the ADEA's particular allowance of legal as well as equitable relief confirmed that the statute probably contemplated jury trials.

---

[91]See, e.g., *Zerbe v. State*, 578 P.2d 597 (Alas. 1978), excerpted and discussed in Eskridge & Frickey 842-47.

[92]See, e.g., *Fogerty v. Fantasy, Inc.*, 510 U.S. 517 (1994), excerpted and discussed in Popkin 674-75.

[93]434 U.S. 575 (1978), excerpted and discussed in Eskridge & Frickey 836-42.

8

Extrinsic Sources for Statutory Interpretation

The *textual sources* examined in Chapter 7 can be distinguished from *extrinsic sources* examined in this chapter. Reasoning from textual sources asks how the ordinary speaker would understand the statutory command, in light of the conventional meaning of the words and syntax used and in light of inferences that can be logically drawn from the whole statute or other texts in the code. Interpretation *x* is better than *y* because it better accords with normal linguistic usage or better fits with the statute as a complete text. Reasoning from extrinsic sources asks what the statutory command means, in light of sources of legal understandings found outside of the four corners of the statute and conventions of linguistics. Interpretation *x* is better than *y* because it is more consistent with a source that the law considers a focal point for filling in the details on a statutory scheme. Such extrinsic sources include the *common law*, *legislative history*, and *agency interpretations*.

As we noted in Chapter 6, *sources* can be distinguished from *goals* in statutory interpretation. For example, two interpreters could agree that the goal is the best interpretation of statutory text but disagree about whether the common law background or legislative history should be considered in addition to that text. Two other interpreters might agree that the touchstone of statutory meaning is legislative intent but nonetheless disagree about whether a source such as legislative history contributes more to that enterprise than it detracts from it. Should extrinsic materials ever be consulted? If so, which ones, and under what circumstances? Consider three different kinds of justifications for these sources, similar to the ones discussed in Chapter 6.

Rule of law justifications would look to the common law, legislative history, and agency regulations as authoritative pronouncements which help make statutory law more determinate, transparent, and objective for the citizenry. Enacted statutes often leave gaps that can be filled or ambiguities that can be resolved by consulting these other sources. If everyone knows about these supplementary sources and they clarify statutory gaps and ambiguities, then they not only render the law clearer for everyone, but also create greater consensus among the citizenry about what the law means.

When the legislature is aware of these conventions of supplementation, legislators can better predict how their statutes will be applied. This subserves the *democratic legitimacy* of statutory interpretation. Because legislative history is created within the legislature, it potentially contributes to the legitimacy of subsequent interpretations, but only insofar as interpreters can distinguish the history reflecting legislative consensus from that reflecting the views of marginal or even troublemaking legislators.

Practical efficacy or more general normative considerations can be promoted if extrinsic sources help the citizenry and other interpreters to understand how the statute is supposed to operate. The dynamic theories popular among academics (and practiced by judges and agencies) would find extrinsic sources particularly useful as a means of applying statutes to new circumstances in ways that fit with larger legal policies or principles. Unlike purely textual conventions, these extrinsic ones can sometimes improve the statute's operation — but likewise they can derail or sidetrack it.

Each of these potential justifications plays out differently for the different extrinsic sources for statutory interpretation, as we shall explain in this chapter. A challenge for each source of meaning is to assure that the particular kind of extrinsic evidence contributes to the rule of law and other boons, and at not too great an expense. Or, to put it another way, those advocating use of extrinsic sources must demonstrate that they decrease *error costs* without substantially increasing *decision costs*. For example, under this efficiency perspective, an interpreter who considers legislative intent the touchstone of statutory interpretation will consult legislative history, which increases the decision costs, only if its use produces a correspondingly greater reduction in error costs (measured by the increased congruence between the resulting interpretation and legislative intent). The responsibility for making these assessments falls to the U.S. Supreme Court (for the federal system) and with each of the state high courts.

A recurring issue is the relationship between these extrinsic sources and textual sources. The *plain meaning rule* suggests that extrinsic sources are not needed, and perhaps should not be consulted, unless textual sources fail to yield a clear answer to the statutory question. In the easy case, interpreters often follow this approach. A lawyer asked to render a quick legal opinion will consult the statutory text and check her interpretation against other parts of the statute and perhaps against a dictionary. Should she do more? Typically, the answer is yes. At the very least, she needs to consult relevant agency regulations.[1] It would usually be malpractice if she did not and her answer got her client into trouble with the agency for violating its regulations. For federal statutes, the attorney is also well advised to consult the statute's committee reports, as they are readily available and often contain valuable guidance.[2] The practitioner would benefit from evaluating the common law background as well. If her understanding of the statute is inconsistent with the traditional common law rule, she should reconsider the firmness with which she holds that view. On the other hand, legislative drafters often intend to overturn or modify the common law practice, so understanding the *status quo ante* can provide insight into the purposes behind the law.

If ordinary lawyers ignore extrinsic evidence at their peril, even in the easy cases, what about ordinary judges? The traditional approach to statutory interpretation by American judges routinely includes consideration of the common law, legislative history, and agency interpretations even when the statutory text has an apparent plain meaning. Consistent with the plain meaning rule, however, these extrinsic sources usually do not trump a clear text, and a dedicated group of judges and law professors maintain that judges

---

[1] At the federal level, formal agency regulations are published in the Code of Federal Regulations and are also on-line. Most tax and environmental law is found in the agency regulations rather than the detailed statutes. Informal regulations, "guidances," and opinion letters are also frequently published or on-line and, in areas such as securities, constitute the main usable source of legal direction. The authoritative weight of these sources is sometimes limited, however.

[2] The *United States Code Congressional and Administrative News* (*USCCAN*), produced by the West Publishing Company, reproduces statutes enacted by Congress and most key committee reports. It is available on-line (as are more recent issues of the *Congressional Record*) and is in many law libraries.

should deemphasize the extrinsic sources generally and ignore them when the text is clear (Chapter 6).

In considering the value of these extrinsic sources, we shall draw from the theories of representation, legislation, and interpretation posed in earlier chapters. We shall apply those theories in the context of leading Supreme Court decisions treating extrinsic sources, as well as the classics introduced in Chapter 6: *Church of the Holy Trinity v. United States*,[3] where the Court ruled that a Christian minister was not an alien imported to "perform labor or service of any kind" for purposes of the Alien Contract Labor Act of 1885; and *United Steelworkers v. Weber*,[4] where the Court ruled that Title VII's rule that employers and unions not "discriminate . . . because of . . . race" allows at least some voluntary race-based affirmative action programs.

I. The Common Law[5]

One of the oldest rules in Anglo-American legisprudence was that statutes in derogation of the common law should be narrowly construed. Just as common law baselines have eroded in constitutional law, so they have eroded in statutory interpretation, and this form of the canon has been extensively criticized and, in many jurisdictions, rejected.[6] On the other hand, the common law remains highly relevant to the interpretation of statutes regulating traditional

---

[3]143 U.S. 457 (1892), excerpted and discussed in Eskridge & Frickey 518-24; Mikva & Lane 828-35; Popkin 230-35.

[4]443 U.S. 193 (1979), excerpted and discussed in Eskridge & Frickey 71-99; Hetzel, Libonati & Williams 456-82; Mikva & Lane 835-55; Popkin 472-76. As in Chapter 6, our analysis of *Weber* draws from William Eskridge, Jr., *Dynamic Statutory Interpretation* 14-31, 37-44 (1994).

[5]Common law rules as background guides for statutory meaning are explored in Eskridge & Frickey 716-32; Hetzel, Libonati & Williams 675-85; Popkin 376-81.

[6]See Antonin Scalia, *A Matter of Interpretation: Federal Courts and the Law* 29 (1997) (terming the canon a "sheer judicial power grab"); Jefferson Fordham & J. Russell Leach, *Interpretation of Statutes in Derogation of the Common Law*, 3 Vand. L. Rev. 438 (1950). But see *Norfolk Redev. & Hous. Auth. v. Chesapeake & Potomac Tel. Co.*, 464 U.S. 30, 35 (1983), which described the derogation canon as "well-established." For more on this canon, see Chapter 9, Part I.

common law areas (tort, contract, property, maritime matters), especially where the legislature has adopted or merely codified common law terms and principles. In a classic example, drafter Karl Llewellyn viewed Article 2 of the Uniform Commercial Code as a "common law code," for it deployed familiar common law concepts and terms and its rules continued evolutionary paths paved by the common law — sometimes, in Llewellyn's view, speeding up salutary evolution. "Statutes which invade the common law or the general maritime law are to be read with a presumption favoring the retention of long-established and familiar principles, except when a statutory purpose to the contrary is evident."[7]

In federal law, this precept has been most dramatically applied in cases interpreting the Civil Rights Act of 1871, current § 1983 of U.S. Code title 42. The statute subjects any "person" acting "under color of" state law to liability in law and equity when that person deprives others of rights secured by the "Constitution and laws" of the United States. The Supreme Court has treated this statute as creating a species of tort liability. Because neither the statutory language nor the legislative history of § 1983 gives much direction as to the details of such public tort liability, the Court has looked to the common law as the source of what might be termed *gap-filling* or *default rules* for filling in the details of the statute. Although the statutory language is all-embracing, the Court has relied on the common law to carve out immunities from suit for various officials.[8] Similarly, in determining what damages relief to afford successful plaintiffs, the Court has started with the normal recoveries allowed by tort law, in some cases adjusted to fit the policies involved in § 1983.[9]

The Court has justified its use of common law baselines in interpreting the scope of § 1983 on both rule of law and policy grounds, which have generated an interesting conflict. The baseline for the drafters of the civil rights law would have been the tort law of

---

[7]*Isbrandtsen Co. v. Johnson*, 343 U.S. 779, 783 (1952).

[8]See *Pierson v. Ray*, 386 U.S. 547 (1967) (judges); *Imbler v. Pachtman*, 424 U.S. 409 (1976) (prosecutors); *Briscoe v. LaHue*, 460 U.S. 325 (1983) (witnesses); cf. *Tower v. Glover*, 467 U.S. 914 (1984) (no immunity for public defenders).

[9]See *Carey v. Piphus*, 435 U.S. 247, 258-64 (1978); *City of Newport v. Fact Concerns, Inc.*, 453 U.S. 247, 258 (1981).

1871, and it is plausible to think that tort law consists of a compre-hensive set of well-developed, time-tested rules. Moreover, tort law rules, as they have evolved over time, are well known to lawyers and many lay people today. These are persuasive justifications for using common law principles to narrow the ambit of the seemingly broad language of § 1983, but they do not clearly reveal *which* common law tort rules to follow — those established in 1871 or those accepted today. The Court has usually followed the latter, albeit nervously (and unpersuasively) seeking to justify them by reference to 1871 sources as well.[10]

A particularly subtle, and controversial, use of the common law came in the famous case of *Bob Jones University v. United States*.[11] The Internal Revenue Code exempts from taxation institutions "organized and operated exclusively for religious, charitable, scientific, testing for public safety, literary, or educational purposes."[12] Bob Jones University had long enjoyed tax-exempt status because it always operated exclusively for educational purposes. After lengthy investigations and negotiations, the Internal Revenue Service ("IRS") revoked its exemption on the ground that Bob Jones discriminated in admissions based upon race, a practice that is strongly contrary to public policy. Bob Jones appealed that ruling, but the Supreme Court agreed with the IRS. The Court started with the proposition that the policy of the exemption was to codify the common law doctrine that charitable trusts be given special privileges. At common law, such privileges were not allowed to institutions that violated local public policies, and so the same disqualification should be read into the federal statutory exemption. Certainly, by the late twentieth century, no conduct could be more

---

[10]Judicial immunity (*Ray*) was recognized at common law in 1871, but prosecutorial immunity (*Imbler*) was not recognized anywhere until the 1890s, and of course public defenders (*Tower*) did not exist until this century. The nervous dynamics of the Court's approach to damages is illustrated by the debate among the Justices in *Smith v. Wade*, 461 U.S. 30 (1983), excerpted and discussed in Eskridge & Frickey 719-31.

[11]461 U.S. 574 (1983), excerpted and discussed in Eskridge & Frickey 815-28; Popkin 377-78.

[12]See 26 U.S.C. § 501(c)(3).

disfavored by American public policy than racial discrimination, as Chief Justice Burger's opinion observed at length.

Most students of legislation find it hard to reject the Court's conclusion in *Bob Jones*, but few have found the Court's reasoning entirely persuasive. The main objection is that the result is at odds with the plain meaning of the statutory text. The law grants the exemption to any institution operated exclusively for "educational" purposes (and also to those operated for "charitable" purposes), without any caveat, suggesting initially that Congress has made a policy judgment that all educational institutions serve the nation's interests *or* that sifting through the many educational institutions and choosing which ones deserve exemption is too much trouble and threatens some degree of state censorship. Moreover, the section granting tax exemption carries with it specific provisos, excluding from the favorable treatment otherwise qualified institutions that generate benefits (even in part) for private individuals or that seek to influence legislation or participate in political campaigns for specific candidates for public office. To the extent that *inclusio unius est exclusio alterius* (the inclusion of one thing suggests the exclusion of all others) is a legitimate guide to interpretation (Chapter 7, Part IC), it supports the idea that the congressional list of exceptions to the tax exemption is an exhaustive list, to which the Court should be reluctant to add new exceptions.

Contributing to the textual argument is that Congress *had* responded to this problem in 1976 when it amended the Code to deny tax-exempt status to social clubs that discriminate on the basis of race, color, or religion.[13] The argument by negative implication is strengthened by the fact that Congress knew how to expand the provision denying tax-exempt status to institutions that discriminate but chose to do so only for social clubs, which might be thought less deserving of deference than schools and colleges. Lamentably, the Chief Justice's opinion for the Court slighted these textual arguments.[14] Thus an initial query raised by the case is whether or

---

[13]*Id.* § 501(i).

[14]Instead, the Chief Justice made this rather weak textual argument: § 170 of the Code allows tax deductions for "charitable contributions" and is in *pari materia* with § 501, which identifies the kinds of institutions to which such contributions

under what circumstances common law rules, or extrinsic evidence more generally, can trump the apparent plain meaning of the statute.

Although he led with the common law and the statutory purpose, the Chief Justice relied on two other kinds of extrinsic evidence as support for creating a nontextual exception to the statutory exemptions. Because Congress had granted the IRS rulemaking authority to elaborate on the requirements of the Internal Revenue Code, the Court deferred to the agency's approach. More important, the Court considered the extensive history of legislative deliberations on this precise issue. After the IRS had adopted the antidiscrimination policy in 1970, Congress immediately and repeatedly deliberated its wisdom in hearings. As a result of those hearings, committees declined to report even one of the thirteen bills introduced to override the IRS's position. Instead, Congress in 1976 arguably reinforced the IRS' position by enacting the exclusion of discriminating social clubs. The committee reports to the 1976 law strongly endorsed the general idea that the government should not subsidize private institutions that discriminate and the specific idea that "discrimination on account of race is inconsistent with an educational institution's tax-exempt status."[15] The reason Congress only addressed discriminating social clubs in the 1976 amendment was to override a lower court decision giving one of them the tax exemption.[16] Prior case law as well as the IRS had since 1970 denied such exemptions to discriminating educational institutions, so there was no need for legislation as to them.

Does this further extrinsic evidence make you more comfortable with the Court's interpretation of the tax statute? Keep your mind open on this question as we consider, in some detail, the role of

---

are tax deductible. Because § 170 uses the broader common law terminology, carrying with it the public policy exception, the concept and the exception should be read into § 501 as well. The problem is that § 170(c)(2)(B) defines *charitable contributions* to be gifts to institutions "organized and operated exclusively for religious, charitable, scientific, literary, or educational purposes." Again, Congress has defined precisely what kinds of contributions it considers "charitable," and the Chief Justice's common law gloss ran up against the plain statutory text.

[15]See 461 U.S. at 601.

[16]See *McGlotten v. Connally*, 338 F. Supp. 448 (D.D.C. 1972), overridden by Pub. L. No. 94-568, 90 Stat. 2697 (1976).

legislative history and agency interpretations, which are the primary sources of extrinsic evidence in the modern administrative state.

II. Legislative History[17]

The legislative history of a statute is the record of deliberations surrounding, and generally prior to, the law's enactment.[18] Most legislative history is created at one of the chief vetogates through which bills must pass to become law (Chapter 3): *hearings* and *reports* are generated by committees reporting bills to the chamber floor; *sponsor statements* and *legislator colloquies* usually occur during the course of floor debate; *conference reports* are developed when the two chambers iron out the differences between bills adopted by the two chambers before they can be presented to the President. In some cases, legislative history has also included *drafting documents* prepared before a bill was introduced in the legislature; *presidential veto or signing statements*; and discussion of a bill after it has passed through the legislature or even signed into law, the oxymoronic *subsequent legislative history*. In Chapter 6, we surveyed the debate about whether legislative history should *ever* be consulted. Assuming that it should be in some cases, this chapter

---

[17]The role of legislative history in construing statutes is treated in Eskridge & Frickey 733-832; Hetzel, Libonati & Williams 437-534; Popkin 404-87. See generally Eskridge, *supra* note 4, at 207-38; Stephen Breyer, *On the Uses of Legislative History in Interpreting Statutes*, 65 S. Cal. L. Rev. 845 (1992); James Brudney, *Congressional Commentary on Judicial Interpretations of Statutes: Idle Chatter or Telling Response?*, 93 Mich. L. Rev. 1 (1994); Daniel Farber & Philip Frickey, *Legislative Intent and Public Choice*, 74 Va. L. Rev. 423 (1988); Jane Schacter, *The Confounding Common Law Originalism in Recent Supreme Court Statutory Interpretation: Implications for the Legislative History Debate and Beyond*, 51 Stan. L. Rev. 1 (1998); Peter Schanck, *The Only Game in Town: An Introduction to Interpretive Theory, Statutory Construction, and Legislative Histories*, 38 Kan. L. Rev. 815 (1990); W. David Slawson, *Legislative History and the Need To Bring Statutory Interpretation Under the Rule of Law*, 44 Stan. L. Rev. 383 (1992); Patricia Wald, *The Sizzling Sleeper: The Use of Legislative History in Construing Statutes in the 1988-89 Term of the United States Supreme Court*, 39 Am. U. L. Rev. 277 (1990); Nicholas Zeppos, *Legislative History and the Interpretation of Statutes: Toward a Fact-Finding Model of Statutory Interpretation*, 76 Va. L. Rev. 1295 (1990).

[18]A great checklist of various documents that might count as legislative history is in Hetzel, Libonati & Williams 438.

examines criteria that might be applied to determine what legislative history is admissible and for what purposes, the hierarchy of legislative history sources, and the conditions (if any) under which legislative history might trump a statutory plain meaning.

A. *Criteria for Using Legislative History*

If legislative history is not entirely off-limits as a theoretical or constitutional matter, one must still figure out what history might be consulted and what value it might have for one's interpretive deliberation. A moderate position would be that legislative history should be consulted only if it is readily *available* to the average lawyer, *relevant* to the precise interpretive question, and *reliable* evidence of consensus within the legislature that can be routinely discerned by interpreters at *reasonable cost*.[19] Consider these criteria in some detail.

The statutory text is readily available to citizens and their lawyers, and the rule of law would require that usable legislative history be similarly available. At the federal level, most legislative history is not only relatively easy for ordinary attorneys to find, but it is also much easier to collect than it was ten years ago because so much of it is on the Internet and microfiche, as well as in published form available in law libraries. Of course, some legislative history of federal statutes is usually not widely available from official sources, including the early drafting history of bills, especially those written outside the legislature; communications between executive department officials and legislators; and committee mark-ups of bills.

Although the unavailability of these materials has made courts reluctant to cite them, judges sometimes do rely on them for what they are worth.[20] In a striking example, the Supreme Court in *Kosak*

---

[19]Cf. Henry Hart, Jr. & Albert Sacks, *The Legal Process: Basic Problems in the Making and Application of Law* 1253-54 (William Eskridge, Jr. & Philip Frickey publication editors, 1994) (from the 1958 "tentative edition"); George Costello, *Average Voting Members and Other "Benign Fictions": The Relative Reliability of Committee Reports, Floor Debates, and Other Sources of Legislative History*, 1990 Duke L.J. 39; Farber & Frickey, *supra* note 17.

[20]See Wald, *supra* note 17, at 202-03.

v. United States[21] ruled that the United States could not be sued under the Federal Tort Claims Act for allowing valuable art to be damaged while in its custody during customs proceedings. The Court found applicable a statutory exception to suit for claims "arising *in respect of* . . . the detention of any goods or merchandise by any officer of customs."[22] Justice Marshall's opinion for the Court conceded some ambiguity as to whether the exception applied only when the claim was for wrongful detention per se *or* applied more broadly to any kind of injury related to the customs detention. Justice Marshall resolved the ambiguity by reference to an unpublished Department of Justice memorandum by the drafter of the bill — written 15 years before the bill was enacted! In dissent, Justice Stevens objected to the Court's reliance on evidence that was accessible only to one party and that was basically the viewpoint of a lobbyist, even if a public-spirited one. *Kosak* seems inconsistent not only with the rule of law, but also with democratic considerations because there was no evidence that even Congress was or could have been aware of the secret memorandum. Thankfully, it is a rare exception to the accessibility rule at the federal level.

The situation at the state level is complex. The legislative history of statutes is published and widely available in some states, such as California and New York, while it is unpublished and available only after some effort in states like Texas and Kansas.[23] There is some correlation between availability of such materials and the willingness of state courts to consider them as a source of statutory meaning. For example, most state courts will not consider legislative colloquies, in part because they are either not recorded or only tape-recorded and therefore not easily available to lawyers at reasonable cost. The Texas Court of Criminal Appeals came up with an ingenious answer to the accessibility (but not the cost) question when it published as an appendix to an opinion a guide to researching legislative history in

---

[21]465 U.S. 848 (1984), excerpted and discussed in Eskridge & Frickey 792-97; Popkin 479-81.

[22]28 U.S.C. § 2680(c) (emphasis added).

[23]For a state-by-state guide, see National Conference of State Legislatures, *Inside the Legislative Process* (1992).

that state.[24] As for legislative debates, the court instructed attorneys to listen to the tapes.

The relevance question is more complex: relevant to *what*? What is the point of looking at legislative history? Recall, from Chapter 6, the legislative history of the alien contract labor statute construed in *Holy Trinity*. Justice Brewer read the exclusion of aliens performing "labor or service of any kind" narrowly, not only exempting the Christian minister from its ambit but also assuming that "brain toilers" generally were exempted. He relied on committee reports for two different kinds of reasons. One was to discern the *general intent* of Congress, namely, the purpose of the statute. Consistent with contemporaneous press accounts, an early lower court construction, and even the title of the act, the House and Senate committee reports identified the statute's purpose as excluding the "class of immigrants" who were "generally from the lowest social stratum"[25] and who were brought over to the United States by employers seeking to depress wage rates. If the general intent of Congress were "simply to stay the influx of this cheap unskilled labor,"[26] as these materials suggested, then the Court should have been reluctant to read the statutory prohibition broadly, according to Justice Brewer. This was arguably both a practical and democratically legitimate use of legislative history, to help inform the Court of the mischief that Congress wanted the statutory scheme to target. Using legislative history to figure out statutory purpose can be objected to on rule of law grounds, however, if the purpose impels the Court to read the statute in a way not suggested by its text, which arguably was also the case in *Holy Trinity*.

Perhaps mindful of this kind of objection, Justice Brewer also invoked the Senate report as support for the idea that excluding "brain toilers" would have been contrary to the *specific intent* of Congress. (In other words, the Court would have been thwarting the will of the branch entrusted with lawmaking, thereby undermining democracy, by uncritically following the apparent plain meaning of the text.) In addition to its discussion of the general problem the bill was sup-

---

[24]See *Dillehey v. State*, 815 S.W.2d 623, 627-33 (Tex. Crim. App. 1991).

[25]See *Holy Trinity*, 143 U.S. at 465.

[26]*Id.*

posed to solve, the Senate committee pointed out that the bill's exclusion of immigrants brought over for "labor or service of any kind" was broader than the members of Congress intended. The report opined that, but for the lateness of the session, the committee would have amended the bill to apply only to *manual* labor and service. The Court used this "singular circumstance" as a clinching argument for its narrow view of the statute. Looking at the Senate report, the Court was able to support its equitable exception for ministers as democratically and lawfully supportable.

Unhappily for the Court, Professor Vermeule has shown that this use of the Senate report has problems of *reliability*.[27] Congress did not enact the alien contract labor bill during the session in which the report apologized for the impossible-to-correct breadth of the bill. Instead, it took up the measure in February 1885, when it was extensively debated in the Senate. Not one senator proposed an amendment to limit the bill to manual labor or service, and the House and Senate floor managers represented the bill as excluding all aliens who came within its admittedly broad textual description. Invoking *unreliable* legislative history is worse than ignoring such history altogether. It is undemocratic to seize upon the views of a legislative subgroup when the entire chamber was told something quite different, and it results in erroneous interpretation as measured from the baseline of intentionalism. Such an approach also arguably violates the constitutional structure that requires bicameral consensus to enact legislation (Article I, Section 7) and precludes judges from legislating and rewriting statutes (Article III). For judges committed to looking at legislative history, the reliability problem can be a big one.

Some legislative history is not reliable because it is generated early in the process and does not reflect the ultimate deals entered to get the statute through Congress. Justice Brennan's opinion for the Court in *Weber* criticized the dissent's parade of anti-quota colloquies, in part on the ground that those colloquies came before the bill was rewritten on the floor of the Senate to add a compromise provision, § 703(j), that implicitly allowed private voluntary but not

---

[27]See Adrian Vermeule, *Legislative History and the Limits of Judicial Competence: The Untold Story of* Holy Trinity Church, 50 Stan. L. Rev. 1833 (1998).

state-required affirmative action.[28] Other legislative history is not reliable because it may reflect the views of legislative outliers, namely representatives who are seeking to give the proposed legislation a slant that they or their allies favor. *Holy Trinity* itself introduced this latter reliability problem with legislative history, because the Court's decision in that and later cases introduced a new self-consciousness into the legislative process. Knowing that courts and agencies will read and may rely on what committees and legislators say about a bill's meaning, interest groups will seek to plant friendly comments in the reports and induce their legislative allies to engage in planned colloquies that reflect a slanted understanding of the statute.[29] Thus, legislative history produced in this century, after *Holy Trinity,* might be more unreliable than that produced before the Supreme Court's landmark decision.

Consider this paradox: there may be a tradeoff between *reliability* and *usefulness* of legislative history. Committee reports and sponsor statements confirming the apparent plain meaning of a statutory text are usually most reliable (they are most likely to reflect the legislative deal) but are not very useful (they just confirm what the interpreter already "knows"). In contrast, committee reports and sponsor statements that take positions on issues not clearly resolved by the statutory text are useful (they help decide the case), but may be less reliable, as may have been the case in *Holy Trinity*.

Professor Vermeule is most critical of Justice Brewer's approach to *Holy Trinity*. Other commentators agree with him about the Court's clumsy invocation of specific intent but disagree with his conclusion that an exclusionary rule is the only solution to avoid sloppy and unprincipled use of legislative materials. Perhaps the relevance of the legislative history is not best tied to specific

---

[28]See *Weber*, 443 U.S. at 207 n.7, responding to *id.* at 231-44 (Rehnquist, J., dissenting). The dissent replied that § 703(j) and its history were just as anti-quota as the previous discussions. See *id.* at 244-51.

[29]The most famous confession of this practice is Congressman William Moorhead, *A Congressman Looks at the Planned Colloquy and Its Effect in the Interpretation of Statutes*, 45 A.B.A. J. 1314 (1959), but no systematic study has shown this to be as troublesome a practice as some have assumed. Compare *Blanchard v. Bergeron*, 489 U.S. 87, 98-99 (1989) (Scalia, J., concurring in part).

legislative intent, but instead to general intent or purpose.[30] The committee reports' understanding of the goal of the statute — to stop depression of wages by employers bringing over cheap labor from abroad — was widely and apparently sincerely shared by legislators supporting the law. Legislative history is more likely to yield reliable evidence of statutory purpose because purpose is at a higher level of generality than specific intent and there is likely to be agreement within the enacting coalition.[31] For the same reason, however, highly general purpose-based arguments will often be even more malleable than specific intent-based arguments. Hence, rule of law concerns might militate against giving evidence of legislative purpose heavy or dispositive weight in statutory interpretation, as the Court did in both *Holy Trinity* and *Weber*.

One of us has suggested a further role for consulting legislative history in cases like *Holy Trinity*: especially for statutes adopted long ago, it is instructive for the current interpreter to see how the legislators used the statutory terms. A notable thing about the debates over the alien contract labor bill was that the supporters focused overwhelmingly on people brought over to do "labor" (with "service" implicitly left as ancillary) and understood labor in the way Justice Brewer did, as manual work.[32] Even a textualist might find something of value in legislative history, which might be a more democratically legitimate guide to meaning than the commonly deployed dictionaries that so fascinate the current Supreme Court.

---

[30]See Carol Chomsky, *The True History of the* Holy Trinity *(Case)*, 100 Colum. L. Rev. ___ (2000) (forthcoming); William Eskridge, Jr., *Textualism, The Unknown Ideal?*, 96 Mich. L. Rev. 1509 (1998).

[31]Recall the suggestion of Hart & Sacks, discussed near the end of Part IIC of Chapter 6: the interpreter should identify the plausible organizing purposes for the statute using all traditional tools other than legislative history, and then consult the legislative history only to see whether it identifies any plausible purposes that were missed the first time around and to ascertain whether it helps sort out which plausible purpose to prefer.

[32]See, e.g., 16 Cong. Rec. 1628, 1630 (Sen. Blair, the floor manager); *id.* at 1781-82 (Sen. Platt); *id.* at 1784 (Sen. Sherman). This point, and more sources, are in Eskridge, *supra* note 30, at 1539. Contrast Vermeule, *supra* note 27, at 1853 & n.89, who asserts that *service* was more bruited about by the legislators, with Chomsky, *supra* note 30, who argues that *labor* was overwhelmingly the operative term.

B. *Hierarchy of Legislative History Sources*

If we are right that legislative history should be used only when it is accessible, relevant, and reliable, there ought to be — and we think there is — a hierarchy of sources for that history. Some legislative history is more weighty and cost-effective than other kinds, namely that legislative history which is accessible, relevant to the interpretive issue, and reasonably reliable. And materials that are not accessible or reliable should rarely, perhaps never, be consulted, even if they are otherwise relevant to the statutory issue. Complicating matters is the possibility of interactions among the factors. For example, material that is accessible and relevant, and thus apt to be used by courts, may become less reliable as lawmakers act strategically to include favorable legislative history that does not accurately reflect the legislative deal.

Committee reports are the most useful legislative history, as reflected in *Holy Trinity*. Almost half the Supreme Court's references to legislative history are to committee reports,[33] and similar documents are the primary legislative history invoked by state courts as well. Is the predominance of committee reports defensible? At the federal level, committee reports are not only publicly available, and now available online, but are reprinted in the widely available *USCCAN*.[34] The reports are also typically quite useful, for they provide an overview of the policy need for the statute (general intent) as well as analysis of each provision and how it relates to other parts of the statute (specific intent). Committee reports are thus accessible and often speak to relevant issues.

The main objection to their use is that they are not always reliable because committees may have their own agendas not reflecting that of the chamber, which may not adequately monitor committee rent-seeking.[35] This concern seems overstated, however. Recent empiri-

---

[33]See Jorge Carro & Andrew Brann, *The U.S. Supreme Court and the Use of Legislative Histories: A Statistical Analysis*, 22 Jurimetrics J. 294, 304 (1982).

[34]See note 2, *supra*.

[35]Justice Scalia also objects that committee reports are written by staff and not read by the legislators, but the same is true of the statutes themselves. More important, there is thus far little or no evidence that congressional staff smuggle in policy statements that do not reflect legislators' preferences and the deals put

cal evidence suggests that congressional committees are relatively representative of their chamber and are monitored not only by the chamber majority but also by whistle-blowers in the minority.[36] It may be too early to conclude that committees actually as well as theoretically operate as information-generating institutions whose members have repeat-play incentives to be responsive to chamber preferences and constraints, but this theory remains lively and persuasive to many neutral observers knowledgeable about the legislative process. For now, it seems safe to say that committee reports have weathered the most cynical critiques of judicial reliance and that careful use of them in interpretation is justified.

Almost as important as committee reports are *explanatory statements by the sponsors or floor managers* of legislation. Justice Rehnquist's *Weber* dissent made much of the facts that the primary Senate and House sponsors insisted that the civil rights bill would not force quotas onto employers and that the Senate managers of the jobs title explicitly assured their colleagues that "any deliberate attempt to maintain a racial balance" would violate the law because it "would require an employer to hire or to refuse to hire on the basis of race."[37] Although he only attracted one other vote in *Weber*, Justice Rehnquist's deft deployment of floor manager statements is widely considered one of his most powerful moments on the Court.

Elsewhere, such evidence has been persuasive to the Court majority. In *North Haven Board of Education v. Bell*,[38] the Court held that Title IX's prohibition of sex discrimination in programs receiving federal funds includes employment discrimination by institutions running such programs. Key evidence for the Court

---

together to get the law through troublesome vetogates. On the contrary, the judgment of informed commentators is that staff faithfully carry out legislator directives. See Brudney, *supra* note 17.

[36]See Thomas Gilligan & Keith Krehbiel, *Organization of Informative Committees by a Rational Legislature*, 34 Am. J. Pol. Sci. 531 (1990); Keith Krehbiel, *Information and Legislative Organization* (1991). See also Chapter 3, Part IA (discussing various theories of congressional committees, some suggesting that members have outlying preferences).

[37]*Weber*, 443 U.S. at 239 (Rehnquist, J., dissenting).

[38]456 U.S. 512 (1982), excerpted and discussed in Popkin 466-70.

included repeated statements by the Senate sponsor that proposed Title IX would cover three kinds of discrimination: admission of students, provision of services and courses of study for admitted students, and employment of faculty and other staff. (Three Justices — including Justice Rehnquist — dissented on the ground that the sponsor's statements were themselves ambiguous.) Like committee reports, sponsor statements — especially the formal statements invoked in *North Haven* and the *Weber* dissent — presumptively reflect the views of the enacting coalition. The speakers are motivated to be truthful because any overstatement may be seized upon by opponents or corrected by the speaker's allies. Moreover, if a sponsor misrepresents the deal in an important way, her reputation may suffer, and with it her effectiveness as a legislator.

After committee reports and sponsor statements, the reliability of legislative history falls off markedly. There is less reason to think that such material reflects the views of the enacting coalition and more reason to worry that it might have been strategically planted in the record. Courts almost never rely on representations about legislation by opponents, who have every incentive to misstate the bill's effect. Even *statements by supporters*, standing alone, are not very reliable. Unlike sponsors, mere supporters have not assumed a leadership role for the enacting coalition. Supporters without institutional responsibilities for the bill face few sanctions for inaccuracies or misrepresentations, and their misstatements are less likely to be monitored and corrected. In *Landgraf v. USI Film Products*,[39] the Court refused to rely on various statements in the Congressional Record by a variety of Senators expressing opinions about the retroactive effect of the Civil Rights Act of 1991, which overrode many of the Court's Title VII decisions. On the other hand, both the majority opinion and the dissent in *Weber* assembled a variety of quotations from minor supporters as well as sponsors of the civil rights law. The goal of each opinion was to show that there was an actual, not just hypothetical, consensus within the enacting coalition as to the statutory purpose of desegregating workplaces (the majority opinion) and the general understanding that the law would not impose or even allow racial quota programs (the dissent).

---

[39]511 U.S. 244 (1994), excerpted and discussed in Eskridge & Frickey 465-77; Mikva & Lane 984-1003; Popkin 297-313.

Although unimpressed with statements by individual legislators, Justice Stevens' opinion in *Landgraf* did consider *drafting and deliberation history*. The Court found it relevant that the President had vetoed the 1990 bill because it overrode the Court's decisions retroactively and that the successful 1991 bill omitted those explicit retroactivity provisions. This is an argument based upon the presumption that Congress does not intend to enact policies that were clearly reflected in earlier versions of the proposed legislation but then withdrawn or (more persuasively) rejected in one chamber or both. The Court more strongly relied on such an argument in *North Haven*, noting that both Houses of Congress in 1975 failed to adopt proposals to override agency regulations applying Title IX to educational employment.[40] There are, however, a significant number of cases where rejected-proposal evidence was unpersuasive because the reasons for rejection were unclear.[41]

Although the Court in *Kosak* relied on *statements by a nonlegislative drafter* of legislation, such evidence usually has little probative value because it is relatively unaccessible and does not necessarily reflect the views of the enacting coalition. Moreover, the possibility of exaggeration or misrepresentation is high. These concerns are greatly abated when legislation is drafted by legislative study commissions or private organizations such as the National Conference of Commissioners on Uniform State Laws. The commentaries provided by such groups are published and widely available, and legislatures adopting their measures are on notice that the commentaries will be used as authoritative sources of meaning. While such materials threaten to smuggle private deals into public law through the back door, state courts will usually consider this kind of background evidence, for some of the same reasons they consider committee reports.[42]

---

[40]See *North Haven*, 456 U.S. at 532-33.

[41]See, e.g., *NLRB v. Catholic Bishop of Chicago*, 440 U.S. 490 (1979), excerpted and discussed in Eskridge & Frickey 676-87. See generally William Eskridge, Jr., *Interpreting Legislative Inaction*, 87 Mich. L. Rev. 67, 84-89, 132-37 (1988) (analysis and appendix collecting the cases).

[42]Compare Laurens Walker, *Writings on the Margin of American Law: Committee Notes, Comments, and Commentary*, 29 Ga. L. Rev. 993 (1995), with *Kaplan v. Superior Court of Orange County*, 491 P.2d 1, 5 n.4 (Cal. 1971)

One nonlegislative official, the President, plays a key role in all federal enactments. *Presidential signing statements* issued when bills are signed into law generally serve political purposes, but it has become an increasingly common practice for them to be designed as well to provide guidance to administrative actors who will implement the laws and to influence the judicial interpretation of the legislation. Courts have struggled with whether to consider such statements in the interpretive calculus. On the one hand, the President is often a major player in negotiating the terms of a bill, and his views might be uniquely well informed.[43] Moreover, as a repeat player on Capitol Hill, the President has incentives not to misrepresent the nature of the compromise. On the other hand, presidential signing statements come at a point when the other players cannot respond, rendering them subject to error or manipulation. In light of this factor, such statements should be treated with caution.

Because they come after the bill has passed Congress, presidential signing statements might be considered *subsequent legislative history*, which is highly disfavored for both rule of law and policy reasons.[44] After-the-fact statements seem particularly prone to insincerity and are not as likely to be refuted if misleading. But recall Chapter 3's discussion of *Montana Wilderness Association v. United States Forest Service*,[45] where Judge Norris withdrew an earlier opinion in light of subsequent legislative history. What persuaded him was a conference committee report for a subsequent statute, which demonstrated a congressional reliance on the interpretation of federal land law that he had previously rejected. The strongest case

---

(considering such evidence because it was endorsed by legislative committees).

[43]See, e.g., *United States v. Story*, 891 F.2d 988, 994 (2d Cir. 1989) (presidential signing statement credited because President was involved in negotiations yielding compromise statute).

[44]The Burger Court sometimes looked at post-enactment history, as when it relied on congressional rejection of bills to override agency regulations in *North Haven*. The Rehnquist Court has taken a harder rhetorical line against subsequent legislative history. See, e.g., *Central Bank v. First Interstate Bank*, 511 U.S. 164, 185-86 (1994). See also Eskridge & Frickey 811-13 & n.1; Brudney, *supra* note 17.

[45]655 F.2d 951 (9th Cir. 1981), excerpted and discussed in Eskridge & Frickey 806-13.

for relying on such history is when Congress has built on a certain construction of federal law when enacting a subsequent statute.[46] In those circumstances, deferring to the subsequent legislative history promotes coherence and can serve to reconcile the two statutes.

In light of the this discussion, consider this diagram, patterned on our *funnel of abstraction* in Chapter 6.[47] This diagram is derived from the federal cases but has application to states where legislative history is available and considered by judges, for the precepts inspiring the Supreme Court cases operate at the state level as well.

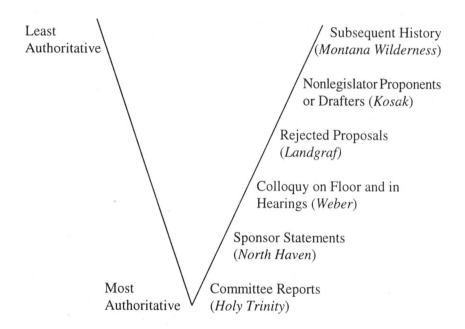

Least
Authoritative

Subsequent History
(*Montana Wilderness*)

Nonlegislator Proponents
or Drafters (*Kosak*)

Rejected Proposals
(*Landgraf*)

Colloquy on Floor and in
Hearings (*Weber*)

Sponsor Statements
(*North Haven*)

Most
Authoritative

Committee Reports
(*Holy Trinity*)

---

[46]See, e.g., *Franklin v. Gwinnett County Pub. Sch.*, 503 U.S. 60 (1992) (discussed in Chapter 7); *Gozlon-Peretz v. United States*, 498 U.S. 395 (1991).

[47]The diagram is developed and explained in Eskridge, *supra* note 4, at 218-22. See also Reed Dickerson, *Statutory Interpretation: Dipping Into Legislative History*, 11 Hofstra L. Rev. 1125 (1983).

C. *The Relationship Between Legislative History and Plain Meaning*

Unhappily, the diagram developed above does not solve some of the most vexing statutory questions because the deepest puzzles address the relationship of text and context and involve normative as well as archaeological issues. Consider *Western Communications, Inc. v. Deschutes County.*[48] An Oregon trial court directed the county to provide a newspaper with information about certain tax payments of some private entities. While the case was on appeal, the legislature enacted a statute exempting such materials from public disclosure on privacy grounds. The senate sponsor of the statute explained it to the house committee as a measure to " 'fix' the statute to address the Court's interpretation, and offer the protection that I believe was and is intended by state and local government." A committee member asked the next witness for the bill, "Wouldn't emergency clause be good in bill, retroactive clause?"[49] The witness agreed, and the committee added an emergency clause which assured that the bill would take effect immediately. The issue on appeal was whether the new statute applied to the pending case. Writing for the Oregon Court of Appeals, Judge Riggs ruled that it did. Because the point of the statute was, according to its sponsor, to override the lower court and protect against disclosure of private tax information, the law should be applied to the pending case. The committee colloquy confirmed that conclusion, showing that the issue had been flagged and was the reason the law was amended to take effect immediately.

Dissenting Chief Judge Joseph assailed the majority for its "Creative (and Absurd)" use of legislative history. The history itself was ambiguous: it supported the idea that the statute would override the lower court's rule of law, but not so clear that the legislators expected to alter the judgment in that particular case. Moreover, emergency clauses have traditionally been viewed by Oregon courts as not affecting past events. This point by the chief judge reveals

---

[48]788 P.2d 1013 (Or. App. 1990), excerpted and discussed in Popkin 447-50.

[49]As is typical at the state (but not the federal) level, there was no verbatim published report of the house hearing. The majority's quotations were taken from the "bill report" assembled by the staff and consisting of written statements submitted for the record (the senator's quote) and summaries of oral testimony and colloquies (the exchange between the witness and the house member). There are often reliability concerns with such materials.

difficult normative issues underlying the judges' debate. Essential to the holding of the U.S. Supreme Court in *Landgraf* was a normative presumption that statutes not be applied retroactively to past events, a canon of interpretation with constitutional undertones that would support Chief Judge Joseph's approach. Supporting Judge Riggs, however, *Landgraf* also contained an explication of what "retroactivity" itself meant. Thus, "application of new statutes passed after the events in suit is unquestionably proper in many situations. When the intervening statute authorizes or affects the propriety of prospective relief, application of the new provision is not retroactive."[50] Under this language, is the application of a statute to injunctive relief in a pending case properly considered to be "retroactive"? Recall, too, that the result reached in *Holy Trinity* was, in effect, to read the 1885 statute to include an exemption provided by an 1891 amendment that by its explicit terms did not apply to pending cases. Clearly in *Holy Trinity*, and perhaps also in *Deschutes County*, the Court was influenced by its view of the reasonableness of the application of the statute to the pending case in determining whether the application was even "retroactive" for purposes of the traditional canon.

Assume that the statute had an unambiguous plain meaning. Should the court then also consider legislative history? Shortly after *Deschutes County*, the Oregon Supreme Court ruled that legislative history should be examined only if the text and canons of statutory construction (such as the presumption against retroactivity) leave the interpreter uncertain as to legislative intent.[51] Generally speaking, this is the rule at the federal level and in virtually all the states whose courts consider legislative history at all. But if meaning depends on context, as is widely believed, how can you be sure the text is "plain" and the legislative intent "clear" if you do not consider probative legislative history (if any exists)? This intuition is why Justice Brewer looked at committee reports and other extrinsic evidence, notwithstanding his concession that the government's insistence on statutory plain meaning had "great force." It is also why Justice Rehnquist's *Weber* dissent delved extensively into Title VII's

---

[50]*Landgraf*, 511 U.S. at 273. See *Bradley v. School Bd. of Richmond*, 416 U.S. 696 (1974).

[51]See *Portland Gen. Elec. Co. v. Bureau of Labor & Indus.*, 859 P.2d 1143 (Or. 1993).

legislative history even though the dissent initially, and powerfully, maintained that, "Were Congress to act today specifically to prohibit the type of racial discrimination suffered by Weber, it would be hard pressed to draft language better tailored to the task than that found in . . . Title VII."[52]

Neither we nor other commentators can resolve this dilemma for you, but some light may be shed on it by the recent House of Lords decision in *Pepper v. Hart.*[53] The issue on appeal was how much taxable income should be imputed to employees of educational institutions who are allowed to enroll their children at reduced tuition rates. The Finance Act of 1976 imposed an income tax on the "cost of the benefit" to the employer (minus any fee paid by the employee), which was defined as the "expense incurred in or in connection with [the fringe benefit's] provision." The government attributed to the taxpayers income in the amount of the *average cost* of educating a student at the school in question (minus the fee). In contrast, the taxpayers asserted that their income was only the *marginal cost* of educating one additional student, an amount that would often be less than the fee paid. Reread the previous sentences carefully and ask yourself: What is the plain or even likely textual meaning of this statute as applied to these facts? Would you want to know more about the context of the legislation? The House of Lords traditionally has not. Following the "British rule" against considering any evidence drawn from the proceedings in Parliament, a panel of Law Lords voted that the statutory text had a plain meaning supporting the government's position.

The Law Lords ordered a rehearing. The taxpayers' brief presented evidence that the Law Lords had misconstrued the deal cut by the government to enact the statute. The original finance bill introduced by the government contained, in addition to the provision for taxing employees for the employer "cost" of a fringe benefit, a provision taxing in-house benefits based on the price that the general

---

[52]*Weber*, 443 U.S. at 226 (Rehnquist, J., dissenting). Echoing Justice Brewer's concession a century earlier, Justice Brennan's opinion for the Court in *Weber* conceded that the plain meaning argument was "not without force." *Id.* at 201.

[53][1993] 1 All E.R. 42 (H.L. 1992), excerpted and discussed in Eskridge & Frickey 758-73; Popkin 451-65.

public paid for the benefits (minus any fee the employee paid). This special provision would have steeply taxed discounted fares given transport employees and education provided to the children of school employees. Railway employee groups immediately complained, and at a parliamentary hearing a chastened Financial Secretary withdrew that special provision from the bill and announced that the law governing in-house benefits (taxable at the employer's marginal cost) would be left unchanged. A Member of Parliament queried whether the withdrawal of the special provision meant that discounted tuition would also remain subject to the old rule, and the Secretary replied: "The removal of [the special provision] will affect the position of a child of one of the teachers at the child's school, because now the benefit will be assessed on the cost to the employer, which would be very small indeed in this case." No speaker for the government nor any Member of Parliament disagreed with any of these statements, and the bill as amended was enacted.

How can your view of the statutory language not be affected by this background information? It certainly affected their Lordships. A slightly different panel of Law Lords voted 7-0 in favor of the taxpayers on rehearing. The Lord Chancellor alone relied on the plain meaning of the text. Everyone else considered the legislative history, and five of those six thought it dispositive. The lead opinion, by Lord Browne-Wilkinson, announced that British courts would henceforth consider the parliamentary history of legislation if, and only if, (1) the statute is ambiguous or leads to an absurd result, (2) the parliamentary materials focus on representations by a "minister or other promoter of the Bill," and (3) the materials clearly answer the precise interpretive question. This formulation is bound to engender debate and likely confusion, as the lower courts sort out admissible from inadmissible parliamentary history.

Pepper v. Hart may end up being the United Kingdom's version of *Holy Trinity*: once a little legislative history is admissible, all of it ultimately gets researched and introduced, which in turn causes more of it to get generated. It is like eating potato chips: you can't eat just one. The potato-chip feature of using legislative history is a chief reason for the instability of the soft plain meaning rule followed by the U.S. Supreme Court and now by the U.K. House of Lords.

Once legislative history gets researched, how can a court not be influenced by smoking guns that the research turns up?

In cases like *Pepper v. Hart*, would it be proper for a court, knowing that the legislative "deal" was to allow school teachers to use marginal cost for tuition benefits, nonetheless to require average cost on the basis of the statute's plain meaning? To many judges that sounds willful,[54] but to some it sounds like routine application of the rule of law. (Note that an approach that excludes such history in *Pepper* might look unfair *ex post* (in retrospect) but might create the best rule *ex ante*.) A final lesson of *Pepper* is that "plain meaning" is itself highly artifactual. It depends upon conventions. If one of the conventions is that statutory language should be understood in the context of the legislature's general or specific expectations, then legislative history becomes *intrinsic to* — rather than *extrinsic to* — a textual inquiry. (Hence, our division of chapters into separate treatments of *textual* and *extrinsic* sources is itself artifactual. We defend our decision on the basis of the convenience of our readers.)

III.   Administrative Interpretations[55]

Most government-based statutory interpretations are nowadays rendered by administrative agencies and departments, and courts are second-order interpreters, examining the issues against the backdrop of what agencies have already said (and in some cases have said for a long time). In *Weber* (Chapter 6), in *Sweet Home* (Chapter 7), and in *Bob Jones, Kosak, Montana Wilderness*, and *North Haven* (all in this chapter), the Supreme Court was not only reviewing agency interpretations, but it followed and upheld those interpretations in each case. This is not a new phenomenon, for the Court has long taken the position that "[w]hen faced with a problem of statutory construction, this Court shows great deference to the interpretation

---

[54]See *Director of Public Prosecutions v. Bull*, [1994] 4 All E.R. 411, holding that a man could not be a "common prostitute" under a 1959 statute. The judge opined that he would not be willing, under *Pepper* or even under the previous exclusionary rule, to apply a plain meaning which he felt was contrary to the legislature's expectations.

[55]Agency views as sources of statutory meaning are explored in Eskridge & Frickey 854-79; Hetzel, Libonati & Williams 571-89; Mikva & Lane 797-804; Popkin 488-516.

given the statute by the officers or agency charged with its administration."[56] At first glance, this is unremarkable. In construing statutes, agencies consider the same sources private lawyers and public judges do (statutory text, legislative history, and purpose), but they are also better informed about the statutory history and the practicality of competing policies than courts are. Yet another look suggests that deference to agency views on matters of law presses statutory policy in particular and, for some, troubling directions.

Because agencies generally give greater weight to policy and statutory purpose and may be swayed by political pressure from the President, Congress, and interest groups, they may be more likely than courts to bend the text and supersede the original legislative expectations than courts. This phenomenon is well illustrated in cases such as *Weber, Sweet Home,* and *Bob Jones,* as dissenting Justices argued in those cases. Scholars have supported deference, in part because of and not in spite of agencies' tendency to interpret statutes flexibly and even dynamically.[57] This Part provides a detailed introduction to the leading Supreme Court case counseling deference even to relatively dynamic agency interpretations. We also assess several cautions about how far courts will or should go in deferring to agencies. As before, the analysis is driven by considerations about the rule of law, democratic legitimacy, and pragmatic assessments concerning the allocation of responsibilities among governmental institutions.

A. *The* Chevron *Revolution?*

Since the New Deal, the U.S. Supreme Court has required the federal judiciary to defer to some extent to administrative constructions of statutes, especially when those constructions were rendered

---

[56]*Udall v. Tallman,* 380 U.S. 1, 16 (1965).

[57]See T. Alexander Aleinikoff, *Updating Statutory Interpretation,* 87 Mich. L. Rev. 20, 42-46 (1988); Colin Diver, *Statutory Interpretation in the Administrative State,* 133 U. Pa. L. Rev. 549 (1985); Jerry Mashaw, *Prodelegation: Why Administrators Should Make Political Decisions,* 1 J.L. Econ. & Org. 81 (1985); Peter Strauss, *When the Judge Is Not the Primary Official With Responsibility to Read: Agency Interpretation and the Problem of Legislative History,* 66 Chi.-Kent L. Rev. 321 (1990).

at or soon after the enactment of the statute.[58] Conversely, agency interpretations well after the statute's enactment were sometimes accorded less deference, and, if the agency actually changed its mind, the Supreme Court was much less likely to defer. For example, in *General Electric Co. v. Gilbert*,[59] the Court refused to defer to the EEOC's view that Title VII's prohibition of "discriminat[ion] . . . because of . . . sex" includes pregnancy-based discrimination. A key reason for the decision was the agency's flip-flop: in 1966 the EEOC had taken the public position that pregnancy-based discrimination does not fall under the 1964 statute and only in 1972 (eight years after the law was enacted) adopted the more liberal view.

Today, the leading case is *Chevron U.S.A., Inc. v. Natural Resources Defense Council*,[60] a precedent that established a more dynamic justification for judicial deference to agency interpretations of statutes. The Clean Air Amendments of 1977 impose certain requirements on states that have not achieved the national air quality standards established by the Environmental Protection Agency (EPA). Under earlier legislation, the EPA required "nonattainment" states to operate permit programs which typically prevent "new or modified major stationary sources" from increasing their level of air pollution. Manufacturing groups urged the EPA to define "major stationary source" to include an entire industrial plant, so that, if one smokestack or device increased its pollution level, the manufacturer could still comply with the law by reducing the level produced by other smokestacks or devices. In 1980, the Carter Administration's EPA rejected this *bubble concept* (based on the notion that the entire plant was under a bubble), and the Court of Appeals for the D.C. Circuit (dominated by Carter appointees) ruled that the EPA properly rejected the idea. The Reagan Administration took a dimmer view of all regulations imposing arguably inflexible burdens on business, and the White House stimulated a rethinking in the EPA that led to its adoption of the bubble concept in 1981. Following its earlier

---

[58]See, e.g., *Norwegian Nitrogen Prods. Co. v. United States*, 288 U.S. 294, 311-15 (1933); *Udall v. Tallman*, 380 U.S. 1, 16 (1965). See also *Skidmore v. Swift & Co.*, 323 U.S. 134, 140 (1944) (deference to informal agency views).

[59]429 U.S. 125 (1976), excerpted and discussed in Eskridge & Frickey 855-57.

[60]467 U.S. 837 (1984), excerpted and discussed in Eskridge & Frickey 857-63; Hetzel, Libonati & Williams 576-79; Mikva & Lane 797-803; Popkin 495-98

precedents, the D.C. Circuit rejected the agency's new interpretation and disallowed the bubble concept.

The U.S. Supreme Court reversed. Justice Stevens' opinion for a unanimous Court (with three Justices not participating) set forth the governing analytical framework in a particularly clear way:[61]

> First, always, is the question whether Congress has directly spoken to the precise question at issue. If the intent of Congress is clear, that is the end of the matter; for the court, as well as the agency, must give effect to the unambiguously expressed intent of Congress. If, however, the court determines Congress has not directly addressed the precise question at issue, the court does not simply impose its own construction on the statute, as would be necessary in the absence of an administrative interpretation. Rather, if the statute is silent or ambiguous with respect to the specific issue, the question for the court is whether the agency's answer is based on a permissible construction of the statute.

In an important footnote following the Court's pronouncement that the clear intent of Congress should prevail above all else, the Court noted: "The judiciary is the final authority on issues of statutory construction and must reject administrative constructions which are contrary to clear congressional intent. If a court, *employing traditional tools of statutory construction*, ascertains that Congress had an intention on the precise question at issue, that intention is the law and must be given effect."[62]

Congress did not define "major stationary source" in the 1977 Amendments, nor did the legislative debates address the meaning of that term as applied to the bubble concept, even though the idea was effervescing in 1977. Given such a dearth of legislative guidance, Justice Stevens insisted that the judiciary defer and reprimanded the lower court for substituting its judgment for that of the agency. That the agency had changed its interpretation in 1981 bothered the Justices in no discernible way. "An initial agency interpretation is not instantly carved in stone. On the contrary, the agency, to engage in

---

[61]*Chevron*, 467 U.S. at 842-43.

[62]*Id.* at 843 n.9 (citations omitted, emphasis added).

informed rulemaking, must consider varying interpretations and the wisdom of its policy on a continuing basis."[63]

Most important, Justice Stevens' opinion suggested normative reasons for judicial deference to agency interpretations, including dynamic ones such as the EPA's in *Chevron*. To begin with, he stressed the formal authorization Congress gave the EPA to fill in the details of the statutory scheme, reflected most obviously in an explicit statutory authorization for the EPA to promulgate rules implementing clean air legislation. (This feature also could distinguish *Gilbert*, for the EEOC has no substantive rulemaking authority under Title VII.) While the legislative history of the 1977 Amendments did not suggest a particular legislative intent as to the bubble concept, it did suggest a congressional consensus that the EPA "should have broad discretion in implementing the policies of the 1977 Amendments."[64] Rule of law values support the idea that published agency rules filling in the details of an open-ended statute should presumptively be followed, but do not so easily support the notion that the same deference should be shown an agency that changes its rule 180 degrees.

Justice Stevens' second argument for deferring to agencies appealed to the New Deal notion that agencies will bring special expertise to bear on regulatory issues. The legislative history of the 1977 Amendments made clear that Congress sought a balance between cleaner air and reasonable costs for industry, and that Congress expected the EPA — and not the courts — to fine-tune that balance. Especially where, as in *Chevron*, "the regulatory scheme is technical and complex, the agency considered the matter in a detailed and reasoned fashion, and the decision involves reconciling conflicting policies,"[65] courts will presumptively not be as institutionally capable as agencies to figure out the best answer. The Natural

---

[63]*Id.* at 863-64. There is a very important qualification to *Chevron*'s relative tolerance of agency dynamism: when the rule of agency deference runs up against the super-strong rule of stare decisis for statutory precedents (Chapter 7, Part IIIA). If the Supreme Court itself has authoritatively construed the statute, the agency may not update the statute, even when circumstances have changed. See *Maislin Indus., U.S., Inc. v. Primary Steel, Inc.*, 497 U.S. 116, 130-31 (1990).

[64]*Chevron*, 467 U.S. at 862.

[65]*Id.* at 865.

Resources Defense Council, of course, took the position that the Reagan Administration's EPA was not engaged in a process of reasoned analysis or scientific policy balancing, but rather exercised raw political power in favor of the business interests that supported the Reagan presidential candidacy. The Supreme Court felt that was an overly simple view of the matter. Although the Court has been hesitant to accept purely political justifications as legitimate reasons for agency policy, it did suggest a third rationale for deference even if there was some truth to the NRDC position.

The third reason appealed to democratic legitimacy. Even if the EPA made a raw political choice in 1981, Justice Stevens was not sure that the D.C. Circuit had not done the same thing in 1982. That contrast was fatal to the lower court's judgment. Whereas judges must be nervous about choosing among competing political interests, lest they be swayed by their "personal policy preferences[,] an agency to which Congress has delegated policymaking responsibilities may, within the limits of that delegation, properly rely upon the incumbent administration's views of wise policy to inform its judgments."[66] As part of the "political branches," agencies are, relatively speaking, more accountable to We the People than life-tenured federal judges are. Not only are agencies directly or indirectly accountable to the elected President,[67] they are also accountable to the elected Congress, which not only confirms their chiefs but also oversees their administration, potentially amends the statutes they are charged with enforcing, and (most important) determines their annual budget.[68]

---

[66]*Id.*

[67]Agencies located within the executive branch itself are perhaps most accountable, as the President can remove as well as appoint their heads. But *independent* as well as *executive* agencies have for almost a generation been subject to White House control through review of their rulemaking. See Terry Moe & Scott Wilson, *Presidents and the Politics of Structure*, Law & Contemp. Probs., Spring 1994 at 1.

[68]The budget point is particularly important, even though agencies rarely say, "We are adopting this interpretation because Congress will cut off our money if we don't." (Congress sometimes attaches substantive riders to appropriations measures, a clearer basis for pressuring agencies.) The budget constraint operates as a background consideration motivating agencies to be interested in as well as responsive to the preferences of Congress or its committees and subcommittees. Among other things, it means the agency heads will return the phone calls of

Perhaps the best way to understand *Chevron* is as articulating a default rule of statutory construction: if statutory text is ambiguous, courts should conclusively presume that Congress intended to delegate to the agency the power to say what the law is. Such a presumption transfers power from the countermajoritarian judiciary to the politically responsible administrative agencies; moreover, it reflects judicial deference to the wishes of the most politically accountable branch, Congress. The legislature always has the power to vary the default rule by expressly indicating that it wishes to delegate the law-interpreting function to the courts, rather than to the agency charged with carrying out the statutory scheme.

Chevron is now the leading case regarding deference to agencies, and its two-step inquiry is widely followed: Does the statute clearly answer the interpretive inquiry? If so, apply the statute by its terms, either to affirm or reverse the agency. If not, the courts should defer to the agency unless its interpretation is "unreasonable." The Supreme Court has reversed an agency interpretation as unreasonable under Step Two only once,[69] so most of the judicial focus has targeted Step One and the search for unambiguous statutory meaning.

Some scholars have treated *Chevron* as though it ushered in a revolution in statutory interpretation. It does appear contrary to the traditional judicial role as the primary interpreter of statutes,[70] and it seems incompatible with the Administrative Procedure Act's directive that courts "shall decide all relevant questions of law, interpret constitutional and statutory provisions, and determine the meaning or applicability of the terms of an agency action."[71] Nonetheless, it is by no means clear that *Chevron* has radically altered outcomes in cases involving agencies and statutory interpretation. On the one hand, Professors Schuck and Elliott have shown that deference to agencies was on the upswing well before *Chevron*, which suggests that the revolution, if any, came from below and *Chevron* has been (over)read to recognize and ratify those preexisting

---

congressional staff and will listen to their gripes. See Chapter 5, Part IIIC.

[69]See *AT&T Corp. v. Iowa Utilities Bd.*, 525 U.S. 366 (1999).

[70]See, e.g., Stephen Breyer, *Judicial Review of Questions of Law and Policy*, 38 Admin. L. Rev. 363 (1986).

[71]5 U.S.C. § 706.

trends.[72] On the other hand, Professor Merrill worries that the post-*Chevron* Supreme Court has not deferred enough. Specifically, he is concerned that the new textualism is trumping *Chevron* too often by finding, at Step One, that the agency interpretation is inconsistent with the statutory text.[73] Professors Cohen and Spitzer offer an openly political theory of *Chevron*: it was a signal from the conservative Court to appeals courts populated with Carter judges to defer more often to Reagan Administration policies.[74] Has the Republican Supreme Court required the Republican courts of appeals to defer to Clinton Administration agencies? If not, Cohen and Spitzer's thesis is powerfully supported; if so, it is powerfully undermined.[75]

B. *Scope and Details of the Agency-Deference Doctrine*

Chevron has not entirely eliminated judicial discomfort with agency *volte-faces*, or shifts in interpretation.[76] More generally, it remains to be seen how much deference *Chevron* requires. Consider some of the doctrinal questions raised by *Chevron* and subsequent Supreme Court opinions.

---

[72]See Peter Schuck & E. Donald Elliott, *To the* Chevron *Station: An Empirical Study of Federal Administrative Law*, 1990 Duke L.J. 984.

[73]See Thomas Merrill, *Judicial Deference to Executive Precedent*, 101 Yale L.J. 969 (1992); Merrill, *Textualism and the Future of the* Chevron *Doctrine*, 72 Wash. U. L.Q. 351 (1994). For an example of Merrill's thesis, see the complicated debate among the Justices in *K Mart Corp. v. Cartier, Inc.*, 486 U.S. 281 (1988), excerpted and discussed in Eskridge & Frickey 863-78. See also Antonin Scalia, *Judicial Deference to Administrative Interpretations of Law*, 1989 Duke L.J. 511, 521, conceding that he is more likely to find a plain meaning than other Justices, which would mean not reaching Step Two of *Chevron* in many cases.

[74]See Linda Cohen & Matthew Spitzer, *Solving the* Chevron *Puzzle*, 57 Law & Contemp. Probs. 65 (Spring 1994).

[75]For some preliminary, partially supportive, findings, see William Eskridge, Jr. & Philip Frickey, *The Supreme Court, 1993 Term — Foreword: Law as Equilibrium*, 108 Harv. L. Rev. 26, 71-76 (1994) (low rate of deference in 1993 Term, when the Court might have been hazing the rookie Clinton Administration).

[76]See, e.g., *INS v. Cardoza-Fonseca*, 480 U.S. 421, 446 n.30 (1987); *Commodity Futures Trading Comm'n v. Schor*, 478 U.S. 833, 846 (1986) (agency cannot change an interpretation Congress has implicitly ratified). But see David Gossett, Chevron, *Take Two: Deference to Revised Agency Interpretations of Statutes*, 64 U. Chi. L. Rev. 681 (1997) (arguing that courts are generally as deferential to revised interpretations as to unchanged ones).

1. *Are agency positions entitled to* Chevron *deference even if the agency is not clearly operating within an area of formally delegated authority?* The *Chevron* case was the classic situation for deference, as the agency had been delegated substantive rulemaking authority by Congress and had adopted a rule easily within the scope of that delegation. The reasoning in Justice Stevens' opinion echoed the facts of the case: "an agency to which Congress has delegated policy-making responsibilities may, within the limits of that delegation, properly rely upon the incumbent administration's views of wise policy to inform its judgments."[77] Often these conditions do not hold, and such cases ask the courts to elaborate on the "meaning" of *Chevron*. Consider three different variations on the classic (*Chevron*) scenario.

To begin with, are agencies entitled to deference when Congress has not delegated them substantive rulemaking authority? *Gilbert* held that the EEOC's interpretation of Title VII was not a good case for deference, in part because the statute authorized the agency to make procedural but not substantive rules.[78] Although *Gilbert* survives as good law, *Chevron*'s reasoning could support a more generous rule: whenever Congress has truly left the matter open, it is more democratically legitimate and in most cases more practical to let the agency make the policy choice — whether or not Congress has given it formal rulemaking authority. The absence of congressional delegation, however, at least reduces the legitimacy of circumscribing the judiciary's traditional role of saying what the law is.

In the alternative, *Chevron* and *Gilbert* could be reconciled by calibrating the idea of deference. Sometimes, for example, the Supreme Court has relied on the EEOC's views as persuasive authority from an expert body. Justice Rehnquist's opinion interpreting Title VII to provide a claim for sexual harassment in the workplace relied on the EEOC's 1980 guidelines as a basis for recognizing

---

[77]*Chevron*, 467 U.S. at 865.

[78]*Gilbert*, 429 U.S. at 141 & n.20 (relying on 42 U.S.C. § 713(a), granting authority only for procedural rules). Accord, *EEOC v. Arabian Am. Oil Co.*, 499 U.S. 244 (1991) (majority of the Court followed *Gilbert* in declining to defer to EEOC views; concurring Justice Scalia assumed, without deciding, that *Chevron* deference should be accorded EEOC but then concluded that agency interpretation was not reasonable).

and conceptualizing the new claim for relief. Consistent with *Gilbert*, Justice Rehnquist ruled that guidelines unmoored to formal rule-making, " ' "while not controlling upon the courts by reason of their authority, do constitute a body of experience and informed judgment to which courts and litigants may properly resort for guidance." ' "[79]

From this contrast you could come up with a rule of thumb: if the court is pretty sure (say, 80%) that traditional statutory materials (text, precedent, possibly legislative history) contradict the agency, then the court will overturn the agency's interpretation under any standard. If the traditional materials do not allow the court to discern an unambiguous statutory meaning but, to a level of, say, 40% certainty, suggest a particular interpretation that the agency adopts, the court should defer if the agency is exercising its delegated rulemaking authority (*Chevron*) but perhaps not defer if the agency is acting informally (*Gilbert*). Note that in such a case outside the regulatory context, the court would adopt its own interpretation, perhaps one that it finds more consistent with the inconclusive statutory material. Where statutory materials completely fail to address the interpretive issue, the court should defer to an agency interpretation made pursuant to its delegated authority as long as the interpretation is not outrageous, but should make an independent assessment, taking some consideration of the agency's opinion, in a *Gilbert* situation. Of course, where the statutory materials substantially support the agency position, the deference issue is moot: the agency is merely following the intent of Congress.

Would *Chevron* or *Gilbert* require deference to agency *litigating positions?* Recall that the church in *Holy Trinity* was prosecuted by the Justice Department for violating one of the 1885 alien contract labor law's criminal prohibitions. Not only did the 1892 Court give

---

[79] *Meritor Sav. Bank, FSB v. Vinson*, 477 U.S. 57, 65 (1986), quoting *Gilbert*, 429 U.S. at 141-42, which in turn was quoting the leading case for reliance on informal agency guidance, *Skidmore v. Swift & Co.*, 323 U.S. 134, 140 (1944). The Court has even more strongly relied on such EEOC guidelines in the wake of the Civil Rights Act of 1991, which overrode the Court's most conservative Title VII decisions but left its sexual harassment case intact. See *Faragher v. City of Boca Raton*, 118 S.Ct. 2275, 2291 n.4, 2292 (1998), where Justice Souter's opinion for the Court credited the guidelines and *Vinson* with some degree of legislative acquiescence or ratification.

no thought of deferring to the department's view that the statute applied to the importation of ministers, the 1992 Court would not have deferred, either. (If the 1992 Court reached a different result than the 1892 Court, it would have been because the Justices viewed the statute as clearly covering the minister's importation.) This idea extends beyond criminal cases, where deference could also be contrary to the rule of lenity (Chapter 9).[80]   Agency litigating positions are generally not entitled to *Chevron* deference, in part because the agency is not exercising delegated authority when it takes litigating positions and in part because of fairness concerns that the agency as advocate will not develop interpretations solely through the use of neutral expertise. Thus, *Kosak* would also not be an appropriate case for deference, because the executive branch's position in that case was adopted mainly as a litigating posture.

Finally, should *Chevron* require deference when agencies are defining, or redefining, their own jurisdiction? Would the rationales underlying deference apply to an agency's determination of whether it was acting "within the limits of that delegation" (the *Chevron* language quoted above)? Possibly so in cases where Congress has formally authorized the agency to regulate interstitially, for the agency brings the same expertise and bears the same democracy advantage in jurisdictional cases as in *Chevron*-type cases.[81] The main objection to deference in defining jurisdictional rules — agency bias or self-interest — is just as applicable to *Chevron*-type cases. Finally, because many asserted errors of agency interpretation can be characterized either as exceeding the agency's jurisdiction or as violating a statutory command, the jurisdiction/substance distinction may be too artificial. For example, is the Food and Drug Administration's decision to regulate tobacco as a "drug" or an "article [] . . .

---

[80]See *Bowen v. Georgetown Univ. Hosp.*, 488 U.S. 204 (1988); *United States v. Western Elec. Co.*, 900 F.2d 283, 297 (D.C. Cir. 1990) (no deference for Department of Justice interpretations in civil or criminal cases). But see Dan Kahan, *Is* Chevron *Relevant to Federal Criminal Law?*, 110 Harv. L. Rev. 469 (1996) (arguing that courts should defer to certain Department of Justice interpretations of ambiguous criminal statutes).

[81]See *Dole v. United Steelworkers*, 494 U.S. 26, 54-55 (1990) (White, J., dissenting); *Mississippi Power & Light Co. v. Mississippi ex rel. Moore*, 487 U.S. 354, 377-83 (1988) (Scalia, J., concurring in the judgment).

intended to affect the structure or any function of the body" a jurisdictional decision?[82] If it is, virtually all decisions to regulate particular actions or products have a jurisdictional flavor. Notwithstanding these excellent arguments, the Court has ruled that an agency " 'may not bootstrap itself into an area in which it has no jurisdiction.' "[83]

2. What can or should the court consult to determine whether the statute is "unclear" and therefore requires deference to agency interpretations? Justice Stevens' opinion in *Chevron* examined the statutory text and, more extensively, the legislative history of the 1977 Amendments before concluding that the statute did not clearly address the interpretive issue. (His opinion in *Sweet Home* similarly backed up his deferential attitude with supportive textual analysis, legislative history, and dicta in Supreme Court precedent.) Most reasonable minds would agree with Justice Stevens, but many of those same reasonable minds would blanch at Chief Justice Burger's reliance in *Bob Jones* on the common law, statutory purpose, and some subsequent legislative history to back up deference to the IRS's rewrite of relatively clear language in the tax code.

Most of the post-*Chevron* Supreme Court decisions have similarly examined both text and legislative history in determining statutory clarity, but there is some debate within the Court as to this matter. There is *no* debate about the proposition that the Court's own statutory precedents, like Congress' text, can trump inconsistent agency rules.[84] In addition, many of the canons of interpretation are

---

[82]See *Brown & Williamson Tobacco Corp. v. FDA*, 161 F.3d 764 (4th Cir. 1998), *cert. granted*, 119 S.Ct. 1495 (1999). See also Richard Merrill, *The FDA May Not Regulate Tobacco Products as "Drugs" or as "Medical Devices,"* 47 Duke L.J. 1071 (1998); Cass Sunstein, *Is Tobacco a Drug? Administrative Agencies as Common Law Courts*, 47 Duke L.J. 1013 (1998).

[83]*Adams Fruit Co. v. Barrett*, 494 U.S. 638, 650 (1990), quoting *Federal Maritime Comm'n v. Seatrain Lines, Inc.*, 411 U.S. 726, 745 (1973). The clarity of this statement is impaired by language in other cases suggesting that the court will defer to such an interpretation of law. See *Mississippi Power & Light Co. v. Mississippi ex rel. Moore*, 487 U.S. 354, 377-83 (1988) (Scalia, J., concurring in the judgment).

[84]See *Neal v. United States*, 516 U.S. 284 (1996); *Maislin Indus., U.S., Inc. v. Primary Steel, Inc.*, 497 U.S. 116 (1990).

considered to be part of the traditional tools available to the Court at Step One.

A leading case concerning reference to legislative history is *City of Chicago v. Environmental Defense Fund.*[85] The issue in the case was whether waste combustion ash generated by a municipal resource recovery incinerator is exempt from hazardous waste regulation under Subtitle C of the Resource Conservation and Recovery Act (RCRA). Without explicit statutory support, the EPA had supported a RCRA exemption for municipal waste incineration in the early 1980s, and in 1984 Congress added § 3001(i) to provide that "[a] resource recovery facility recovering energy from the mass burning of municipal solid waste" would not be "deemed to be treating, storing, disposing of, or otherwise managing hazardous wastes for the purposes of [Subtitle C]."[86] Municipalities assumed that § 3001(i) also allowed them to dispose of the ash created in such process without the expensive protections required by Subtitle C. The EPA sent wholly mixed signals on the ash issue before siding with the municipalities in a 1992 memorandum developed in connection with the *City of Chicago* case. The EPA memorandum argued that the statutory balance of environmental protection and reasonable costs could best be achieved through a broad exemption, for cities faced enormous costs if they had to dispose of ash under Subtitle C. Moreover, the legislative history of § 3001(i) strongly supported this balance. The Senate report accompanying § 3001(i) said that "[a]ll waste management activities of such a facility, including the *generation*, transportation, treatment, storage and disposal of waste shall be covered by the exclusion."[87] Based on this evidence of the 1984 deal, the deference everyone expected for the EPA's final position based on *Chevron*, and the supposed anti-environmental bias of a right-wing Supreme Court, everyone expected Chicago to win the case.

---

[85]511 U.S. 328 (1994). Our discussion of *City of Chicago* draws from Richard Lazarus & Claudia Newman, City of Chicago v. Environmental Defense Fund: *Searching for Plain Meaning in Unambiguous Ambiguity*, 4 N.Y.U. Env. L.J. 1 (1995).

[86]42 U.S.C. § 6921(i).

[87]S. Rep. No. 284, 98th Cong., 1st Sess. 61 (1983) (emphasis added).

Chicago lost, the EPA lost, the EDF won, and one of the most conservative Justices wrote the opinion. Justice Scalia's opinion for the Court found § 3001(i) unambiguous: the *facility* is exempt from Subtitle C, but there is no mention and therefore no exemption for the *ash* produced in the facility and subsequently disposed of by the city. Justice Stevens, the author of *Chevron* and a big fan of legislative history, dissented on the ground that the legislative history revealed a congressional deal not only suggesting some ambiguity in the text (and triggering *Chevron* deference), but suggesting that the EPA memorandum was the best understanding of the statutory text. Justice Scalia not only refused to credit the Senate report with any value, but he deployed it to prove his point: the report included *generation* of waste as one of the activities exempted by § 3001(i), a term notably absent from the statute itself. Perhaps this was a strong case for the use of the maxim *inclusio unius est exclusio alterius* (Chapter 7, Part IC), because of the evidence that lawmakers knew how to include this term in the text if they wished. Although most of the Supreme Court cases will consider legislative history in determining *Chevron* deference, *City of Chicago* is not alone in considering only the statutory text and pointedly refusing to consider legislative history.[88]

3. *When is an agency interpretation of an ambiguous statute "unreasonable"?* Neither *Chevron* nor many of the post-*Chevron* cases address the Step Two inquiry: If the statute is ambiguous, under what circumstances should a court nonetheless set aside an agency interpretation because it is *unreasonable*? The Court did find part of the FCC regulations implementing the Telecommunications Act of 1996 unreasonable in *AT&T Corp. v. Iowa Utilities Board.*[89] The regulations concerned the conditions under which local exchange carriers had to share their networks with competitors. In determining what network elements must be made available, the Act instructed the FCC to consider which access is necessary for the competitor and whether failure to provide access would impair the competitor's ability to provide services. The Court determined that the regulations

---

[88]See also *K Mart Corp. v. Cartier, Inc.*, 486 U.S. 281 (1988) (Kennedy, J., delivering the judgment of the Court).

[89]119 S.Ct. 721 (1999).

represented an abdication by the Commission of its responsibilities to make this "necessary and impair" consideration, allowing the competitor access if it produced minimal evidence of need. "We cannot avoid the conclusion that, if Congress had wanted to give blanket access to incumbents' networks on a basis as unrestricted as the scheme the Commission has come up with, it would not have included [the necessary and impair standard] in the statute at all."[90] Thus, even though the meaning of the necessary and impair requirement was ambiguous, the agency's regulation promulgated under its delegated authority was unreasonable. Otherwise, the Supreme Court has given little guidance as to the proper application of Step Two.

The reasonableness requirement threatens to reintroduce the problem of antidemocratic and under-informed judicial value choices that *Chevron* claimed to have headed off. Viewed another way, the reasonableness requirement's underdeveloped status may reveal central problems with the *Chevron* framework itself.

C. *Critique of Strong Judicial Deference to Agency Interpretations*

The main criticism of a vigorous application of *Chevron* deference is that it unbalances government, allowing the executive department to announce major shifts in public policy even when such shifts are contrary to the popular will as reflected in Congress[91] or when they detract from the rule of law and constitutional values the courts are supposed to protect.[92] *City of Chicago* can be read as a caution against the second prong of this concern: courts ought to insist on agency adherence to the rule of law and clear statutory texts even in a deferential regime. As we shall explain, however, the

---

[90]*Id.* at 735.

[91]See William Eskridge, Jr. & John Ferejohn, *The Article I, Section 7 Game*, 80 Geo. L.J. 523 (1992).

[92]See Cynthia Farina, *Statutory Interpretation and the Balance of Power in the Administrative State*, 89 Colum. L. Rev. 452 (1989). See also Stephen Breyer, *Judicial Review of Questions of Law and Policy*, 38 Admin. L. Rev. 363 (1986); Clark Byse, *Judicial Review of Administrative Interpretation of Statutes: An Analysis of* Chevron's *Step Two*, 2 Admin. L.J. 255 (1988); Cass Sunstein, *Law and Administration After* Chevron, 90 Colum. L. Rev. 2071 (1990).

Court's decision in *Rust v. Sullivan*[93] may be an example of the Court's insensitivity to the first concern and its selective solicitude toward the second.

Congress in 1970 enacted the Public Health Service Act, Title X of which seeks to help people plan their families through medical counseling and providing useful information. The law grants the Department of Health and Human Services (HHS) rulemaking authority. One provision prohibits using Title X "in programs where abortion is a method of family planning."[94] The HHS regulations in the 1970s and early 1980s precluded programs from performing abortions but did not regulate the form of counseling in Title X family planning offices. In 1988, the Reagan Administration's HHS promulgated new regulations prohibiting "counseling concerning the use of abortion as a method of family planning" in Title X programs.[95] Even if families asked for advice or referrals for abortions, the medical staff could not help them. This striking departure from prior policy would never have been enacted by Congress, which voted by wide margins to override the new rule but whose will was thwarted by a presidential veto.[96] The new rule also raised constitutional concerns: its restrictions on medical counseling not only arguably abridged medical personnel's First Amendment speech rights, but also burdened women's privacy rights to choose abortions and obtain information relevant to that choice. Is *Chevron* deference appropriate here?

The Supreme Court upheld the agency rules in *Rust v. Sullivan*. Chief Justice Rehnquist's opinion for the Court held that HHS's new interpretation of the statute was allowable, because the statute was ambiguous. As *Chevron* held, the agency in such situations has discretion to change its interpretation of the statute, in light of

---

[93]500 U.S. 173 (1991), discussed in Eskridge & Frickey 878-79; Popkin 498; and excerpted and discussed in Hetzel, Libonati & Williams 582-89.

[94]Pub. L. No. 91-572, § 1008, 84 Stat. 1508 (1970).

[95]42 C.F.R. § 59.8(a)(1) (1988). This so-called "gag rule" was revoked by the Clinton Administration by executive order in January 1993.

[96]See 138 Cong. Rec. H10,678 (daily ed. Oct. 2, 1992) (House voted 266-148 to override President's veto, short of the two-thirds majority constitutionally required).

changed circumstances and the agency's experience with statutory implementation.[97] Four Justices dissented from this holding, on the ground that the agency's interpretation unnecessarily introduced constitutional doubts into the statutory scheme. Even if the statute, so construed, were able to pass muster, the constitutional questions were troubling enough to insist that Congress, not the agency, clearly make the choice to venture so close to the constitutional periphery.[98]

Rust v. Sullivan is best understood as a chapter in the Court's ongoing struggle with the level of constitutional protection to afford a woman's right to choose abortions and to apply when the government imposes speech-restrictive "conditions" on its employees, its agents, and recipients of its state funds. It reflects a lesson suggested in Chapter 6: the substantive dimensions of the cases cannot be divorced from the statutory interpretation moves and decisions made. But the decision poses dilemmas generated by *Chevron*. On the one hand, *Rust* concretely illustrates the dynamic potential of *Chevron*, giving agencies and the political process legal space to experiment with novel statutory policies. On the other hand, *Rust* also illustrates the ways *Chevron*'s dynamism can empower the executive vis-à-vis Congress and leave citizens insecure in some of their most fundamental liberties.

---

[97]See *Rust*, 500 U.S. at 186-87.

[98]See *id.* at 204-07 (Blackmun, J., dissenting); *id.* at 223-25 (O'Connor, J., dissenting). Three of the four dissenters (all but Justice O'Connor) found the statute unconstitutional as thus interpreted. The Court majority ruled that the statute survived constitutional attack by a wide enough margin to avoid the canon that statutes should be construed to avoid *serious* constitutional difficulties. On that canon, see Chapter 9, Part IIA.

9

Substantive Canons of Statutory Interpretation

Chapter 7 discussed *textual* canons of statutory interpretation, which are guidelines for evaluating linguistic or syntactic meaning. These canons easily coincide with the traditional approaches to statutory interpretation developed in Chapter 6: textual meaning is either alone the touchstone of statutory interpretation or a helpful indicator of legislative intent or statutory purpose. Probably the most basic questions raised by their use are (1) how accurately they identify ordinary textual meaning (do they advance our understanding of the textual perspective to statutes?), (2) whether the legislature drafts statutes with these canons in mind (do they enhance our understanding of the institutional legislative perspective by revealing what the legislature either knew or should have known would be the judicial interpretation of certain textual formulations?), and (3) whether they should be given a rule-like quality or merely serve as a checklist of potential textual meanings that might otherwise be overlooked. These questions indicate that the application of the textual canons is not entirely policy-neutral. As in all things, judges must make some choices about the bases for and roles of these canons. Nonetheless, because the canons have longstanding pedigrees and reflect linguistic and syntactic understandings that may be useful in context, their role in statutory interpretation is relatively uncontroversial.

Chapter 8 introduced a variety of other principles rooted in institutional relationships. It raised such questions as whether judges should consider the documentary history developed by the legislature during the process of enactment and whether they should defer to a plausible interpretation of a statute by the administrative agency charged with implementing it. These approaches may be labeled *extrinsic* or *referential* canons of interpretation because they direct judicial interpreters to refer to a variety of factors extrinsic to the statutory text as aids in attributing meaning to it. As Chapter 8 indicated, these principles are controversial. Some of the concerns are normative. For example, some textualist approaches to statutory meaning would consider legislative history irrelevant and agency interpretations lawful only if they embrace the best textual under-standing of the statute. Other concerns are descriptive. For example, even if one is attracted to intentionalist theory, one might have doubts whether consulting legislative history is likely to clarify statutory meaning more than confuse it. It is apparent that one's attitude toward these principles depends upon their congruence with one's preferred overall interpretive theory and one's sense whether any given principle advances that theory.

The *substantive* canons of interpretation, the subjects of this chapter, are even more controversial, because they are rooted in broader policy or value judgments. These canons attempt to harmo-nize statutory meaning with policies rooted in the common law, other statutes, or the Constitution. The substantive canons are numerous and multifaceted, and they significantly affect statutory interpretation in federal and state courts. Because we cannot provide an analysis of each one, we have included an Appendix to this book that contains a list of canons of interpretation, including the substantive ones, recently used by the Supreme Court.[1] As this list indicates, some-times these canons are phrased as directions that certain kinds of statutes are to be construed "liberally" or "strictly," while other substantive canons operate as presumptions, or default rules, about statutory meaning. Some of the presumptions are so forceful as to amount to *clear statement rules* that mandate an interpretive conclu-sion unless clear statutory text dictates the opposite interpretation.

Part I of this chapter considers each of these categories of canons and then examines the importance of identifying the underlying values that substantive canons are designed to promote. Part II provides a detailed examination of several of the most important substantive canons. The chapter then concludes, in Part III, with some final thoughts about the contributions the canons make to the overall process of statutory interpretation.

---

[1]In many instances, the easiest way to identify cases applying the canons is through the digests. For example, West's key number system, under the heading "statutes," has a key number for each of the major canons.

I. An Overview of the Substantive Canons

Like Chapter 6, this chapter combines descriptive and prescriptive elements. For the most part, we seek to describe the canonical regime followed in the federal and most state court systems. The description itself contains a normative feature — namely, what values the judiciary thinks, or might think, the canons, or particular canons, serve. We invite students of legislation to think even more prescriptively. Ask yourself at various points: What should be the overall role(s) or goal(s) of the substantive canons? What should be their relationship to other public law norms, especially constitutional ones? Are there some canons that do not fit those goals, or whose costs to the system exceed likely benefits, and therefore that should be jettisoned? Are there some canons that should be added?[2]

A. *Liberal versus Strict Construction — Change versus Continuity in Legal Regimes*

Many canons purport to direct the interpreter to construe particular kinds of statutes either broadly or narrowly. Among the oldest and most general formulations of this kind state that "remedial" statutes are to be broadly construed and "statutes in derogation of the common law" are to be narrowly construed. On the surface, these canons seem not merely obscure as to the values they might serve, but mutually contradictory — for every statute that alters the common law would seem an attempt to remedy a defect in the common law. Thus, any reconciliation of these canons requires fine-tuning their application,

---

[2]For speculations along these lines, see William Eskridge, Jr., *Public Values in Statutory Interpretation*, 137 U. Pa. L. Rev. 1007 (1989); Cass Sunstein, *Interpreting Statutes in the Regulatory State*, 103 Harv. L. Rev. 407 (1989); Symposium, *A Reevaluation of the Canons of Statutory Interpretation*, 45 Vand. L. Rev. 529 (1992), all lucidly criticized in John Nagle, *Waiving Sovereign Immunity in an Age of Clear Statement Rules*, 1995 Wis. L. Rev. 771. For books that treat the canons within the larger framework of statutory interpretation theory, see William Eskridge, Jr., *Dynamic Statutory Interpretation* ch. 9 (1994); Henry Hart, Jr. & Albert Sacks, *The Legal Process: Basic Problems in the Making and Application of Law* ch. 7 (William Eskridge, Jr. & Philip Frickey publication eds., 1994) (from 1958 "tentative edition"); J. Willard Hurst, *Dealing with Statutes* 56-65 (1982); Samuel Mermin, *Law and the Legal System: An Introduction* 237-70 (2d ed. 1982). For casebook discussions, see Eskridge & Frickey 652-716; Hetzel, Libonati & Williams 648-703; Lane & Mikva 770-75; Popkin 274-338.

which can only be done by attributing public-policy purposes to each of them.

Illustratively, recall that the common law did not outlaw employment discrimination on grounds of race or gender — it allowed employers great autonomy to make even discriminatory decisions about their workforces. By the mid-twentieth century, many Americans came to view the freedom of racial minorities and women to engage in work free from discriminatory barriers as more important to our society than the autonomy that the common law had accorded to employers. Accordingly, many state legislatures, and eventually Congress in the 1964 Civil Rights Act, passed employment discrimination statutes. These laws are equally "remedial" and "in derogation of the common law." How should they be construed?

Probably the most natural response is to say that one of the canons should retain contemporary vitality and the other one be discarded. It seems mindless, though, to say that any statute changing the common law should be liberally construed; because virtually every statutory change alters the pre-existing legal baseline, the maxim ends up looking like nearly all statutes should be liberally construed. It seems equally mindless to prefer the derogation canon, which can work to ossify an obsolete status quo and, in any event, is probably rooted historically in a selfish desire by English judges to limit Parliament's capacity to intrude upon the common law. Perhaps, then, the remedial canon and the derogation canon just cancel each other out and both should be jettisoned — employment discrimination statutes, for example, should be interpreted "reasonably," not liberally or strictly. This may be too facile a conclusion, however.

Centrist judges attuned to the traditions of Anglo-American statutory interpretation sometimes may intuit that a remedial statute deserves broad construction. For example, our centrist judge might understand the herculean effort required of the supporters of civil rights legislation to work through all the vetogates and persuade Congress to enact the Civil Rights Act of 1964.[3] Thus, from the institutional perspective reflected in intentionalist and purposive

---

[3]See Charles & Barbara Whalen, *The Longest Debate: A Legislative History of the 1964 Civil Rights Act* (1985); Eskridge & Frickey 26. On *vetogates*, see our discussion in Chapter 3, Part I.

theories of statutory interpretation,[4] our judge may sense that the political system and the legislature *really* wanted this fundamental change in law. She might, therefore, feel that the passage of this law was an important moment, even a turning point, in fundamental national policy, and that the new approach to human rights embodies a legislative purpose worthy of broad construction. She might believe that Congress was now acting in harmony with the judicial branch, which since *Brown v. Board of Education* had worked toward ameliorating the great American dilemma of racial inequality. On these understandings, the adoption of the statute remedied an obsolete approach to employer autonomy no longer even arguably consistent with contemporary values. It would not be surprising for our centrist judge to conclude that a civil rights statute of this sort should be broadly construed. And, indeed, the Supreme Court has sometimes taken this liberal-construction approach to federal civil rights laws.[5] Some state civil rights laws even expressly state that their provisions shall be construed liberally to promote their purposes.[6]

Contrast our hypothetical centrist judge's reaction to a different kind of statute altering a common law approach. Suppose that a state legislature adopts a statute sharply limiting the procedural and substantive rights of victims of medical malpractice. The public-regarding purpose for the statute is to ensure the continued provision of health care and to rid the system of the distorting effects of a plethora of often-weak malpractice actions filed by opportunistic plaintiffs' lawyers on behalf of unlucky persons injured by medical procedures that were in fact competently provided. Our centrist judge might have some qualms about this "reform." Public choice theory suggests that it would be easy for physicians — a relatively small, easily organized, and wealthy group — to lobby the legislature for this measure, along with easily organized and politically powerful insurance companies. The members of the diffuse public who might someday suffer injury at the hands of physicians will be virtually

---

[4] See Chapter 6, Part I.

[5] See, e.g., *Griggs v. Duke Power Co.*, 401 U.S. 424 (1971); *Allen v. State Bd. of Elections*, 393 U.S. 544 (1969).

[6] See, e.g., 3A *Sutherland Statutory Construction* § 74.03 (Norman Singer ed. 1992).

impossible to organize to lobby for the continuation of the common law status quo.[7] It is probable that our centrist judge has some ideological attachment to traditional tort approaches (law school imprints such things, if nothing else) and believes that the presence of customary common law remedies serves to deter negligence and to shift the loss of careless conduct to the most efficient loss avoider. Our judge may well worry that the legislature, under one-sided political pressure, jettisoned a tried-and-true, if somewhat flawed, approach rather than fine-tuned it to correct specific problems — that it threw the baby out with the bathwater. In such circumstances, it would not be surprising for our centrist judge to feel that the malpractice reform statute should be narrowly construed.[8]

Note that these intuitions about this hypothetical centrist judge do not support an absolute rule that remedial statutes are to be broadly construed or statutes in derogation of the common law are to be narrowly construed. Rather, implicit in our suggestions is the notion that broad or narrow construction should turn on the extent of reliable political support for a change in the status quo and the extent to which the judiciary intuits that a shift in societal values has rendered certain common law principles obsolete. On this understanding, the remedial canon and the derogation canon are simply crude, unreliable indicators of the ubiquitous tension between change and continuity in law that can be resolved only in particular contexts, not by global rules. As Professor Shapiro has argued, the derogation canon, which is usually treated as anathema by contemporary commentators, is best understood as a sign that our legal process tradition favors continuity

---

[7]See Chapter 3, Part IIB-C.

[8]See, e.g., *Hutchinson v. Patel*, 637 So.2d 415 (La. 1994) (ambiguities in medical malpractice reform act should be strictly construed).

Of course, there are other ways to understand the legislative processes required to pass the civil rights law and the medical malpractice reform law. For example, a judge might conclude from the difficulty of passing the Civil Rights Act that important compromises were required to negotiate all the vetogates successfully. Perhaps a broadly written anti-discrimination law could not have been enacted; is it then legitimate for the court to construe the statute contrary to the likely intention of the median or pivotal voter necessary to the winning coalition? In the case of the malpractice reform bill, the well organized and politically powerful trial lawyers association no doubt opposed the law. Perhaps this group has served as an effective proxy for the interests of the diffuse and unorganized public.

and gradual evolution to rapid, discontinuous change. He rightly points out that many canons more specifically implement this preference. In general, he proposes that "close questions of construction should be resolved in favor of continuity and against change."[9] We agree with Shapiro descriptively — that our traditions favor continuity to change — but are concerned that his proposed principle might more often ossify an unworthy status quo than protect against ill-advised legislative changes.

In addition to civil rights statutes, the Supreme Court has sometimes applied the generous liberal-construction canon to such statutes as those promoting workplace safety[10] and providing benefits to seaworkers[11] and veterans.[12] In contrast, the Court has applied the grudging strict-construction canon to statutes waiving the sovereign immunity of the United States[13] and providing public grants to private parties.[14] These latter instances of narrow construction are especially worth consideration because they demonstrate how liberal- or strict-construction canons can be based on political-process assumptions and can evolve over time.

The narrow construction of public grants seems rooted in judicial suspicion of the legislative process when it allocates public benefits to narrow interests. Anticipating public choice theory by more than a half-century, the Supreme Court once wrote that, when a public grant to a private party is ambiguous,

> [i]t must be, therefore, uncertain whether the legislators voted for this act upon one construction or the other. It may be that the very

---

[9]David Shapiro, *Continuity and Change in Statutory Interpretation*, 67 N.Y.U. L. Rev. 921, 925 (1992).

[10]See *Whirlpool Corp. v. Marshall*, 445 U.S. 1 (1980).

[11]See *Cox v. Roth*, 348 U.S. 207 (1955).

[12]See *King v. St. Vincent's Hosp.*, 502 U.S. 215, 220 n. 9 (1991); *Coffy v. Republic Steel Corp.*, 447 U.S. 191 (1980).

[13]See, e.g., *West v. Gibson*, 119 S.Ct. 1906 (1999); *Lane v. Pena*, 518 U.S. 187 (1996); *United States v. Nordic Village, Inc.*, 503 U.S. 30 (1992). More generally, state and federal courts will often construe statutes in derogation of sovereignty narrowly, holding, for example, that a statute regulating private parties presumptively does not apply to the government.

[14]See, e.g., *Andrus v. Charlestone Stone Prods. Co.*, 436 U.S. 604, 617 (1978).

ambiguity of the act was the means of securing its passage. Legislative grants of this character should be in such unequivocal form of expression that the legislative mind may be distinctly impressed with their character and import, in order that the privileges may be intelligently granted or purposely withheld. It is matter of common knowledge that grants of this character are usually prepared by those interested in them, and submitted to the legislature with a view to obtain from such bodies the most liberal grant of privileges which they are willing to give. This is one among many reasons why they are to be strictly construed.[15]

The Court has applied the canon less rigidly when the public grant, although awarded to a narrow private interest, clearly promotes a public value.[16] Moreover, consistent with public choice theory, when the costs and benefits of the grant are spread widely across the public, such as when a widespread benefit such as Medicaid and other safety net programs are funded by general taxation, courts are less likely to follow the beady-eyed public grants canon and, in fact, may flip their approach such that the benefits statute is broadly construed to promote its social-welfare purpose.[17]

Like the public grants canon, the sovereign immunity canon protects the public fisc from unintended obligations. At common law, the government was immune from suit without its consent. Accordingly, any statute waiving sovereign immunity is in derogation

---

[15]*Blair v. City of Chicago*, 201 U.S. 400, 471 (1906). See also Frank Easterbrook, *Statutes' Domains*, 50 U. Chi. L. Rev. 533 (1983) (making a similar argument from a public choice perspective and applying it generally to statutory interpretation).

[16]See, e.g., *Leo Sheep Co. v. United States*, 440 U.S. 668 (1979) (declining to follow narrow construction rule in case involving land grant made as consideration for construction of transcontinental railroad).

[17]Compare *Rosado v. Wyman*, 397 U.S. 397 (1970) (liberal construction of welfare law allowing recipients to sue state officials for failure to comply with statutory requirements), with *Pennhurst State Sch. & Hosp. v. Halderman*, 451 U.S. 1 (1981) (narrow construction of laws announcing rights for the disabled). See Rand Rosenblatt, *Statutory Interpretation and Distributive Justice: Medicaid Hospital Reimbursement and the Debate Over Public Choice*, 35 St. Louis U. L.J. 793 (1991). See also Jonathan Macey, *Promoting Public-Regarding Legislation Through Statutory Interpretation: An Interest Group Model*, 86 Colum. L. Rev. 223 (1986) (considering liberal and strict construction from the perspective of public choice theory).

of the common law. As we have seen, however, that is no reason, standing alone, to construe such a statute narrowly; strict construction must be justified on more finely tuned grounds. Some commentators have argued that sovereign immunity is obsolete — that in modern times, government should be as amenable as private parties to suit for harm it causes.[18] Indeed, all states and the federal government have embraced this proposition in part, by enacting statutes allowing suit against the government for tort and breach of contract.[19] But these statutes generally do not subject the government to common-law-like suits to the same extent as private parties, for in many instances damages are limited (e.g., no punitive damages, a cap on actual damages), certain special defenses are available (e.g., that the tort injury resulted from a discretionary government function), and so on.

Based on the earlier analysis assessing when liberal or strict construction might make contextual sense, one might wonder whether the limited retention of sovereign immunity supports any plausible contemporary value that might have emerged from a reasonably fair legislative process. The almost universal retention of the canon of narrow construction of waivers of sovereign immunity at the federal and state levels suggests that the judiciary is unwilling to assume that the current state of affairs flunks these inquiries. Nonetheless, nothing prevents a state supreme court that is confident that local public values favor recovery against the government from flipping the canon into one of liberal construction of immunity waivers.[20]

---

[18]See Kenneth Culp Davis, *Administrative Law Treatise* § 25.01, at 435-36 (1958); Akhil Amar, *Of Sovereignty and Federalism*, 96 Yale L.J. 1425 (1987); John Paul Stevens, *Is Justice Irrelevant?*, 87 Nw. U. L. Rev. 1121 (1993). For an argument defending sovereign immunity, see note 26 *infra*.

[19]Greater problems arise, however, when the legislature creates new statutory rights but fails to clarify whether the government as well as private parties is subject to the new duties and remedies. See, e.g., *Lane v. Pena*, 518 U.S. 187 (1996) (because the Rehabilitation Act contains no unequivocal waiver of immunity of United States to money damages, federal court concluding that cadet had been dismissed by U.S. Merchant Marine Academy in violation of the statute's prohibition of discrimination on account of disability could order him reinstated, but could not award compensatory damages).

[20]Cf. *Zerbe v. State*, 578 P.2d 597 (Alaska 1978) (narrowly construing exceptions to Alaska's tort claims statute to promote recovery for citizens harmed by their government).

Given the apparent tension between the sovereign immunity canon and contemporary values supporting compensation for victims of wrongdoing, it seems surprising that the Supreme Court, which only a few years ago seemed well on the way to diluting, if not abandoning, the canon,[21] has recently reembraced the canon with great enthusiasm.[22] Indeed, it appears to have transformed the canon from one of narrow construction into one that requires a very clear statement in statutory text before a waiver of immunity is found. In *United States v. Nordic Village, Inc.*,[23] for example, Justice Scalia's opinion for the court began with the narrow-construction canon: "[T]he traditional principle" is that "the Government's consent to be sued must be construed strictly in favor of the sovereign, and not enlarge[d] . . . beyond what the language requires."[24] Yet the Court treated the absence of a clear waiver in statutory text to be the end of the inquiry, refusing to consider legislative history or other factors. Justice Scalia stated that "the 'unequivocal expression' of elimination of sovereign immunity that we insist upon is an expression in statutory text."[25] It seems remarkable that the Court did not explain what values might justify this great expansion in the power of the canon.[26]

---

[21]In *United States v. Kubrick*, 444 U.S. 111 (1979), the Court stated that "we should not take it upon ourselves to extend the waiver beyond that which Congress intended. Neither, however, should we assume the authority to narrow the waiver that Congress intended." *Id.* at 117-18 (citations omitted). Accordingly, the Court in *Kubrick* treated the question as one of routine statutory interpretation under which it should consider statutory text, legislative history, purpose, and so on.

[22]See Nagle, *supra* note 2, as well as William Eskridge, Jr. & Philip Frickey, *Quasi-Constitutional Law: Clear Statement Rules as Constitutional Lawmaking*, 45 Vand. L. Rev. 593 (1992).

[23]503 U.S. 30 (1992).

[24]*Id.* at 34 (multiple quotation marks and citations omitted).

[25]*Id.* at 37.

[26]For an extended discussion, see Nagle, *supra* note 2.

As Part IIB of this chapter indicates, clear statement rules are sometimes rooted in structural constitutional principles. Perhaps the separation of powers provides some basis for sovereign immunity. See Harold Krent, *Reconceptualizing Sovereign Immunity*, 45 Vand. L. Rev. 1529 (1992). Arguably, it is a uniquely legislative function to establish a process for compensating victims of government wrongdoing, and any judicial overthrow of sovereign immunity would make public

Nordic Village teaches several general lessons about the substantive canons. No matter how longstanding the canon, its salience in interpretation will vary over time depending upon the values that judges find underlying it. In particular, the procedural impact of a canon — whether it functions as a broad- or narrow-construction directive or, as the next section discusses, as some kind of presumption about statutory meaning — is subject to fluidity over time. As the sovereign immunity example indicates, hoary canons sit like loaded guns, to be picked up and even modified to produce more firepower by skillful advocates and opportunistic judges. Regrettably, because the canons are rule-like in form, judges may rely upon them without acknowledging that the canons are rooted in controversial values, may have been phrased in different ways in prior cases, and can evolve over time on a case-by-case basis. We will return to these qualities that strip the rule-like veneer from the substantive canons when we examine several of the most important canonical presumptions throughout the remainder of this chapter.

B. *Presumptions and Clear Statement Rules*

The liberal- or strict-construction canons are linked to certain kinds of statutes (remedial, waivers of sovereign immunity, and so on). Other canons are phrased as embodying presumptions of policies that the legislature intends to promote throughout its statutes. As with all other canons, these canons are based on the judicial embrace of some value found in the Constitution, the common law, or other

---

officials subject to suit for injunctive relief in ways that would interfere with their capacity to exercise appropriate discretion. Someone who suffers injury at the hands of the government and cannot avail herself of an existing waiver of sovereign immunity is remediless in court, but not necessarily in the legislature: she may take her claim there, and the legislature may pay it off (most state legislatures have standing committees to handle just such problems) or enact a special waiver of immunity allowing her to proceed in court. Limited sovereign immunity protects small subdivisions, like towns, from ruinous liability from perhaps a single instance of wrongdoing. In contemporary America, those who suffer personal injury often have other means of covering their expenses and lost wages (e.g., insurance), and those who do not are likely to be eligible for benefits like unemployment compensation and welfare from the government in any event. Although such arguments may not persuade everyone that limited waivers of sovereign immunity are good policy, they may be powerful enough to dissuade judges from construing ambiguities in waiver statutes against the government.

statutes. For example, based on the separation of powers, the Court presumes that Congress does not intend to erode the traditional powers of the President[27] or the federal courts.[28] Based on the constitutional value of federalism, the Court presumes that Congress does not intend that federal regulatory statutes preempt state authority beyond that necessary to achieve congressional objectives.[29]

Frequently the distinction between a liberal- or strict-construction canon and a presumption is more form than substance. For example, a longstanding interpretive principle is that ambiguities in federal Indian treaties and statutes involving Indian affairs will be construed in favor of Native Americans.[30] Sometimes the Supreme Court has phrased the canon as requiring a liberal construction of text benefitting Indians;[31] sometimes it has treated the canon as requiring a narrow construction of text harming Indians;[32] sometimes it has simply assumed that there is a presumption favoring the textual reading benefiting Indians.[33] Obviously, each formulation just seems to require that Native Americans get the benefit of the doubt as to textual uncertainty.

---

[27]See, e.g., *Haig v. Agee*, 453 U.S. 280, 297-98 (1981).

[28]See, e.g., *Weinberger v. Romero-Barcelo*, 456 U.S. 305, 313 (1982); *Hecht Co. v. Bowles*, 321 U.S. 321, 330 (1944) (presumption that Congress would not withdraw the courts' traditional equitable discretion). See also *Dunlop v. Bachowski*, 421 U.S. 560, 567-68 (1975) (presumption of judicial review of government action).

[29]See, e.g., *Cipollone v. Liggett Group, Inc.*, 505 U.S. 504, 518-20 (1992); *Ray v. Atlantic Richfield Co.*, 435 U.S. 151 (1978).

[30]See, e.g., Philip Frickey, *Marshalling Past and Present: Colonialism, Constitutionalism, and Interpretation in Federal Indian Law*, 107 Harv. L. Rev. 381 (1993).

[31]See, e.g., *Washington v. Washington State Commercial Passenger Fishing Vessel Ass'n*, 443 U.S. 658, 676 (1979).

[32]The reciprocal nature of the canon is reflected in *Bryan v. Itasca County*, 426 U.S. 373, 392 (1976), where the Court articulated the canon as mandating the liberal construction of statutes benefiting Indians but applied it to construe narrowly a statute invading tribal prerogatives.

[33]See, e.g., *Minnesota v. Mille Lacs Band of Chippewa Indians*, 119 S.Ct. 1187, 1200 n.5 (1999).

Moreover, in many circumstances the interpretive effect of a canon may be similar regardless of whether it is phrased as one directing liberal or strict construction or creating a presumption of textual meaning. The weakest kind of substantive canon operates merely as a *tiebreaker* at the end of the interpretive analysis. A court following such a canon first uses the traditional tools of statutory interpretation (for pragmatists: text, legislative history, statutory purpose, policy) to determine statutory meaning; only if the court is left in great doubt does the canon become relevant and control the outcome. Such canons could be formulated as liberal- or strict-interpretation directions or as presumptions. For example, if a state appellate court takes a fairly flexible view of the sovereign immunity canon, it might first construe the text potentially waiving immunity with the traditional tools. If, on balance, the court believes that a waiver is fairly clearly present or not present, that is the end of the matter. If, instead, the court concludes that the question is a very close one, it would apply the canon as essentially a tiebreaker and hold that no waiver existed. The court could phrase the canon either as requiring a narrow construction of ambiguities in potential waiver statutes or as creating a presumption that the legislature did not intend to waive immunity in doubtful circumstances.

Substantive canons with more interpretive bite amount to *rebuttable presumptions* about statutory meaning that affect interpretation at the outset rather than merely at the end of the analysis. A court following this approach begins by presuming that the legislature intended the statute to have a certain meaning (e.g., not to waive sovereign immunity) and places the burden of overcoming that interpretation upon the unfortunate advocate on that side of the case. Whether the advocate can bring all the traditional tools of interpretation to bear on the problem or only a subset of such tools depends upon how the controlling precedents implementing the canon have treated it. For example, sometimes the Supreme Court has suggested that only text,[34] or only the combination of text and legislative history,[35] can reveal statutory meaning sufficient to overcome the canon favoring Native Americans. Obviously, it is more natural to

---

[34]See *Worcester v. Georgia*, 31 U.S. (6 Pet.) 515, 554 (1832).

[35]See *United States v. Dion*, 476 U.S. 734, 739-40 (1986).

phrase such a canon as a presumption rather than as a liberal- or strict-interpretation directive, but, as the canon involving Native Americans indicates, courts are often not careful or consistent about such formulations.

If a presumption of statutory meaning is sufficiently powerful, it can rise to the level of a *clear statement rule*. Illustratively, recall that, in *Nordic Village*, the Court announced that "the 'unequivocal expression' of elimination of sovereign immunity that we insist upon is an expression in statutory text."[36] In such instances, the Court is announcing a rule of law: in the absence of clear statutory text speaking to the precise issue, judges must interpret the statute a certain way. Sometimes the courts impose such a stringent requirement of statutory textual clarity as to require the legislature to draft statutes with highly targeted text containing what amounts to "magic language" if the legislature wishes to overcome the canon. For example, Congress is well advised, after *Nordic Village*, to include such language as "the sovereign immunity of the United States is hereby waived" in its statutes in addition to more general language indicating that the government is amenable to suit. Such steroidal canons dictating special language might be labeled *super-strong clear statement rules*.[37] We will examine one cluster of such canons, which concern federalism, in Part IIB below.

C. *Policies Potentially Served by Substantive Canons*

Having assessed the nature and interpretive effects of substantive canons, it is next important to consider what justifications might exist for these canons.[38] One way of defending the canons is on grounds of efficiency. It is impossible for a legislature to draft statutes to cover all contingencies. The established canons may provide a predictable *interpretive regime* that embodies gap-filling rules accessible to the legislature and the bar. If courts adhere to the

---

[36]*Nordic Village*, 503 U.S. at 37.

[37]Eskridge & Frickey, *supra* note 22, at 597, 611-12; see Nagle, *supra* note 2 (criticism of *Nordic Village* and related clear statement rules from an originalist perspective).

[38]The discussion in text is drawn from Eskridge, *Dynamic Statutory Interpretation, supra* note 2, at 275-306.

canons, over time all the relevant actors will become familiar with the legal effects that particular statutory language will have, allowing more knowledgeable legislative drafting, bargaining, and lobbying to occur. Perhaps, as the Supreme Court once stated, "[w]hat is of paramount importance is that Congress be able to legislate against a background of clear interpretive rules, so that it may know the effect of the language it adopts."[39]

Note several characteristics of this economic defense of canons. The justification applies to all canons, not merely substantive ones. It does not depend upon the courts' picking the best canons, only that the canons be transparent and consistently applied. For the textual canons, this argument might make some sense, although it begs the question whether legislatures and lobbyists are institutionally capable of drafting and bargaining with such maxims in mind. For the substantive canons, however, we think that this justification is less compelling.

Unlike the textual canons, which are probably relatively neutral in their allocational effects, the substantive canons reflect judicially articulated policies that are sometimes enforced very vigorously by strong presumptions or clear statement rules and thus do affect the allocation of power, rights, and property in our society. For example, it may well be that the current Supreme Court is a good deal stingier about allowing recovery against the federal government than is Congress or the citizenry at large. Of course, in theory, at least, legislative drafters can work around the obstacles created by the canons. But even in this theoretical world (which may be far removed from the sloppy reality of the legislative process), the obstacles are more formidable to one set of drafters than others. For example, clear statement rules concerning federalism impose higher costs on those wishing to enact obligations binding state and local officials than on those who favor less intrusion on subnational governments. Furthermore, meeting interpretive requirements becomes hard, if not impossible, when the canons undergo unpredict-

---

[39] *Finley v. United States*, 490 U.S. 545, 556 (1989) (Scalia, J.). The idea of the canons as an "interpretive regime" is developed in William Eskridge, Jr. & John Ferejohn, *Politics, Interpretation, and the Rule of Law*, in *The Rule of Law* 265 (Ian Shapiro ed. 1994) (NOMOS XXXVI).

able evolution in the case law, as occurred when the Court in recent years transformed the sovereign immunity canon from a presumption into a clear statement rule.[40] In any event, even in a transparent and static interpretive regime, the value judgments rooted in the substantive canons — like all value judgments in legal analysis — require normative justification.

What might such normative justifications be? A straightforward argument would be that the values reflected in the substantive canons are normatively attractive in some relatively objective fashion, not merely reflective of judicial bias. Thus, if a substantive canon has been followed across several generations of judges who have differed in their ideological outlooks, the premises supporting the canon may have some time-tested value. Moreover, especially if the values supporting the canon seem commonsensical or reflect something approximating a consensus in American values, they might serve as reasonable, off-the-shelf predictions about legislative intent.[41] In addition, the canons may correlate with basic values embedded in the Constitution, the common law, or longstanding public policies. All of these justifications point outside the judge's own values to potentially more durable foundations.

Another normative justification might be that the canons can correct legislative failure and can promote legislative deliberation, thereby serving republican and due-process-of-lawmaking values.[42] As the models of the political process examined in Chapter 3 indicate, legislatures may be systematically biased towards certain interests and in ways that undermine the public good. For example, as already noted, the public grants canon seems designed to protect the public fisc against predictable, if improvident, grants of public assets to narrow, well organized, politically powerful private interests. Similarly, the rule of lenity in criminal cases, which counsels that ambiguities are to be interpreted against the government and in favor

---

[40]See Nagle, *supra* note 2, at 819-29, for a detailed exposition of the difficulty Congress sometimes has in following the new sovereign immunity rules.

[41]See Antonin Scalia, *A Matter of Interpretation: Federal Courts and the Law* 29 (1997).

[42]On the republican theory of lawmaking, see Chapter 2; on due process of lawmaking, see Chapter 5, Part IIB.

of the criminal defendant, might reflect a commonsense notion that potential criminal defendants are virtually impossible to organize for political action. On the other hand, if it is in the public interest for the criminal law to reach conduct that the courts have held to be outside the criminal prohibition, prosecutors are easily organized to propose such an amendment and have great legitimacy in making such a case to a legislature, which is unlikely to want to be viewed as "soft on crime." Similar justifications might support a *"Carolene* canon,"[43] under which civil rights statutes should be interpreted to promote the lot of politically powerless minorities. Thus, the substantive canons might be capable of serving as methods for judicial "remands" of statutory problems to the legislative arena for reconsideration in a potentially more politically balanced and informative environment — the sort of judicial-legislative interaction captured by the discussion of due process of lawmaking in Chapter 5.

This canonical quality of enhancing judicial and legislative deliberation might be especially important when fundamental constitutional values are at stake. For instance, one justification for the rule of lenity is that constitutional notions of due process counsel that a criminal statute must provide clear notice before someone may be incarcerated for violating its commands. Rather than striking down an unclear criminal statute as void for vagueness — thereby possibly depriving the public of its protections against persons clearly acting wrongfully — the court may simply narrowly interpret the statute so that it avoids the hardest constitutional problems.[44] Such an outcome allows the court to avoid an unnecessary decision about what might be a difficult constitutional question and remands the controversy to the legislature for potential reconsideration in light of the court's constitutional qualms. Moreover, this kind of strategy

---

[43]See Eskridge, *Public Values, supra* note 2, at 1032-34, arguing that Warren and Burger Court constructions of civil rights laws reflected the idea, gleaned from *United States v. Carolene Prods. Co.*, 304 U.S. 144, 152 n.4 (1938), that the judiciary should guard against statutory discriminations against "discrete and insular minorities" such as people of color.

[44]See, e.g., *United States v. Vuitch*, 402 U.S. 62 (1971) (upholding D.C. abortion law against vagueness attack, but construing law to place burden of proof on prosecutors to show that abortion was *not* necessary for preservation of the mother's life *or* health).

might allow the Court to give some bite to "underenforced constitutional norms" — norms derived from the Constitution but that the Court, for prudential or institutional reasons, feels it ought not enforce very often through direct judicial review.[45]

Take another example: the Court rarely invalidates a congressional enactment on the ground that it invades domains reserved by the Constitution to the President or the Court. That norm is more often enforced by the canon, mentioned in Part IB, that presumes Congress does not intend to invade traditional executive and judicial prerogatives. Narrow construction allows courts to protect the executive and judicial branches from potentially unconstitutional congressional intrusions that might have been inadvertent in the first place. This result also kicks the issue back to Congress and encourages its members to deliberate conscientiously about the constitutional separation of powers before adopting similar legislation in the future. In this way, the canons may generally serve the republican value of fostering deliberation, both within the legislature and across the legislative and judicial divide. This approach also might be defended as democracy-enhancing, for it gives the legislature greater opportunities to deliberate and respond to judicial decisions.

Each of the foregoing justifications can be questioned, however. The efficiency justification depends on a potentially unrealistic capacity of legislatures, lobbyists, and others to understand an interpretive regime and act in sophisticated ways in response to it.[46] (This is going to be true especially in state legislatures that have little support staff.) Turning to normative concerns, some of the values

---

[45]On underenforced constitutional norms, see Lawrence Sager, *Fair Measure: The Legal Status of Underenforced Constitutional Norms*, 91 Harv. L. Rev. 1212 (1978). Perhaps the most sustained leakage of constitutional norms into statutory interpretation has occurred in immigration law. See Hiroshi Motomura, *Immigration Law After a Century of Plenary Power: Phantom Constitutional Norms and Statutory Interpretation*, 100 Yale L.J. 545 (1990).

[46]For thoughtful analyses of court-legislature communications of this sort, see Shirley Abrahamson & Robert Hughes, *Shall We Dance?: Steps for Legislators and Judges in Statutory Interpretation*, 75 Minn. L. Rev. 1045 (1991); *Judges and Legislators: Toward Institutional Comity* (Robert Katzmann ed. 1988). See also Elizabeth Garrett, *Legal Scholarship in the Age of Legislation*, 34 Tulsa L.J. 676 (1999) (discussing need for empirical study into democracy-forcing justifications for clear statement rules).

reflected in the substantive canons are unlikely to correlate with probable legislative intent. For example, it is unlikely that Congress thinks potential criminals should get a break in the interpretation of criminal statutes or that Indian tribes should be preferred to other interests. If these values are defensible, it must be in spite of, not because of, their linkage to probable congressional preferences. That judges have enthusiastically embraced certain values across the generations does not guarantee the current appropriateness of the canons, as the sovereign immunity canon might well demonstrate. Judicial intervention based on impressions about internal legislative processes will strike many as anti-democratic intermeddling, not a healthy correction for legislative failure. Indeed, the whole thrust of the substantive canons may seem as countermajoritarian as judicial review, for skewing the interpretation of a statute may involve as much judicial activism as declaring it unconstitutional. To be sure, a critical difference between canonical interpretation and constitutional invalidation is that in the former instance the legislature can reenact the statute without ambiguities, but this safety valve may simply encourage a greater degree of judicial activism through the use of the canonical strategy.[47]

In the final analysis, the promise and problematics of the substantive canons should be assessed locally, not globally. The substantive canons might work better in some areas of law than in others. And some canons may function better than others in achieving these potential benefits without incurring the potential costs. The next Part considers three important substantive canons in light of these concerns.

II. Three Important Substantive Canons

As the Appendix to this book indicates, the Constitution serves as the source for many of the important substantive canons. Three such canons are worthy of extended consideration, in part because they illustrate the plasticity of the canons as well as their potential for an

---

[47]See William Eskridge, Jr. & Philip Frickey, *The Supreme Court, 1993 Term — Foreword: Law as Equilibrium*, 108 Harv. L. Rev. 26, 81-87 (1994), for examples of the Court's "stealth activism," and Motomura, *supra* note 45, at 600-13, for an example (immigration law) where "phantom norms" have arguably created both too much and not enough judicial activism.

effective dialogue with the legislature, and in part because they provide good contexts for critically assessing the utility of substantive canons in practice. They might help you answer the age-old question: Does the U.S. Supreme Court or state high courts deploy *lucid* canons, or are their weapons *loose* canons instead?

A. *Avoiding Serious Constitutional Issues*

A fundamental principle of American public law is that courts should decide constitutional issues only when necessary. In the most famous discussion of this principle, Justice Brandeis wrote that "[t]he Court will not pass upon a constitutional question although properly presented by the record, if there is also present some other ground upon which the case may be disposed of. . . . Thus, if a case can be decided on either of two grounds, one involving a constitutional question, the other a question of statutory construction or general law, the Court will decide only the latter."[48] He articulated the resulting canon of interpretation as follows: " 'When the validity of an act of the Congress is drawn in question, and even if a serious doubt of constitutionality is raised, it is a cardinal principle that this Court will first ascertain whether a construction of the statute is fairly possible by which the question may be avoided.' "[49]

Professor Schauer attributes this approach to the absence of any clear constitutional authorization of the practice of judicial review and to the countermajoritarian difficulty that arises when unelected federal judges with life tenure invalidate a statute enacted by democratically elected legislators.[50] We would add a third, related, concern. Even if judicial review is considered a well-settled and legitimate practice, the Court's constitutional decisions raise several practical legal process issues relating to the comparative institutional competence of courts and legislatures. Because many constitutional

---

[48]*Ashwander v. Tennessee Valley Auth.*, 297 U.S. 288, 347 (1936) (Brandeis, J., concurring).

[49]*Id.* at 348 (quoting *Crowell v. Benson*, 285 U.S. 22, 62 (1932)).

[50]See Frederick Schauer, Ashwander *Revisited*, 1995 Sup. Ct. Rev. 71, 71-72. For other useful recent discussions, see Lisa Kloppenberg, *Avoiding Constitutional Questions*, 35 B.C. L. Rev. 1003 (1994); Adrian Vermeule, *Saving Constructions*, 85 Geo. L.J. 1945 (1997).

prohibitions, such as due process and equal protection, provide only vague standards, the Court is frequently required to elaborate doctrines and tests that go well beyond anything that can be mechanically gleaned from constitutional text. Perhaps courts should avoid such nuanced, debatable case-by-case elaboration if possible. This may be especially true in constitutional law, where legislatures generally cannot reenact the statute in question if they disagree with the Court's constitutional understanding. Because the only remedies for a faulty constitutional invalidation are cumbersome — either the Court must overrule itself or the U.S. Constitution must be amended — perhaps the Court should embrace the "avoidance canon" with Brandeisian enthusiasm.

At first glance, the avoidance canon may seem to serve the goals for the substantive canons. When a statute is interpreted to avoid a serious constitutional question, the legislature is free to return to the issue. The Court's constitutional discussion may enhance later legislative deliberations on this or related subjects, and at least it should encourage legislators to address the responsibility they undertook when they took their oaths to uphold the Constitution.[51] An interbranch dialogue concerning constitutional meaning might be fostered that would enrich the perspectives of both the judiciary and the legislature. Meanwhile, the narrowing interpretation protects the underlying constitutional values and puts the often-difficult burden of surmounting all the legislative vetogates[52] upon those who would trench upon them. This allocation of the burden of legislative inertia might seem particularly important when the underlying constitutional values involve the protection of the politically powerless.

Because these justifications have a strong superficial appeal and because the avoidance canon has a longstanding pedigree,[53] it is

---

[51]For discussions of how conscientious legislators might approach constitutional interpretation, see Paul Brest, *The Conscientious Legislator's Guide to Constitutional Interpretation*, 27 Stan. L. Rev. 585 (1975); Stephen Ross, *Legislative Enforcement of Equal Protection*, 72 Minn. L. Rev. 311 (1987).

[52]See Chapter 3, Part I.

[53]Even before the Court in *Marbury v. Madison*, 5 U.S. (1 Cranch) 137 (1803), established the principle of judicial review, it had narrowly interpreted the Judiciary Act of 1789 on the ground that the statute must "receive a construction, consistent with the constitution." *Mossman v. Higginson*, 4 U.S. (4 Dall.) 12, 14

tempting to view it as a well settled, legitimate, and uncontroversial aspect of the American practice of statutory interpretation. Indeed, a decade ago the Supreme Court stated that the canon "has for so long been applied by this Court that it is beyond debate."[54] Even Justice Scalia — whom one would expect to be dubious about any canon encouraging a court to deviate from the best textual reading of a statute — recently chided the majority of his colleagues for refusing to apply the canon because they believed that the constitutional issue was not sufficiently close and the statute not sufficiently ambiguous.[55]

Academics like nothing better than attacking the conventional wisdom, however. For example, Professor Schauer argues that the costs of applying the avoidance canon are substantial and the benefits flowing from it minimal.[56] When the canon is invoked, the best interpretation of the statute is jettisoned in favor of any alternative that is "fairly possible," a slippery requirement that in the hands of lazy or willful judges might provide little barrier to truly implausible attributions of statutory meaning. This cost is incurred to avoid constitutional inquiry, but in fact it cannot be undertaken until at least a preliminary constitutional analysis has been conducted — for how else can the judge determine whether the preferred interpretation of the statute raises a serious constitutional question? While the court need not technically decide the constitutional issue once and for all time, the conscientious judge must come close enough to doing so to satisfy herself that the issue is genuinely a close one. This judicial effort is supposed to lead to a canonically inspired interpretation rather than judicial invalidation of the statute so that the legislature can deliberate and respond if it wishes. But because the court has

---

(1800). See Vermeule, *supra* note 50, at 1948. For an early invocation of a related principle, that courts should avoid statutory interpretations inconsistent with the law of nations, see *Murray v. Schooner Charming Betsy*, 6 U.S. (2 Cranch) 64, 118 (1804) (Marshall, C.J.). See generally Ralph Steinhardt, *The Role of International Law as a Canon of Domestic Statutory Construction*, 43 Vand. L. Rev. 1103 (1990).

[54]*Edward J. DeBartolo Corp. v. Florida Gulf Coast Bldg. & Constr. Trades Council*, 485 U.S. 568, 575 (1988).

[55]See *Almendarez-Torres v. United States*, 118 S.Ct. 1219, 1234 (1998) (Scalia, J., dissenting).

[56]See Schauer, *supra* note 50.

signaled that any restorative amendment stands a good chance of being struck down, why would a legislature bother? Moreover, how likely are legislators to concern themselves with relatively abstract questions of constitutional meaning, as opposed to their perceptions of good public policy and what is in their own political interest?

Indeed, perhaps the only practical difference between invalidating the statute as unconstitutional and imaginatively interpreting it canonically is that in the latter instance the court may well do a slipshod job of constitutional analysis, failing to think through the constitutional issues because, after all, it is supposedly avoiding them.[57] Especially in light of the seemingly uncontroversial nature of the canon, we might expect at least some judges who would carefully deliberate before holding a statute unconstitutional to search reflexively for any remotely plausible interpretation to avoid the constitutional issue. In any event, for Professor Schauer, it is not clear that judicial rewriting is any less an affront to the legislature than judicial invalidation. He would jettison the avoidance canon entirely or weaken its effect.

Judge Posner and others have objected that the canon cuts off potentially constitutional statutory applications, for it leads a court to interpret a statute to avoid a constitutional question even though the more natural construction of the statute might survive constitutional review.[58] Indeed, "[t]he case law is rife with constitutional questions that the Court has avoided by construction, only later to hold, when forced to confront the question under a different statute, that the constitutional claim should not prevail."[59] While some critics lament that the canon is too deeply entrenched in our public law to be dislodged, this does not excuse scholars from asking normative questions: Does this pattern amount to an illegitimate judicial invasion into legislative supremacy? Is it, on balance, an "over-protection" of constitutional norms?

---

[57]For a good example of such poor judicial craftsmanship, consider the Court's disastrous opinion in *United States v. Harriss*, 347 U.S. 612 (1954), interpreting the 1946 federal statute regulating lobbying. As discussed in Chapter 5, Part IIIA, it took decades for Congress to reenact meaningful legislation on lobbying.

[58]See, e.g., Richard Posner, *The Federal Courts: Crisis and Reform* 284-85 (1985).

[59]Vermeule, *supra* note 50, at 1960.

Recall that the canons of statutory interpretation can protect constitutional values that are underenforced by courts through judicial review, such as the rule of lenity, the separation of powers canons, and the federalism canons.[60] Moreover, canons, including the avoidance one, may be prudential devices for the protection of constitutional norms that are under particular attack due to short-term political factors.

For example, during the McCarthy Era of the 1950s and its aftermath, the Court used the avoidance canon to protect the rights of persons who were under a cloud because of their supposed Communist affiliation or sympathies. In *Kent v. Dulles,*[61] the Court held that the executive branch could not withhold passports from "subversives" without express congressional authorization. The Court thus protected the constitutional right of foreign travel by narrow interpretation rather than by judicial invalidation. This suspensive veto worked: Congress never enacted the explicit authorization, despite pleas from President Eisenhower to do so.[62] Similarly, in a series of cases, the Court narrowly interpreted the notorious anti-Communist Smith Act — which made it a federal crime for someone "to knowingly or willfully advocate, abet, advise, or teach the duty,

---

[60]See Parts IB & IIB of this chapter. Consider another potential example. As Chapter 2, Part IC indicated, there are potentially serious tensions between the constitutional requirement that each state have a republican form of government and the use of direct democracy in the American states to enact statutes and amend state constitutions. Many years ago, the Supreme Court ducked the issue, labeling it a nonjusticiable political question. See *Pacific States Tel. & Tel. Co. v. Oregon,* 223 U.S. 118 (1912). Technically, state courts are not bound by the limitations upon judicial authority instinct in Article III, and therefore they could consider the constitutionality of direct democracy. See Hans Linde, *Who is Responsible for Republican Government?,* 65 U. Colo. L. Rev. 709 (1994). Although for prudential and political reasons it is unlikely that state judges, who are often popularly elected, would outlaw the longstanding practice of direct democracy, the avoidance canon might suggest that measures adopted by initiative or referendum should be interpreted narrowly, especially if they are in tension with other basic constitutional norms such as equal protection. See Philip Frickey, *Interpretation on the Borderline: Constitution, Canons, Direct Democracy,* 1996 Ann. Surv. Am. L. 477.

[61]357 U.S. 116 (1958).

[62]See Daniel Farber, *National Security, the Right to Travel, and the Court,* 1981 Sup. Ct. Rev. 263, 279-81.

necessity, desirability, or propriety of overthrowing or destroying any government in the United States by force or violence" — as outlawing not beliefs, but only actions that were specifically intended to incite the overthrow of the government.[63] As a result of these narrowing interpretations and a gradual change in political climate, prosecutions under the Smith Act ground to a halt.

In a famous essay written a generation ago, Professor Alexander Bickel extolled the Court to use such "passive virtues" to shift the status quo toward protecting important interests of constitutional dimension while allowing Congress the opportunity to reconsider the matter deliberatively.[64] According to Bickel, "the Court exercises a triune function: it checks, it legitimates, or it does neither."[65] Rather than give the Smith Act and the passport statute a broad reading and then either strike them down (perhaps causing a constitutional crisis in the Court's relation with Congress or the society at large) or uphold them (which might have encouraged "Red-baiting"), the Court took an intermediate position seeking to ensure that the status quo respected norms of constitutional magnitude while leaving legislators and executive officials some capacity to respond. To be sure, avoidance in these cases hardly seems "passive." Whether it was a "virtue" probably depends upon what one believes about the supposed countermajoritarian difficulty of judicial review and about the judicial capacity to exercise such nuanced, discretionary techniques in a principled way.[66]

---

[63]See *Scales v. United States*, 367 U.S. 203 (1961); *Yates v. United States*, 354 U.S. 298 (1957). The Court had upheld the Act against direct constitutional attack in *Dennis v. United States*, 341 U.S. 494 (1951).

[64]See Alexander Bickel, *The Supreme Court, 1960 Term — Foreword: The Passive Virtues*, 75 Harv. L. Rev. 40 (1961), recast as Alexander Bickel, *The Least Dangerous Branch: The Supreme Court at the Bar of Politics* ch. 4 (1962). Evidence of a neo-Bickelian impulse among both judges and commentators can be seen in such recent commentary as Neal Katyal, *Judges as Advicegivers*, 50 Stan. L. Rev. 1709 (1998), and Cass Sunstein, *The Supreme Court, 1995 Term — Foreword: Leaving Things Undecided*, 110 Harv. L. Rev. 4 (1996).

[65]Bickel, *The Least Dangerous Branch*, supra note 64, at 200.

[66]Cf. Gerald Gunther, *The Subtle Vices of the "Passive Virtues" — A Comment on Principle and Expediency in Judicial Review*, 64 Colum. L. Rev. 1 (1964), criticizing Bickel's approach as inconsistent with the deeper, principle-based grounds for judicial legitimacy.

Even though most judicial invocations of the avoidance canon are not in such dramatic settings, our sense is that the questions raised by Professor Schauer and others about the costs and benefits of the canon do at least counsel its narrow formulation. The Court has articulated the canon in various ways in different cases. In perhaps the broadest, and most dubious, formulation in recent times, the Court in *National Labor Relations Board v. Catholic Bishop of Chicago*[67] suggested that it would avoid "serious constitutional questions" unless compelled to do so by an "affirmative intention of the Congress clearly expressed."[68] If a "serious constitutional question" is merely one that gives headaches to law students (even if it has a relatively clear answer if thought through carefully), this canon could be invoked in many cases even though the constitutionality of the statute, fairly interpreted, is not in much doubt. More important, a search for an "affirmative intention of the Congress clearly expressed" seems to be satisfied only by express statutory language or crystal-clear legislative history. Such an extraordinarily strong presumption, amounting to a kind of clear statement rule, would allow courts to give statutes suboptimal interpretations in a great many cases, even those where the ordinary tools of interpretation pretty clearly point to a preferred construction. The dissenting opinion in *Catholic Bishop* quoted precedents articulating a narrower formulation that would ascertain "whether a construction of the statute is *fairly possible* by which the question may be avoided."[69] This approach seems preferable, for it "acts as a brake against wholesale judicial dismemberment of congressional enactments."[70]

B. *The Federalism Canons*

The substantive canons designed to protect state authority from federal encroachment provide the most vivid illustrations of canonical evolution in recent decades. The Supreme Court has long attempted

---

[67]440 U.S. 490 (1979), excerpted and discussed in Eskridge & Frickey 676-87.

[68]*Id.* at 501.

[69]*Id.* at 510 (Brennan, J., dissenting) (multiple quotation marks omitted), quoting *Machinists v. Street*, 367 U.S. 740, 749-50 (1961), in turn quoting *Crowell v. Benson*, 285 U.S. 22, 62 (1932).

[70]*Id.* at 510-11.

to use canons to ameliorate the tension between the Supremacy Clause, which provides that federal statutes are the "law of the land" and trump state law, and the underlying principles of federalism reflected in Article I and the Tenth Amendment. The most basic category of such canons concerns *preemption*. When a federal law and a state law are arguably inconsistent, the Court "start[s] with the assumption that the historic police powers of the States were not to be superseded by the Federal Act unless that was the clear and manifest purpose of Congress."[71] In recent years the Court has aggressively distinguished federal preemption of the state's police power over private citizens — which remains subject to the canonical presumption just quoted — from federal interference with the operations of state government, which now requires much clearer congressional authorization. These *intergovernmental immunity* canons have taken three basic forms.

The canon with the most longstanding stature was borne of the peculiar compromises surrounding the interpretation of the Eleventh Amendment, which generally immunizes the states from suit in federal court.[72] Congress has the authority to abrogate the states' immunity to suit when it is acting pursuant to its powers to enforce the Fourteenth Amendment.[73] In the 1980s, the Court transformed what had once been a presumption against congressional abrogation in ambiguous circumstances[74] into a stringent clear statement rule: "Congress may abrogate the States' constitutionally secured immunity from suit in federal court only by making its intention *unmistakably clear in the language of the statute*."[75]

---

[71]*Rice v. Santa Fe Elevator Corp.*, 331 U.S. 218, 230 (1947). The canonical treatment of the preemption issue is enormously complex and beyond the scope of this chapter. A good overview is S. Candice Hoke, *Preemption Pathologies and Civic Republican Values*, 71 B.U. L. Rev. 685 (1991).

[72]See *Hans v. Louisiana*, 134 U.S. 1 (1890).

[73]See *Fitzpatrick v. Bitzer*, 427 U.S. 445 (1976). When Congress legislates under its Article I powers, it lacks the power to abrogate the states' Eleventh Amendment immunity. See *Seminole Tribe of Fla. v. Florida*, 517 U.S. 44 (1996).

[74]See, e.g., *Employees of the Dep't of Pub. Health & Welfare v. Department of Pub. Health & Welfare*, 411 U.S. 279, 285 (1973).

[75]*Atascadero State Hosp. v. Scanlon*, 473 U.S. 234, 242 (1985) (emphasis added), excerpted and discussed in Hetzel, Libonati & Williams 650-52.

Note that this canon cannot be defended as a simple invocation of the rule about avoiding serious constitutional questions: the Court conceded that, if Congress acted with the requisite clarity, the statute would be constitutional. Instead, the canon seems based on the premise that state immunity to suit in federal court is a constitutional norm that the Court will not enforce to its limits, instead giving Congress some discretion to alter the traditional balance between federal and state power. This judicial willingness to defer to Congress comes at a price, however. Apparently the Court expects Congress to deliberate carefully about such intrusions upon core state functions, and only the most explicit decisions by Congress may take lawful effect.

Two other intergovernmental immunity canons involve even starker disjunctions between what the Court will strike down as unconstitutional and what it will narrow by interpretation in the absence of congressional clarity. The Court applies only minimal constitutional scrutiny when Congress attaches conditions to its grants of federal money to the states,[76] yet the conditions take legal effect only if they are unambiguous.[77] Similarly, during a period when the Court had (perhaps temporarily) abandoned serious constitutional scrutiny of federal statutes enacted pursuant to Congress's commerce powers that regulate core state functions,[78] the Court created a new canon that required Congress to express itself clearly if it wished to impose such regulations on the states.

The case imposing this last clear statement requirement, *Gregory v. Ashcroft*,[79] illustrates the problematic aspects of canonical evolution and shifting interpretive regimes. The issue in the case was

---

[76]See *South Dakota v. Dole*, 483 U.S. 203 (1987).

[77]See *Pennhurst State Sch. & Hosp. v. Halderman*, 451 U.S. 1, 22-24 (1981), excerpted and discussed in Hetzel, Libonati & Williams 648-50.

[78]See *Garcia v. San Antonio Metro. Transit Auth.*, 469 U.S. 528 (1985), overruling *National League of Cities v. Usery*, 426 U.S. 833 (1976), which had itself overruled *Maryland v. Wirtz*, 392 U.S. 183 (1968). In light of recent federalism decisions, *Garcia*, in its turn, may be narrowed or overruled in the future.

[79]501 U.S. 452 (1991), excerpted and discussed in Eskridge & Frickey 687-700.

whether a state could require its judges to retire at age seventy. The judges contended that the federal Age Discrimination in Employment Act[80] (ADEA) protected them against mandatory retirement. The Act covered "employees" of states, but it provided that

> "employee" shall not include any person elected to public office in any State or political subdivision of any State by the qualified voters thereof, or any person chosen by such officer to be on such officer's personal staff, or an appointee on the policymaking level or an immediate adviser with respect to the exercise of the constitutional or legal powers of the office.[81]

The judges were not elected officials. They would seem to be "appointees on the policymaking level," however. To be sure, the canon *noscitur a sociis*[82] might suggest that, because the other two kinds of appointed officials unprotected by the Act had close working relationships with elected officials, so too only those "appointees" with such a relationship were unprotected. In addition, perhaps judges are not on "the policymaking level," if by *noscitur a sociis* we understand that to mean the kind of policymaking undertaken by elected officials.

But even if it is not clear that appointed judges were included in this exemption, it is far from clear that they were excluded. The language of the exemption seems poorly chosen to capture the situation of appointed judges, one way or the other, and could easily be read as a rather clumsy way of excluding all high-level appointees in state government. State judges who were elected were clearly excepted from the ADEA's coverage, and there is no compelling reason to treat appointed judges differently. Apparently Congress gave the provision little attention, with the legislative history perhaps supporting the conclusion that the exemption was intended to keep the ADEA out of conflict with the state's ability to control its high-level appointees.[83] Moreover, a basic purpose of the ADEA — to protect older workers against competition in the workplace from

---

[80]29 U.S.C. §§ 621-34.

[81]*Id.* at § 630(f).

[82]See Chapter 7, Part IB.

[83]See *Gregory*, 501 U.S. at 484-85 (White, J., concurring in part and dissenting in part).

younger persons willing to work for lower wages — is inapposite to judges, who receive a fixed salary regardless of seniority, come from a class that is hardly politically powerless or subject to victimization, and may in fact have some sort of protected tenure of office under state law that serves as a *quid pro quo* for eventual mandatory retirement. Thus, the traditional tools of interpretation suggest that the coverage provision of the ADEA was at best ambiguous. In our judgment, the Court in *Gregory* could have invoked the longstanding traditional preemption canon, which creates a presumption that Congress does not intend its statutes to trump state authority,[84] and reached the uncontroversial conclusion that the judges had no federal statutory protection against mandatory retirement.

The Court reached that result, but by a far more aggressive canonical stance. Although Justice O'Connor's majority opinion certainly imposes upon Congress the burden of substantial exactitude, the opinion itself is hardly a model of clarity. It left unclear both what conditions trigger the new canon and the interpretive consequences that flow from it. At various points in the opinion, Justice O'Connor suggested that any federal law "intrud[ing] on traditional state authority"[85] or even merely "on state governmental functions"[86] was subject to the canon. Other passages, however, contain much more limiting language, such that the canon might apply only to federal law invading decisions "of the most fundamental sort for a sovereign entity"[87] or even just those involving a state's definition of its "constitutional officers."[88] The interpretive effect of the canon might be satisfied only if Congress chose "unmistakably clear"[89] statutory language — the same test as the Eleventh Amendment canon — or something less might do, such as when the traditional tools of interpretation make it "absolutely certain that Congress

---

[84]See text at note 71, *supra*.

[85]*Gregory*, 501 U.S. at 469.

[86]*Id.* at 470.

[87]*Id.* at 460.

[88]*Id.* Elsewhere, Justice O'Connor suggested that the concern focused on the state's "most important government officials." *Id.* at 463.

[89]*Id.* at 460 (multiple quotation marks and citations omitted).

intended such an exercise"[90] or "plain to anyone reading the Act that it covers judges."[91]

Note the relationship between the triggering requirement and the interpretive command contained in the *Gregory* canon. If the canon is invoked any time a federal statute might intrude on traditional state authority, then the canon is similar to the traditional preemption canon; it would seemingly apply even when the federal and state regulations apply only to private persons, not state governmental operations. As such, the interpretive effect of the canon should be modest, lest Congress be thwarted from regulating the private sector at all. Conversely, if the canon is only triggered when a federal law arguably regulates a state's constitutional officers, the canon has a limited sweep that is targeted at a potentially severe intrusion upon the values of federalism, for surely at the core of self-government is the citizenry's right to design the offices of their high governmental officials. If the canon is targeted that narrowly, it might make sense to enforce it very vigorously with a stringent clear statement rule similar to that in place to protect the states' Eleventh Amendment immunity. Indeed, if the canon were that narrow, it would also gain strength from the avoidance canon, for surely at least some federal interferences with state self-government — such as a federal statute requiring Minnesota to move the state capitol from St. Paul to St. Peter — could violate the Constitution.[92]

Perhaps in part due to the vagaries of *Gregory*, its canon has had a checkered history in its short life. In *BFP v. Resolution Trust Corp.*,[93] Justice Scalia's majority opinion invoked *Gregory* in partial support of reading the federal bankruptcy code, which allows a trustee to set aside fraudulent transfers of real estate, to be consistent with the definition of fraudulent conveyances under state law. Because this case involved the usual preemption question — whether federal law trumped state law concerning private rights — rather than federal regulation of core state operations, its invocation of the *Gregory*

---

[90]*Id.* at 464.

[91]*Id.* at 467.

[92]See *National League of Cities v. Usery*, 426 U.S. 833, 845 (1976) (quoting *Coyle v. Smith*, 221 U.S. 559, 565 (1911)).

[93]511 U.S. 531 (1994), excerpted and discussed in Eskridge & Frickey 700-02.

canon may indicate that the conditions triggering it are much wider than the facts of the *Gregory* case would suggest. In a second case, *Pennsylvania Department of Corrections v. Yeskey*,[94] Justice Scalia, this time for a unanimous Court, assumed *arguendo* that the operation of state prisons "is a traditional and essential State function subject to the plain-statement rule of *Gregory*."[95] He then concluded, however, that the coverage provision of the Americans with Disabilities Act satisfied the clear statement requirement.[96]

Whatever might be the reach and effect of *Gregory*, it vividly demonstrates three fundamental characteristics of the federalism canons. First, by imposing a stringent clear statement rule upon existing statutes, *Gregory* demonstrates that canonical evolution can amount to a "bait and switch." Congress may have frequently legislated in ways that would have been interpreted as reaching the states under the interpretive regime in place when Congress acted, only to discover that because of canonical evolution it must formally amend the statutes to reach the states today.[97]

---

[94]118 S.Ct. 1952 (1998), excerpted and discussed in Eskridge, Frickey & Garrett 1998 Supp. 129-31.

[95]*Id.* at 1954.

[96]Justice Scalia wrote in part:

> * * * The situation here is not comparable to that in *Gregory*. There, although the ADEA plainly covered state employees, it contained an exception for " 'appointee[s] on the policymaking level' " which made it impossible for us to "conclude that the state plainly cover[ed] appointed state judges." Here, the ADA plainly covers state institutions *without* any exception that could cast the coverage of prisons into doubt.

Id. (citations omitted). For the argument, developed before the Court decided *Yeskey*, that *Gregory* should be limited to situations in which a seemingly universal statutory coverage provision is qualified by an ambiguous exception, see Michael Lee, Comment, *How Clear Is "Clear"?: A Lenient Interpretation of the* Gregory v. Ashcroft *Clear Statement Rule*, 65 U. Chi. L. Rev. 255 (1998).

[97]For a vivid example of this bait-and-switch problem, consider *Dellmuth v. Muth*, 491 U.S. 223 (1989). The case involved the Education of the Handicapped Act, enacted in 1975, which probably would have abrogated the states' Eleventh Amendment immunity by the standards of that time. When, in 1985, in the *Atascadero* case, the Court imposed a stringent clear statement rule concerning the abrogation of Eleventh Amendment immunity, Congress responded in 1986 by amending the EHA so that it contained a clear abrogation. But the *Dellmuth* case

Second, it is difficult to escape the conclusion that the federalism canons are driven as much by the Justices' own values as by a belief that Congress may invade state interests so long as it deliberates carefully (the republican justification) or by the sense that the Court is merely constructing a transparent interpretive regime to promote predictability and certainty in law (the economic justification). The evolution of the federalism canons has been a small part of an overall judicial plan to limit federal power in modern America. The current Court is more sensitive to states' rights than any of its predecessors for at least two generations. For the first time in sixty years, it struck down a federal statute as beyond Congress' commerce powers.[98] It has invalidated congressional attempts to "commandeer" state legislatures[99] and state executive officials[100] to carry out federal programs. The Court has not only prevented Congress from using its Article I powers to abrogate state immunity to suit in federal court by invoking the Eleventh Amendment,[101] it has interpreted the Constitution's federalism values as preventing Congress from subjecting the states to suit in *their own state courts*.[102] Canonical interpretive moves may be a kinder and gentler way than judicial review to implement the values of federalism, but both the canonical and the constitutional strategies remain based on a hotly contested vision of the appropriate balance of federal and state power.

Third, the evolution of a set of canons can have its own gravitational pull, altering the roles played by other substantive canons that come into contact with it. For example, the canon promoting

---

involved matters arising before this 1986 amendment, and the Court retroactively imposed the *Atascadero* clear statement rule and said that the pre-1986 version did not amount to an abrogation. The Court even cited the 1986 amendment as containing the sort of drafting clarity required. See William Eskridge, Jr., *The New Textualism*, 37 UCLA L. Rev. 621, 684 (1990).

[98]See *United States v. Lopez*, 514 U.S. 549 (1995).

[99]See *New York v. United States*, 505 U.S. 144 (1992), explicated in Deborah Merritt, *Three Faces of Federalism: Finding a Formula for the Future*, 47 Vand. L. Rev. 1563 (1994).

[100]See *Printz v. United States*, 521 U.S. 898 (1997).

[101]See *Seminole Tribe of Fla. v. Florida*, 517 U.S. 44 (1996).

[102]See *Alden v. Maine*, 119 S.Ct. 2240 (1999). Note that the text of Eleventh Amendment does not apply to state courts.

interpretations favoring Native Americans has weakened considerably in recent years, in the aftermath of jurisdictional disputes where states have prevailed over tribes.[103]   Conversely, the expansive force accorded the values of federalism has sometimes invigorated another traditional canon, the rule of lenity, the subject to which we now turn.

C. *The Rule of Lenity*

Like the avoidance canon, and unlike the federalism clear statement rules, the notion that ambiguities in criminal statutes should be construed to the benefit of the defendant is of longstanding vintage.[104]   The most commonly articulated justifications for the canon are rooted in constitutional values. Reflecting due process concerns, the canon is designed to promote fair notice to the citizenry about what conduct subjects them to criminal sanctions. Reflecting both due process and equal protection values, the canon provides courts a way to limit prosecutorial discretion by thwarting arbitrary or discriminatory applications of a criminal statute. Reflecting separation of powers concerns, the canon may serve a nondelegation

---

[103]See, e.g., *South Dakota v. Yankton Sioux Tribe*, 118 S.Ct. 789 (1998) (Indian reservation was diminished when Congress later opened it to non-Indian settlement, and most areas are now subject to state, not tribal, jurisdiction); *Blatchford v. Native Village of Noatak*, 501 U.S. 775 (1991) (federal statute potentially authorizing tribe to sue state in federal court was subjected to Eleventh Amendment clear statement rule rather than canon favoring interpretations benefitting Indians); *Cotton Petroleum Corp. v. New Mexico*, 490 U.S. 163 (1989) (federal statutory scheme allowed a state to impose its severance tax upon the extraction of oil and gas on an Indian reservation). For the argument that the Court has drifted away from a canonical approach to federal Indian law toward case-by-case common-law-like analysis, see Philip Frickey, *A Common Law for Our Age of Colonialism: The Judicial Divestiture of Indian Tribal Authority over Nonmembers*, 109 Yale L.J. 1 (1999).

[104]See, e.g., *United States v. Wiltberger*, 18 U.S. (5 Wheat.) 76, 95 (1820) (Marshall, C.J.): "The rule that penal laws are to be construed strictly, is perhaps not much less old than construction itself. It is founded on the tenderness of the law for the rights of individuals; and on the plain principle that the power of punishment is vested in the legislative, not in the judicial department. It is the legislature, not the Court, which is to define a crime, and ordain its punishment."

Most of the legislation casebooks focus a great deal of attention on the rule of lenity. See Eskridge & Frickey 655-75; Hetzel, Libonati & Williams 653-75; Popkin 110-18, 378-81.

function by presuming that it is the legislative, not the judicial, function to define crimes. The canon also may reflect a basic libertarian bias in favor of freedom versus regulation. As one would expect, our reading of the cases suggests that criminal defendants are much less likely to get the benefit of the rule of lenity when their allegedly criminal conduct was *malum in se* (obviously evil in itself, like murder) rather than *malum prohibitum* (conduct arguably innocent in itself but made criminal for regulatory purposes, such as doing electrical repairs without the proper license).

In the abstract, it may seem hard to quarrel with these concerns. In a recent study, however, Professor Kahan has contended that the rule of lenity has been applied erratically by the federal courts,[105] thus undermining the economic justification that the canon establishes a predictable interpretive regime for the criminal law. Consider a series of cases that illustrate the unpredictable quality of the canon.

If someone trades a gun for drugs, has he violated a federal statute providing that "[w]hoever, during and in relation to any crime of violence or drug trafficking crime * * * uses or carries a firearm, shall, in addition to the punishment provided for such crime of violence or drug trafficking crime, be sentenced to imprisonment for five years"?[106] In an opinion by Justice O'Connor, the Court held in the affirmative, concluding that this constituted "using" the gun in relation to a drug offense, citing dictionary definitions defining "use" as "to employ."[107] Justice Scalia dissented, contending that the ordinary meaning of "uses a firearm" is using a gun as a gun, not as a medium of exchange like money.[108] In a second case, however, where both a gun and drugs were found in a vehicle, the Court unanimously rejected the argument that the defendant had "used" the gun.[109] Justice O'Connor, again writing for the Court, concluded that the statute required an active use — apparently, like trading the gun for drugs — rather than the passive employment of the gun in this

---

[105]See Dan Kahan, *Lenity and Federal Common Law Crimes*, 1994 Sup. Ct. Rev. 345.

[106]18 U.S.C. § 924(c)(1).

[107]See *Smith v. United States*, 508 U.S. 223, 229 (1993).

[108]See *id.* at 242 (Scalia, J., dissenting).

[109]See *Bailey v. United States*, 516 U.S. 137 (1995).

circumstance.[110] Yet in a third case with essentially the same facts as this one, a bare majority of the Court accepted the argument that the defendant had violated the statute because he had "carried" a gun in relation to a drug offense.[111]

Among other things,[112] the majority and dissenting opinions in the third, most recent case are notable for their starkly different deployments of the rule of lenity. Justice Breyer, writing for the majority, treated the canon as of little interpretive significance:

> The simple existence of some statutory ambiguity . . . is not sufficient to warrant application of [the rule of lenity], for most statutes are ambiguous to some degree. "The rule of lenity applies only if, after seizing everything from which aid can be derived, . . . we can make no more than a guess as to what Congress intended." To invoke the rule, we must conclude that there is a "grievous ambiguity or uncertainty in the statute."[113]

---

[110]See *id.* at 143, 148-51.

[111]See *Muscarello v. United States*, 524 U.S. 125 (1998), excerpted and discussed in Eskridge, Frickey & Garrett 1998 Supp. 117-27.

[112]In *Muscarello*, even the lineup of Justices suggested that something strange was at work. The majority opinion by Justice Breyer was joined by Justices Stevens, O'Connor, Kennedy, and Thomas; the dissenting opinion by Justice Ginsburg was joined by Chief Justice Rehnquist, Justice Scalia, and Justice Souter. So far as we know, this is an unprecedented lineup of Justices on both sides of a question. The opinions also reflected a kind of interpretive weirdness. Justice Breyer, who is ordinarily not much of a formalist, stressed dictionary definitions of "carry" as simply meaning conveying something, and to this effect he also marshaled quotations from the King James version of the Bible, Defoe's *Robinson Crusoe*, Melville's *Moby Dick,* and numerous newspaper articles. See 524 U.S. at 128-31 (opinion for the Court). In dissent, Justice Ginsburg contended that "carrying a gun" means "bearing [it] in such manner as to be ready for use as a weapon" or, more colloquially, "pack[ing] heat," not hauling it in the trunk of a car. *Id.* at 140, 148 (dissenting opinion). She responded to Justice Breyer by citing her own dictionary definitions and biblical passages for this narrower definition of "carry" as meaning carrying an object in one's hand or on one's person. She also quoted poetry by Oliver Goldsmith and Rudyard Kipling, recalled Teddy Roosevelt's famous advice to speak softly and carry a big stick, and even quoted Benjamin Franklin (Hawkeye) Pierce, played by Alan Alda on the popular television series M*A*S*H. See *id.* at 142-44 & n.6.

[113]*Id.* at 138-39 (opinion for the Court) (multiple quotation marks and citations omitted).

Contrast the much more powerful canon articulated by Justice Ginsburg in her dissenting opinion:

> The sharp division in the Court on the proper reading of the measure confirms, "[a]t the very least, . . . that the issue is subject to some doubt. Under these circumstances, we adhere to the familiar rule that, where there is ambiguity in a criminal statute, doubts are resolved in favor of the defendant." . . . "[W]here text, structure, and history fail to establish that the Government's position is unambiguously correct — we apply the rule of lenity and resolve the ambiguity in [the defendant's] favor."[114]

That both Justices constructed their different formulations of the canon by quoting from precedents supports Kahan's argument that the canon has led an erratic and unpredictable life in the federal cases. Indeed, the current interpretive effect of the rule is in some doubt. Justice Breyer, for five Justices, treated the canon as a weak tie-breaker; Justice Ginsburg, for four Justices, treated the canon as a strong presumption that can be rebutted by the traditional sources of statutory meaning; both cited ample precedents for their conflicting approaches. A third possibility has also been floated: that textually ambiguous criminal statutes cannot be rendered clear by the use of legislative history or other nontextual sources of meaning.[115]

Professor Kahan's solution to this confusion is to jettison the canon at the federal level. He contends that the canon is inconsistent with the inherently dynamic quality of the federal criminal law. In his judgment, Congress often delegates a common-law-like power to the federal courts to mold federal criminal statutes — many of which are vaguely worded, encouraging judicial elaboration[116] — to fit facts

---

[114]*Id.* at 148 (dissenting opinion) (multiple quotation marks and citations omitted).

[115]See *United States v. R.L.C.*, 503 U.S. 291, 307-11 (1992) (Scalia, J., joined by Kennedy & Thomas, JJ., concurring). Of course, the practical effect of the canon will be undercut by the fact that textualist Justices are more confident than their colleagues in attributing unambiguous meaning to statutory language.

[116]For example, 18 U.S.C. § 1341 prohibits use of the U.S. mails to execute "any scheme or artifice to defraud." On its common law evolution, see Jed Rakoff, *The Federal Mail Fraud Statute (Part I)*, 18 Duquesne L. Rev. 771 (1980). Similarly open-ended language can be found in 18 U.S.C. § 371 (crime to "defraud the United States"), *id.* § 1951 (crime to commit "robbery" or "extortion" affecting

unforeseen at the time of enactment. This pattern would seem to endanger the values of fair notice and limiting prosecutorial discretion, but he concludes that these values can be protected by replacing the rule of lenity with the requirement that the Department of Justice promulgate regulations definitively interpreting the federal criminal statutes.[117]

In response, Professor Solan has defended the rule of lenity.[118] Solan usefully traces the history of the canon, showing that it has served different purposes over time. Originally, the canon provided judges the opportunity to ameliorate some of the extraordinary harshness of the old common law. Eventually, the canon became an important tool to temper the vagueness and ambiguity inherent in statutory language. As courts moved beyond purely textual interpretation to include more factors, such as legislative history, in the analysis, however, statutory meaning became more easily ascertained, and the canon became accordingly less significant. By the mid-twentieth century, according to Solan, the Supreme Court treated the canon as a tiebreaker, giving the defendant the benefit of the interpretive doubt after all other interpretive aids had been exhausted. In Solan's judgment, this modest form of the canon is worth preserving, for it protects defendants against the inherent uncertainties of criminal regulation. That the canon serves these important purposes, he contends, is reflected in the fact that jurisdictions that have formally abandoned the rule of lenity by statute end up, in effect, recreating it by judicial decision to protect these values.

We suspect that the debate about the appropriateness and interpretive effect of the rule of lenity will continue at the federal level. In the state courts, our perception is that the rule is alive and well, usually operating as a tiebreaker along the lines that Solan described. An important difference might be that state courts are less likely to view criminal statutes as having common-law-like qualities, in part out of respect for legislative intent (state legislatures have

---

commerce).

[117]See Dan Kahan, *Is* Chevron *Relevant to Federal Criminal Law?*, 110 Harv. L. Rev. 469 (1996).

[118]See Lawrence Solan, *Law, Language, and Lenity*, 40 Wm. & Mary L. Rev. 57 (1998).

generally not effectively delegated authority in the criminal realm to their courts) and in part out of a more formal conception of the separation of powers (under which it is the legislative function to define crimes). Another difference may be the perception that state legislatures and state appellate courts have closer working relationships than do Congress and the federal courts, so that problems in criminal statutes are more likely to receive legislative reconsideration at the state level. Nonetheless, as our discussion of the *Marsh* case in Chapter 1 indicates, state judges will sometimes elaborate upon poorly chosen text in criminal statutes rather than invoke the rule of lenity and leave the ultimate resolution of the problem to the state legislature.

Another important difference between the federal rule of lenity and its state counterparts is rooted in the values of federalism. As Part IIB of this chapter demonstrated, the current Supreme Court views the protection of state authority from federal encroachment as a fundamental constitutional value. Because federal law often criminalizes conduct that is also subject to state regulation, there is substantial potential for overlap and inconsistency. If the federal statutes effectively displace local and state decisions about such matters, that would be a serious blow to the values of federalism that are now so judicially salient. These concerns can translate into an elevated rule of lenity in the federal system that is designed to protect state authority.

Perhaps the best recent example of this phenomenon is *McNally v. United States*.[119] During a time when the Democratic Party dominated Kentucky politics, state officers and party officials who controlled the purchase of insurance for the state developed a scheme under which they received kickbacks from the insurance agencies to which they funneled the business. The United States Attorney prosecuted them under the federal mail fraud statute, which provides that "[w]hoever, having devised or intending to devise any scheme or artifice to defraud, or for obtaining money or property by means of false or fraudulent pretenses, representations, or promises," is guilty of violating the statute if the U.S. mail is used as part of the

---

[119]483 U.S. 350 (1987), excerpted and discussed in Eskridge & Frickey 666-75.

scheme.[120] The problem for the prosecutor was that it could not be shown that the state had lost any money from the scheme. Accordingly, the theory of the prosecution was that the state had been defrauded of its intangible rights to an honest government and to fiduciary conduct by government officials.

The majority of the Court, in an opinion by Justice White, applied the rule of lenity and held that the mail fraud statute applied only when the mail was used to promote fraudulent schemes causing deprivation of money or property. In dissent, Justice Stevens castigated this result. He argued that none of the values associated with the rule of lenity counseled against this prosecution. The statutory text gave no hint that only monetary frauds came within the language outlawing any "scheme or artifice to defraud." Many decisions of lower federal courts had applied the mail fraud statute to similar schemes, indicating that defendants had fair notice that their conduct — which was *malum in se* in any event — was criminal and that the United States Attorney was not acting arbitrarily in prosecuting them.

McNally is a puzzle when viewed within the narrow framework customarily associated with the rule of lenity. When the analysis is enlarged to consider the values of federalism, however, the decision may make more sense. Defendants' conduct apparently did not violate state law. The majority of the Court was reluctant to fill this void by transforming the old, vague, federal mail fraud statute into an all-purpose honesty-in-state-government regulation enforceable by federal prison terms. Indeed, Justice White expressly invoked the rule of lenity to avoid an interpretation that "involves the Federal Government in setting standards of disclosure and good government for local and state officials."[121] In other cases, as well, the Court has

---

[120]18 U.S.C. § 1341.

[121]*McNally*, 483 U.S. at 360. Justice White could also have stressed the potential unseemliness of the partisan nature of the prosecution, brought by the Republican United States Attorney in Kentucky against state Democratic Party activists and officeholders. Of course, in response one might contend that partisan prosecutions of political corruption are better than no prosecutions at all, and that the cyclical holding of the Presidency by Republicans and Democrats generally ensures that United States Attorneys from different parties will be in office over time. Notwithstanding all these factors, however, it is interesting to note that

sometimes invoked the rule of lenity to protect state political activities from prosecution under vague federal criminal statutes,[122] as well as more generally trimmed the sails of federal criminal statutes when the conduct in question is subject to the state police power as well and there is no obvious reason to federalize the criminal regulation of it.[123]

III. Conclusions About the Canons — and About Statutory Interpretation

In a famous article published almost a half-century ago, the great legal realist Karl Llewellyn contended that "there are two opposing canons on almost every point" and illustrated his argument with a list of canons and counter-canons. "[T]o make any canon take hold in a particular instance," Llewellyn continued, "the construction contended for must be sold, essentially, by means other than the use of canon: The good sense of the situation and a *simple* construction of the available language to achieve that sense, *by tenable means, out of the statutory language*."[124]

Although we defer to few in our allegiance to legal realism, we have some qualms about the way the Llewellyn analysis might be understood. For one thing, most of his examples of "opposing canons" are best understood as simply general rules (such as the plain meaning rule) and exceptions (such as the absurd result exception to that rule). As such, although they do not dictate results, they structure the adversarial dialogue between the attorneys in the case in predict-

---

Congress immediately overturned the result in *McNally*, clarifying that deprivation of the intangible right of honest services is covered by the mail fraud statute. See 18 U.S.C. § 1346.

[122]See, e.g., *McCormick v. United States*, 500 U.S. 257 (1991) ("extortion," as defined in federal Hobbs Act, requires clear proof of a *quid pro quo*, not simply that state legislator received contributions from private party for whom the legislator had introduced legislation in the past and had promised to do so again in the future).

[123]See, e.g., Eskridge & Frickey, *Law as Equilibrium, supra* note 47, at 65-71.

[124]Karl Llewellyn, *Remarks on the Theory of Appellate Decision and the Rules or Canons About How Statutes Are To Be Construed*, 3 Vand. L. Rev. 395, 401 (1950), excerpted and discussed in Eskridge & Frickey 705-13; Hetzel, Libonati & Williams 691-700; Mikva & Lane 770-73.

able and potentially useful ways. More important, we view the canons as, at least, a handy checklist of possibilities for advocates. It may well be, for example, that upon first analyzing statutory text the attorney missed not only that the words had an *ejusdem generis* formulation,[125] but missed the entire argument for narrow construction of broad catch-all phrases upon which that canon is based. Familiarity with the canons helps advocates identify the relevant possibilities of statutory meaning for which one might want to contend.

We do endorse Llewellyn's argument that the application of canons must depend upon context. The canons are rooted in assumptions about the normal usage of language (Chapter 7), the institutional relationships of legislatures and courts (Chapter 8), and basic systemic values (this chapter). Consistent with our pragmatic perspective, the weight accorded a canon in a given situation should vary depending upon how these assumptions fit that context. Canons should ordinarily be conceptualized as potentially useful guidelines, not rules of law.

Regrettably, the judicial practice with the canons has raised deep pragmatic concerns along both empirical and normative lines. The defense that the substantive canons serve rule-of-law values by creating a predictable interpretive regime has been undermined by the inconsistent judicial application of them and by the absence of any empirical evidence that legislative actors can respond to the incentives provided by a predictable interpretive regime. Moreover, the rule-like façade of the canons tends to conceal the value choices that underlie them and encourages judges and advocates to attempt to formulate their debatable propositions in canonical form to shield themselves from critical analysis. If (as we think) interpretation is an inherently normative enterprise, its practices need to be defended in those terms.

Formalists, too, might have concerns about the canons. For example, theorists concerned with judicial lawmaking would presumably find most of the canons to be distracting at best or an invitation to illicit judicial lawmaking at worst. Professor Nagle has

---

[125]See Chapter 7, Part IB.

made a strong originalist case against the Court's canonical activism along these lines,[126] and even Justice Scalia (the author of such possibly activist decisions as *Nordic Village* and *BFP*) has questioned the validity of the canons. "To the honest textualist, all of these preferential rules and presumptions are a lot of trouble," both because they are based on debatable values and because they may actually increase the unpredictability of judicial decisions by forcing resolution of such precious questions as how much lack of clarity is needed for there to be "ambiguity" and how much clarity is needed for there to be "unmistakably clear" meaning.[127]

Alternatively, imagine a formalist who believes that the canons have established pedigrees and provide a reasonably predictable interpretive regime that the interpreter can usefully deploy to fill gaps in meaning caused by ambiguous statutory text without having to resort to nebulous statutory purposes and free-wheeling judicial value judgments. Such a formalist might propose this formula for statutory interpretation:

> [F]irst, find the ordinary meaning of the language in its textual context; and second, using established canons of construction, ask whether there is any clear indication that some permissible meaning other than the ordinary one applies. If not — and especially if a good reason for the ordinary meaning appears plain — we apply that ordinary meaning.[128]

This formulation — ironically, also written by Justice Scalia — illustrates dilemmas posed by the canons for formalist theories such as original intent and textualism.

If the canons are background rules known (or imputed) to legislators and the citizenry, don't the ideas of original intent and plain meaning *depend* on the canons? If the canons reflect *shared assumptions* about statutory meaning, wouldn't it be negligent to ignore them? But because they are also under the control of judges

---

[126]See Nagle, *supra* note 2.

[127]See Scalia, *supra* note 41, at 28-29.

[128]*Chisom v. Roemer*, 501 U.S. 380, 404 (1991) (Scalia, J., dissenting), excerpted and discussed in Eskridge & Frickey 613-28; Popkin 250-62. For a similar formulation from a purpose-based viewpoint, see Hart & Sacks, *supra* note 2, at 1374, 1376-77.

and are notoriously manipulable and dynamic, don't loose canons undermine the democracy-enhancing and rule-of-law features of statutory interpretation? Recall how some of the substantive canons discussed in this chapter — the sovereign immunity canon, the canon concerning Native Americans, the Eleventh Amendment canon, and the rule of lenity — have dramatically evolved over time. Indeed, the Court sometimes even invents new canons, as it did in *Gregory v. Ashcroft*, and applies them retroactively.

The canons pose unhappy tradeoffs that at least some formalists do not want to acknowledge.[129] Do the canons contribute to greater legal certainty?[130] If so, does the value of certainty justify using the canons even where textual integrity is sacrificed? If not, do the canons contribute some other, quasi-constitutional value worth preserving in our system? Can they be defended as part of a judicially constructed and enforced due-process-of-lawmaking principle? Or are the canons based on debatable values and too erratically applied to subserve any noncontroversial public value?

Our experience with the canons suggests a final point. If an advocate has a good hunch about how a court should go about interpreting the statute, she should assiduously research the cases to see whether that hunch has ever been formulated as a canon of interpretation. She might have forgotten about one of the longstanding canons that serves this purpose, or she might get lucky and find an obscure case or two that fits her insight. But even if she cannot find precedential support for the argument, she should assert it anyway and cite whatever she can in support of the proposition. If its justification is normatively attractive and its formulation sounds sufficiently canonical, the court might just canonize it.[131]

---

[129]Justice O'Connor, a fan of original intent in statutory interpretation, devised the new canon in *Gregory v. Ashcroft*. More dramatically, archtextualist Justice Scalia joined her openly normative opinion rather than Justice White's concurring opinion, which relied on traditional principles to reach the same result.

[130]This is, of course, ultimately an empirical question, but unfortunately one that would be hard to test. See William Eskridge, Jr., *Norms, Empiricism, and Canons in Statutory Construction*, 66 U. Chi. L. Rev. 671 (1999).

[131]For a student note advocating a new clear statement rule for "linked statutes," see John Flynn, *Mixed-Motive Causation Under the ADA: Linked Statutes, Fuzzy Thinking, and Clear Statements*, 83 Geo. L.J. 2009 (1995).

For example, in 1989 the Court stated that "[a] party contending that legislative action changed settled law has the burden of showing that the legislature intended such a change."[132] This proposition has obvious similarities to Professor Shapiro's point about many canons preferring legal continuity over change, which was discussed in Part IA of this chapter. But the Court's only citation in support of its conclusion was to one case introduced by "*Cf.*", indicating that the precedent did not directly support the proposition. Just six years later, the Court treated this maxim as an established canon of interpretation, this time simply quoting the 1989 case in support.[133]

*   *   *

As Chapter 1 pointed out, in the 1950s Henry Hart and Albert Sacks had this to say about techniques of statutory interpretation:

> Do not expect anybody's theory of statutory interpretation, whether it is your own or somebody else's, to be an accurate statement of what courts actually do with statutes. The hard truth of the matter is that American courts have no intelligible, generally accepted, and consistently applied theory of statutory interpretation.[134]

Whatever else might be said about statutory interpretation at the millennium, we are confident that these comments remain descriptively accurate. Consider as well the normative conclusion Hart and Sacks drew from this observation:

> When an effort is made to formulate a sound and workable theory, therefore, the most that can be hoped for is that it will have some foundation in experience and in the best practice of the wisest judges, and that it will be well calculated to serve the ultimate purposes of law.[135]

---

[132]*Green v. Bock Laundry Mach. Co.*, 490 U.S. 504, 521 (1989), excerpted and discussed in Eskridge & Frickey 589-603.

[133]*Tome v. United States*, 513 U.S. 150, 163 (1995) (quoting *Bock Laundry, supra* note 132).

[134]Hart & Sacks, *supra* note 2, at 1169.

[135]*Id.*

We would add that, when an effort is made to develop the practical skills necessary for the practice of law in the new century, which promises to be even more "statutorified" than the last, the ability to interpret statutes should be near the top of the list.

We hope that your study of this book has provided a timely and useful introduction to both the theory and the practice of statutory interpretation, understood within its broader institutional context.

APPENDIX:
THE REHNQUIST COURT'S CANONS
OF STATUTORY CONSTRUCTION

A study by two of us collected the canons used by the Supreme Court in the 1986 through 1993 Terms and divided the canons into categories that essentially parallel the typology provided in this book. The list is reprinted below, stripped of the footnotes citing the relevant cases.[a]

TEXTUAL CANONS

- Plain meaning rule: follow the plain meaning of the statutory text, except when text suggests an absurd result or a scrivener's error.

LINGUISTIC INFERENCES

- *Expressio unius*: expression of one thing suggests the exclusion of others.

- *Noscitur a sociis*: interpret a general term to be similar to more specific terms in a series.

- *Ejusdem generis*: interpret a general term to reflect the class of objects reflected in more specific terms accompanying it.

- Follow ordinary usage of terms, unless Congress gives them a specified or technical meaning.

- Follow dictionary definitions of terms, unless Congress has provided a specific definition. Consider dictionaries of the era in which the statute was enacted. Do not consider "idiosyncratic" dictionary definitions.

- "May" is usually precatory, while "shall" is usually mandatory.

- "Or" means in the alternative.

---

[a]William Eskridge, Jr. & Philip Frickey, *The Supreme Court, 1993 Term — Foreword: Law as Equilibrium*, 108 Harv. L. Rev. 26, 97-108 (1994). Copyright © 1994 by the Harvard Law Review Association. Reprinted by permission.

GRAMMAR AND SYNTAX

- Punctuation rule: Congress is presumed to follow accepted punctuation standards, so that placements of commas and other punctuation are assumed to be meaningful.

- Do not have to apply the "rule of the last antecedent" if not practical.

TEXTUAL INTEGRITY

- Each statutory provision should be read by reference to the whole act. Statutory interpretation is a "holistic" endeavor.

- Avoid interpreting a provision in a way that would render other provisions of the Act superfluous or unnecessary.

- Avoid interpreting a provision in a way inconsistent with the policy of another provision.

- Avoid interpreting a provision in a way that is inconsistent with a necessary assumption of another provision.

- Avoid interpreting a provision in a way that is inconsistent with the structure of the statute.

- Avoid broad readings of statutory provisions if Congress has specifically provided for the broader policy in more specific language elsewhere.

- Interpret the same or similar terms in a statute the same way.

- Specific provisions targeting a particular issue apply instead of provisions more generally covering the issue.

- Provisos and statutory exceptions should be read narrowly.

- Do not create exceptions in addition to those specified by Congress.

EXTRINSIC SOURCE CANONS

AGENCY INTERPRETATIONS

- Rule of deference to agency interpretations, unless contrary to plain meaning of statute or unreasonable.

- Rule of extreme deference when there is express delegation of law-making duties to agency.

- Presumption that agency interpretation of its own regulations is correct.

CONTINUITY IN LAW

- Rule of continuity: assume that Congress does not create discontinuities in legal rights and obligations without some clear statement.

- Presumption that Congress uses same term consistently in different statutes.

- Super-strong presumption of correctness for statutory precedents.

- Presumption that international agreements do not displace federal law.

- Borrowed statute rule: when Congress borrows a statute, it adopts by implication interpretations placed on that statute, absent express statement to the contrary.

- Re-enactment rule: when Congress re-enacts a statute, it incorporates settled interpretations of the re-enacted statute. The rule is inapplicable when there is no settled standard Congress could have known.

- Acquiescence rule: consider unbroken line of lower court decisions interpreting statute, but do not give them decisive weight.

EXTRINSIC LEGISLATIVE SOURCES

- Interpret provision consistent with subsequent statutory amendments, but do not consider subsequent legislative discussions.

- Consider legislative history if the statute is ambiguous.

- Committee reports are authoritative legislative history, but cannot trump a textual plain meaning, and should not be relied on if they are "imprecise."

- Committee report language that cannot be tied to a specific statutory provision cannot be credited. House and Senate reports inconsistent with one another should be discounted.

- Presumption against interpretation considered and rejected by floor vote of a chamber of Congress or committee.

- Floor statements can be used to confirm apparent meaning.

- Contemporaneous and subsequent understandings of a statutory scheme (including understandings by President and Department of Justice) may sometimes be admissible.

- The "dog didn't bark" canon: presumption that prior legal rule should be retained if no one in legislative deliberations even mentioned the rule or discussed any changes in the rule.

SUBSTANTIVE POLICY CANONS

CONSTITUTION-BASED CANONS

- Avoid interpretations that would render a statute unconstitutional. Inapplicable if statute would survive constitutional attack, or if statutory text is clear.

1. Separation of Powers

- Super-strong rule against congressional interference with President's authority over foreign affairs and national security.

- Rule against congressional invasion of the President's core executive powers.

- Rule against review of President's core executive actions for "abuse of discretion."

- Rule against congressional curtailment of the judiciary's "inherent powers" or its "equity" powers.

- Rule against congressional expansion of Article III injury in fact to include intangible and procedural injuries.

- Presumption that Congress does not delegate authority without sufficient guidelines.

- Presumption against "implying" causes of action into federal statutes.

- Presumption that U.S. law conforms to U.S. international obligations.

- Rule against congressional abrogation of Indian treaty rights.

- Presumption favoring severability of unconstitutional provisions.

2. Federalism

- Super-strong rule against federal invasion of "core state functions."

- Super-strong rule against federal abrogation of states' Eleventh Amendment immunity from lawsuits in federal courts.

- Rule against inferring enforceable conditions on federal grants to the states.

- Rule against congressional expansion of federal court jurisdiction that would siphon cases away from state courts.

- Rule against reading a federal statute to authorize states to engage in activities that would violate the dormant commerce clause.

- Rule favoring concurrent state and federal court jurisdiction over federal claims.

- Rule against federal pre-emption of traditional state functions, or against federal disruption of area of traditional state regulation.

- Presumption against federal pre-emption of state-assured family support obligations.

- Presumption against federal regulation of intergovernmental taxation by the states.

- Presumption against application of federal statutes to state and local political processes.

- Presumption that states can tax activities within their borders, including Indian tribal activities, but also presumption that states cannot tax on Indian lands.

- Presumption against congressional derogation from state's land claims based upon its entry into Union on an "equal footing" with all other states.

- Presumption against federal habeas review of state criminal convictions supported by independent state ground.

- Presumption of finality of state convictions for purposes of habeas review.

- Principle that federal equitable remedies must consider interests of state and local authorities.

- Presumption that Congress borrows state statutes of limitations for federal statutory schemes, unless otherwise provided.

3. Due Process

- Rule of lenity: rule against applying punitive sanctions if there is ambiguity as to underlying criminal liability or criminal penalty.

- Rule of lenity applies to civil sanction that is punitive or when underlying liability is criminal.

- Rule against criminal penalties imposed without showing of specific intent.

- Rule against interpreting statutes to be retroactive, even if statute is curative or restorative.

- Rule against interpreting statutes to deny a right to jury trial.

- Presumption in favor of judicial review, especially for constitutional questions, but not for agency decisions not to prosecute.

- Presumption against pre-enforcement challenges to implementation.

- Presumption against exhaustion of remedies requirement for lawsuit to enforce constitutional rights.

- Presumption that judgments will not be binding upon persons not party to adjudication.

- Presumption against national service of process unless authorized by Congress.

- Presumption against foreclosure of private enforcement of important federal rights.

- Presumption that preponderance of the evidence standard applies in civil cases.

STATUTE-BASED CANONS

- *In pari materia*: similar statutes should be interpreted similarly, unless legislative history or purpose suggests material differences.

- Presumption against repeals by implication.

- Purpose rule: interpret ambiguous statutes so as best to carry out their statutory purposes.

- Narrow interpretation of statutory exemptions.

- Presumption against creating exemptions in a statute that has none.

- Allow *de minimis* exceptions to statutory rules, so long as they do not undermine statutory policy.

- Presumption that federal private right of action (express or implied) carries with it all traditional remedies.

- Presumption that court will not supply a sanction for failure to follow a timing provision when the statute has no sanction.

- Rule against state taxation of Indian tribes and reservation activities.

- Presumption against national "diminishment" of Indian lands.

- Narrow interpretation of exemptions from federal taxation.

- Presumption against taxpayer claiming income tax deduction.

- Presumption that the Bankruptcy Act of 1978 preserved prior bankruptcy doctrines.

- Federal court deference to arbitral awards, even where the Federal Arbitration Act is not by its terms applicable.

- Strong presumption in favor of enforcing labor arbitration agreements.

- Rule favoring arbitration of federal statutory claims.

- Strict construction of statutes authorizing appeals.

- Rule that Court of Claims is proper forum for Tucker Act claims against federal government.

- Rule that "sue and be sued" clauses waive sovereign immunity and should be liberally construed.

- Presumption that statute creating agency and authorizing it to "sue and be sued" also creates federal subject matter jurisdiction for lawsuits by and against the agency.

- Construe ambiguities in deportation statutes in favor of aliens.

- Principle that veterans' benefits statutes be construed liberally for their beneficiaries.

- Liberal application of antitrust policy.

- Presumption against application of Sherman Act to activities authorized by states.

- Principle that statutes should not be interpreted to create anticompetitive effects.

- Strong presumption that federal grand juries operate within legitimate spheres of their authority.

COMMON LAW-BASED CANONS

- Presumption in favor of following common law usage where Congress has employed words or concepts with well settled common law traditions. Follow evolving common law unless inconsistent with statutory purposes.

- Rule against extraterritorial application of U.S. law, except for antitrust laws.

- Super-strong rule against waivers of United States sovereign immunity.

- Rule that debts to the United States shall bear interest.

- Super-strong rule against conveyance of U.S. public lands to private parties.

- Rule presuming against attorney fee-shifting in federal courts and federal statutes, and narrow construction of fee-shifting statutes to exclude unmentioned costs.

- Presumption that jury finds facts, judge declares law.

- Rule presuming that law takes effect on date of enactment.

- Presumption that public (government) interest not be prejudiced by negligence of federal officials.

- Presumption that federal agencies launched into commercial world with power to "sue and be sued" are not entitled to sovereign immunity.

- Presumption favoring enforcement of forum selection clauses.

- Presumption against criminal jurisdiction by an Indian tribe over a nonmember.

- Presumption that party cannot invoke federal jurisdiction until she has exhausted her remedies in Indian tribal courts.

- Presumption that federal judgment has preclusive effect in state administrative proceedings.

- Presumption importing common law immunities into federal civil rights statutes.

Index